English Literature in Schools

Exploring the Curriculum

This book is one of a series designed to assist teachers to review practice in schools and classrooms. The series has been prepared by members of the Open University team for the course: *Applied Studies in Curriculum and Teaching*. Each volume follows a common sequence of issues relating to the nature of an area of specialization, its place in contemporary society, its treatment in schools, particular features of its teaching and learning, and consequences for organization and evaluation.

The titles in the series are:

J. Brown, A. Cooper, T. Horton, F. Toates and D. Zeldin (Eds.):
Science in Schools
A. Cross and R. McCormick (Eds.): *Technology in Schools*
V. J. Lee (Ed.): *English Literature in Schools*

English Literature in Schools

Edited by
Victor J. Lee
at the Open University

Open University Press
Milton Keynes • Philadelphia

Open University Press
Open University Educational Enterprises Limited
12 Cofferidge Close
Stony Stratford
Milton Keynes MK11 1BY, England

and
242 Cherry Street
Philadelphia, PA 19106, USA

First Published 1987

British Library Cataloguing in Publication Data

English literature in schools. — (Exploring
  the curriculum)
  1. English literature — Study and
  teaching (Secondary) — Great Britain
  I. Lee, V.J.   II. Series
  820'.7'1241   PR51.G7

  ISBN 0-335-15246-5
  ISBN 0-335-15245-7 Pbk

Library of Congress Cataloguing in Publication Data
Main entry under title:

English literature in schools.
  (Exploring the curriculum series)
  Includes index.
  1. English literature — Study and teachings (Secondary)
  — Great Britain.   I. Lee, V.J. (Victor J.)
  II. Series.
  PR51.G7E54 1987   820'.7'1241   86-18127

  ISBN 0-335-15246-5
  ISBN 0-335-15245-7 (pbk.)

Text design by Carlton Hill
Typeset by Burns & Smith
Printed in Great Britain
by Butler & Tanner Ltd, Frome and London.

Contents

Acknowledgements

The Editor would like to thank each of the publishers for permission to reproduce material from the sources listed below:

SECTION I
1. Joseph Conrad (1897), *The Nigger of the 'Narcissus'*. Everyman's Library edn., Dent, London 1974, pp. xxiii–xxviii.
2. Terry Eagleton, *Literary Theory: An Introduction*. Basil Blackwell, Oxford 1983, pp. 1–16.
3. William Wordsworth (1802) in *William Wordsworth*. Ed. S. Gill, Oxford University Press, Oxford 1984, pp. 603–612.
4. Lionel Trilling in *The Liberal Imagination*. Secker and Warburg, London and Viking Penguin Inc., New York 1951 edn., pp. 34–57. First published in 1940, revised 1947.
5. I.A. Richards, *Principles of Literary Criticism*. Routledge & Kegan Paul, London 1976, pp. 17–23. First published 1924.
6. Laurence Lerner in *Reconstructing Literature*. Ed. L. Lerner, Basil Blackwell, Oxford 1983, pp. 1–9.
7. David Lodge, *Working with Structuralism*. Routledge & Kegan Paul, London 1981, pp. 37–45.

SECTION II
8. Terry Eagleton, *Literary Theory: An Introduction*. Basil Blackwell, Oxford 1983, pp. 22–37.
9. J. Middleton Murry, *The Problem of Style*. Oxford University Press, London 1960, pp. 22–28. First published 1922.
10. Raymond Williams, *Modern Tragedy*. Verso, revised edition 1979, pp. 45–61. First published 1966.
11. T.S. Eliot from *Selected Essays*. Faber and Faber Ltd., London, 3rd edn. 1951, pp. 388–401.
12. Richard Hoggart in *Arts Express*, No. 12, 1985, pp. 12–14.
13. Carol MacDougall in *English in Education*, Vol. 15, No. 13, 1981, pp. 19–24.
14. Elaine Showalter in *Critical Approaches to the Fiction of Thomas Hardy*. Ed. D. Kramer, The Macmillan Press Ltd., London and Barnes and Noble, New York 1979, pp. 99–115.

SECTION III

15. Martin Esslin, *The Age of Television*. W.H. Freeman and Company, San Francisco 1982, pp. 3–10.
16. John Ellis in *Screen*. Vol. 23, No. 1, 1982, pp. 3–5.
17. Phillip Simpson in *Screen*. Vol. 23, No. 1, 1982, pp. 20–30.
18. David Lusted with Richard Exton from 'The school and the street' in *The English Magazine*. No. 6, Spring 1981, pp. 25–29.
19. Morris Beja, *Film and Literature*. Longman Group Ltd., London 1979, pp. 51–59.
20. David Lodge, *The Modes of Modern Writing*, Edward Arnold, London 1977, pp. 81–87.
21. John Drakakis in *Radio Drama*. Ed. Peter Lewis, Longman Group Ltd., Harlow 1981, pp. 118–123.

SECTION IV

22. Margaret Mathieson, *The Preachers of Culture*. George Allen & Unwin Ltd., London 1975, pp. 69–82.
23. John Dixon in *Growth through English*. Published for the National Association for the Teaching of English by the Oxford University Press, 3rd edn. 1975, pp. 1–13.
24. David Allen, *English Teaching since 1965: How Much Growth?* Heinemann Educational Books, London 1980, pp. 27–44.
25. Department of Education and Science, *A Language for Life*. HMSO, London 1975, pp. 124–138.
26. Rex Gibson, *Structuralism and Education*. Hodder and Stoughton, London 1984, pp. 88–104.

SECTION V

27. D.W. Harding in *The British Journal of Aesthetics*. Vol. 2, No. 2, 1962, pp. 133–147.
28. Michael Benton and Geoff Fox, *Teaching Literature: Nine to Fourteen*. Oxford University Press 1985, pp. 19–32.
29. Robert Protherough in *The Development of Readers, Aspects of Education 30*. Institute of Education, University of Hull 1983, pp. 55–71.
30. Paul Zindel in *Teenage Reading*. Ed. Peter Kennerley, Ward Lock Educational, London 1979, pp. 43–48.
31. Louise M. Rosenblatt from 'The transactional theory of the literary work: implications for research' in *Researching Response to Literature and the Teaching of Literature: Points of Departure*. Ed. Charles R. Cooper, Ablex Publishing Corporation, Norwood, New Jersey 1985, pp. 37–40.

SECTION VI

32. M. Raleigh and M. Simons from *The English Magazine*. ILEA English Centre, Sutherland Street, London 1982, pp. 66–77.

33. Richard Exton in *Eccentric Propositions*. Ed. J. Miller, Routledge and Kegan Paul, London 1984, pp. 70–79.
34. S. Brownjohn in *Does It Have To Rhyme?* Hodder and Stoughton, London 1980, pp. 7–9, 18–19, 76–77.
35. Chris Woodhead in *The Times Educational Supplement*. July 11, 1980, p. 42.
36. Geoff Fox and Brian Merrick in *Children, Language and Literature*. The Open University Press, Milton Keynes 1982, pp. 90–93.
37. Mike Hayhoe and Stephen Parker, *Working with Fiction*. Edward Arnold, London 1984, pp. 49–58.
38. Paul Ashton, Andrew Bethell *et al.* in *Macbeth*. ILEA English Centre, Sutherland Street, London 1981, pp. 29–46.
39. Richard Exton with David Lusted from 'The school and the street' in *The English Magazine*. No. 6, Spring 1981, pp. 30–32.
40. John Brown and Terry Gifford in *English Studies 11–18: An Arts-Based Approach*. Hodder and Stoughton, London 1983, pp. 139–150.

SECTION VII
41. David Jackson, *Continuity in Secondary English*. Methuen, London 1982, pp. 123–131.
42. Department of Education and Science. General Certificate of Secondary Education: The National Criteria, English, D.E.S. 1985, pp. 1, 5–6.
43. John Dixon and Leslie Stratta in *English in Education*. Vol. 19, No. 2, Summer 1985, pp. 1–11.
44. G.C.E. Boards of England, Wales and Northern Ireland in *Common Cores at Advanced Level*. Autumn 1983, pp. 3–5.
45. John Dixon in *The English Magazine*. Spring 1984, pp. 21–24, 29–30.
46. Terry Gifford in *Teaching Literature for Examinations*. Ed. Robert Protherough, Open University Press, Milton Keynes 1986, pp. 61–69.

The editor wishes to thank the following who read all or part of an earlier draft of this Reader:.

Pamela Barnard, Richard Ball, Janet Brennan, Brian Caws, Christopher Cooper, Keith Davidson, Celia de Piro, Richard Gill, Gill Goldenburg, Steve Goldenburg, Barbara Kinnes, Anita Miles, Alex Moore, Arthur Parker, Carol Robson.

General Introduction

This is a particularly appropriate time to produce a reader concerned with the teaching of English Literature in secondary schools, because the subject is in a state of flux. Many of the old certainties have gone. Not so long ago there was an accepted canon, agreed by many if not by all. Now what constitutes the subject of English is under constant debate, as are the relationships between literature and the media and its place in education. Upstart crows, foreign ones at that, such as structuralism and deconstruction, challenge the very edifices upon which the traditional view of English Literature is built. A continuing concern with accountability has been one of the factors leading to an increased interest in the way it is taught and learned, and there is a constant endeavour to find new means of assessment, the G.C.S.E. being a good example of this.

This reader attempts to reflect some of these current issues and debates. Of course, choices have to be made, because a single reader cannot reflect all the facets of the many debates. So, for example, the interesting model of English as communication studies has not been included. Mostly secondary rather than primary sources have been used. By this I mean that in a subject such as structuralism/deconstruction, original papers of the various combatants have not been included. There are two main reasons for that. First, there simply is not enough space. Secondly, many of the original papers are abstruse. Instead, there is a gentle introduction to structuralism in general (Chapter 26); an assessment of some of the main issues of structuralism and deconstruction (6); an example of a moderate form of structuralism applied to Dickens's *Hard Times* (7); and consideration of possible practical implications for teachers in secondary schools (33).

Any anthology of readings must reveal certain personal choices of the editor. In addition, this particular set of readings has other constraints because it is intended to form a central part of EA 803, the Literature option of the Open University *Advanced Diploma in Curriculum and Teaching*. This means that the editor has inherited the basic divisions into sections, so that the Literature Reader can fit into a series of readers in different subjects planned for the Advanced Diploma as a whole.

While keeping in mind the needs of the Open University students in the selection of the articles and extracts, the editor has also borne in mind a larger group of readers who may be interested in English Literature in the educational context. It is intended, then, that this selection can act as a source book, for example, for those who are being trained as teachers of English and also for those who are practising teachers. This latter group will find articles here that they have already encountered, but they will also find, it is hoped, articles new to them which will help them revalue their own knowledge in the light of new ideas and current thinking.

The sections are not sacrosanct compartments. Any consideration of 'What is Literature?' for example, must to some extent be concerned with questions of human values. In Section II, however, particular values are highlighted in each case. In the first Eagleton extract (2), for instance, the nature of English is considered in a number of ways, the conclusion being that it is a question of ideology, but the second Eagleton extract (8) traces the development of English specifically as an ideology. This is followed by Middleton Murry's polished treatment of some of the 'traditional' concerns of English Literature (9), and Williams's interpretation of drama as ideology (10). A further four articles see literature in relation to religion (T.S. Eliot, 11); social class differences (Hoggart, 12); its role in a multicultural society (MacDougall, 13); and feminist objectives (14). The MacDougall article, for example, could be in Section VI, because it is concerned with the teaching of English. However, it does set out to promulgate a particular set of values and rests happily in the company of articles where particular values are stressed.

The main aim in the reader is to present a collection of articles and extracts which form a coherent whole. At times, this has meant selecting a particular article which may not be regarded by all as central to a writer's work. Eliot's extract on religion (11) is a case in point. However, it serves as a useful foil to other articles in that section such as the Eagleton, and, above all, makes valid points about an area important in its own right.

The length of the chapters depends upon a variety of factors. First, there is some attempt overall to create a balance among the genres, so that poetry, the novel and drama are reasonably represented across the chapters, although not in a pedantically symmetric way. Secondly, most articles are selected because they strike the editor as being particularly effective, but some are chosen because they represent a viewpoint considered to be important. Most of the articles in the teaching of English (Section VI) belong to the former category, while the MacDougall (13), for example, belongs to the latter. Length of chapter is to some degree arbitrary. In the editor's view, it is most useful to make Section VI on the teaching of English the longest section with most articles, but this was a straightforward value judgement.

The division of the responding to and the teaching of English

Literature into two sections (V and VI) does allow different parts of the process of teaching English Literature to be emphasized.

A discussion which is having increasing significance for the teacher of English is the relationship between literature and the media. Some of the ramifications of this relationship are reflected in Section III where such problems as what happens to literary works when they are adapted for television and radio are investigated. Such investigations range from interpretations of Shakespeare plays for radio (21) to evaluations of a television presentation of Bradbury's *The History Man* (17). Film, too, gives its own perspective to literary works, and this is evaluated in Chapters 19 and 20.

At different times in its history different emphases have been given to English in education, and in Section IV some of these debates are reflected, starting with *The Newbolt Report* and Sampson's *English for the English* (22). The flow of ideas following in the wake of the Dartmouth Seminar of 1966 is discussed and evaluated (23, 24). The official voice is represented in *The Bullock Report*. One of the most recent debates concerns structuralism and deconstruction, and the section concludes with discussion of these issues, linking up with the articles at the end of the first section.

As a general trend, the movement of the articles in this reader is from the abstract to the practical. Important as the theoretical concerns undoubtedly are, the sections on learning and teaching (Sections V and VI) should be of particular significance to the practising teacher. The aim of Section V is eclectic: it includes the views of psychologists and teachers, of the children themselves and of a 'practising' novelist in the art of the adolescent novel.

It is hoped that Section VI is particularly rich. In an important and central sense, the other sections meet here. The texts range from *Macbeth* (38) to *Coronation Street* (39), implicitly raising Section I issues as to the nature of literature. Of course, *Coronation Street* could be included in the media section (Section III), but the emphasis of the extract is on classroom purposes, so it is included here. These are important links, but joining them all together is the need for good practice.

'Assessment' (Section VII) is an area of almost constant change. Here, an attempt is made to include issues that are not only current but are also likely to prove fundamental and long lasting.

1 WHAT IS LITERATURE?

The Reader opens with a celebration, a celebration of the beauty and mystery of literature. Conrad's preface is a fitting start.

Verve and panache are the hallmarks of the second article where Eagleton raises a host of issues concerned with the definition of literature in a particularly economic way. It is not offered as a definitive statement of what literature is because Eagleton has a particular story to tell, but it is a touchstone for lively ideas. Eagleton stresses the importance of ideology in any definition of literature.

The Wordsworth extract is of a different time and a different thrust. It sheds a poet's light on what constitutes poetic art, discussing such issues as poetry — the 'spontaneous overflow of powerful feelings' — and style, giving a Romantic prescription whose afterglow we still live in today.

One of the powerful influences on literature in the twentieth century has been the work of the psychoanalyst, Sigmund Freud. Trilling investigates some of the strengths and weaknesses of this tradition in approaches to literature.

In a major statement on the function of twentieth-century criticism, Richards attacks the value of psychoanalysis as a tool for exploring literature. In his attack and in his argument that accounts of value and communication are the basis of criticism, he reveals important insights into what he regards literature to be.

The last two extracts deal with particularly modern trends in looking at the nature of literature, structuralism and deconstruction. Lerner attempts to analyse the nature of the debate between structuralism/deconstruction and 'traditional' English literature, seeing deconstruction as a combination of structuralism and the radicalism of its practitioners. Here there is a link back to the Eagleton article, because deconstructionists stress the ideology of literary judgements. Structuralism and deconstruction are often considered difficult ideas for those working outside these traditions. The last article, by Lodge, is an example of structuralism at work, although it must be stressed that it is a gentle example.

1 *Preface to* The Nigger of the 'Narcissus'

● Joseph Conrad

A work that aspires, however humbly, to the condition of art should carry its justification in every line. And art itself may be defined as a single-minded attempt to render the highest kind of justice to the visible universe, by bringing to light the truth, manifold and one, underlying its every aspect. It is an attempt to find in its forms, in its colours, in its light, in its shadows, in the aspects of matter and in the facts of life what of each is fundamental, what is enduring and essential — their one illuminating and convincing quality — the very truth of their existence. The artist, then, like the thinker or the scientist, seeks the truth and makes his appeal. Impressed by the aspect of the world the thinker plunges into ideas, the scientist into facts — whence, presently, emerging they make their appeal to those qualities of our being that fit us best for the hazardous enterprise of living. They speak authoritatively to our common-sense, to our intelligence, to our desire of peace or to our desire of unrest; not seldom to our prejudices, sometimes to our fears, often to our egoism — but always to our credulity. And their words are heard with reverence, for their concern is with weighty matters: with the cultivation of our minds and the proper care of our bodies, with the attainment of our ambitions, with the perfection of the means and the glorification of our precious aims.

It is otherwise with the artist.

Confronted by the same enigmatical spectacle the artist descends within himself, and in that lonely region of stress and strife, if he be deserving and fortunate, he finds the terms of his appeal. His appeal is made to our less obvious capacities: to that part of our nature which, because of the warlike conditions of existence, is necessarily kept out of sight within the more resisting and hard qualities — like the vulnerable body within a steel armour. His appeal is less loud, more profound, less distinct, more stirring — and sooner forgotten. Yet its effect endures forever. The changing wisdom of successive generations discards ideas, questions facts, demolishes theories. But the artist appeals to that part of our being which is not dependent on wisdom; to that in us which is a gift and not an acquisition — and, therefore, more permanently enduring. He speaks to our capacity for delight and wonder, to the sense of mystery surrounding our lives; to our sense of pity, and beauty, and pain; to the latent feeling of fellowship with all creation — and to the subtle but invincible conviction of solidarity that knits together the loneliness of innumerable hearts, to the solidarity in dreams, in joy, in sorrow, in aspirations, in illusions, in hope, in fear, which binds men to each other, which binds together all humanity — the dead to the living and the living to the unborn.

[...] Fiction — if it at all aspires to be art — appeals to temperament. And in truth it must be, like painting, like music, like all art, the appeal of one temperament to all the other innumerable temperaments whose subtle and resistless power endows passing events with their true meaning, and creates the moral, the emotional atmosphere of the place and time. Such an appeal to be effective must be an impression conveyed through the senses; and, in fact, it cannot be made in any other way, because temperament, whether individual or collective, is not amenable to persuasion. All art, therefore, appeals primarily to the senses, and the artistic aim when expressing itself in written words must also make its appeal through the senses, if its high desire is to reach the secret spring of responsive emotions. It must strenuously aspire to the plasticity of sculpture, to the colour of painting, and to the magic suggestiveness of music — which is the art of arts. And it is only through complete, unswerving devotion to the perfect blending of form and substance; it is only through an unremitting never-discouraged care for the shape and ring of sentences that an approach can be made to plasticity, to colour, and that the light of magic suggestiveness may be brought to play for an evanescent instant over the commonplace surface of words: of the old, old words, worn thin, defaced by ages of careless usage.

The sincere endeavour to accomplish that creative task, to go as far on that road as his strength will carry him, to go undeterred by faltering, weariness or reproach, is the only valid justification for the worker in prose. And if his conscience is clear, his answer to those who in the fulness of a wisdom which looks for immediate profit, demand specifically to be edified, consoled, amused; who demand to be promptly improved, or encouraged, or frightened, or shocked, or charmed, must run thus: My task which I am trying to achieve is, by the power of the written word to make you hear, to make you feel — it is, before all, to make you *see*. That — and no more, and it is everything. If I succeed, you shall find there according to your deserts: encouragement, consolation, fear, charm — all you demand — and, perhaps, also that glimpse of truth for which you have forgotten to ask.

To snatch in a moment of courage, from the remorseless rush of time, a passing phase of life, is only the beginning of the task. The task approached in tenderness and faith is to hold up unquestioningly, without choice and without fear, the rescued fragment before all eyes in the light of a sincere mood. It is to show its vibration, its colour, its form; and through its movement, its form, and its colour, reveal the substance of its truth — disclose its inspiring secret: the stress and passion within the core of each convincing moment. In a single-minded attempt of that kind, if one be deserving and fortunate, one may perchance attain to such clearness of sincerity that at last the presented vision of regret or pity, of terror or mirth, shall awaken in the hearts of the beholders that feeling of unavoidable solidarity; of the solidarity in mysterious origin, in toil, in joy, in hope, in uncertain fate, which binds men to each other and all mankind to the visible world.

It is evident that he who, rightly or wrongly, holds by the convictions expressed above cannot be faithful to any one of the temporary formulas of his craft. The enduring part of them — the truth which each only imperfectly veils — should abide with him as the most precious of his possessions, but they all: Realism, Romanticism, Naturalism, even the unofficial sentimentalism (which like the poor, is exceedingly difficult to get rid of), all these gods must, after a short period of fellowship, abandon him — even on the very threshold of the temple — to the stammerings of his conscience and to the outspoken consciousness of the difficulties of his work. In that uneasy solitude the supreme cry of Art for Art, itself, loses the exciting ring of its apparent immorality. It sounds far off. It has ceased to be a cry, and is heard only as a whisper, often incomprehensible, but at times and faintly encouraging.

Sometimes, stretched at ease in the shade of a roadside tree, we watch the motions of a labourer in a distant field, and after a time, begin to wonder languidly as to what the fellow may be at. We watch the movements of his body, the waving of his arms, we see him bend down, stand up, hesitate, begin again. It may add to the charm of an idle hour to be told the purpose of his exertions. If we know he is trying to lift a stone, to dig a ditch, to uproot a stump, we look with a more real interest at his efforts; we are disposed to condone the jar of his agitation upon the restfulness of the landscape; and even, if in a brotherly frame of mind, we may bring ourselves to forgive his failure. We understood his object, and, after all, the fellow has tried, and perhaps he had not the strength — and perhaps he had not the knowledge. We forgive, go on our way — and forget.

And so it is with the workman of art. Art is long and life is short, and success is very far off. And thus, doubtful of strength to travel so far, we talk a little about the aim — the aim of art, which like life itself, is inspiring, difficult — obscured by mists. It is not in the clear logic of a triumphant conclusion; it is not in the unveiling of one of those heartless secrets which are called the Laws of Nature. It is not less great, but only more difficult.

To arrest, for the space of a breath, the hands busy about the work of the earth, and compel men entranced by the sight of distant goals to glance for a moment at the surrounding vision of form and colour, of sunshine and shadows; to make them pause for a look, for a sigh, for a smile — such is the aim, difficult and evanescent, and reserved only for a very few to achieve. But sometimes, by the deserving and the fortunate, even that task is accomplished. And when it is accomplished — behold! — all the truth of life is there: a moment of vision, a sigh, a smile — and the return to an eternal rest.

2 *What is Literature?*

● Terry Eagleton

There have been various attempts to define literature. You can define it, for example, as 'imaginative' writing in the sense of fiction — writing which is not literally true. But even the briefest reflection on what people commonly include under the heading of literature suggests that this will not do. Seventeenth-century English literature includes Shakespeare, Webster, Marvell and Milton; but it also stretches to the essays of Francis Bacon, the sermons of John Donne, Bunyan's spiritual autobiography and whatever it was that Sir Thomas Browne wrote. It might even at a pinch be taken to encompass Hobbes's *Leviathan* or Clarendon's *History of the Rebellion*. French seventeenth-century literature contains, along with Corneille and Racine, La Rochefoucauld's maxims, Bossuet's funeral speeches, Boileau's treatise on poetry, Madame de Sévigné's letters to her daughter and the philosophy of Descartes and Pascal. Nineteenth-century English literature usually includes Lamb (though not Bentham), Macaulay (but not Marx), Mill (but not Darwin or Herbert Spencer).

A distinction between 'fact' and 'fiction', then, seems unlikely to get us very far, not least because the distinction itself is often a questionable one. It has been argued, for instance, that our own opposition between 'historical' and 'artistic' truth does not apply at all to the early Icelandic sagas.[1] In the English late sixteenth and early seventeenth centuries, the word 'novel' seems to have been used about both true and fictional events, and even news reports were hardly to be considered factual. Novels and news reports were neither clearly factual nor clearly fictional: our own sharp discriminations between these categories simply did not apply.[2] Gibbon no doubt thought that he was writing the historical truth, and so perhaps did the authors of Genesis, but they are now read as 'fact' by some and 'fiction' by others; Newman certainly thought his theological meditations were true but is now for many readers 'literature'. Moreover, if 'literature' includes much 'factual' writing, it also excludes quite a lot of fiction. *Superman* comic and Mills and Boon novels are fictional but not generally regarded as literature, and certainly not as Literature. If literature is 'creative' or 'imaginative' writing, does this imply that history, philosophy and natural science are uncreative and unimaginative?

Perhaps one needs a different kind of approach altogether. Perhaps literature is definable not according to whether it is fictional or 'imaginative', but because it uses language in peculiar ways. On this theory, literature is a kind of writing which, in the words of the Russian critic Roman Jakobson, represents an 'organized violence committed on ordinary speech'. Literature transforms and intensifies ordinary language, deviates systematically from everyday speech. If you approach me at a bus stop and murmur 'Thou still unravished bride of quietness,' then I am instantly aware that I am in the presence of the literary. I know this because the texture, rhythm and resonance of your words are in excess of their abstractable meaning — or, as the linguists might more technically put it, there is a disproportion between the signifiers and the signifieds. Your language draws attention to itself, flaunts its material being, as statements like 'Don't you know the drivers are on strike?' do not.

This, in effect, was the definition of the 'literary' advanced by the Russian formalists who emerged in Russia in the years before the 1917 Bolshevik revolution, and flourished throughout the 1920s, until they were effectively silenced by Stalinism. A militant, polemical group of critics, they rejected the quasi-mystical symbolist doctrines which had influenced literary criticism before them, and in a practical, scientific spirit shifted attention to the material reality of the literary text itself. Criticism should dissociate art from mystery and concern itself with how literary texts actually worked: literature was not pseudo-religion or psychology or sociology but a particular organization of language. It had its own specific laws, structures and devices, which were to be studied in themselves rather than reduced to something else. The literary work was neither a vehicle for ideas, a reflection of social reality nor the incarnation of some transcendental truth: it was a material fact, whose functioning could be analysed rather as one could examine a machine. It was made of words, not of objects or feelings, and it was a mistake to see it as the expression of an author's mind. Pushkin's *Eugene Onegin*, Osip Brik once airily remarked, would have been written even if Pushkin had not lived.

Formalism was essentially the application of linguistics to the study of literature; and because the linguistics in question were of a formal kind, concerned with the structures of language rather than with what one might actually say, the Formalists passed over the analysis of literary 'content' (where one might always be tempted into psychology or sociology) for the study of literary form. Far from seeing form as the expression of content, they stood the relationship on its head: content was merely the 'motivation' of form, an occasion or convenience for a particular kind of formal exercise. *Don Quixote* is not 'about' the character of that name: the character is just a device for holding together different kinds of narrative technique. *Animal Farm* for the Formalists would not be an allegory of Stalinism; on the contrary, Stalinism would simply provide a useful opportunity for the construction of an allegory. It was this perverse insistence which won for the Formalists their derogatory name from their antagonists; and though they did not deny that art had a relation to social reality — indeed some of them were closely associated with the Bolsheviks — they provocatively claimed that this relation was not the critic's business.

The Formalists started out by seeing the literary work as a more or less arbitrary assemblage of 'devices', and only later came to see these devices as interrelated elements or 'functions' within a total textual system. 'Devices' included sound, imagery, rhythm, syntax, metre, rhyme, narrative techniques, in fact the whole stock of formal literary elements; and what all of these elements had in common was their 'estranging' or 'defamiliarizing' effect. What was specific to literary language, what distinguished it from other forms of discourse, was that it 'deformed' ordinary language in various ways. Under the pressure of literary devices, ordinary language was intensified, condensed, twisted, telescoped, drawn out, turned on its head. It was language 'made strange'; and because of this estrangement, the everyday world was also suddenly made unfamiliar. In the routines of everyday speech, our perceptions of and responses to reality become stale, blunted, or, as the Formalists would say, 'automatized'. Literature, by forcing us into a dramatic awareness of language, refreshes these habitual responses and renders objects more 'perceptible'. By having to grapple with language in a more strenuous, self-conscious way than usual, the world which that language contains is vividly renewed. The poetry of Gerard Manley Hopkins might provide a particularly graphic example of this. Literary discourse estranges or alienates ordinary speech, but in doing so, paradoxically, brings us into a fuller, more intimate possession of experience. Most of the time we breathe in air without being conscious of it: like language, it is the very medium in which we move. But if the air is suddenly thickened or infected we are forced to attend to our breathing with new vigilance, and the effect of this may be a heightened experience of our bodily life. We read a scribbled note from a friend without paying much attention to its narrative structure; but if a story breaks off and begins again, switches constantly from one narrative level to another and delays its climax to keep us in suspense, we become freshly conscious of how it is constructed at the same time as our engagement with it may be intensified. The story, as the Formalists would argue, uses 'impeding' or 'retarding' devices to hold our attention; and in literary language, these devices are 'laid bare'. It was this which moved Viktor Shklovsky to remark mischievously of Laurence Sterne's *Tristram Shandy*, a novel which impedes its own story-line so much that it hardly gets off the ground, that it was 'the most typical novel in world literature'.

The Formalists, then, saw literary language as a set of deviations from a norm, a kind of linguistic violence: literature is a 'special' kind of language, in contrast to the 'ordinary' language we commonly use. But to spot a deviation implies being able to identify the norm from which it swerves. Though 'ordinary language' is a concept beloved of some Oxford philosophers, the ordinary language of Oxford philosophers has little in common with the ordinary language of Glaswegian dockers. The language both social groups use to write love letters usually differs from the way they talk to the local vicar. The idea that there is a single 'normal' language, a common currency shared equally by all members of society, is an illusion. Any actual language consists of a highly complex range of discourses, differentiated according to class, region, gender, status and so on, which can by no means be neatly unified into a single homogeneous linguistic community. One person's norm may be another's deviation: 'ginnel' for 'alleyway' may be poetic in Brighton but ordinary language in Barnsley. Even the most 'prosaic' text of the fifteenth century may sound 'poetic' to us today because of its archaism. If we were to stumble across an isolated scrap of writing from some long-vanished civilization, we could not tell whether it was 'poetry' merely by inspecting it, since we might have no access to that society's 'ordinary' discourses; and even if further research were to reveal that it was 'deviatory', this would still not prove that it was poetry as not all linguistic deviations are poetic. Slang, for example: we would not be able to tell just by looking at it that it was not a piece of 'realist' literature, without much more information about the way it actually functioned as a piece of writing within the society in question.

It is not that the Russian Formalists did not realize all this. They recognized that norms and deviations shifted around from one social or historical context to another — that 'poetry' in this sense depends on where you happen to be standing at the time. The fact that a piece of language was 'estranging' did not guarantee that it was always and everywhere so: it was estranging only against a certain normative linguistic background, and if this altered then the writing might cease to be perceptible as literary. If everyone used phrases like 'unravished bride of quietness' in ordinary pub conversation, this kind of language might cease to be poetic. For the Formalists, in other words, 'literariness' was a function of the *differential* relations between one sort of discourse and another; it was not an eternally given property. They were not out to define 'literature', but 'literariness' — special uses of language, which could be found in 'literary' texts but also in many places outside them. Anyone who believes that 'literature' can be defined by such special uses of language has to face the fact that there is more metaphor in Manchester than there is in Marvell. There is no 'literary' device — metonymy, synecdoche, litotes, chiasmus and so on — which is not quite intensively used in daily discourse.

Nevertheless, the Formalists still presumed that 'making strange' was the essence of the literary. It was just that they relativized this use of language, saw it as a matter of contrast between one type of speech and another. But what if I were to hear someone at the next pub table remark 'This is awfully squiggly handwriting!' Is this 'literary' or 'non-literary' language? As a matter of fact it is 'literary' language, because it comes from Knut Hamsun's novel *Hunger*. But how do I know that it is literary? It doesn't, after all, focus any particular attention on itself as a verbal performance. One answer to the question of how I know that this is literary is that it comes from Knut Hamsun's novel *Hunger*. It is part of a text which I read as 'fictional', which announces itself as a 'novel', which may be put on university literature syllabuses and so on. The *context* tells me that it is literary; but the language itself has no inherent properties or qualities which might distinguish it from other kinds of discourse, and someone might well say this in a pub without being admired for their literary dexterity. To think of literature as the Formalists do is really to think of all literature as *poetry*. Significantly, when the Formalists came to consider prose writing, they often simply extended to it the kinds of technique they had used with poetry. But literature is usually judged to contain much besides poetry — to include, for example, realist or naturalistic writing which is not linguistically self-conscious or self-exhibiting in any striking way. People sometimes call writing 'fine' precisely because it *doesn't* draw undue attention to itself: they admire its laconic plainness or low-keyed sobriety. And what about jokes, football chants and slogans, newspaper headlines, advertisements, which are often verbally flamboyant but not generally classified as literature?

Another problem with the 'estrangement' case is that there is no kind of writing which cannot, given sufficient ingenuity, be read as estranging. Consider a prosaic, quite unambiguous statement like the one sometimes seen in the London underground system: 'Dogs must be carried on the escalator.' This is not perhaps quite as unambiguous as it seems at first sight: does it mean that you *must* carry a dog on the escalator? Are you likely to be banned from the escalator unless you can find some stray mongrel to clutch in your arms on the way up? Many apparently straightforward notices contain such ambiguities: 'Refuse to be put in this basket', for instance, or the British road-sign 'Way Out' as read by a Californian. But even leaving such troubling ambiguities aside, it is surely obvious that the underground notice could be read as literature. One could let oneself be arrested by the abrupt, minatory *staccato* of the first ponderous monosyllables; find one's mind drifting, by the time it had reached the rich allusiveness of 'carried', to suggestive resonances of helping lame dogs through life; and perhaps even detect in the very lilt and inflection of the word 'escalator' a miming of the rolling, up-and-down motion of the thing itself. This may well be a fruitless sort of pursuit, but it is not significantly more fruitless than claiming to hear the cut and thrust of the rapiers in some poetic description of a duel, and it at least has the advantage of suggesting that 'literature' may be at least as much a question of what people do to writing as of what writing does to them.

But even if someone were to read the notice in this way, it would still be a matter of reading it as *poetry*, which is only part of what is usually included in literature. Let us therefore consider another way of 'misreading' the sign which might move us a little beyond this. Imagine a late-night drunk doubled over the escalator handrail who reads the notice with laborious attentiveness for several minutes and then mutters to himself 'How true!' What kind of mistake is occurring here? What the drunk is doing, in fact, is taking the sign as some statement of general, even cosmic significance. By applying certain conventions of reading to its words, he prises them loose from their immediate context and generalizes them beyond their pragmatic purpose to something of wider and probably deeper import. This would certainly seem to be one operation involved in what people call literature. When the poet tells us that his love is like a red rose, we know by the very fact that he puts this statement in metre that we are not supposed to ask whether he actually had a lover who for some bizarre reason seemed to him to resemble a rose. He is telling us something about women and love in general. Literature, then, we might say, is 'non-pragmatic' discourse: unlike biology textbooks and notes to the milkman it serves no immediate practical purpose, but is to be taken as referring to a general state of affairs. Sometimes, though not always, it may employ peculiar language as though to make this fact obvious — to signal that what is at stake is a *way of talking* about a woman, rather than any particular real-life woman. This focusing on the way of talking, rather than on the reality of what is talked about, is sometimes taken to indicate that we mean by literature a kind of *self-referential* language, a language which talks about itself.

There are, however, problems with this way of defining literature too. For one thing, it would probably have come as a surprise to George Orwell to hear that his essays were to be read as though the topics he discussed were less important than the way he discussed them. In much that is classified as literature, the truth-value and practical relevance of what is said *is* considered important to the overall effect. But even if treating discourse 'non-pragmatically' is part of what is meant by 'literature', then it follows from this 'definition' that literature cannot in fact be 'objectively' defined. It leaves the definition of literature up to how somebody decides to *read*, not to the nature of what is written. There are certain kinds of writing — poems, plays, novels — which are fairly obviously intended to be 'non-pragmatic' in this sense, but this does not guarantee that they will actually be read in this way. I might well read Gibbon's account of the Roman empire not because I am misguided enough to believe that it will be reliably informative about ancient Rome but because I enjoy Gibbon's prose style, or revel in images of human corruption whatever their historical source. But I might read Robert Burns's poem because it is not clear to me, as a Japanese horticulturalist, whether or not the red rose flourished in eighteenth-century Britain. This, it will be said, is not reading it 'as literature'; but am I reading Orwell's essays as literature only if I generalize what he says about the Spanish civil war to some cosmic utterance about human life? It is true that many of the works studied as literature in academic institutions were 'constructed' to be read as literature, but it is also true that many of them were not. A piece of writing may start off life as history or philosophy and then come to be ranked as literature; or it may start off as literature and then come to be valued for its archaeological significance. Some texts are born literary, some achieve literariness, and some have literariness thrust upon them. Breeding in this respect may count for a good deal more than birth. What matters may not be where you came from but how people treat you. If they decide that you are literature then it seems that you are, irrespective of what you thought you were.

In this sense, one can think of literature less as some inherent quality or set of qualities displayed by certain kinds of writing all the way from *Beowulf* to Virginia Woolf, than as a number of ways in which people *relate themselves* to writing. It would not be easy to isolate, from all that has been variously called 'literature', some constant set of inherent features. In fact it would be as impossible as trying to identify the single distinguishing feature which all games have in common. There is no 'essence' of literature whatsoever. Any bit of writing may be read 'non-pragmatically', if that is what reading a text as literature means, just as any writing may be read 'poetically'. If I pore over the railway timetable not to discover a train connection but to stimulate in myself general reflections on the speed and complexity of modern existence, then I might be said to be reading it as literature. John M. Ellis has argued that the term 'literature' operates rather like the word 'weed': weeds are not particular kinds of plant, but just any kind of plant which for some reason or another a gardener does not want around.[3] Perhaps 'literature' means something like the opposite: any kind of writing which for some reason or another somebody values highly. As the philosophers might say, 'literature' and 'weed' are *functional* rather than *ontological* terms: they tell us about what we do, not about the fixed being of things. They tell us about the role of a text or a thistle in a social context, its relations with and differences from its surroundings, the ways it behaves, the purposes it may be put to and the human practices clustered around it. 'Literature' is in this sense a purely formal, empty sort of definition. Even if we claim that it is a non-pragmatic treatment of language, we have still not arrived at an 'essence' of literature because this is also so of other linguistic practices such as jokes. In any case, it is far from clear that we can discriminate neatly between 'practical' and 'non-practical' ways of relating ourselves to language. Reading a novel for pleasure obviously differs from reading a road sign for information, but how about reading a biology textbook to improve your mind? Is that a 'pragmatic' treatment of language or not? In many societies, 'literature' has served highly practical functions such as religious ones; distinguishing sharply between 'practical' and 'non-practical' may only be possible in a society like ours, where literature has ceased to have much practical function at all. We may be offering as a general definition a sense of the 'literary' which is in fact historically specific.

We may have still not discovered the secret, then, of why Lamb, Macaulay and Mill are literature but not, generally speaking, Bentham, Marx and Darwin. Perhaps the simple answer is that the first three are examples of 'fine writing', whereas the last three are not. This answer has the disadvantage of being largely untrue, at least in my judgement, but it has the advantage of suggesting that by and large people term 'literature' writing which they think is *good*. An obvious objection to this is that if it were entirely true there would be no such thing as 'bad literature'. I may consider Lamb and Macaulay overrated, but that does not necessarily mean that I stop regarding them as literature. You may consider Raymond Chandler 'good of his kind', but not exactly literature. On the other hand, if Macaulay were a *really* bad writer — if he had no grasp at all of grammar and seemed interested in nothing but white mice — then people might well not call his work literature at all, even bad literature. Value-judgements would certainly seem to have a lot to do with what is judged literature and what is not — not necessarily in the sense that writing has to be 'fine' to be literary, but that it has to be *of the kind* that is judged fine: it may be an inferior example of a generally valued mode. Nobody would bother to say that a bus ticket was an example of inferior literature, but someone might well say that the poetry of Ernest Dowson was. The term 'fine writing', or *belles lettres*, is in this sense ambiguous: it denotes a sort of writing which is generally highly regarded, while not necessarily committing you to the opinion that a particular specimen of it is 'good'.

With this reservation, the suggestion that 'literature' is a highly valued kind of writing is an illuminating one. But it has one fairly devastating consequence. It means that we can drop once and for all the illusion that the category 'literature' is 'objective', in the sense of being eternally given and immutable. Anything can be literature, and anything which is regarded as unalterably and unquestionably literature — Shakespeare, for example — can cease to be literature. Any belief that the study of literature is the study of a stable, well-definable entity, as entomology is the study of insects, can be abandoned as a chimera. Some kinds of fiction are literature and some are not; some literature is fictional and some is not; some literature is verbally self-regarding, while some highly-wrought rhetoric is not literature. Literature, in the sense of a set of works of assured and unalterable value, distinguished by certain shared inherent properties, does not exist. When I use the words 'literary' and 'literature', then, I place them under an invisible crossing-out mark, to indicate that these terms will not really do but that we have no better ones at the moment.

The reason why it follows from the definition of literature as highly valued writing that it is not a stable entity is that value-judgements are notoriously variable. 'Times change, values don't,' announces an advertisement for a daily newspaper, as though we still believed in killing off infirm infants or putting the mentally ill on public show. Just as people may treat a work as philosophy in one century and as literature in the next, or vice versa, so they may change their minds about what writing they consider valuable. They may even change their minds about the grounds they use for judging what is valuable and what is not. This, as I have suggested, does not necessarily mean that they will refuse the title of literature to a work which they have come to deem inferior: they may still call it literature, meaning roughly that it belongs to the *type* of writing which they generally value. But it does mean that the so-called 'literary canon', the unquestioned 'great tradition' of the 'national literature', has to be recognized as a *construct*, fashioned by particular people for particular reasons at a certain time. There is no such thing as a literary work or tradition which is valuable *in itself*, regardless of what anyone might have said or come to say about it. 'Value' is a transitive term: it means whatever is valued by certain people in specific situations, according to particular criteria and in the light of given purposes.[...]

The fact that we always interpret literary works to some extent in the light of our own concerns — indeed that in one sense of 'our own concerns' we are incapable of doing anything else — might be one reason why certain works of literature seem to retain their value across the centuries. It may be, of course, that we still share many preoccupations with the work itself; but it may also be that people have not actually been valuing the 'same' work at all, even though they may think they have. 'Our' Homer is not identical with the Homer of the Middle Ages, nor 'our' Shakespeare with that of his contemporaries; it is rather that different historical periods have constructed a 'different' Homer and Shakespeare for their own purposes, and found in these texts elements to value or devalue, though not necessarily the same ones. All literary works, in other words, are 'rewritten', if only unconsciously, by the societies which read them; indeed there is no reading of a work which is not also a 're-writing'. No work, and no current evaluation of it, can simply be extended to new groups of people without being changed, perhaps almost unrecognizably, in the process; and this is one reason why what counts as literature is a notably unstable affair.

I do not mean that it is unstable because value-judgements are 'subjective'. According to this view, the world is divided between solid facts 'out there' like Grand Central station, and arbitrary value-judgements 'in here' such as liking bananas or feeling that the tone of a Yeats poem veers from defensive hectoring to grimly resilient resignation. Facts are public and unimpeachable, values are private and gratuitous. There is an obvious difference between recounting a fact, such as 'This cathedral was built in 1612,' and registering a value-judgement, such as 'This cathedral is a magnificent specimen of baroque architecture.' But suppose I made the first kind of statement while showing an overseas visitor around England, and found that it puzzled her considerably. Why, she might ask, do you keep telling me the dates of the foundation of all these buildings? Why this obsession with origins? In the society I live in, she might go on, we keep no record at all of such events: we classify our buildings instead according to whether they face north-west or south-east. What this might do would be to demonstrate part of the unconscious system of value-judgements which underlies my own descriptive statements. Such value-judgements are not necessarily of the same kind as 'This cathedral is a magnificent specimen of baroque architecture,' but they are value-judgements nonetheless, and no factual pronouncement I make can escape them. Statements of fact are after all *statements*, which presumes a number of questionable judgements: that those statements are worth making, perhaps more worth making than certain others, that I am the sort of person entitled to make them and perhaps able to guarantee their truth, that you are the kind of person worth making them to, that something useful is accomplished by making them, and so on. A pub conversation may well transmit information, but what also bulks large in such dialogue is a strong element of what linguists would call the 'phatic', a concern with the act of communication itself. In chatting to you about the weather I am also signalling that I regard conversation with you as valuable, that I consider you a worthwhile person to talk to, that I am not myself anti-social or about to embark on a detailed critique of your personal appearance.

In this sense, there is no possibility of a wholly disinterested statement. Of course stating when a cathedral was built is reckoned to be more disinterested in our own culture than passing an opinion about its architecture, but one could also imagine situations in which the former statement would be more 'value-laden' than the latter. Perhaps 'baroque' and 'magnificent' have come to be more or less synonymous, whereas only a stubborn rump of us cling to the belief that the date when a building was founded is significant, and my statement is taken as a coded way of signalling this partisanship. All of our descriptive statements move within an often invisible network of value-categories, and indeed without such categories we would have nothing to say to each other at all. It is not just as though we have something called factual knowledge which may then be distorted by particular interests and judgements, although this is certainly possible; it is also that without particular interests we would have no knowledge at all, because we would not see the point of bothering to get to know anything. Interests are *constitutive* of our knowledge, not merely prejudices which imperil it. The claim that knowledge should be 'value-free' is itself a value-judgement.

It may well be that a liking for bananas is a merely private matter, though this is in fact questionable. A thorough analysis of my tastes in food would probably reveal how deeply relevant they are to certain formative experiences in early childhood, to my relations with my parents and siblings and to a good many other cultural factors which are quite as social and 'non-subjective' as railway stations. This is even more true of that fundamental structure of beliefs and interests which I am born into as a member of a particular society, such as the belief that I should try to keep in good health, that differences of sexual role are rooted in human biology or that human beings are more important than crocodiles. We may disagree on this or that, but we can only do so because we share certain 'deep' ways of seeing and valuing which are bound up with our social life, and which could not be changed without transforming that life. Nobody will penalize me heavily if I dislike a particular Donne poem but if I argue that Donne is not literature at all then in certain circumstances I might risk losing my job. I am free to vote Labour or Conservative, but if I try to act on the belief that this choice itself merely masks a deeper prejudice — the prejudice that the meaning of democracy is confined to putting a cross on a ballot paper every few years — then in certain unusual circumstances I might end up in prison.

The largely concealed structure of values which informs and underlies our factual statements is part of what is meant by 'ideology'. By 'ideology' I mean, roughly, the ways in which what we say and believe connects with the power-structure and power-relations of the society we live in. It follows from such a rough definition of ideology that not all of our underlying judgements and categories can usefully be said to be ideological. It is deeply ingrained in us to imagine ourselves moving forwards into the future (at least one other society sees itself as moving backwards into it), but though this way of seeing *may* connect significantly with the power-structure of our society, it need not always and everywhere do so. I do not mean by 'ideology' simply the deeply entrenched, often unconscious beliefs which people hold; I mean more particularly those modes of feeling, valuing, perceiving and believing which have some kind of relation to the maintenance and reproduction of social power. The fact that such beliefs are by no means merely private quirks may be illustrated by a literary example.

In his famous study *Practical Criticism* (1929), the Cambridge critic I. A. Richards sought to demonstrate just how whimsical and subjective literary value-judgements could actually be by giving his undergraduates a set of poems, withholding from them the titles and authors' names, and asking them to evaluate them. The resulting judgements, notoriously, were highly variable: time-honoured poets were marked down and obscure authors celebrated. To my mind, however, much the most interesting aspect of this project, and one apparently quite invisible to Richards himself, is just how tight a consensus of unconscious valuations underlies these particular differences of opinion. Reading Richards' undergraduates' accounts of literary works, one is struck by the habits of perception and interpretation which they spontaneously share — what they expect literature to be, what assumptions they bring to a poem and what fulfilments they anticipate they will derive from it. None of this is really surprising: for all the participants in this experiment were, presumably, young, white, upper- or upper middle-class, privately educated English people of the 1920s, and how they responded to a poem depended on a good deal more than purely 'literary' factors. Their critical responses were deeply entwined with their broader prejudices and beliefs. This is not a matter of *blame*: there is no critical response which is not so entwined, and thus no such thing as a 'pure' literary critical judgement or interpretation. If anybody is to be blamed it is I. A. Richards himself, who as a young, white, upper-middle-class male Cambridge don was unable to objectify a context of interests which he himself largely shared, and was thus unable to recognize fully that local, 'subjective' differences of evaluation work within a particular, socially structured way of perceiving the world.

If it will not do to see literature as an 'objective', descriptive category, neither will it do to say that literature is just what people whimsically choose to call literature. For there is nothing at all whimsical about such kinds of value-judgement: they have their roots in deeper structures of belief which are as apparently unshakeable as the Empire State building. What we have uncovered, then, is not only that literature does not exist in the sense that insects do, and that the value-judgements by which it is constituted are historically variable, but that these value-judgements themselves have a close relation to social ideologies. They refer in the end not simply to private taste, but to the assumptions by which certain social groups exercise and maintain power over others.

NOTES

1. See M. I. Steblin-Kamenskij, *The Saga Mind* (Odense, 1973).
2. See Lennard J. Davis, 'A Social History of Fact and Fiction: Authorial Disavowal in the Early English Novel', in Edward W. Said (ed.), *Literature and Society* (Baltimore and London, 1980).
3. *The Theory of Literary Criticism: A Logical Analysis* (Berkeley, 1974), pp. 37–42.

3 *Preface to* Lyrical Ballads

● William Wordsworth

[...] Taking up the subject upon general grounds, I ask what is meant by the word Poet? What is a Poet? To whom does he address himself? And what language is to be expected from him? He is a man speaking to men: a man, it is true, endued with more lively sensibility, more enthusiasm and tenderness, who has a greater knowledge of human nature, and a more comprehensive soul, than are supposed to be common among mankind; a man pleased with his own passions and volitions, and who rejoices more than other men in the spirit of life that is in him; delighting to contemplate similar volitions and passions as manifested in the goings-on of the Universe, and habitually impelled to create them where he does not find them. To these qualities he has added a disposition to be affected more than other men by absent things as if they were present; an ability of conjuring up in himself passions, which are indeed far from being the same as those produced by real events, yet (especially in those parts of the general sympathy which are pleasing and delightful) do more nearly resemble the passions produced by real events, than any thing which, from the motions of their own minds merely, other men are accustomed to feel in themselves; whence, and from practice, he has acquired a greater readiness and power in expressing what he thinks and feels, and especially those thoughts and feelings which, by his own choice, or from the structure of his own mind, arise in him without immediate external excitement.

But, whatever portion of this faculty we may suppose even the greatest Poet to possess, there cannot be a doubt but that the language which it will suggest to him, must, in liveliness and truth, fall far short of that which is uttered by men in real life, under the actual pressure of those passions, certain shadows of which the Poet thus produces, or feels to be produced, in himself. However exalted a notion we would wish to cherish of the character of a Poet, it is obvious, that, while he describes and imitates passions, his situation is altogether slavish and mechanical, compared with the freedom and power of real and substantial action and suffering. So that it will be the wish of the Poet to bring his feelings near to those of the persons whose feelings he describes, nay, for short spaces of time perhaps, to let himself slip into an entire delusion, and even confound and identify his own feelings with theirs; modifying only the language which is thus suggested to him, by a consideration that he describes for a particular purpose, that of giving pleasure. Here, then, he will apply the principle [...] of selection; on this he will depend for removing what would otherwise be painful or disgusting in the passion; he will feel that there is no necessity to trick out or elevate nature: and, the more industriously he applies this principle, the deeper will be his faith that no words, which his fancy or imagination can suggest, will be to be compared with those which are in the emanations of reality and truth.

But it may be said by those who do not object to the general spirit of these remarks, that, as it is impossible for the Poet to produce upon all occasions language as exquisitely fitted for the passion as that which the real passion itself suggests, it is proper that he should consider himself as in the situation of a translator, who deems himself justified when he substitutes excellences of another kind for those which are unattainable by him; and endeavours occasionally to surpass his original, in order to make some amends for the general inferiority to which he feels that he must submit. But this would be to encourage idleness and unmanly despair. Further, it is the language of men who speak of what they do not understand; who talk of Poetry as of a matter of amusement and idle pleasure; who will converse with us as gravely about a *taste* for Poetry, as they express it, as if it were a thing as indifferent as a taste for Rope-dancing, or Frontiniac or Sherry. Aristotle, I have been told, hath said, that Poetry is the most philosophic of all writing: it is so: its object is truth, not individual and local, but general, and operative; not standing upon external testimony, but carried alive into the heart by passion; truth which is its own testimony, which gives strength and divinity to the tribunal to which it appeals, and receives them from the same tribunal. Poetry is the image of man and nature. The obstacles which stand in the way of the fidelity of the Biographer and Historian, and of their consequent utility, are incalculably greater than those which are to be encountered by the Poet who has an adequate notion of the dignity of his art. The Poet writes under one restriction only, namely, that of the necessity of giving immediate pleasure to a human Being possessed of that information which may be expected from him, not as a lawyer, a physician, a mariner, an astronomer or a natural philosopher, but as a Man. Except this one restriction, there is no object standing between the Poet and the image of things; between this, and the Biographer and Historian there are a thousand.

Nor let this necessity of producing immediate pleasure be considered as a degradation of the Poet's art. It is far otherwise. It is an acknowledgement of the beauty of the universe, an acknowledgement the more sincere, because it is not formal, but indirect; it is a task light and easy to him who looks at the world in the spirit of love: further, it is a homage paid to the native and naked dignity of man, to the grand elementary principle of pleasure, by which he knows, and feels, and lives, and moves. We have no sympathy but what is propagated by pleasure: I would not be misunderstood; but wherever we sympathize with pain it will be found that the sympathy is produced and carried on by subtle combinations with pleasure. We have no knowledge, that is, no general principles drawn from the contemplation of particular facts, but what has been built up by pleasure, and exists in us by pleasure alone. The Man of Science, the Chemist and Mathematician, whatever difficulties and disgusts they may have had to struggle with, know and feel this. However painful may be the objects with which the Anatomist's knowledge is connected, he feels that his knowledge is pleasure; and where he has no pleasure he has no knowledge. What then does the Poet? He considers man and the objects that surround him as acting and re-acting upon each other, so as to produce an infinite complexity of pain and pleasure; he considers man in his own nature and in his ordinary life as contemplating this with a certain quantity of immediate knowledge, with certain convictions, intuitions, and deductions which by habit become of the nature of intuitions; he considers him as looking upon this complex scene of ideas and sensations, and finding every where objects that immediately excite in him sympathies which, from the necessities of his nature, are accompanied by an overbalance of enjoyment.

To this knowledge which all men carry about with them, and to these sympathies in which without any other discipline than that of our daily life we are fitted to take delight, the Poet principally directs his attention. He considers man and nature as essentially adapted to each other, and the mind of man as naturally the mirror of the fairest and most interesting qualities of nature. And thus the Poet, prompted by this feeling of pleasure which accompanies him through the whole course of his studies, converses with general nature with affections akin to those, which, through labour and length of time, the Man of Science has raised up in himself, by conversing with those particular parts of nature which are the objects of his studies. The knowledge both of the Poet and the Man of Science is pleasure; but the knowledge of the one cleaves to us as a necessary part of our existence, our natural and unalienable inheritance; the other is a personal and individual acquisition, slow to come to us, and by no habitual and direct sympathy connecting us with our fellow-beings. The Man of Science seeks truth as a remote and unknown benefactor; he cherishes and loves it in his solitude: the Poet, singing a song in which all human beings join with him, rejoices in the presence of truth as our visible friend and hourly companion. Poetry is the breath and finer spirit of all knowledge; it is the impassioned expression which is in the countenance of all Science. Emphatically may it be said of the Poet, as Shakespeare hath said of man, 'that he looks before and after.' He is the rock of defence of human nature; an upholder and preserver, carrying every where with him relationship and love. In spite of difference of soil and climate, of language and manners, of laws and customs, in spite of things silently gone out of mind and things violently destroyed, the Poet binds together by passion and knowledge the vast empire of human society, as it is spread over the whole earth, and over all time. The objects of the Poet's thoughts are every where; though the eyes and senses of man are, it is true, his favorite guides, yet he will follow wheresoever he can find an atmosphere of sensation in which to move his wings. Poetry is the first and last of all knowledge — it is as immortal as the heart of man. If the labours of Men of Science should ever create any material revolution, direct or indirect, in our condition, and in the impressions which we habitually receive, the Poet will sleep then no more than at present, but he will be ready to follow the steps of the Man of Science, not only in those general indirect effects, but he will be at his side, carrying sensation into the midst of the objects of the Science itself. The remotest discoveries of the Chemist, the Botanist, or Mineralogist, will be as proper objects of the Poet's art as any upon which it can be employed, if the time should ever come when these things shall be familiar to us, and the relations under which they are contemplated by the followers of these respective Sciences shall be manifestly and palpably material to us as enjoying and suffering beings. If the time should ever come when what is now called Science, thus familiarized to men, shall be ready to put on, as it were, a form of flesh and blood, the Poet will lend his divine spirit to aid the transfiguration, and will welcome the Being thus produced, as a dear and genuine inmate of the household of man. — It is not, then, to be supposed that any one, who holds that sublime notion of Poetry which I have attempted to convey, will break in upon the sanctity and truth of his pictures by transitory and accidental ornaments, and endeavour to excite admiration of himself by arts, the necessity of which must manifestly depend upon the assumed meanness of his subject.

What I have thus far said applies to Poetry in general; but especially to those parts of composition where the Poet speaks through the mouths of his characters; and upon this point it appears to have such weight that I will conclude, there are few persons of good sense, who would not allow that the dramatic parts of composition are defective, in proportion as they deviate from the real language of nature, and are coloured by a diction of the Poet's own, either peculiar to him as an individual Poet, or belonging simply to Poets in general, to a body of men who, from the circumstance of their compositions being in metre, it is expected will employ a particular language.

It is not, then, in the dramatic parts of composition that we look for this distinction of language; but still it may be proper and necessary where the Poet speaks to us in his own person and character. To this I answer by referring my Reader to the description which I have before given of a Poet. Among the qualities which I have enumerated as principally conducing to form a Poet, is implied nothing differing in kind from other men, but only in degree. The sum of what I have there said is, that the Poet is chiefly distinguished from other men by a greater promptness to think and feel without immediate external excitement, and a greater power in expressing such thoughts and feelings as are produced in him in that manner. But these passions and thoughts and feelings are the general passions and thoughts and feelings of men. And with what are they connected? Undoubtedly with our moral sentiments and animal sensations, and with the causes which excite these; with the operations of the elements and the appearances of the visible universe; with storm and sun-shine, with the revolutions of the seasons, with cold and heat, with loss of friends and kindred, with injuries and resentments, gratitude and hope, with fear and sorrow. These, and the like, are the sensations and objects which the Poet describes, as they are the sensations of other men, and the objects which interest them. The Poet thinks and feels in the spirit of the passions of men. How, then, can his language differ in any material degree from that of all other men who feel vividly and see clearly? It might be *proved* that it is impossible. But supposing that this were not the case, the Poet might then be allowed to use a peculiar language when expressing his feelings for his own gratification, or that of men like himself. But Poets do not write for Poets alone, but for men. Unless therefore we are advocates for that admiration which depends upon ignorance, and that pleasure which arises from hearing what we do not understand, the Poet must descend from this supposed height, and, in order to excite rational sympathy, he must express himself as other men express themselves. To this it may be added, that while he is only selecting from the real language of men, or, which amounts to the same thing, composing accurately in the spirit of such selection, he is treading upon safe ground, and we know what we are to expect from him. Our feelings are the same with respect to metre; for, as it may be proper to remind the Reader, the distinction of metre is regular and uniform, and not like that which is produced by what is usually called poetic diction, arbitrary, and subject to infinite caprices upon which no calculation whatever can be made. In the one case, the Reader is utterly at the mercy of the Poet respecting what imagery or diction he may choose to connect with the passion, whereas, in the other, the metre obeys certain laws, to which the Poet and Reader both willingly submit because they are certain, and because no interference is made by them with the passion but such as the concurring testimony of ages has shown to heighten and improve the pleasure which co-exists with it.

It will now be proper to answer an obvious question, namely, Why, professing these opinions, have I written in verse? To this, in addition to such answer as is included in what I have already said, I reply in the first place, because, however I may have restricted myself, there is still left open to me what confessedly constitutes the most valuable object of all writing, whether in prose or verse, the great and universal passions of men, the most general and interesting of their occupations, and the entire world of nature, from which I am at liberty to supply myself with endless combinations of forms and imagery. Now, supposing for a moment that whatever is interesting in these objects may be as vividly described in prose, why am I to be condemned, if to such description I have endeavoured to superadd the charm which, by the consent of all nations, is acknowledged to exist in metrical language? To this, by such as are unconvinced by what I have already said, it may be answered, that a very small part of the pleasure given by Poetry depends upon the metre, and that it is injudicious to write in metre, unless it be accompanied with the other artificial distinctions of style with which metre is usually accompanied, and that by such deviation more will be lost from the shock which will be thereby given to the Reader's associations, than will be counterbalanced by any pleasure which he can derive from the general power of numbers. In answer to those who still contend for the necessity of accompanying metre with certain appropriate colours of style in order to the accomplishment of its appropriate end, and who also, in my opinion, greatly under-rate the power of metre in itself, it might perhaps, as far as relates to these Poems, have been almost sufficient to observe, that poems are extant, written upon more humble subjects, and in a more naked and simple style than I have aimed at, which poems have continued to give pleasure from generation to generation. Now, if nakedness and simplicity be a defect, the fact here mentioned affords a strong presumption that poems somewhat less naked and simple are capable of affording pleasure at the present day; and, what I wished *chiefly* to attempt, at present, was to justify myself for having written under the impression of this belief.

But I might point out various causes why, when the style is manly, and the subject of some importance, words metrically arranged will long continue to impart such a pleasure to mankind as he who is sensible of the extent of that pleasure will be desirous to impart. The end of Poetry is to produce excitement in co-existence with an over-balance of pleasure. Now, by the supposition, excitement is an unusual and irregular state of the mind; ideas and feelings do not in that state succeed each other in accustomed order. But, if the words by which this excitement is produced are in themselves powerful, or the images and feelings have an undue proportion of pain connected with them, there is some danger that the excitement may be carried beyond its proper bounds. Now the co-presence of something regular, something to which the mind has been accustomed in various moods and in a less excited state, cannot but have great efficacy in tempering and restraining the passion by an intertexture of ordinary feeling, and of feeling not strictly and necessarily connected with the passion. This is unquestionably true, and hence, though the opinion will at first appear paradoxical, from the tendency of metre to divest language in a certain degree of its reality, and thus to throw a sort of half consciousness of unsubstantial existence over the whole composition, there can be little doubt but that more pathetic situations and sentiments, that is, those which have a greater proportion of pain connected with them, may be endured in metrical composition, especially in rhyme, than in prose. The metre of the old Ballads is very artless; yet they contain many passages which would illustrate this opinion. This opinion may be further illustrated by appealing to the Reader's own experience of the reluctance with which he comes to the re-perusal of the distressful parts of Clarissa Harlowe, or the Gamester. While Shakespeare's writings, in the most pathetic scenes, never act upon us as pathetic beyond the bounds of pleasure — an effect which, in a much greater degree than might at first be imagined, is to be ascribed to small, but continual and regular impulses of pleasurable surprise from the metrical arrangement. — On the other hand (what it must be allowed will much more frequently happen) if the Poet's words should be incommensurate with the passion, and inadequate to raise the Reader to a height of desirable excitement, then (unless the Poet's choice of his metre has been grossly injudicious), in the feelings of pleasure which the Reader has been accustomed to connect with metre in general, and in the feeling, whether cheerful or melancholy, which he has been accustomed to connect with that particular movement of metre, there will be found something which will greatly contribute to impart passion to the words, and to effect the complex end which the Poet proposes to himself.

If I had undertaken a systematic defence of the theory upon which these poems [the *Lyrical Ballads*] are written, it would have been my duty to develope the various causes upon which the pleasure received from metrical language depends. Among the chief of these causes is to be reckoned a principle which must be well known to those who have made any of the Arts the object of accurate reflection; I mean the pleasure which the mind derives from the perception of similitude in dissimilitude. This principle is the great spring of the activity of our minds, and their chief feeder. From this principle the direction of the sexual appetite, and all the passions connected with it, take their origin: it is the life of our ordinary conversation; and upon the accuracy with which similitude in dissimilitude, and dissimilitude in similitude are perceived, depend our taste and our moral feelings. It would not have been a useless employment to have applied this principle to the consideration of metre, and to have shown that metre is hence enabled to afford much pleasure, and to have pointed out in what manner that pleasure is produced. But my limits will not permit me to enter upon this subject, and I must content myself with a general summary.

[...] Poetry is the spontaneous overflow of powerful feelings: it takes its origin from emotion recollected in tranquillity: the emotion is contemplated till by a species of reaction the tranquillity disappears, and an emotion, kindred to that which was before the subject of contemplation, is gradually produced, and does itself actually exist in the mind. In this mood successful composition generally begins, and in a mood similar to this it is carried on; but the emotion, of whatever kind and in whatever degree, from various causes is qualified by various pleasures, so that in describing any passions whatsoever, which are voluntarily described, the mind will upon the whole be in a state of enjoyment. Now, if Nature be thus cautious in preserving in a state of enjoyment a being thus employed, the Poet ought to profit by the lesson thus held forth to him, and ought especially to take care, that whatever passions he communicates to his Reader, those passions, if his Reader's mind be sound and vigorous, should always be accompanied with an overbalance of pleasure. Now the music of harmonious metrical language, the sense of difficulty overcome, and the blind association of pleasure which has been previously received from works of rhyme or metre of the same or similar construction, an indistinct perception perpetually renewed of language closely resembling that of real life, and yet, in the circumstance of metre, differing from it so widely, all these imperceptibly make up a complex feeling of delight, which is of the most important use in tempering the painful feeling which will always be found intermingled with powerful descriptions of the deeper passions. This effect is always produced in pathetic and impassioned poetry; while, in lighter compositions, the ease and gracefulness with which the Poet manages his numbers are themselves confessedly a principal source of the gratification of the Reader. I might perhaps include all which it is *necessary* to say upon this subject by affirming, what few persons will deny, that, of two descriptions, either of passions, manners, or characters, each of them equally well executed, the one in prose and the other in verse, the verse will be read a hundred times where the prose is read once.

4 **Freud and Literature**

● Lionel Trilling

i

The Freudian psychology is the only systematic account of the human mind which, in point of subtlety and complexity, of interest and tragic power, deserves to stand beside the chaotic mass of psychological insights which literature has accumulated through the centuries. To pass from the reading of a great literary work to a treatise of academic psychology is to pass from one order of perception to another, but the human nature of the Freudian psychology is exactly the stuff upon which the poet has always exercised his art. It is therefore not surprising that the psychoanalytical theory has had a great effect upon literature. Yet the relationship is reciprocal, and the effect of Freud upon literature has been no greater than the effect of literature upon Freud. When, on the occasion of the celebration of his seventieth birthday, Freud was greeted as the 'discoverer of the unconscious,' he corrected the speaker and disclaimed the title. 'The poets and philosophers before me discovered the unconscious,' he said. 'What I discovered was the scientific method by which the unconscious can be studied.' [...]

ii

[...] Now Freud has, I believe, much to tell us about art, but whatever is suggestive in him is not likely to be found in those of his works in which he deals expressly with art itself. Freud is not insensitive to art — on the contrary — nor does he ever intend to speak of it with contempt. Indeed, he speaks of it with a real tenderness and counts it one of the true charms of the good life. Of artists, especially of writers, he speaks with admiration and even a kind of awe, though perhaps what he most appreciates in literature are specific emotional insights and observations; he speaks of literary men, because they have understood the part played in life by the hidden motives, as the precursors and coadjutors of his own science.

And yet eventually Freud speaks of art with what we must indeed call contempt. Art, he tells us, is a 'substitute gratification,' and as such is 'an illusion in contrast to reality.' Unlike most illusions, however, art is 'almost always harmless and beneficent' for the reason that 'it does not seek to be anything but an illusion. Save in the case of a few people who are, one might say, obsessed by Art, it never dares make any attack on the realm of reality.' One of its chief functions is to serve as a 'narcotic.' It shares the characteristics of the dream, whose element of distortion Freud calls a 'sort of inner dishonesty.' As for the artist, he is virtually in the same category with the neurotic. 'By such separation of imagination and intellectual capacity,' Freud says of the hero of a novel, 'he is destined to be a poet or a neurotic, and he belongs to that race of beings whose realm is not of this world.'

Now there is nothing in the logic of psychoanalytical thought which requires Freud to have these opinions. But there is a great deal in the practice of the psychoanalytical therapy which makes it understandable that Freud, unprotected by an adequate philosophy, should be tempted to take the line he does. The analytical therapy deals with illusion. The patient comes to the physician to be cured, let us say, of a fear of walking in the street. The fear is real enough, there is no illusion on that score, and it produces all the physical symptoms of a more rational fear, the sweating palms, pounding heart, and shortened breath. But the patient knows that there is no cause for the fear, or rather that there is, as he says, no 'real cause': there are no machine guns, man traps, or tigers in the street. The physician knows, however, that there is indeed a 'real' cause for the fear, though it has nothing at all to do with what is or is not in the street; the cause is within the patient, and the process of the therapy will be to discover, by gradual steps, what this real cause is and so free the patient from its effects.

Now the patient in coming to the physician, and the physician in accepting the patient, make a tacit compact about reality; for their purpose they agree to the limited reality by which we get our living, win our loves, catch our trains and our colds. The therapy will undertake to train the patient in proper ways of coping with this reality. The patient, of course, has been dealing with this reality all along, but in the wrong way. For Freud there are two ways of dealing with external reality. One is practical, effective, positive; this is the way of the conscious self, of the ego which must be made independent of the super-ego and extend its organization over the id, and it is the right way. The antithetical way may be called, for our purpose now, the 'fictional' way. Instead of doing something about, or to, external reality, the individual who uses this way does something to, or about, his affective states. The most common and 'normal' example of this is daydreaming, in which we give ourselves a certain pleasure by imagining our difficulties solved or our desires gratified. Then, too, as Freud discovered, sleeping dreams are, in much more complicated ways, and even though quite unpleasant, at the service of this same 'fictional' activity. And in ways yet more complicated and yet more unpleasant, the actual neurosis from which our patient suffers deals with an external reality which the mind considers still more unpleasant than the painful neurosis itself.

For Freud as psychoanalytic practitioner there are, we may say, the polar extremes of reality and illusion. Reality is an honorific word, and it means what is *there*; illusion is a pejorative word, and it means a response to what is *not there*. The didactic nature of a course of psychoanalysis no doubt requires a certain firm crudeness in making the distinction; it is after all aimed not at theoretical refinement but at practical effectiveness. The polar extremes are practical reality and neurotic illusion, the latter judged by the former. This, no doubt, is as it should be; the patient is not being trained in metaphysics and epistemology.

This practical assumption is not Freud's only view of the mind in its relation to reality. Indeed what may be called the essentially Freudian view assumes that the mind, for good as well as bad, helps create its reality by selection and evaluation. In this view, reality is malleable and subject to creation; it is not static but is rather a series of situations which are dealt with in their own terms. But beside this conception of the mind stands the conception which arises from Freud's therapeutic-practical assumptions; in this view, the mind deals with a reality which is quite fixed and static, a reality that is wholly 'given' and not (to use a phrase of Dewey's) 'taken.' In his epistemological utterances, Freud insists on this second view, although it is not easy to see why he should do so. For the reality to which he wishes to reconcile the neurotic patient is, after all, a 'taken' and not a 'given' reality. It is the reality of social life and of value, conceived and maintained by the human mind and will. Love, morality, honor, esteem — these are the components of a created reality. If we are to call art an illusion then we must call most of the activities and satisfactions of the ego illusions; Freud, of course, has no desire to call them that.

What, then, is the difference between, on the one hand, the dream and the neurosis, and, on the other hand, art? That they have certain common elements is of course clear; that unconscious processes are at work in both would be denied by no poet or critic; they share too, though in different degrees, the element of fantasy. But there is a vital difference between them which Charles Lamb saw so clearly in his defense of the sanity of true genius: 'The . . . poet dreams being awake. He is not possessed by his subject but he has dominion over it.'

That is the whole difference: the poet is in command of his fantasy, while it is exactly the mark of the neurotic that he is possessed by his fantasy. And there is a further difference which Lamb states; speaking of the poet's relation to reality (he calls it Nature), he says, 'He is beautifully loyal to that sovereign directress, even when he appears most to betray her'; the illusions of art are made to serve the purpose of a closer and truer relation with reality. Jacques Barzun, in an acute and sympathetic discussion of Freud, puts the matter well: 'A good analogy between art and *dreaming* has led him to a false one between art and *sleeping*. But the difference between a work of art and a dream is precisely this, that the work of art *leads us back to the outer reality by taking account of it.*' Freud's assumption of the almost exclusively hedonistic nature and purpose of art bar him from the perception of this.

Of the distinction that must be made between the artist and the neurotic Freud is of course aware; he tells us that the artist is not like the neurotic in that he knows how to find a way back from the world of imagination and 'once more get a firm foothold in reality.' This however seems to mean no more than that reality is to be dealt with when the artist suspends the practice of his art; and at least once when Freud speaks of art dealing with reality he actually means the rewards that a successful artist can win. He does not deny to art its function and its usefulness; it has a therapeutic effect in releasing mental tension; it serves the cultural purpose of acting as a 'substitute gratification' to reconcile men to the sacrifices they have made for culture's sake; it promotes the social sharing of highly valued emotional experiences; and it recalls men to their cultural ideals. This is not everything that some of us would find that art does, yet even this is a good deal for a 'narcotic' to do.

iii

I started by saying that Freud's ideas could tell us something about art, but so far I have done little more than try to show that Freud's very conception of art is inadequate. Perhaps, then, the suggestiveness lies in the application of the analytic method to specific works of art or to the artist himself? I do not think so, and it is only fair to say that Freud himself was aware both of the limits and the limitations of psychoanalysis in art, even though he does not always in practice submit to the former or admit the latter.

Freud has, for example, no desire to encroach upon the artist's autonomy; he does not wish us to read his monograph on Leonardo and then say of the 'Madonna of the Rocks' that it is a fine example of homosexual, autoerotic painting. If he asserts that in investigation the 'psychiatrist cannot yield to the author,' he immediately insists that the 'author cannot yield to the psychiatrist,' and he warns the latter not to 'coarsen everything' by using for all human manifestations the 'substantially useless and awkward terms' of clinical procedure. He admits, even while asserting that the sense of beauty probably derives from sexual feeling, that psychoanalysis 'has less to say about beauty than about most other things.' He confesses to a theoretical indifference to the form of art and restricts himself to its content. Tone, feeling, style, and the modification that part makes upon part he does not consider. 'The layman,' he says, 'may expect perhaps too much from analysis . . . for it must be admitted that it throws no light upon the two problems which probably interest him the most. It can do nothing toward elucidating the nature of the artistic gift, nor can it explain the means by which the artist works — artistic technique.'

What, then, does Freud believe that the analytical method can do? Two things: explain the 'inner meanings' of the work of art and explain the temperament of the artist as man.

A famous example of the method is the attempt to solve the 'problem' of *Hamlet* as suggested by Freud and as carried out by Dr Ernest Jones, his early and distinguished follower. Dr Jones's monograph is a work of painstaking scholarship and of really masterly ingenuity. The research undertakes not only the clearing up of the mystery of Hamlet's character, but also the discovery of 'the clue to much of the deeper workings of Shakespeare's mind.' Part of the mystery in question is of course why Hamlet, after he had so definitely resolved to do so, did not avenge upon his hated uncle his father's death. But there is another mystery to the play — what Freud calls 'the mystery of its effect,' its magical appeal that draws so much interest toward it. Recalling the many failures to solve the riddle of the play's charm, he wonders if we are to be driven to the conclusion 'that its magical appeal rests solely upon the impressive thoughts in it and the splendor of its language.' Freud believes that we can find a source of power beyond this.

We remember that Freud has told us that the meaning of a dream is its intention, and we may assume that the meaning of a drama is its intention, too. The Jones research undertakes to discover what it was that Shakespeare intended to say about Hamlet. It finds that the intention was wrapped by the author in a dreamlike obscurity because it touched so deeply both his personal life and the moral life of the world; what Shakespeare intended to say is that Hamlet cannot act because he is incapacitated by the guilt he feels at his unconscious attachment to his mother. There is, I think, nothing to be quarreled with in the statement that there is an Oedipus situation in *Hamlet*; and if psychoanalysis has indeed added a new point of interest to the play, that is to its credit.[1]. And, just so, there is no reason to quarrel with Freud's conclusion when he undertakes to give us the meaning of *King Lear* by a tortuous tracing of the mythological implications of the theme of the three caskets, of the relation of the caskets to the Norns, the Fates, and the Graces, of the connection of these triadic females with Lear's daughters, of the transmogrification of the death goddess into the love goddess and the identification of Cordelia with both, all to the conclusion that the meaning of *King Lear* is to be found in the tragic refusal of an old man to 'renounce love, choose death, and make friends with the necessity of dying.' There is something both beautiful and suggestive in this, but it is not *the* meaning of *King Lear* any more than the Oedipus motive is *the* meaning of *Hamlet*.

It is not here a question of the validity of the evidence, though that is of course important. We must rather object to the conclusions of Freud and Dr Jones on the ground that their proponents do not have an adequate conception of what an artistic meaning is. There is no single meaning to any work of art; this is true not merely because it is better that it should be true, that is, because it makes art a richer thing, but because historical and personal experience show it to be true. Changes in historical context and in personal mood change the meaning of a work and indicate to us that artistic understanding is not a question of fact but of value. Even if the author's intention were, as it cannot be, precisely determinable, the meaning of a work cannot lie in the author's intention alone. It must also lie in its effect. We can say of a volcanic eruption on an inhabited island that it 'means terrible suffering,' but if the island is uninhabited or easily evacuated it means something else. In short, the audience partly determines the meaning of the work. But although Freud sees something of this when he says that in addition to the author's intention we must take into account the mystery of *Hamlet's* effect, he nevertheless goes on to speak as if, historically, *Hamlet's* effect had been single and brought about solely by the 'magical' power of the Oedipus motive to which, unconsciously, we so violently respond. Yet there was, we know, a period when *Hamlet* was relatively in eclipse, and it has always been scandalously true of the French, a people not without filial feeling, that they have been somewhat indifferent to the 'magical appeal' of *Hamlet*.

I do not think that anything I have said about the inadequacies of the Freudian method of interpretation limits the number of ways we can deal with a work of art. Bacon remarked that experiment may twist nature on the rack to wring out its secrets, and criticism may use any instruments upon a work of art to find its meanings. The elements of art are not limited to the world of art. They reach into life, and whatever extraneous knowledge of them we gain — for example, by research into the historical context of the work — may quicken our feelings for the work itself and even enter legitimately into those feelings. Then, too, anything we may learn about the artist himself may be enriching and legitimate. But one research into the mind of the artist is simply not practicable, however legitimate it may theoretically be. That is, the investigation of his unconscious intention as it exists apart from the work itself. Criticism understands that the artist's statement of his conscious intention, though it is sometimes useful, cannot finally determine meaning. How much less can we know from his unconscious intention considered as something apart from the whole work? Surely very little that can be called conclusive or scientific. For, as Freud himself points out, we are not in a position to question the artist; we must apply the technique of dream analysis to his symbols, but, as Freud says with some heat, those people do not understand his theory who think that a dream may be interpreted without the dreamer's free association with the multitudinous details of his dream.

We have so far ignored the aspect of the method which finds the

solution to the 'mystery' of such a play as *Hamlet* in the temperament of
Shakespeare himself and then illuminates the mystery of Shakespeare's
temperament by means of the solved mystery of the play. Here it will be
amusing to remember that by 1935 Freud had become converted to the
theory that it was not Shakespeare of Stratford but the Earl of Oxford
who wrote the plays, thus invalidating the important bit of evidence that
Shakespeare's father died shortly before the composition of *Hamlet*. This
is destructive enough to Dr Jones's argument, but the evidence from
which Dr Jones draws conclusions about literature fails on grounds
more relevant to literature itself. For when Dr Jones, by means of his
analysis of *Hamlet*, takes us into 'the deeper workings of Shakespeare's
mind,' he does so with a perfect confidence that he knows what *Hamlet*
is and what its relation to Shakespeare is. It is, he tells us, Shakespeare's
'chief masterpiece,' so far superior to all his other works that it may be
placed on 'an entirely separate level.' And then, having established his
ground on an entirely subjective literary judgment, Dr Jones goes on to
tell us that *Hamlet* 'probably expresses the core of Shakespeare's
philosophy and outlook as no other work of his does.' That is, all the
contradictory or complicating or modifying testimony of the other plays
is dismissed on the basis of Dr Jones's acceptance of the peculiar
position which, he believes, *Hamlet* occupies in the Shakespeare canon.
And it is upon this quite inadmissible judgment that Dr Jones bases his
argument: 'It may be expected *therefore* that anything which will give us
the key to the inner meaning of the play will *necessarily* give us the clue
to much of the deeper workings of Shakespeare's mind.' (The italics are
mine.)

I should be sorry if it appeared that I am trying to say that
psychoanalysis can have nothing to do with literature. I am sure that the
opposite is so. For example, the whole notion of rich ambiguity in
literature, of the interplay between the apparent meaning and the latent
— not 'hidden' — meaning, has been reinforced by the Freudian
concepts, perhaps even received its first impetus from them. Of late
years, the more perceptive psychoanalysts have surrendered the early
pretensions of their teachers to deal 'scientifically' with literature. That
is all to the good, and when a study as modest and precise as Dr Franz
Alexander's essay on *Henry IV* comes along, an essay which pretends
not to 'solve' but only to illuminate the subject, we have something
worth having. Dr Alexander undertakes nothing more than to say that
in the development of Prince Hal we see the classic struggle of the ego to
come to normal adjustment, beginning with the rebellion against the
father, going on to the conquest of the super-ego (Hotspur, with his
rigid notions of honor and glory), then to the conquests of the *id*
(Falstaff, with his anarchic self-indulgence), then to the identification
with the father (the crown scene) and the assumption of mature
responsibility. An analysis of this sort is not momentous and not
exclusive of other meanings; perhaps it does no more than point up and

formulate what we all have already seen. It has the tact to *accept* the play and does not, like Dr Jones's study of *Hamlet*, search for a 'hidden motive' and a 'deeper working,' which implies that there is a reality to which the play stands in the relation that a dream stands to the wish that generates it and from which it is separable; it is this reality, this 'deeper working,' which, according to Dr Jones, produced the play. But *Hamlet* is not merely the product of Shakespeare's thought, it is the very instrument of his thought, and if meaning is intention, Shakespeare did not intend the Oedipus motive or anything less than *Hamlet*; if meaning is effect then it is *Hamlet* which affects us, not the Oedipus motive. *Coriolanus* also deals, and very terribly, with the Oedipus motive, but the effect of the one drama is very different from the effect of the other.

iv

If, then, we can accept neither Freud's conception of the place of art in life nor his application of the analytical method, what is it that he contributes to our understanding of art or to its practice? In my opinion, what he contributes outweighs his errors; it is of the greatest importance, and it lies in no specific statement that he makes about art but is, rather, implicit in his whole conception of the mind.

For, of all mental systems, the Freudian psychology is the one which makes poetry indigenous to the very constitution of the mind. Indeed, the mind, as Freud sees it, is in the greater part of its tendency exactly a poetry-making organ. This puts the case too strongly, no doubt, for it seems to make the working of the unconscious mind equivalent to poetry itself, forgetting that between the unconscious mind and the finished poem there supervene the social intention and the formal control of the conscious mind. Yet the statement has at least the virtue of counterbalancing the belief, so commonly expressed or implied, that the very opposite is true, and that poetry is a kind of beneficent aberration of the mind's right course.

Freud has not merely naturalized poetry; he has discovered its status as a pioneer settler, and he sees it as a method of thought. Often enough he tries to show how, as a method of thought, it is unreliable and ineffective for conquering reality; yet he himself is forced to use it in the very shaping of his own science, as when he speaks of the topography of the mind and tells us with a kind of defiant apology that the metaphors of space relationship which he is using are really most inexact since the mind is not a thing of space at all, but that there is no other way of conceiving the difficult idea except by metaphor. In the eighteenth century Vico spoke of the metaphorical, imagistic language of the early stages of culture; it was left to Freud to discover how, in a scientific age, we still feel and think in figurative formations, and to create, what psychoanalysis is, a science of tropes, of metaphor and its variants, synecdoche and metonomy.

Freud showed, too, how the mind, in one of its parts, could work without logic, yet not without that directing purpose, that control of intent from which, perhaps it might be said, logic springs. For the unconscious mind works without the syntactical conjunctions which are logic's essence. It recognizes no *because*, no *therefore*, no *but*; such ideas as similarity, agreement, and community are expressed in dreams imagistically by compressing the elements into a unity. The unconscious mind in its struggle with the conscious always turns from the general to the concrete and finds the tangible trifle more congenial than the large abstraction. Freud discovered in the very organization of the mind those mechanisms by which art makes its effects, such devices as the condensations of meanings and the displacement of accent.

All this is perhaps obvious enough and, though I should like to develop it in proportion both to its importance and to the space I have given to disagreement with Freud, I will not press it further. For there are two other elements in Freud's thought which, in conclusion, I should like to introduce as of great weight in their bearing on art.

Of these, one is a specific idea which, in the middle of his career (1920), Freud put forward in his essay *Beyond the Pleasure Principle*. The essay itself is a speculative attempt to solve a perplexing problem in clinical analysis, but its relevance to literature is inescapable, as Freud sees well enough, even though his perception of its critical importance is not sufficiently strong to make him revise his earlier views of the nature and function of art. The idea is one which stands besides Aristotle's notion of the catharsis, in part to supplement, in part to modify it.

Freud has come upon certain facts which are not to be reconciled with his earlier theory of the dream. According to this theory, all dreams, even the unpleasant ones, could be understood upon analysis to have the intention of fulfilling the dreamer's wishes. They are in the service of what Freud calls the pleasure principle, which is opposed to the reality principle. It is, of course, this explanation of the dream which had so largely conditioned Freud's theory of art. But now there is thrust upon him the necessity for reconsidering the theory of the dream, for it was found that in cases of war neurosis — what we once called shellshock — the patient, with the utmost anguish, recurred in his dreams to the very situation, distressing as it was, which had precipitated his neurosis. It seemed impossible to interpret these dreams by any assumption of a hedonistic intent. Nor did there seem to be the usual amount of distortion in them: the patient recurred to the terrible initiatory situation with great literalness. And the same pattern of psychic behavior could be observed in the play of children; there were some games which, far from fulfilling wishes, seemed to concentrate upon the representation of those aspects of the child's life which were most unpleasant and threatening to his happiness.

To explain such mental activities Freud evolved a theory for which he at first refused to claim much but to which, with the years, he attached an increasing importance. He first makes the assumption that there is indeed in the psychic life a repetition-compulsion which goes beyond the pleasure principle. Such a compulsion cannot be meaningless, it must have an intent. And that intent, Freud comes to believe, is exactly and literally the developing of fear. 'These dreams,' he says, 'are attempts at restoring control of the stimuli by developing apprehension, the pretermission of which caused the traumatic neurosis.' The dream, that is, is the effort to reconstruct the bad situation in order that the failure to meet it may be recouped; in these dreams there is no obscured intent to evade but only an attempt to meet the situation, to make a new effort of control. And in the play of children it seems to be that 'the child repeats even the unpleasant experiences because through his own activity he gains a far more thorough mastery of the strong impression than was possible by mere passive experience.'

Freud, at this point, can scarcely help being put in mind of tragic drama; nevertheless, he does not wish to believe that this effort to come to mental grips with a situation is involved in the attraction of tragedy. He is, we might say, under the influence of the Aristotelian tragic theory which emphasizes a qualified hedonism through suffering. But the pleasure involved in tragedy is perhaps an ambiguous one; and sometimes we must feel that the famous sense of cathartic resolution is perhaps the result of glossing over terror with beautiful language rather than an evacuation of it. And sometimes the terror even bursts through the language to stand stark and isolated from the play, as does Oedipus's sightless and bleeding face. At any rate, the Aristotelian theory does not deny another function for tragedy (and for comedy, too) which is suggested by Freud's theory of the traumatic neurosis — what might be called the mithridatic function, by which tragedy is used as the homeopathic administration of pain to inure ourselves to the greater pain which life will force upon us. There is in the cathartic theory of tragedy, as it is usually understood, a conception of tragedy's function which is too negative and which inadequately suggests the sense of active mastery which tragedy can give.

In the same essay in which he sets forth the conception of the mind embracing its own pain for some vital purpose, Freud also expresses a provisional assent to the idea (earlier stated, as he reminds us, by Schopenhauer) that there is perhaps a human drive which makes of death the final and desired goal. The death instinct is a conception that is rejected by many of even the most thoroughgoing Freudian theorists (as, in his last book, Freud mildly noted); the late Otto Fenichel in his authoritative work on the neurosis argues cogently against it. Yet even if we reject the theory as not fitting the facts in any operatively useful way, we still cannot miss its grandeur, its ultimate tragic courage in acquiescence to fate. The idea of the reality principle and the idea of the death instinct form the crown of Freud's broader speculation on the life of man. Their quality of grim poetry is characteristic of Freud's system and the ideas it generates for him.

And as much as anything else that Freud gives to literature, this quality of his thought is important. Although the artist is never finally determined in his work by the intellectual systems about him, he cannot avoid their influence; and it can be said of various competing systems that some hold more promise for the artist than others. When, for example, we think of the simple humanitarian optimism which, for two decades, has been so pervasive, we must see that not only has it been politically and philosophically inadequate, but also that it implies, by the smallness of its view of the varieties of human possibility, a kind of check on the creative faculties. In Freud's view of life no such limitation is implied. To be sure, certain elements of his system seem hostile to the usual notions of man's dignity. Like every great critic of human nature — and Freud is that — he finds in human pride the ultimate cause of human wretchedness, and he takes pleasure in knowing that his ideas stand with those of Copernicus and Darwin in making pride more difficult to maintain. Yet the Freudian man is, I venture to think, a creature of far more dignity and far more interest than the man which any other modern system has been able to conceive. Despite popular belief to the contrary, man, as Freud conceives him, is not to be understood by any simple formula (such as sex) but is rather an inextricable tangle of culture and biology. And not being simple, he is not simply good; he has, as Freud says somewhere, a kind of hell within him from which rise everlastingly the impulses which threaten his civilization. He has the faculty of imagining for himself more in the way of pleasure and satisfaction than he can possibly achieve. Everything that he gains he pays for in more than equal coin; compromise and the compounding with defeat constitute his best way of getting through the world. His best qualities are the result of a struggle whose outcome is tragic. Yet he is a creature of love; it is Freud's sharpest criticism of the Adlerian psychology that to aggression it gives everything and to love nothing at all.

One is always aware in reading Freud how little cynicism there is in his thought. His desire for man is only that he should be human, and to this end his science is devoted. No view of life to which the artist responds can insure the quality of his work, but the poetic qualities of Freud's own principles, which are so clearly in the line of the classic tragic realism, suggest that this is a view which does not narrow and simplify the human world for the artist but on the contrary opens and complicates it.

NOTE

1. However, A.C. Bradley, in his discussion of Hamlet *(Shakespearean Tragedy)*, states clearly the intense sexual disgust which Hamlet feels and which, for Bradley, helps account for his uncertain purpose; and Bradley was anticipated in this view by Löning. It is well known, and Dover Wilson has lately emphasized the point, that to an Elizabethan audience Hamlet's mother was not merely tasteless, as to a modern audience she seems, in hurrying to marry Claudius, but actually adulterous in marrying him at all because he was, as her brother-in-law, within the forbidden degrees.

5 *Communication and the Artist*

- I. A. Richards

Poetry is the record of the best and happiest moments of the happiest and best minds. — *The Defence of Poetry*

The two pillars upon which a theory of criticism must rest are an account of value and an account of communication. We do not sufficiently realize how great a part of our experience takes the form it does, because we are social beings and accustomed to communication from infancy. That we acquire many of our ways of thinking and feeling from parents and others is, of course, a commonplace. But the effects of communication go much deeper than this. The very structure of our minds is largely determined by the fact that man has been engaged in communicating for so many hundreds of thousands of years, throughout the course of his human development and beyond even that. A large part of the distinctive features of the mind are due to its being an instrument for communication. An experience has to be formed, no doubt, before it is communicated, but it takes the form it does largely because it may have to be communicated. The emphasis which natural selection has put upon communicative ability is overwhelming.

There are very many problems of psychology, from those with which some of the exponents of *Gestalt theorie* are grappling to those by which psychoanalysts are bewildered, for which this neglected, this almost overlooked aspect of the mind may provide a key, but it is pre-eminently in regard to the arts that it is of service. For the arts are the supreme form of the communicative activity. Most of the difficult and obscure points about the structures of the arts, for example the priority of formal elements to content, or the impersonality and detachment so much stressed by aestheticians, become easily intelligible as soon as we consider them from this angle. But a possible misunderstanding must be guarded against. Although it is as a communicator that it is most profitable to consider the artist, it is by no means true that he commonly looks upon himself in this light. In the course of his work he is not as a rule deliberately and consciously engaged in a communicative endeavour. When asked, he is more likely than not to reply that communication is an irrelevant or at best a minor issue, and that what he is making is something which is beautiful in itself, or satisfying to him personally, or something expressive, in a more or less vague sense, of his emotions, or of himself, something personal and individual. That other people are going to study it, and to receive experiences from it may seem to him a merely accidental, inessential circumstance. More modestly still, he may say that when he works he is merely amusing himself.

That the artist is not as a rule consciously concerned with communication, but with getting the work, the poem or play or statue or painting or whatever it is, 'right', apparently regardless of its communicative efficacy, is easily explained. To make the work 'embody', accord with, and represent the precise experience upon which its value depends is his major preoccupation, in difficult cases an overmastering preoccupation, and the dissipation of attention which would be involved if he considered the communicative side as a separate issue would be fatal in most serious work. He cannot stop to consider how the public or even how especially well qualified sections of the public may like it or respond to it. He is wise, therefore, to keep all such considerations out of mind altogether. Those artists and poets who can be suspected of close separate attention to the communicative aspect tend (there are exceptions to this, of which Shakespeare might be one) to fall into a subordinate rank.

But this conscious neglect of communication does not in the least diminish the importance of the communicative aspect. It would only do so if we were prepared to admit that only our conscious activities matter. The very process of getting the work 'right' has itself, so far as the artist is normal, immense communicative consequences. Apart from certain special cases, it will, when 'right', have much greater communicative power than it would have if 'wrong'. The degree to which it accords with the relevant experience of the artist is a measure of the degree to which it will arouse similar experiences in others.

But more narrowly the reluctance of the artist to consider communication as one of his main aims, and his denial that he is at all influenced in his work by a desire to affect other people, is no evidence that communication is not actually his principal object. On a simple view of psychology, which overlooked unconscious motives, it would be, but not on any view of human behaviour which is in the least adequate. When we find the artist constantly struggling towards impersonality, towards a structure for his work which excludes his private, eccentric, momentary idiosyncrasies, and using always as its basis those elements which are most uniform in their effects upon impulses; when we find private works of art, works which satisfy the artist,[1] but are incomprehensible to everybody else, so rare, and the publicity of the work so constantly and so intimately bound up with its appeal to the artist himself, it is difficult to believe that efficacy for communication is not a main part of the 'rightness'[2] which the artist may suppose to be something quite different.

How far desire actually to communicate, as distinguished from desire to produce something with communicative efficacy (however disguised), is an 'unconscious motive' in the artist is a question to which we need not hazard an answer. Doubtless individual artists vary enormously. To some the lure of 'immortality' of enduring fame, of a permanent place in the influences which govern the human mind, appears to be very strong. To others it is often negligible. The degree to which such notions are avowed certainly varies with current social and intellectual fashions. At present the appeal to posterity, the 'nurslings of immortality' attitude to works of art appears to be much out of favour. 'How do we know what posterity will be like? They may be awful people!' a contemporary is likely to remark, thus confusing the issue. For the appeal is not to posterity merely as living at a certain date, but as especially qualified to judge, a qualification most posterities have lacked.

What concerns criticism is not the avowed or unavowed motives of the artist, however interesting these may be to psychology, but the fact that his procedure does, in the majority of instances, make the communicative efficacy of his work correspond with his own satisfaction and sense of its rightness. This may be due merely to his normality, or it may be due to unavowed motives. The first suggestion is the more plausible. In any case it is certain that no mere careful study of communicative possibilities, together with any desire to communicate, however intense, is ever sufficient without close natural correspondence between the poet's impulses and possible impulses in his reader. All supremely successful communication involves this correspondence, and no planning can take its place. Nor is the deliberate conscious attempt directed to communication so successful as the unconscious indirect method.

Thus the artist is entirely justified in his apparent neglect of the main purpose of his work. And when in what follows he is alluded to without qualification as being primarily concerned with communication, the reservations here made should be recalled.

Since the poet's unconscious motives have been alluded to, it may be well at this point to make a few additional remarks. Whatever psychoanalysts may aver, the mental processes of the poet are not a very profitable field for investigation. They offer far too happy a hunting-ground for uncontrollable conjecture. Much that goes to produce a poem is, of course, unconscious. Very likely the unconscious processes are more important than the conscious, but even if we knew far more than we do about how the mind works, the attempt to display the inner working of the artist's mind by the evidence of his work alone must be subject to the gravest dangers. And to judge by the published work of Freud upon Leonardo da Vinci or of Jung upon Goethe (e.g. *The Psychology of the Unconscious*, p. 305), psychoanalysts tend to be peculiarly inept as critics.

The difficulty is that nearly all speculations as to what went on in the artist's mind are unverifiable, even more unverifiable than the similar speculations as to the dreamer's mind. The most plausible explanations are apt to depend upon features whose actual causation is otherwise. I do not know whether anyone but Mr Graves has attempted to analyse *Kubla Khan*, a poem which by its mode of composition and by its subject suggests itself as well fitted for analysis. The reader acquainted with current methods of analysis can imagine the results of a thoroughgoing Freudian onslaught.

If he will then open *Paradise Lost*, Book IV, at line 223, and read onwards for sixty lines, he will encounter the actual sources of not a few of the images and phrases of the poem. In spite of —

> Southward through *Eden* went a River large,
> Nor changed his course, but through the shaggie hill
> Pass'd underneath ingulft . . .

in spite of —

> Rose a fresh Fountain, and with many a rill
> Watered the Garden; thence united fell
> Down the steep glade, and met the neather Flood . . .

in spite of —

> Rowling on Orient Pearl and sands of Gold
> With mazie error under pendant shades
> Ran Nectar . . .

in spite of —

> Meanwhile murmuring waters fall
> Down the slope hills, disperst . . .

his doubts may still linger until he reaches

> Nor where *Abassin* Kings their issue Guard,
> Mount Amara.

and one of the most cryptic points in Coleridge's poem, the Abyssinian maid, singing of Mount Abora, finds its simple explanation. The closing line of the poem perhaps hardly needs this kind of derivation.

From one source or another almost all the matter of *Kubla Khan* came to Coleridge in a similar fashion. I do not know whether this particular indebtedness has been remarked before, but *Purchas his Pilgrimage*, Bartram's *Travels in North and South Carolina*, and Maurice's *History of Hindostan* are well-known sources, some of them indicated by Coleridge himself.

This very representative instance of the unconscious working of a poet's mind may serve as a not inapposite warning against one kind at least of possible applications of psychology in criticism.

The extent to which the arts and their place in the whole scheme of human affairs have been misunderstood, by Critics, Moralists, Educators, Aestheticians . . . is somewhat difficult to explain. Often those who most misunderstand have been perfect in their taste and ability to respond, Ruskin for example. Those who both knew what to do with a work of art and also understood what they were doing, have been for the most part artists and little inclined for, or capable of, the rather special task of explaining. It may have seemed to them too obvious to need explanation. Those who have tried have as a rule been foiled by language. For the difficulty which has always prevented the arts from being explained as well as 'enjoyed' (to use an inadequate word in default of an adequate) is language.

> 'Happy who can
> Appease this virtuous enemy of man!'

It was perhaps never so necessary as now that we should know why the arts are important and avoid inadequate answers. It will probably become increasingly more important in the future. Remarks such as these, it is true, are often uttered by enthusiastic persons, and are apt to be greeted with the same smile as the assertion that the future of England is bound up with Hunting. Yet their full substantiation will be found to involve issues which are nowhere lightly regarded.

The arts are our storehouse of recorded values. They spring from and perpetuate hours in the lives of exceptional people, when their control and command of experience is at its highest, hours when the varying possibilities of existence are most clearly seen and the different activities which may arise are most exquisitely reconciled, hours when habitual narrowness of interests or confused bewilderment are replaced by an intricately wrought composure. Both in the genesis of a work of art, in the creative moment, and in its aspect as a vehicle of communication, reasons can be found for giving to the arts a very important place in the theory of Value. They record the most important judgements we possess as to the values of experience. They form a body of evidence which, for lack of a serviceable psychology by which to interpret it, and through the desiccating influence of abstract Ethics, has been left almost untouched by professed students of value. An odd omission, for without the assistance of the arts we could compare very few of our experiences, and without such comparison we could hardly hope to agree as to which are to be preferred. Very simple experiences — a cold bath in an enamelled tin, or running for a train — may to some extent be compared without elaborate vehicles; and friends exceptionally well acquainted with one another may manage some rough comparisons in ordinary conversation. But subtle or recondite experiences are for most men incommunicable and indescribable, though social conventions or terror of the loneliness of the human situation may make us pretend the contrary. In the arts we find the record in the only form in which these things can be recorded of the experiences which have seemed worth having to the most sensitive and discriminating persons. Through the obscure perception of this fact the poet has been regarded as a seer and the artist as a priest, suffering from usurpations. The arts, if rightly approached, supply the best data available for deciding which experiences are more valuable than others. The qualifying clause is all-important however. Happily there is no lack of glaring examples to remind us of the difficulty of approaching them rightly.

NOTES

1. Again the normality of the artist has to be considered.
2. As will be seen, I am not going to identify 'beauty' with 'communicative efficacy'. This is a trap which it is easy to fall into. A number of the exoteric followers of Croce may be found in it, though not Croce himself.

6 *La Nouvelle Critique*

● Laurence Lerner

In a society which does not stand still, one would not expect theories of literature to remain unchanged; so before trying to assess recent movements in literary criticism, we should perhaps begin by admitting that they are inevitable. The new movements of the last two decades, however, have caused more stir and challenged more preconceptions than is usual; they have also caused much bewilderment, to the point where a clear summary of the main issues is difficult and even, to some, suspect.

But since any contribution to the debate must begin by asking what it is about, I will make bold to suggest that an account of *la nouvelle critique* should be organized round two main ideas (I use the French phrase because 'New Criticism' has of course a precise and different referent in English; and since France has contributed so much to the movement, it can lend us a name for it too). The first is structuralism, which is defined by Barthes as the application to other disciplines of the methods of linguistics. For linguistics is surely the one discipline that must necessarily study structure and not content, for the simple reason that if it concerned itself with content it would be taking all human knowledge as its province, since all knowledge, with the possible exception of mathematical physics, is in language. The study of language cannot be concerned with the rightness or wrongness of what is said in language, but must deal with the rules of language itself, and that, since Saussure, has meant the establishing of differences. The study of anything else (marriage customs and kinship patterns, law, advertising or literature) as a language — that is, as a system of signs — must therefore mean the attempt to discover the structures that make meaning possible within that system. In the case of literature, this will not differ greatly from the traditional study of literary conventions if the structures that are found are conscious; but once the critic looks for deep structures that operate below the awareness of writer and reader (as the deep rules of grammar, syntax and phonology operate below the awareness of competent speakers) then he will require a new terminology that will not, at first, seem to be using literary concepts. The quest for homologies between the devices of style and those of narrative organization, for instance, as carried out by Todorov, will seem to the old-fashioned reader to be using a barbarous and non-literary jargon, but the object of its pursuit is soon seen to be a specifically literary effect. Indeed, because structuralist criticism is not concerned with subject matter, it is in one way very literary indeed. Its aim, as Jakobson claimed, is to establish the nature of literariness; so that whereas the biographical, the sociological and the moral critics move continually from the universe of literature to that of society or the individual reader or writer, the structuralist will deny himself such excursions. His travels are from the nature of language in general to one particular kind of language.

The second central element in *la nouvelle critique* is its radicalism. Its practitioners are usually on the Left, and are often Marxists. They tend to claim that nothing is politically neutral, and that the purpose of criticism should be to reveal the ideological implications of the literary work: either to show how the apparent neutrality of the work conceals a commitment to the status quo, or to show how the professed conservatism of a great writer cannot prevent him from revealing conflicts in his society through contradictions in his world view. The former will normally take the form of a hostile critique, the latter of a sympathetic one, and the same writer (Shakespeare, Voltaire, Heine, Dickens, Dostoievsky, Eliot) may be seen by one critic as bourgeois and reactionary, by another as emancipatory and radical.

There is no necessary connection between these two tendencies. Both a conservative structuralism and a non-structuralist radicalism are easy to conceive: the former would study the deep structures of literary convention in the belief that to understand them better can strengthen them (as the grammarian will not seek to overthrow the rules he discovers), and the latter would attack the status quo and advocate political revolution without using the analogy with language, or claiming that the very processes of representation have an ideological function — indeed, the radical may claim that semiotic analysis distracts from the urgent practical tasks of political change, just as he may see the often very obscure terminology of structuralism as a new form of elitism.

None the less, the two elements have often been joined lately, and their combination produces deconstruction, the form of criticism which sets out to analyse either a particular work or the very concept of literature so as to reveal its ideological basis. The deconstructionist, by calling our attention to the ideological prison of literary assumptions, and even of language itself, hopes to free us from it. He (or she) often regards the traditional conception of literature as elitist, and claims that its ideological function has been to maintain bourgeois hegemony; and by deconstructing it he rejects the view that literature is a 'natural' activity which criticism studies, in favour of the view that it is criticism which decides which texts shall be regarded as literary.

Such in brief is how the situation can be viewed. [...] [Yet] the age of reason did not come to a sudden end twenty years ago, and *la nouvelle critique* has not rendered 'traditional literary criticism' suddenly obsolete. Indeed, there is no such thing as 'traditional literary criticism': to run together the enormous variety of critical positions and theories from Plato to Leavis into a single mass of overcooked rice pudding will prevent us from reading any of it with discrimination, and if a 'new' movement has to be seen as a rejection of all that has gone before, it will have to take up extreme positions that no one has previously been crazy enough to adopt. This is fine for a gossip columnist scenting battle and scandal in the hitherto remote lecture rooms of academies, but its effect on understanding can only be reductive of both elements. The 'traditional' will be dead, the 'new' will be lunatic.

For suppose we tried to find a single basic contrast that would justify this crude division? We might begin from an attempt by George Steiner to be helpful:

> Let me try and put very simply what the 'new way' of reading literature which we associate with such awkward words as 'structuralism' or 'semiotics' is fundamentally about. Instead of looking at a poem or passage from a novel in terms of what it says about 'the world out there', in terms of how the words represent or produce external experience, the 'structuralist' critic takes the text to be a complete experience in itself. The action, the only possible truth, is 'inside' the words. We don't ask how they relate to some supposed evidence 'out there', but we look at the manifold ways in which they relate to each other or to comparable verbal structures.[1]

Perhaps this is as good an account in ordinary language as we are likely to get of this central point; and we can add to it a rather similar assertion by Antony Easthope:

> Poetry is not to be read for truth or falsity of reference. . . . The poet as historical author is typically dead or absent; what we have as the poem is the message itself, *writing*. . . . Poetry consists *only* of artifice. . . .We never have the 'presence' of a poet; what we have is language, fiction, artifice, means of representation, poem.[2]

And Easthope couples this with an attack on the view of poetry as the expression of individual experience, and on the view that the reader 'recreates or relives this experience which is communicated to him or her'.

Does this then mean that 'traditional' criticism denied that poetry was artifice, or that the action of a poem was 'inside' the verbal structure? The first reply to this is that the doctrine of expression is not very old: it derives from the Romantics, and the consequent disparagement of the 'artificial' as that which lacks the expression of personal feeling only becomes prominent in criticism in the nineteenth century: 'artificial' is not a pejorative term for the Elizabethans, who had no difficulty in believing that poetry consists of artifice. But we do not even need to go back behind the Romantic movement:

> The aesthetic experience cares nothing for the reality or unreality of its object. It is neither true nor false of set purpose: it simply ignores the distinction. There is no such thing as the so-called artistic illusion, for illusion means believing in the reality of that which is unreal, and art does not believe in the reality of anything at all.[3]

> The 'objective orientation' . . . on principle regards the work of art in isolation from all . . . external points of reference, analyses it as a self-sufficient entity constituted by its parts in their internal relations, and sets out to judge it solely by criteria intrinsic to its own mode of being.[4]

Both these views sound very similar to what Steiner and Easthope see as central to structuralism. The first is from *Speculum Mentis* (1924) by Collingwood, who also held a view of art as the expression of emotion very close to the Romantic view which Easthope attacks; the second is from *The Mirror and the Lamp* (1953), Abrams' magisterial account of Romantic literary theory, and this 'objective orientation', which sounds even stronger than Steiner's statement ('the poem as heterocosm, a world of its own, independent of the world into which we are born') is supported from the central figures of the New Criticism, whom deconstructionists attack so vigorously.

And there is quite a different position that can lead to the view of literature as self-contained: that is the school of literary history that regards literature as an institution, and which we can represent by, say, the work of Leo Spitzer. Spitzer interprets literary works by relating them to tradition, and by reducing, if not eliminating, the personal element: thus his brilliant essay on Milton's sonnet 'Methought I saw my late espoused saint' attempts to remove the poet's blindness from the meaning of the poem by showing how well it can be understood in terms of conventions that were publicly available to poet and reader.[5]

There is a further complication. Not only is the view of literature as self-contained system represented in 'traditional' criticism, it is also attacked by the 'new'. Ellen Cantarow, for instance, attacks the 'literary professionalism' of the American university of the 1950s which tried to teach her to eliminate her own feelings and talk about the form of a poem; instead of such 'objectivity' she pleads for a response which thinks about what the poem is saying 'about me, or about my friend's mother, or about my friend'.[6] Ellen Cantarow represents what I have classified as non-structuralist radicalism, but she is so representative a voice of the revolutionaries of 1968 ('It was the fact of my womanhood, the war, the American education that made me a radical') that she can hardly be placed among the 'traditionalists'.

The division between those who see literature as a more or less self-contained system, and those who see it as interacting with real, extra-literary experience (that of the author, or of the reader, or the social reality of the author's or the reader's world) is a profoundly important one — perhaps as important as any other distinction: but it cuts across any division into two congealed rice puddings of the old and the new. Old-fashioned literary history and new-fashioned intertextuality fall on one side of the divide, as old-fashioned realism and new-fashioned demystification of literature fall on the other. And whatever other criterion was proposed for dividing the pre-historic (or pre-1960s) rice pudding from the new would equally mislead and oversimplify. [...] What makes a new movement valuable is its ability to re-animate old controversies by feeding in new social insights, a new psychology, or a new theoretical context. Psychoanalysis gave a new dimension to the very old doctrine of inspiration; and the view (derived from Foucault and Derrida) that there is no reality outside discourse gives a new dimension to the doctrine that literature is self-contained. If all language is self-contained because there is no external world for it to reach out to, [...] then the claim that literature is self-contained becomes more far-reaching, merely a particular case of a general rule.

Yet such an extension, simply because its philosophical claim is so absolute, may not make much difference to our way of seeing literature. If it were necessary to settle fundamental questions on the nature of reality before being able to understand and interpret literature, we would find ourselves in the position of Browning's Grammarian, putting off living until he had first mastered the knowledge that was its necessary preliminary, and finding that he had put it off for ever.

There is another reason for refusing to believe that true literary criticism began in the 1960s: that is the relation between criticism and reading. It is not difficult to accept that a paradigm shift in physics can render earlier physics obsolete, because the phenomena which physics explains (the behaviour of matter) do not depend for their functioning on our understanding of them. But if a new and scientific form of criticism has now rendered the old kinds obsolete, what is its relation to reading? The claim that reading has in the past been a naive activity which we can now explain (replace?) by deconstructing it seems to go against all we know of literature. Almost everyone who reads likes to talk about what he reads: when that talk becomes systematic it is called criticism. Criticism has always been judged by whether in its enthusiasm for system it loses touch with the reading experience: when this happens, we have neo-classic systems which are eventually rejected as mere abstract schemata. Structuralism can only claim exemption from this danger by claiming that a scientific criticism can dispense with the concept of the reading experience. But structuralism's parent, linguistics, cannot study a language unless there are native speakers, whose experience provides the criteria for meaning; and the native speaker of literature is the reader who responds. Any systematic theory of literature must therefore base itself on understanding, which is as old as the literary work: it can reorganize such understanding (which is complex and changing) but it cannot abolish it.

Let us for instance take the idea of a code, much used by *la nouvelle critique*, and, indeed, the basis of Barthes' *S/Z*. In some circles it has become so accepted that interpretation is referred to as decoding. Is this a mere change in terminology? The defining factor in a code is that the meaning is hidden, so that we cannot understand without the key. Interpreting and decoding can merge into each other, but are not the same, as we can see if we think about learning a foreign language. At first, we need to decode: we understand nothing without dictionary and grammar-book. Then, as we get to know the language, it gradually loses its code-like character. If we apply this distinction to literature, we will see that the code-like elements are those which cannot form part of our reading experience until we are taught them; perhaps they never can. A wholly innocent reader of a sonnet, not noticing how many lines there were, and not knowing that the number of lines had any significance, would have to have the sonnet form decoded for him. Are there any elements in poetry that remain encoded, even for the most sophisticated reader? In principle, the answer has to be no, since we can learn to notice anything, but there are certainly elements which the reader of any one period, or group, may never think of attending to. If Alastair Fowler is right in finding numerological patterns of astonishing intricacy in Renaissance poetry, then he is telling us that as far as we are concerned Surrey and Spenser wrote in code. A sophisticated Elizabethan might — just — have noticed that the first three stanzas of *Prothalamion* contain six rhymes each, stanzas 4–6 and 8–10 seven each, and stanza 7 five rhymes; but to go on and deduce a 'double symmetry', one of which places the bride at the centre and the other does not, to relate this to two almost totally concealed 'half-zodiacs' and conclude 'the half-zodiac of stanzas 8–10, like the 180 degrees mimed by the line-total, suggests the incompleteness of betrothal' would mean that he would have to operate on the poem like a cryptographer.[7]

Decoding differs from interpreting in that it does not spell out to us the meaning of what we have read, it adds new elements to that meaning. If it were not for psychoanalysis, we could even say that it contributes precisely the elements we did not read, but once we dissolve the distinction between conscious and unconscious meaning, we must allow that what the decoder tells us could have been part of the reading experience — though if our reason for saying this is psychoanalytic, we shall only say it of elements that have some cathectic charge because they activate repressed material: which is very hard indeed to say of the fact that Surrey's sonnet on Clere contains four personal and seven place names (of which three have family connections), offsetting the figure 7 by the 'tetrad of alliance'.[8]

There are three possible positions on decoding, two tenable and one untenable. The first is that decoding, and interpreting the meaning of what we read, are opposites; that the former only begins where the latter leaves off. This would deprive it of all interest. The second is that decoding identifies elements in our reading of which we were unaware, and so increases self-knowledge: the decoding formula we use would then depend on the mechanism of concealment that we postulate — superego, class ideology, *mauvaise foi*, Apollonian dream, numerological game. The untenable position is that interpreting *is* decoding, and no other term is needed. That could only be true if no one had previously understood what he read.

NOTES

1. George Steiner, *Sunday Times*, 4 May 1980, p. 43.
2. Anthony Easthope, 'Poetry and the Politics of Reading', in *Re-reading English*, ed. Peter Widdowson (1982), p. 141.
3. R. G. Collingwood, *Speculum Mentis* (1924), III.i.
4. M. H. Abrams, *The Mirror and the Lamp* (1953), I.v.
5. See Leo Spitzer, *Linguistics and Literary History* (1948); 'Understanding Milton', *The Hopkins Review* (1951), pp. 16–27.
6. Ellen Cantarow, 'Why Teach Literature? An Account of How I Came to Ask That Question' in *The Politics of Literature*, ed. Louis Kampf and Paul Laker (1970).
7. Alastair Fowler, *Conceitful Thought: the Interpretation of English Renaissance Poems* (1975), ch. 4.
8. *Ibid.*, ch. 2.

7 *How Successful is* Hard Times?

● David Lodge

The so-called industrial novels of the Victorian period, like *Hard Times*, offer a special problem, or trap, for literary criticism. Because these novels comment directly upon contemporary social issues, they open themselves to evaluation according to the 'truthfulness' with which they reflect the 'facts' of social history. Modern criticism of *Hard Times* shows this tendency very clearly. Humphrey House, in *The Dickens World* (1941), for instance, argued that the novel was a failure because Dickens had taken on subject-matter that he either could not or would not treat adequately: Dickens did not understand Utilitarianism well enough to attack it effectively, and in handling the theme of industrial relations falsified his own observations, as recorded in his report on the Preston strike in *Household Words* (11 February 1854). Dr Leavis, in advancing a (then) startlingly high evaluation of the novel in *The Great Tradition* (1948), conceded Dickens's failure on the latter score, but minimized its significance. For him, the centre of the novel was its critique of Utilitarianism, through the characterisation of Gradgrind and Bounderby. In his treatment of the latter, Leavis claimed, 'Dickens . . . makes a just observation about the affinities and practical tendency of Utilitarianism, as, in his presentment of the Gradgrind home and the Gradgrind elementary school, he does about the Utilitarian spirit in Victorian education'.[1] John Holloway contested this view in his essay, '*Hard Times*, A History and a Criticism'. Documenting his case extensively from contemporary encyclopedias, textbooks and government reports, Holloway argued forcefully that Dickens's account of Utilitarianism, and of the various practices that derived from it, was both unfair and internally inconsistent; and as regards the industrial theme he followed House in stressing Dickens's 'deliberate falsification of what [he] knew from his visit to Preston'.[2] In his introduction to the Penguin English library edition of the novel, the Marxist critic David Craig swung back to the opposite pole. Affirming the 'deep and manifold rootedness of *Hard Times* in its age', he sought to demonstrate the essential truthfulness of Dickens's critique of Gradgrind's philosophy of education by culling from the work of the Hammonds and other social historians descriptions of contemporary board schools that correspond closely to the early chapters of *Hard Times*. 'The schooling systems favoured by go-ahead cotton masters', says Craig, 'were themselves like living satires on Utilitarianism in practice, even before Dickens had recreated them in the mode of satire'.[3] But the 'mode' of the novel is less acceptable to Craig when it comes to the treatment of the working class, and his claims for the novel's truthfulness become progressively more tortuous and equivocal as his introduction proceeds. His conclusion reads almost like a parody of Stalinist Socialist Realism: 'if one tried to imagine the great industrial novel that never did get written, one might suggest that the masters cried out to be satirized, the mass of the people presented with clear-eyed realism. Insofar as Dickens fails in the latter, his novel sags; insofar as he excels in the former, it succeeds . . .'[4]

The history of critical commentary on *Hard Times* demonstrates that no amount of comparison between a novel and its social-historical sources (whether specific or general) can ever settle the question of how successful it is as a work of art. The reason is not that criteria of empirical truthfulness are wholly irrelevant (they are not); but that in referring from fiction to fact and back again, the critics are ignoring a vitally important stage in the creative process by which narratives are composed, viz. the transformation of the deep structure of the text into its surface structure. We must consider, that is to say, not just the transformation of historical data into fictional narrative, but the transformation of the narrative *fabula*, a story potentially realizable in an infinite number of ways, into a particular *sjuzet*, or text. It is in this process that the particular literary identity of a novel, and therefore the range of reader-responses appropriate to it, are determined.

In an earlier essay on *Hard Times*[5] I tried to mediate between conflicting evaluations of the novel by a formalistic analysis of its surface structure — that is, its characteristic style or rhetoric — suggesting that persuasiveness rather than truthfulness should be the criterion of success or failure. In this essay I aim to complement that earlier study by examining the novel's structure at a deeper level, that of narrative technique. The object is to answer the question, how successful is *Hard Times*, by answering another one: what kind of novel is *Hard Times*?

In advancing his very high estimate of the novel, Dr Leavis classified it as a 'moral fable', which he defined by saying that 'in it the intention is peculiarly insistent, so that the representative significance of everything in the fable — character, episode and so on — is immediately apparent as we read'.[6] But as Robert Garis pointed out, Dr Leavis's reading of *Hard Times* is not perceptibly different from his reading of other novels in *The Great Tradition*, and claims for it qualities which it hardly possesses.[7]

Professor Garis's own term for the exuberant explicitness which Leavis characterized as 'moral fable' is 'theatre', but it is a quality *he* finds permeating all Dickens's writing, whereas most readers of *Hard Times* have felt that there is something quite distinctive about the 'feel' of this novel. In what follows I shall try to analyse in formal terms the moralized theatricality that is specific to *Hard Times*, beginning with the categories of time and 'point of view'.

The most significant aspect of Dickens's handling of time in his novel concerns what Gérard Genette calls 'duration', affecting the *pace* of the narrative. There is not much to comment on with regard to the *ordering* of events — we do not find in *Hard Times* that radical dislocation and rearrangement of chronological order that we encounter, for instance, in *Wuthering Heights* or the novels of Joseph Conrad. Dickens tells his story in a straightforward way, narrating events in the order in which they occurred (except for passages where he shifts attention from one set of characters to another, and must bring us up to date by a brief recapitulation). The pace of the narrative is, however, rapid — considerably more so than Dickens's other novels, and certainly more rapid than other 'industrial novels' of the period, like Mrs Gaskell's *Mary Barton* (1848) or Disraeli's *Sybil* (1845). This rapid pace is partly the result of the condensation of several years' doings into a relatively short text, but it is also the result of the drastic curtailment of *description*, compared with Dickens's usual practice. There are, of course, vivid and memorable descriptions of people and places in *Hard Times*, but they are highly compressed, and overtly symbolic rather than realistic in function. The description of Mr Gradgrind's physiognomy and physique (I,1) and house (I,2) in metaphorical terms of geometrical regularity, mercantile accountancy, etc., is representative. Location is described in the same way, with a few bold strokes: the brick-red and soot-black city of Coketown, with its ugly, uniform civic architecture, its anonymous crowds of workers moving backwards and forwards at fixed intervals between their mean, identical dwellings and the factories that are ironically likened to brightly lit palaces, in which the pistons of the steam engines 'worked monotonously up and down, like the head of an elephant in a state of melancholy madness' (I,5). Dickens's often remarked technique of describing the animate in terms of the inanimate, and vice versa, here attains a stark, cartoon-like simplicity and economy of means. And since description always suspends the onward flow of narrative, this economy has the effect of speeding up the narrative tempo of *Hard Times* — an effect increased by the breaking up of the text into very short chapters. Authorial commentary, too, is more self-denying in terms of space than equivalent passages in, say, *Dombey and Son* or *Bleak House*. These features of *Hard Times* were no doubt partly dictated by the weekly serial publication in *Household Words* for which it was originally written — but only partly. Other novels by Dickens originally published in the same way, such as *The Old Curiosity Shop* or *Great Expectations*, have quite different and more leisurely rhythms. The basic rhythm of *Hard Times* is the alternation of highly compressed and stylized authorial narration/description/commentary with dialogue between the characters, presented in a scenic or dramatic fashion, with comparatively little comment or analysis from the authorial voice. In these dialogue scenes, the tempo of the text approximates to that of 'real life', but it rarely becomes slower, because Dickens does not linger to examine motives and responses in great detail.

I turn now to 'point of view'. *Hard Times* is narrated by an authorial voice who occasionally refers to himself as 'I' and whom it is natural to regard as a literary persona of the 'Charles Dickens' whose name appears on the title page. In other words, he is a reliable narrator, whose values and opinions we are invited to adopt. He is also omniscient, in the sense that he knows all there is to be known about the characters and their actions, though he withholds or postpones the revelation of his knowledge in the interests of narrative. He is intrusive, constantly drawing attention to his mediation of the story by the highly rhetorical language he uses, and by making polemical, didactic comments from time to time on matters of education, politics, social justice, etc. The entire novel, considered as a discourse, is uttered by the authorial voice, except for the direct speech of the characters. But while the author reports everything, he frequently restricts himself to reporting what this or that particular character *perceives*. Thus, by restricting the narrative to the limited and fallible perspective of a character, suspense and mystery are generated, by making the reader share the uncertainty of the character.

The characters in the novel are grouped in various clusters:

1. the Gradgrind family
2. the Bounderby ménage
3. the workers
4. the circus folk

The narrative brings members of these clusters into contact with each other, and occasionally shifts them from one cluster to another (thus, Louisa and Tom move from 1 to 2, Sissy from 4 to 1, and Mrs Pegler from 3 to 2) in ways which generate enigma and suspense, and at the same time illustrate in moral terms certain ideas about culture and society which are explicitly formulated by the authorial voice. Of these effects enigma is probably the least important. It would be a very slow-witted reader who did not guess that Tom committed the robbery, and that Mrs Pegler is Bounderby's mother, long before these facts are made plain to the characters. Compared with Dickens's other novels, the plot of *Hard Times* depends little upon mystery for its interest. The main source of simple narrative interest lies in suspense — in such questions as: will Louisa commit adultery? will Stephen be found and cleared of suspicion? will Tom escape from Bitzer? Most important of all is the didactic, illustrative import of the story, which is principally communicated by a series of ironic reversals or peripeteias.Thus the falsity of Mr Gradgrind's Utilitarian philosophy of life is demonstrated by the failure of his educational system as applied to his own children and to others. Louisa is so emotionally starved by her upbringing that she makes a loveless marriage and is thus rendered vulnerable to seduction by Harthouse, whom Gradgrind has himself introduced to Coketown in pursuance of his Utilitarian political interests; Tom grows up to be a wastrel and a thief, and when Mr Gradgrind tries to rescue him from public disgrace he is almost prevented by the model pupil of his own school, Bitzer, who produces impeccably Utilitarian reasons for his intervention.[8] Sissy Jupe, by contrast, who was ineducable by Gradgrind's system, has developed into a young woman of shining character on whom Gradgrind himself has come to depend heavily for moral support and practical assistance. The motif of ironic reversal permeates the whole novel. Mrs Sparsit's efforts to ingratiate herself with Mr Bounderby and vent her own spleen twice misfire — once in connection with Louisa's suspected elopement and a second time when she arrests Mrs Pegler, a scene which also constitutes a humiliating reversal for Bounderby himself.

The above description of the form of *Hard Times* does not, however, take us very far towards defining what is distinctive about this novel. Most of Dickens's novels concern several clusters of characters drawn from different ranks of society, between whom the plot sets up interesting and instructive connections, and most are narrated by an omniscient and intrusive authorial voice, who, however, often limits himself to articulating what is perceived by certain characters. Indeed, one might say this is the form of most classic English novels from Scott to George Eliot. *Hard Times* is unusual in that there are no characters whose perspectives dominate the novel, which is another way of saying that it has no hero or heroine: no character or pair of characters in whose fortune the reader develops an overriding interest. Sissy, Louisa and Stephen Blackpool are all possible candidates for such a role, but we are never allowed to share their perspectives in a sufficiently sustained way as to really identify with them. Indeed, we hardly ever get inside the girls' heads at all — they are primarily objects in the perceptual fields of other characters; and Stephen, though presented in a more interiorized fashion, is not in the foreground of the novel long enough to dominate it (out of thirty-seven chapters, he appears in only nine). The characters whose viewpoints are adopted by the narrator for any significant length of time are the morally unreliable characters like Mr Gradgrind in the early chapters of Book I, or Harthouse and Mrs Sparsit in Book II. But none of them is allowed to dominate the book either. The overall impression is of rapid and constant shifts of perspective, not only from one chapter to another, but often within a single chapter. No character is allowed to dominate, and no character is interiorized to any significant extent. We learn what they think and feel from what they say — aloud and to each other. The narrative is built up of scenes rather than episodes, explicit verbal interchanges between characters. The scene in the schoolroom, the scene at the Pegasus's Arms, the interview between Louisa and her father to discuss Bounderby's proposal, the corresponding scene in which she returns, a fugitive from Harthouse's attention, to reproach Gradgrind for the way she was brought up, the speeches at the workers' meetings and Stephen Blackpool's two confrontations with Bounderby, Harthouse's insidious *tête-à-têtes* with Louisa and Tom, and his verbal defeat by Sissy in his hotel — these and many similar scenes are the building blocks out of which *Hard Times* is constructed. Even the authorial voice is very much a speaking voice: not a ruminative essayist, or even a fireside conversationalist, but an orator, a pulpit-thumper, a Chorus.

Dickens's lifelong interest in the theatre and theatricals is well known, and the theatrical quality of his literary genius has been remarked by more than one critic. That this influence is particularly evident in *Hard Times*, and that it can alienate readers who expect a more subtle and realistic representation of life in novels, was shrewdly observed by Dickens's great contemporary, John Ruskin:

> The usefulness of that work (to my mind, in several respects, the greatest he has written) is with many persons seriously diminished because Mr Bounderby is a dramatic monster instead of a characteristic example of a worldly master; and Stephen Blackpool a dramatic perfection instead of a characteristic example of an honest workman. But let us not lose the use of Dickens's wit and insight, because he chooses to speak in a circle of stage fire.[9]

A sympathetic reading of *Hard Times*, then (which is not to say an uncritical reading), must recognize that its method is to a considerable extent borrowed from the popular theatre. The point may be illustrated by comparing Dickens's novel with that peculiarly British theatrical institution, the pantomime. Originally a form of mime, with its roots in the Italian Commedia del Arte, the pantomime became in the course of the nineteenth century a mixed form of narrative drama, usually based on some traditional story such as a fairy-tale, combining music, dance, spectacle, broad humour, slapstick and strong melodrama, with audience participation in the form of hissing, booing and cheering. It is still, of course, an extremely popular form of entertainment — indeed, the annual visit to the Christmas pantomime is the only occasion on which the average British family patronizes the live theatre.

There are several reasons why it seems useful to invoke the pantomime in defining the distinctive quality of *Hard Times*. First of all, something very like pantomime is actually represented in the novel. The entertainment provided by Sleary's Horse-Riding is not, like our modern circuses, pure spectacle, but has a strong narrative and dramatic element. Sissy's father, for instance, plays the leading role in 'the novel and laughable hippo-commedietta of the Tailor's Journey to Brentford' (I,4) and Tom is disguised as a black servant in a presentation of 'Jack the Giant-Killer' (III,7). Dickens, then, invites our approval not only of the values which the circus folk embody (loyalty, generosity, spontaneity, etc.) but also of the art which they practise. Secondly, as I have demonstrated elsewhere,[10] the text of *Hard Times* is saturated with allusions to the world of fairy-tale and nursery rhyme with which pantomimes are characteristically concerned: ogres and witches and dragons and fairies, old women on broomsticks, the cow with the crumpled horn, Peter Piper, and so on. Mr Gradgrind's ruthless exclusion of this kind of fantasy from his children's education is a primary index of what is wrong with his system:

> 'And what,' asked Mr Gradgrind, in a still lower voice, 'did you read to your father, Jupe?'
> 'About the Fairies, sir, and the Dwarf, and the Hunchback and the Genies,' she sobbed out; 'and about —'
> 'Hush!' said Mr Gradgrind, 'that is enough. Never breathe a word of such destructive nonsense any more. Bounderby, this is a case for rigid training, and I shall observe it with interest.' (I,8)

Thirdly, and perhaps most importantly, the characters themselves tend to act out roles that derive from the same literary and dramatic traditions. Thus Louisa and Tom first figure as the brother and sister pair who often appear in fairy-tales (e.g. the Babes in the Wood, another item in Sleary's repertoire) threatened by various dangers — in their case, the 'ogre' their father (I, 8). Bounderby is a giant in a castle as far as Stephen Blackpool is concerned ('Stephen . . . turned about and betook himself as in duty bound, to the red brick castle of the giant Bounderby' (II, 5)), but he also owes a lot to the very traditional comic figure of the Braggart or *miles gloriosus*, the boastful soldier who is really a coward. As the Gradgrind children grow up, Louisa becomes a princess threatened with enchantment by a bad fairy or witch (Mrs Sparsit, willing Louisa to descend the 'Giant's Staircase'), Tom is the thieving knave, and Harthouse a demon king invariably wreathed in smoke:

> smoking his cigar in his own easy way, and looking pleasantly at the whelp, as if he knew himself to be a kind of agreeable demon who had only to hover over him, and he must give up his whole soul if required. (II, 3)

The way these characters interact is theatrical in a bold, explicit, conventionalized manner typical of pantomime and other forms of popular theatre. I will give three examples. First, the scene in which Sissy tells Harthouse that he must give up any hope of winning Louisa and leave Coketown immediately. Sissy combines, in the novel, the roles of Cinderella (at first the most despised, later the most valued member of the family) and Fairy Godmother (Mr Gradgrind, in III, 7, 'raised his eyes to where she stood, like a good fairy in his house'), and her success in dispatching the demon tempter Harthouse depends on our acceptance of these stereotypes rather than on the persuasiveness of her arguments or the plausibility of Harthouse's motivation. The second scene is the one in which the mysterious old woman who, Bounderby observes, 'seems to have been flying into the town on a broomstick now and then', and whom he suspects of being involved in the bank robbery, is revealed to be his mother and thus exposes the falsity of his claims to have dragged himself up from the gutter. The highly theatrical feature of this scene, apart from the fact that it is nearly all direct speech, is that a large number of townspeople pour into Bounderby's house to witness the confrontation. It is implausible that they should have been admitted in the first place and still more so that they are permitted to remain after Bounderby has recognized his mother. But realism is sacrificed to a theatrical denouement, the whole 'company' on stage to mark, ritually, Bounderby's exposure. The third scene is when Louisa returns to her father and reproaches him with his failure to educate her emotions in the past. Louisa is given lines and gestures that belong entirely to the stage, and the chapter (the last one in Book II) ends with a strong 'curtain line' and symbolic tableau in which the novel's primary theme is made heavily explicit:

> 'Now, father, you have brought me to this. Save me by some other means!'
> He tightened his hold in time to prevent her sinking on the floor, but she cried out in a terrible voice, 'I shall die if you hold me! Let me fall upon the ground!' And he laid her down there, and saw the pride of his heart and the triumph of his system, lying, an insensible heap, at his feet.

This scene owes more to melodrama than to pantomime, and it is precisely in this respect that Dickens's reliance on the conventions of the popular stage creates most problems for his readers, especially modern ones. To treat the 'Condition of England' theme in the style of pantomime was a brilliantly imaginative stroke. First of all, it relieved Dickens of the obligation to present Utilitarianism, trade unionism or the workings of industrial capitalism, with any kind of objective, detailed verisimilitude — something he lacked the necessary experience and technical knowledge to accomplish in any case. Secondly, by invoking the world of fairy-tale *ironically*, making the inhabitants of this drab, gritty, Victorian mill town re-enact the motifs of folk-tale and legend, he drew attention to that repression or elimination of the human faculty of imagination (he calls it 'Fancy') which he believed was the culturally disastrous effect of governing society according to purely materialistic, empirical criteria of 'utility'. This double effect is epitomized by the recurrent description of the factories of Coketown as 'fairy palaces': instead of á realistic description of a factory, full of documentary detail, we get an ironic metaphor. To complain of the lack of realism is to miss the point of the metaphor. In *Hard Times* Dickens seems to be attempting something comparable to the 'alienation effect' of Bertolt Brecht's plays: to defamiliarize not merely the subject-matter of the story, so that we perceive it freshly, but also the method of presentation itself, so that instead of lapsing into a passive enjoyment of the illusion of life, instead of reacting emotionally to the story, we are compelled to recognize its artificiality and to consider its ideological implications. Dickens is not, however, so consistent and thoroughgoing as Brecht — and it would be anachronistic to expect him to be. In some parts of *Hard Times* — such as Louisa's scene with her father, or Stephen Blackpool's death scene — he exploits the techniques of popular theatre to encourage an emotional, indeed sentimental, response to the story, and seems to evade the awkward questions about class, capitalism and social justice that he himself has raised. *Hard Times* is not a totally satisfactory novel, but when we consider the boldness of Dickens's experiment, we should perhaps be more impressed by the degree of his success than by the novel's imperfections.

NOTES

1. F.R. Leavis, *The Great Tradition* (Harmondsworth, Middx, 1962), p. 251.

2. John Holloway, 'Hard Times, a History and a Criticism' in *Dickens and the Twentieth Century*, ed. John Gross and Gabriel Pearson (1962), p. 167.

3. David Craig, Introduction to *Hard Times* (Harmondsworth, Middx, 1969), p. 22.

4. *Ibid.*, p. 36.

5. 'The Rhetoric of *Hard Times*' in *Language of Fiction* (1966).

6. F. R. Leavis, *op. cit.*, p. 249.

7. Robert Garis, *The Dickens Theatre* (1965).

8. Arguably it would have made a fitter conclusion to the novel if Bitzer's intervention had been successful. There is no natural or poetic justice in allowing Tom to escape, as Dickens seems to acknowledge by killing him off by fever in the epilogue: and all the 'good' characters, even Sissy, seem somewhat compromised morally by their eagerness to save him from prison. Dickens no doubt wanted to bring the circus folk back into the story in a positive role, but the suspicion lingers that he thought it would be too black a conclusion to send a gentleman's son to prison.

9. John Ruskin, *Unto This Last*. Quoted by Robert Garis, *op. cit.*, p. 146.

10. In 'The Rhetoric of *Hard Times*', *op. cit.*, pp. 159–62.

II LITERATURE AND HUMAN VALUES

In the second chapter of the opening section, Eagleton defined literature as ideology. In the opening extract of this section, he sees the rise of English as a discipline as an example of ideology at work.

When you pass on to the Middleton Murry extract, you are in a different world. As you tread his quiet ways, the 'quality of life' becomes a major concern, as well as the relationship between thought and emotion in the creative process. 'The great writer does not really come to conclusions about life...'

Williams follows, and with him there is a return to the ideological emphasis of 'The Rise of English' as he argues that 'the ordinary tradition of tragedy is in fact an ideology'.

The remaining chapters highlight the relationship between literature and important areas of human values: religion, social class differences, the multicultural society and feminism. The Hoggart article, for example, illustrates fundamental issues in the understanding of the debate about high-status versus low-status arts in general and literature in particular. The tradition of English Literature is shot through with Christianity, and in the fourth chapter, Eliot considers the relationship between Religion and Literature, while MacDougall discusses some of the issues concerning the role of English in a multicultural Britain, arguing that American authors seem to have more self-assurance in this context than British writers because of a longer tradition of writing about ethnic minorities. The final chapter in this section deals with a feminist interpretation of Hardy's *The Mayor of Casterbridge*.

8   *The Rise of English*

● Terry Eagleton

[...] To speak of 'literature and ideology' as two separate phenomena which can be interrelated is in one sense quite unnecessary. Literature, in the meaning of the word we have inherited, *is* an ideology. It has the most intimate relations to questions of social power. [...] The narrative of what happens to literature in the later nineteenth century [may] prove [...] persuasive [in this context].

If one were asked to provide a single explanation for the growth of English studies in the later nineteenth century, one could do worse than reply: 'the failure of religion'. By the mid-Victorian period, this traditionally reliable, immensely powerful ideological form was in deep trouble. It was no longer winning the hearts and minds of the masses, and under the twin impacts of scientific discovery and social change its previous unquestioned dominance was in danger of evaporating. This was particularly worrying for the Victorian ruling class, because religion is for all kinds of reasons an extremely effective form of ideological control. Like all successful ideologies, it works much less by explicit concepts or formulated doctrines than by image, symbol, habit, ritual and mythology. It is affective and experiential, entwining itself with the deepest unconscious roots of the human subject; and any social ideology which is unable to engage with such deep-seated a-rational fears and needs, as T. S. Eliot knew, is unlikely to survive very long. Religion, moreover, is capable of operating at every social level: if there is a doctrinal inflection of it for the intellectual elite, there is also a pietistic brand of it for the masses. It provides an excellent social 'cement', encompassing pious peasant, enlightened middle-class liberal and theological intellectual in a single organization. Its ideological power lies in its capacity to 'materialize' beliefs as practices: religion is the sharing of the chalice and the blessing of the harvest, not just abstract argument about consubstantiation or hyperdulia. Its ultimate truths, like those mediated by the literary symbol, are conveniently closed to rational demonstration, and thus absolute in their claims. Finally religion, at least in its Victorian forms, is a *pacifying* influence, fostering meekness, self-sacrifice and the contemplative inner life. It is no wonder that the Victorian ruling class looked on the threatened dissolution of this ideological discourse with something less than equanimity.

Fortunately, however, another, remarkably similar discourse lay to hand: English literature. George Gordon, early Professor of English Literature at Oxford, commented in his inaugural lecture that 'England is sick, and . . . English literature must save it. The Churches (as I understand) having failed, and social remedies being slow, English literature has now a triple function: still I suppose, to delight and instruct us, but also, and above all, to save our souls and heal the State.'[1] Gordon's words were spoken in our own century, but they find a resonance everywhere in Victorian England. It is a striking thought that had it not been for this dramatic crisis in mid-nineteenth-century ideology, we might not today have such a plentiful supply of Jane Austen casebooks and bluffer's guides to Pound. As religion progressively ceases to provide the social 'cement', affective values and basic mythologies by which a socially turbulent class-society can be welded together, 'English' is constructed as a subject to carry this ideological burden from the Victorian period onwards. The key figure here is Matthew Arnold, always preternaturally sensitive to the needs of his social class, and engagingly candid about being so. The urgent social need, as Arnold recognizes, is to 'Hellenize' or cultivate the philistine middle class, who have proved unable to underpin their political and economic power with a suitably rich and subtle ideology. This can be done by transfusing into them something of the traditional style of the aristocracy, who as Arnold shrewdly perceives are ceasing to be the dominant class in England, but who have something of the ideological wherewithal to lend a hand to their middle class masters. State-established schools, by linking the middle-class to 'the best culture of their nation', will confer on them 'a greatness and a noble spirit, which the tone of these classes is not of itself at present adequate to impart'.[2]

The true beauty of this manoeuvre, however, lies in the effect it will have in controlling and incorporating the working class:

> It is of itself a serious calamity for a nation that its tone of feeling and grandeur of spirit should be lowered or dulled. But the calamity appears far more serious still when we consider that the middle classes, remaining as they are now, with their narrow, harsh, unintelligent, and unattractive spirit and culture, will almost certainly fail to mould or assimilate the masses below them, whose sympathies are at the present moment actually wider and more liberal than theirs. They arrive, these masses, eager to enter into possession of the world, to gain a more vivid sense of their own life and activity. In this their irrepressible development, their natural educators and initiators are those immediately above them, the middle classes. If these classes cannot win their sympathy or give them their direction, society is in danger of falling into anarchy.[3]

Arnold is refreshingly unhypocritical: there is no feeble pretence that the education of the working class is to be conducted chiefly for their own benefit, or that his concern with their spiritual condition is, in one of his own most cherished terms, in the least 'disinterested'. In the even more disarmingly candid words of a twentieth-century proponent of this view: 'Deny to working-class children any common share in the immaterial, and presently they will grow into the men who demand with menaces a communism of the material.'[4] If the masses are not thrown a few novels, they may react by throwing up a few barricades.

Literature was in several ways a suitable candidate for this ideological enterprise. As a liberal, 'humanizing' pursuit, it could provide a potent antidote to political bigotry and ideological extremism. Since literature, as we know, deals in universal human values rather than in such historical trivia as civil wars, the oppression of women or the dispossession of the English peasantry, it could serve to place in cosmic perspective the petty demands of working people for decent living conditions or greater control over their own lives, and might even with luck come to render them oblivious of such issues in their high-minded contemplation of eternal truths and beauties. English, as a Victorian handbook for English teachers put it, helps to 'promote sympathy and fellow feeling among all classes': another Victorian writer speaks of literature as opening a 'serene and luminous region of truth where all may meet and expatiate in common', above 'the smoke and stir, the din and turmoil of man's lower life of care and business and debate'.[5] Literature would rehearse the masses in the habits of pluralistic thought and feeling, persuading them to acknowledge that more than one viewpoint than theirs existed — namely, that of their masters. It would communicate to them the moral riches of bourgeois civilization, impress upon them a reverence for middle-class achievements, and, since reading is an essentially solitary, contemplative activity, curb in them any disruptive tendency to collective political action. It would give them a pride in their national language and literature: if scanty education and extensive hours of labour prevented them personally from producing a literary masterpiece, they could take pleasure in the thought that others of their own kind — English people — had done so. The people, according to a study of English literature written in 1891, 'need political culture, instruction, that is to say, in what pertains to their relation to the State, to their duties as citizens; and they need also to be impressed sentimentally by having the presentation in legend and history of heroic and patriotic examples brought vividly and attractively before them'.[6] All of this, moreover, could be achieved without the cost and labour of teaching them the Classics: English literature was written in their own language, and so was conveniently available to them.

Like religion, literature works primarily by emotion and experience, and so was admirably well-fitted to carry through the ideological task which religion left off. Indeed by our own time literature has become effectively identical with the opposite of analytical thought and conceptual enquiry: whereas scientists, philosophers and political theorists are saddled with these drably discursive pursuits, students of literature occupy the more prized territory of feeling and experience. Whose experience, and what kinds of feeling, is a different question. Literature from Arnold onwards is the enemy of 'ideological dogma', an attitude which might have come as a surprise to Dante, Milton and Pope; the truth or falsity of beliefs such as that blacks are inferior to whites is less important than what it feels like to experience them. Arnold himself had beliefs, of course, though like everybody else he regarded his own beliefs as reasoned positions rather than ideological dogmas. Even so, it was not the business of literature to communicate such beliefs directly — to argue openly, for example, that private property is the bulwark of liberty. Instead, literature should convey *timeless* truths, thus distracting the masses from their immediate commitments, nurturing in them a spirit of tolerance and generosity, and so ensuring the survival of private property. Just as Arnold attempted in *Literature and Dogma* and *Gold and the Bible* to dissolve away the embarrassingly doctrinal bits of Christianity into poetically suggestive sonorities, so the pill of middle-class ideology was to be sweetened by the sugar of literature.

There was another sense in which the 'experiential' nature of literature was ideologically convenient. For 'experience' is not only the homeland of ideology, the place where it takes root most effectively; it is also in its literary form a kind of vicarious self-fulfilment. If you do not have the money and leisure to visit the Far East, except perhaps as a soldier in the pay of British imperialism, then you can always 'experience' it at second hand by reading Conrad or Kipling. Indeed according to some literary theories this is even more real than strolling around Bangkok. The actually impoverished experience of the mass of people, an impoverishment bred by their social conditions, can be supplemented by literature: instead of working to change such conditions (which Arnold, to his credit, did more thoroughly than almost any of those who sought to inherit his mantle), you can vicariously fulfil someone's desire for a fuller life by handing them *Pride and Prejudice*.

It is significant, then, that 'English' as an academic subject was first institutionalized not in the Universities, but in the Mechanics' Institutes, working men's colleges and extension lecturing circuits.[7] English was literally the poor man's Classics — a way of providing a cheapish 'liberal' education for those beyond the charmed circles of public school and Oxbridge. From the outset, in the work of 'English' pioneers like F. D. Maurice and Charles Kingsley, the emphasis was on solidarity between the social classes, the cultivation of 'larger sympathies', the instillation of national pride and the transmission of 'moral' values. This last concern — still the distinctive hallmark of literary studies in

England, and a frequent source of bemusement to intellectuals from other cultures — was an essential part of the ideological project; indeed the rise of 'English' is more or less concomitant with an historic shift in the very meaning of the term 'moral', of which Arnold, Henry James and F. R. Leavis are the major critical exponents. Morality is no longer to be grasped as a formulated code or explicit ethical system: it is rather a sensitive preoccupation with the whole quality of life itself, with the oblique, nuanced particulars of human experience. Somewhat rephrased, this can be taken as meaning that the old religious ideologies have lost their force, and that a more subtle communication of moral values, one which works by 'dramatic enactment' rather than rebarbative abstraction, is thus in order. Since such values are nowhere more vividly dramatized than in literature, brought home to 'felt experience' with all the unquestionable reality of a blow on the head, literature becomes more than just a handmaiden of moral ideology: it *is* moral ideology for the modern age, as the work of F. R. Leavis was most graphically to evince.

The working class was not the only oppressed layer of Victorian society at whom 'English' was specifically beamed. English literature, reflected a Royal Commission witness in 1877, might be considered a suitable subject for 'women . . . and the second- and third-rate men who [. . .] become schoolmasters.'[8] The 'softening' and 'humanizing' effects of English, terms recurrently used by its early proponents, are within the existing ideological stereotypes of gender clearly feminine. The rise of English in England ran parallel to the gradual, grudging admission of women to the institutions of higher education; and since English was an untaxing sort of affair, concerned with the finer feelings rather than with the more virile topics of *bona fide* academic 'disciplines', it seemed a convenient sort of non-subject to palm off on the ladies, who were in any case excluded from science and the professions. Sir Arthur Quiller Couch, first Professor of English at Cambridge University, would open with the word 'Gentlemen' lectures addressed to a hall filled largely with women. Though modern male lecturers may have changed their manners, the ideological conditions which make English a popular University subject for women to read have not.

If English had its feminine aspect, however, it also acquired a masculine one as the century drew on. The era of the academic establishment of English is also the era of high imperialism in England. As British capitalism became threatened and progressively outstripped by its younger German and American rivals, the squalid, undignified scramble of too much capital chasing too few overseas territories, which was to culminate in 1914 in the first imperialist world war, created the urgent need for a sense of national mission and identity. What was at stake in English studies was less English *literature* than *English* literature: our great 'national poets' Shakespeare and Milton, the sense of an 'organic' national tradition and identity to which new recruits could be admitted by the study of humane letters. The reports of educational bodies and official enquiries into the teaching of English, in this period and in the early twentieth century, are strewn with nostalgic back-references to the 'organic' community of Elizabethan England in which nobles and groundlings found a common meeting-place in the Shakespearean theatre, and which might still be reinvented today. It is no accident that the author of one of the most influential Government reports in this area, *The Teaching of English in England* (1921), was none other than Sir Henry Newbolt, minor jingoist poet and perpetrator of the immortal line 'Play up! play up! and play the game!' Chris Baldick has pointed to the importance of the admission of English literature to the Civil Service examinations in the Victorian period: armed with this conveniently packaged version of their own cultural treasures, the servants of British imperialism could sally forth overseas secure in a sense of their national identity, and able to display that cultural superiority to their envying colonial peoples.[9]

It took rather longer for English, a subject fit for women, workers and those wishing to impress the natives, to penetrate the bastions of ruling-class power in Oxford and Cambridge. English was an upstart, amateurish affair as academic subjects went, hardly able to compete on equal terms with the rigours of Greats or philology; since every English gentleman read his own literature in his spare time anyway, what was the point of submitting it to systematic study? Fierce rearguard actions were fought by both ancient Universities against this distressingly dilettante subject: the definition of an academic subject was what could be examined, and since English was no more than idle gossip about literary taste it was difficult to know how to make it unpleasant enough to qualify as a proper academic pursuit. This, it might be said, is one of the few problems associated with the study of English which have since been effectively resolved. The frivolous contempt for his subject displayed by the first really 'literary' Oxford professor, Sir Walter Raleigh, has to be read to be believed.[10] Raleigh held his post in the years leading up to the First World War; and his relief at the outbreak of the war, an event which allowed him to abandon the feminine vagaries of literature and put his pen to something more manly — war propaganda — is palpable in his writing. The only way in which English seemed likely to justify its existence in the ancient Universities was by systematically mistaking itself for the Classics; but the classicists were hardly keen to have this pathetic parody of themselves around.

If the first imperialist world war more or less put paid to Sir Walter Raleigh, providing him with an heroic identity more comfortably in line with that of his Elizabethan namesake, it also signalled the final victory of English studies at Oxford and Cambridge. One of the most strenuous antagonists of English — philology — was closely bound up with Germanic influence; and since England happened to be passing through a major war with Germany, it was possible to smear classical philology as a form of ponderous Teutonic nonsense with which no self-respecting Englishman should be caught associating.[11] England's victory over Germany meant a renewal of national pride, an upsurge of patriotism which could only aid English's cause; but at the same time the deep trauma of the war, its almost intolerable questioning of every previously held cultural assumption, gave rise to a 'spiritual hungering', as one contemporary commentator described it, for which poetry seemed to provide an answer. It is a chastening thought that we owe the University study of English, in part at least, to a meaningless massacre. The Great War, with its carnage of ruling-class rhetoric, put paid to some of the more strident forms of chauvinism on which English had previously thrived: there could be few more Walter Raleighs after Wilfred Owen. English Literature rode to power on the back of wartime nationalism; but it also represented a search for spiritual solutions on the part of an English ruling class whose sense of identity had been profoundly shaken, whose psyche was ineradicably scarred by the horrors it had endured. Literature would be at once solace and reaffirmation, a familiar ground on which Englishmen could regroup both to explore, and to find some alternative to, the nightmare of history.

The architects of the new subject at Cambridge were on the whole individuals who could be absolved from the crime and guilt of having led working-class Englishmen over the top. F. R. Leavis had served as a medical orderly at the front; Queenie Dorothy Roth, later Q. D. Leavis, was as a woman exempt from such involvements, and was in any case still a child at the outbreak of war. I. A. Richards entered the army after graduation; the renowned pupils of these pioneers, William Empson and L. C. Knights, were also still children in 1914. The champions of English, moreover, stemmed on the whole from an alternative social class to that which had led Britain into war. F. R. Leavis was the son of a musical instruments dealer, Q. D. Roth the daughter of a draper and hosier, I. A. Richards the son of a works manager in Cheshire. English was to be fashioned not by the patrician dilettantes who occupied the early Chairs of Literature at the ancient universities, but by the offspring of the provincial petty bourgeoisie. They were members of a social class entering the traditional Universities for the first time, able to identify and challenge the social assumptions which informed its literary judgements in a way that the devotees of Sir Arthur Quiller Couch were not. None of them had suffered the crippling disadvantages of a purely literary education of the Quiller Couch kind: F. R. Leavis had migrated to English from history, his pupil Q. D. Roth drew in her work on psychology and cultural anthropology. I. A. Richards had been trained in mental and moral sciences.

In fashioning English into a serious discipline, these men and women blasted apart the assumptions of the pre-war upper-class generation. No subsequent movement within English studies has come near to recapturing the courage and radicalism of their stand. In the early 1920s it was desperately unclear why English was worth studying at all: by the early 1930s it had become a question of why was it worth wasting your time on anything else. English was not only a subject worth studying, but *the* supremely civilizing pursuit, the spiritual essence of the social formation. Far from constituting some amateur or impressionistic enterprise, English was an arena in which the most fundamental questions of human existence — what it meant to be a person, to engage in significant relationship with others, to live from the vital centre of the most essential values — were thrown into vivid relief and made the object of the most intensive scrutiny. *Scrutiny* was the title of the critical journal launched in 1932 by the Leavises, which has yet to be surpassed in its tenacious devotion to the moral centrality of English studies, their crucial relevance to the quality of social life as a whole. Whatever the 'failure' or 'success' of *Scrutiny*, however one might argue the toss between the anti-Leavisian prejudice of the literary establishment and the waspishness of the *Scrutiny* movement itself, the fact remains that English students in England today are 'Leavisites' whether they know it or not, irremediably altered by that historic intervention. There is no more need to be a card-carrying Leavisite today than there is to be a card-carrying Copernican: that current has entered the bloodstream of English studies in England as Copernicus reshaped our astronomical beliefs, has become a form of spontaneous critical wisdom as deep-seated as our conviction that the earth moves round the sun. That the 'Leavis debate' is effectively dead is perhaps the major sign of *Scrutiny*'s victory.

What the Leavises saw was that if the Sir Arthur Quiller Couches were allowed to win out, literary criticism would be shunted into an historical siding of no more inherent significance than the question of whether one preferred potatoes to tomatoes. In the face of such whimsical 'taste', they stressed the centrality of rigorous critical analysis, a disciplined attention to the 'words on the page'. They urged this not simply for technical or aesthetic reasons, but because it had the closest relevance to the spiritual crisis of modern civilization. Literature was important not only in itself, but because it encapsulated creative energies which were everywhere on the defensive in modern 'commercial' society. In literature, and perhaps in literature alone, a vital feel for the creative uses of language was still manifest, in contrast to the philistine devaluing of language and traditional culture blatantly apparent in 'mass society'. The quality of a society's language was the most telling index of the quality of its personal and social life: a society which had ceased to value literature was one lethally closed to the impulses which had created and sustained the best of human civilization. In the civilized manners of eighteenth-century England, or in the 'natural', 'organic' agrarian society of the seventeenth century, one could discern a form of living sensibility without which modern industrial society would atrophy and die.

To be a certain kind of English student in Cambridge in the late 1920s and 1930s was to be caught up in this buoyant, polemical onslaught against the most trivializing features of industrial capitalism. It was rewarding to know that being an English student was not only valuable but the most important way of life one could imagine — that one was contributing in one's own modest way to rolling back twentieth-century society in the direction of the 'organic' community of seventeenth-century England, that one moved at the most progressive tip of civilization itself. Those who came up to Cambridge humbly expecting to read a few poems and novels were quickly demystified: English was not just one discipline among many but the most central subject of all, immeasurably superior to law, science, politics, philosophy or history. These subjects, *Scrutiny* grudgingly conceded, had their place; but it was a place to be assessed by the touchstone of literature, which was less an academic subject than a spiritual exploration coterminous with the fate of civilization itself. With breathtaking boldness, *Scrutiny* redrew the map of English literature in ways from which criticism has never quite recovered. The main thoroughfares on this map ran through Chaucer, Shakespeare, Jonson, the Jacobeans and Metaphysicals, Bunyan, Pope, Samuel Johnson, Blake, Wordsworth, Keats, Austen, George Eliot, Hopkins, Henry James, Joseph Conrad, T. S. Eliot and D. H. Lawrence. This *was* 'English literature': Spencer, Dryden, Restoration drama, Defoe, Fielding, Richardson, Sterne, Shelley, Byron, Tennyson, Browning, most of the Victorian novelists, Joyce, Woolf and most writers after D. H. Lawrence constituted a network of 'B' roads interspersed with a good few cul-de-sacs. Dickens was first out and then in; 'English' included two and a half women, counting Emily Brontë as a marginal case; almost all of its authors were conservatives.

Dismissive of mere 'literary' values, *Scrutiny* insisted that how one evaluated literary works was deeply bound up with deeper judgements about the nature of history and society as a whole. Confronted with critical approaches which saw the dissection of literary texts as somehow discourteous, an equivalent in the literary realm to grievous bodily harm, it promoted the most scrupulous analysis of such sacrosanct objects. Appalled by the complacent assumption that any work written in elegant English was more or less as good as any other, it insisted on the most rigorous discrimination between different literary qualities: some works 'made for life', while others most assuredly did not. Restless with the cloistered aestheticism of conventional criticism, Leavis in his early years saw the need to address social and political questions: he even at one point guardedly entertained a form of economic communism. *Scrutiny* was not just a journal, but the focus of a moral and cultural crusade: its adherents would go out to the schools and universities to do battle there, nurturing through the study of literature the kind of rich, complex, mature, discriminating, morally serious responses (all key *Scrutiny* terms) which would equip individuals to survive in a mechanized society of trashy romances, alienated labour, banal advertisements and vulgarizing mass media.

I say 'survive', because apart from Leavis's brief toying with 'some form of economic communism', there was never any serious consideration of actually trying to *change* such a society. It was less a matter of seeking to transform the mechanized society which gave birth to this withered culture than of seeking to withstand it. In this sense, one might claim, *Scrutiny* had thrown in the towel from the start. The only form of change it contemplated was education: by implanting themselves in the educational institutions, the Scrutineers hoped to develop a rich, organic sensibility in selected individuals here and there, who might then transmit this sensibility to others. In this faith in education, Leavis was the true inheritor of Matthew Arnold. But since such individuals were bound to be few and far between, given the insidious effects of 'mass civilization', the only real hope was that an embattled cultivated minority might keep the torch of culture burning in the contemporary waste land and pass it on, via their pupils, to posterity.

There are real grounds for doubting that education has the transformative power which Arnold and Leavis assigned to it. It is, after all, *part* of society rather than a solution to it; and who, as Marx once asked, will educate the educators? *Scrutiny* espoused this idealist 'solution', however, because it was loath to contemplate a political one. Spending your English lessons alerting schoolchildren to the manipulativeness of advertisements or the linguistic poverty of the popular press is an important task, and certainly more important than getting them to memorize *The Charge of the Light Brigade*. *Scrutiny* actually founded such 'cultural studies' in England, as one of its most enduring achievements. But it is also possible to point out to students that advertisements and the popular press only exist in their present form because of the profit motive. 'Mass' culture is not the inevitable product of 'industrial' society, but the offspring of a particular form of industrialism which organizes production for profit rather than for use, which concerns itself with what will sell rather than with what is valuable. There is no reason to assume that such a social order is unchangeable; but the changes necessary would go far beyond the sensitive reading of *King Lear*. The whole *Scrutiny* project was at once hair-raisingly radical and really rather absurd. As one commentator has shrewdly put it, the Decline of the West was felt to be avertible by close reading.[12] Was it really true that *literature* could roll back the deadening effects of industrial labour and the philistinism of the media? It was doubtless comforting to feel that by reading Henry James one belonged to the moral vanguard of civilization itself; but what of all those people who did not read Henry James, who had never even heard of James, and would no doubt go to their graves complacently ignorant that he had been and gone? These people certainly composed the overwhelming social majority; were they morally callous, humanly banal and imaginatively bankrupt? One was speaking perhaps of one's own parents and friends here, and so needed to be a little circumspect. Many of these people seemed morally serious and sensitive enough: they showed no particular tendency to go around murdering, looting and plundering, and even if they did it seemed implausible to attribute this to the fact they had not read Henry James. The *Scrutiny* case was inescapably elitist: it betrayed a profound ignorance and distrust of the capacities of those not fortunate enough to have read English at Downing College. 'Ordinary' people seemed acceptable if they were seventeenth-century cowherds or 'vital' Australian bushmen.

But there was another problem, too, more or less the reverse of this. For if not all of those who could not recognize an enjambement were nasty and brutish, not all of those who could were morally pure. Many people were indeed deep in high culture, but it would transpire a decade or so after the birth of *Scrutiny* that this had not prevented some of them from engaging in such activities as superintending the murder of Jews in central Europe. The strength of Leavisian criticism was that it was able to provide an answer, as Sir Walter Raleigh was not, to the question, why read Literature? The answer, in a nutshell, was that it made you a better person. Few reasons could have been more persuasive than that. When the Allied troops moved into the concentration camps some years after the founding of *Scrutiny*, to arrest commandants who had whiled away their leisure hours with a volume of Goethe, it appeared that someone had some explaining to do. If reading literature did make you a better person, then it was hardly in the direct ways that this case at its most euphoric had imagined. It was possible to explore the 'great tradition' of the English novel and believe that in doing so you were addressing questions of fundamental value — questions which were of vital relevance to the lives of men and women wasted in fruitless labour in the factories of industrial capitalism. But it was also conceivable that you were destructively cutting yourself off from such men and women, who might be a little slow to recognize how a poetic enjambement enacted a movement of physical balancing.

The lower middle-class origins of the architects of English are perhaps relevant here. Nonconformist, provincial, hardworking and morally conscientious, the Scrutineers had no difficulty in identifying for what it was the frivolous amateurism of the upper-class English gentlemen who filled the early Chairs of Literature at the ancient Universities. These men were not their kind of men: they were not what the son of a shopkeeper or daughter of a draper would be especially inclined to respect, as a social elite who had excluded their own people from the ancient Universities. But if the lower middle class has a deep animus against the effete aristocracy perched above it, it also works hard to discriminate itself from the working class set below it, a class into whose ranks it is always in danger of falling. *Scrutiny* arose out of this social ambivalence: radical in respect of the literary-academic Establishment, coterie-minded with regard to the mass of the people. Its fierce concern with 'standards' challenged the patrician dilettantes who felt that Walter Savage Landor was probably just as charming in his own way as John Milton, at the same time as it posed searching tests for anyone trying to muscle in on the game. The gain was a resolute singleness of purpose, uncontaminated by wine-tasing triviality on the one hand and 'mass' banality on the other. The loss was a profoundly ingrown isolationism: *Scrutiny* became a defensive elite which, like the Romantics, viewed itself as 'central' while being in fact peripheral, believed itself to be the 'real' Cambridge while the real Cambridge was busy denying it academic posts, and perceived itself as the vanguard of civilization while nostalgically lauding the organic wholeness of exploited seventeenth-century farm labourers.

The only sure fact about the organic society, as Raymond Williams has commented, is that it has always gone.[13] Organic societies are just convenient myths for belabouring the mechanized life of modern industrial capitalism. Unable to present a political alternative to this social order, the Scrutineers offered an 'historical' one instead, as the Romantics had done before them. They insisted, of course, that there was no literal returning to the golden age, as almost every English writer who has pressed the claims of some historical utopia has been careful to do. Where the organic society lingered on for the Leavisites was in certain uses of the English language. The language of commercial society was abstract and anaemic: it had lost touch with the living roots of sensuous experience. In really 'English' writing, however, language 'concretely enacted' such felt experience: true English literature was verbally rich, complex, sensuous and particular, and the best poem, to caricature the case a little, was one which read aloud sounded rather like chewing an apple. The 'health' and 'vitality' of such language was the product of a 'sane' civilization: it embodied a creative wholeness which had been historically lost, and to read literature was thus to regain vital touch with the roots of one's own being. Literature *was* in a sense an organic society all of its own: it was important because it was nothing less than a whole social ideology.

NOTES

1. Quoted by Chris Baldick, 'The Social Mission of English Studies' (D. Phil thesis, Oxford 1981), p. 156. I am considerably indebted to this excellent study (published as *The Social Mission of English Criticism 1848–1932*, London, 1983).

2. 'The Popular Education of France', in *Democratic Education*, ed. R. H. Super (Ann Arbor, 1962), p. 22.

3. ibid., p. 26.

4. George Sampson, *English for the English* (1921), quoted by Baldick, 'The Social Mission of English Studies', p. 153.

5. H. G. Robinson, 'On the use of English Classical Literature in the Work of Education', *Macmillan's Magazine* 11 (1860), quoted by Baldick, 'Social Mission', p. 103.

6. J. C. Collins, *The Study of English Literature* (1891), quoted by Baldick, 'Social Mission', p. 100.

7. See Lionel Gossman, 'Literature and Education', *New Literary History*, vol. XIII, no. 2, Winter 1982, pp. 341–71. See also D. J. Palmer, *The Rise of English Studies* (London, 1965).

8. Quoted by Gossman, 'Literature and Education', pp. 341–2.

9. See Baldick, 'The Social Mission of English Studies', pp. 108–11.

10. See ibid., pp. 117–23.

11. See Francis Mulhern, *The Moment of 'Scrutiny'* (London, 1979), pp. 20–2.

12. See Iain Wright, 'F. R. Leavis, the *Scrutiny* movement and the Crisis', in Jon Clarke *et al.* (eds.), *Culture and Crisis in Britain in the Thirties* (London, 1979), p. 48.

13. See *The Country and the City* (London, 1973), pp. 9–12.

9 *The Psychology of Style*

● J. Middleton Murry

[...] Most people would agree that the originating emotion was a prime factor in the genesis of a lyrical poem. There is a profound perturbation of the poet's being, of which the occasion may be an object or event in the real world — a particular woman, the west wind, the smaller celandine — or an object or event in the ideal world — a presentiment of immortality, a vision of death or eternity: to this perturbing emotion the poet gives utterance, that is checked from mere exuberance and lifted above the plane of a sensational reaction, by the discipline of rhythm and metre. If the poem that is the result of this reassertion of conscious control over the disturbed being is a very good poem, each word of it will be absolutely relevant to the originating emotion, not merely in virtue of its logical meaning, but of its suggestion: more than this, the rhythm of the poem will be concordant. As an example of the simple case, let us take one of the finest of modern lyrical poems, Mr Hardy's 'A Broken Appointment':

You did not come,
And marching Time drew on, and wore me numb. —
Yet less for loss of your dear presence there
Than that I thus found lacking in your make
That high compassion which can overbear
Reluctance for pure loving-kindness' sake
Grieved I, when, as the hope-hour stroked its sum,
You did not come.

You love not me,
And love alone can lend you loyalty;
— I know and knew it. But unto the store
Of human deeds divine in all but name
Was it not worth a little hour or more
To add yet this: Once you, a woman, came
To soothe a time-torn man; even though it be
You love me not?

The language in which the emotion is expressed could hardly be more direct and simple. In the first verse there is one inversion — one simple yet tremendous metaphor — 'And marching Time drew on and wore me numb' — and one phrase in which words have been compelled by a force there is no escaping to do the poet's purpose — 'As the hope-hour stroked its sum.' The second verse is limpid. The rhythm is absolutely appropriate to the emotion: we hear the step of marching time, and in the short lines which open and clinch each stanza there are the first and the last strokes of the fatal bell. Even though the actual process of composition may be mysterious, we can see the predominant part played by the originating emotion.

But what of a dramatic poem or a novel? After all, lyric poetry is, almost by definition, the medium for the expression of personal emotion; what of the literature that is impersonal? It is clear that we cannot refer a perfect play — for instance, *Antony and Cleopatra* — to an originating emotion as we can Mr Hardy's poem. *Antony and Cleopatra* had its origin in no single, simple disturbance of the author's being. In the first place, Shakespeare more or less deliberately chose his theme — rather more than less deliberately[1] in this particular case, I think — but, in the crude language of our analysis, that will only mean that the emotional disturbance was self-provoked. The more mysterious aspect is its indubitable complication. It is to cover complicated disturbances of this kind that I introduce the phrase 'modes of experience', and which I will now try to elucidate.

The literary artist begins his career with a more than ordinary sensitiveness. Objects and episodes in life, whether the life of every day or of the mind, produce upon him a deeper and more precise impression than they do upon the ordinary man. As these impressions accumulate, unless the artist is one of the most simple, lyrical types, who reacts directly and completely to each separate impression, they to some extent obliterate and to a greater extent reinforce each other. From them all emerges, at least in the case of an artist destined to mature achievement, a coherent emotional nucleus. This is often consolidated by a kind of speculative thought, which differs from the speculative thought of the philosopher by its working from particular to particular. The creative literary artist does not generalize; or rather, his generalization is not abstract. However much he may think, his attitude to life is predominantly emotional; his thoughts partake much more of the nature of residual emotions, which are symbolized in the objects which aroused them, than of discursive reasoning. Out of the multitude of his vivid perceptions, with their emotional accompaniments, emerges a sense of the quality of life as a whole. It is this sense of, and emphasis upon, a dominant quality pervading the human universe which gives to the work of the great master of literature that unique universality which Matthew Arnold attempted to isolate in his famous criterion of the highest kind of poetry — 'criticism of life'.[2] Though I think it would not be difficult to show that Arnold himself was partly hypnotized by the phrase of his own coining, the conception is in itself most valuable. We have, however, to remember that it is half-metaphorical; that a great creative writer does not 'criticize' life, for criticism is a predominantly intellectual activity. It was because Arnold sometimes forgot that 'criticism of life' was only an analogue to the peculiar achievement of the writer, that he was inclined to choose, as his examples of the highest kind of poetry, lines which contained a poet's formulated judgement upon life, such as Dante's 'Nessun maggior dolore', which, though magnificent, is not really typical of the supreme excellence of Dante's poetry; or Shakespeare's 'We are such stuff as dreams are made on: and our little life is rounded with a sleep'.[2]

The great writer does not really come to conclusions about life; he discerns a quality in it. His emotions, reinforcing one another, gradually form in him a habit of emotion; certain kinds of objects and incidents impress him with a peculiar weight and significance. This emotional bias or predisposition is what I have ventured to call the writer's 'mode of experience'; it is by virtue of this mysterious accumulation of past emotions that the writer, in his maturity, is able to accomplish the miracle of giving to the particular the weight and force of the universal. 'In certain states of the soul', Baudelaire wrote, 'the profound significance of life is revealed completely in the spectacle, however commonplace, that is before one's eyes: it becomes the symbol of this significance.'[3] The greater the writer, the more continuous does that apprehensive condition of the soul become. And Wordsworth, in the preface to the second edition of *Lyrical Ballads*, has a passage which has always seemed to me infinitely precious for the light it throws on the psychology of the creative writer. 'All good poetry', he says, 'is the spontaneous overflow of powerful feelings: and though this be true, poems to which any value can be attached were never produced on any variety of subjects but by a man who, being possessed *of more than usual organic sensibility*, has also thought long and deeply. For our continued influxes of feeling are modified and directed by our thoughts, *which are indeed the representatives of all our past feelings*; and, as by contemplating the relation of these general representatives to each other, we discover what is really important to men, so, by the repetition and continuance of this act, our feelings will be connected with important subjects, till at length, if we be originally possessed of much sensibility, such habits of mind will be produced that, by *obeying blindly and mechanically the impulses of those habits*, we shall describe objects, and utter sentiments, of such a nature and such connexion with each other, that the understanding of the reader must necessarily be in some degree heightened and his affections strengthened and purified.'* Wordsworth seems to lay greater stress on the part played by thought in this

---

* This quotation occurs earlier in the 'Preface to *Lyrical Ballads*' than the extract cited in this Reader. See Gill, *op cit.*, p. 598, for a somewhat differently-worded source. The first part of this quotation is repeated in the Wordsworth extract in Chapter 1 (p. 26).

development of the poetical consciousness than I have done; but, I think that, if you examine more closely the sense in which he is using the words 'thought' and 'thoughts' (which he definitely describes as representatives of all our past feelings) you will see that it is not a rational process with which he is concerned. The thoughts in the mind of a great poet are chiefly the residue of remembered emotions.

I do not wish to imply that discursive thinking plays no part at all in determining the writer's spiritual background, his mental hinterland, as Mr H. G. Wells calls it; but I am convinced that the part it plays is on the whole a small one, and never — even in the case of the most philosophic poets like Lucretius and Dante, or the most philosophic novelists like Dostoevsky and Thomas Hardy — a dominant part. The meditation of a writer is, in spite of all analogies, different in kind from the meditation of the philosopher or the scientist; it is exercised on a different material and produces different results. A tragic poet is not a pessimistic philosopher, however sternly some critics may insist on treating him as one.

The part played by the intellect in the work of literary creation is essentially subordinate, though its subordinate function may be much more important in one writer than another. Its most characteristic employment is to explicate the large and complex emotional conviction, which is sometimes called 'a writer's philosophy', and may with less danger of misinterpretation be called his 'attitude', the element which determines his mode of experience and gives unity to his work as a whole. Lucretius used the philosophy of Epicurus, Dante the mediaeval conception of the Aristotelian cosmogony; but both those great poets used those intellectual systems as a scaffolding upon which to build an emotional structure. A great satirist like Swift uses the intellect, not to reach rational conclusions, but to expound and convey in detail a complex of very violent emotional reactions; and I would even say that Plato used a tremendous logical apparatus in order to impart to posterity an attitude towards the universe that was not logical at all.

Let us now return to the play or the novel. The poet, in whom (according to our theory) the vivid emotions of youth had been refined into a complex but self-consistent attitude to life, and his emotional bias confirmed into a mode of experience, chooses a plot. Aristotle rightly says everything depends on the choice of a plot — but there are different ways of choosing it. If he is an author who has to get his living by his work, he will have to take into account the taste of the age. If it is an active and enthusiastic age, he will to some extent be in sympathy with its taste. He will be able to choose a plot which may not be at all what he would desire in point of delicacy and subtlety, but lends itself to the bent of his own mode of experience, his emotional predisposition; on the whole we may say that this was the good fortune of Shakespeare, though the Sonnets are evidence that at one time in his career he reproached himself bitterly with having prostituted his genius on work that went against the grain. But where the writer is a perfectly free agent, as Shakespeare occasionally was, his choice of plot will be of a subtler and still more important kind.

The plot he chooses will then be one in which — to use Baudelaire's words — 'the deep significance of life reveals itself in its entirety'. Life, in this phrase, means the universe of the writer's experience; its 'deep significance' is the emotional quality which is the common element in the objects and incidents which have habitually made the most precise and profound impression on his mind; a quality that is in part the creation of the poet himself, but in part also a real attribute of the existing world, which needs the sensitiveness of the creative writer in order to be discerned. The plot of the writer of mature genius, who is a completely free agent, will be absolutely in harmony with this quality. For a plot is, after all, in itself only an episode or incident of life, whether it be taken from history or legend, or from the common life of every day, or be the writer's original invention. A plot that is a pure invention is only an incident in an imaginary continuation of the life of history and every day; how little it is the product of an arbitrary fantasy appears from the research of that ingenious Frenchman who tabulated the plots of every work of literature of a certain level of merit, and discovered that there are only thirty-six (or was it thirty-three?) different plots. This incident, then, of historical, actual, or imaginary life, will be as it were saturated with the quality of life which the writer discerns; its various parts and characters will be of such a nature that the writer's accumulation of emotional experience will be able to form itself about them, like crystals about a string dipped into a saturated solution.

NOTES

1. I originally wrote, and really meant, 'rather less than more deliberately'. But the assumptions underlying that use of 'deliberately' are so great and demand so much immediate explanation, that on re-reading I was compelled to put it the other way, and the wrong way, round.

2. How little in his critical practice Arnold followed his own critical theory may be easily seen from these two contrasted passages from his essay on Wordsworth (*Essays in Criticism*, vol.ii).

p. 140. Long ago, in speaking of Homer, I said that the noble and profound application of ideas to life is the most essential part of poetic greatness. I said that a great poet receives his distinctive character of superiority from his application, under the conditions immutably fixed by the laws of poetic beauty and poetic truth, from his application, I say, to his subject, whatever it may be, of the ideas

On man, on nature and on human life

which he has acquired for himself. The line quoted is Wordsworth's own; and his superiority arises from his powerful use, in his best pieces, his powerful application to his subjects of ideas 'on man, on nature and on human life'.

p. 153. Wordsworth's poetry is great because of the extra-ordinary power with which Wordsworth feels the joy offered to us in nature, the joy offered to us in the simple primary affections and duties; and because of the extra-ordinary power with which, in case after case, he shows us this joy, and renders it so as to make us share it.

How far, on the other hand, his theory could warp his judgement may be seen from his dictum on Shakespeare (*Essays in Criticism*, vol. ii, p. 62): 'Shakespeare is divinely strong, rich and attractive. But the sureness of perfect style Shakespeare himself does not possess.'

3. It is this truth which Mr Hardy has emphasized by his choice of a title for the volume which contains his finest lyrical poetry, *Moments of Vision*. I am happy to have his endorsement of the theory in a letter which he wrote to me when I first developed it in an article on his 'Collected Poems' (*Aspects of Literature*, p. 121).

10 *Tragedy and Contemporary Ideas*

● Raymond Williams

In the suffering and confusion of our own century, there has been great pressure to take a body of work from the past and to use it as a way of rejecting the present. That there has been tragedy (or chivalry, or community) but that lacking this belief, that rule, we are now incapable of it, is a common response of this kind. And of course it is necessary, if this position is to be maintained, to reject ordinary contemporary meanings of tragedy, and to insist that they are a misunderstanding.

Yet tragic experience, because of its central importance, commonly attracts the fundamental beliefs and tensions of a period, and tragic theory is interesting mainly in this sense, that through it the shape and set of a particular culture is often deeply realised. If, however, we think of it as a theory about a single and permanent kind of fact, we can end only with the metaphysical conclusions that are built into any such assumption. Chief among these is the assumption of a permanent, universal and essentially unchanging human nature (an assumption taken over from one kind of Christianity to 'ritual' anthropology and the general theory of psychoanalysis). Given such an assumption, we have to explain tragedy in terms of this unchanging human nature or certain of its faculties. But if we reject this assumption (following a different kind of Christianity, a different psychological theory, or the evidence of comparative anthropology), the problem is necessarily transformed. Tragedy is then not a single and permanent kind of fact, but a series of experiences and conventions and institutions. It is not a case of interpreting this series by reference to a permanent and unchanging human nature. Rather, the varieties of tragic experience are to be interpreted by reference to the changing conventions and institutions. The universalist character of most tragic theory is then at the opposite pole from our necessary interest.

The most striking fact about modern tragic theory is that it is rooted in very much the same structure of ideas as modern tragedy itself, yet one of its paradoxical effects is its denial that modern tragedy is possible, after almost a century of important and continuous and insistent tragic art. It is very difficult to explain why this should be so. Part of the explanation seems to be the incapacity to make connections which is characteristic of this whole structure. But it is also significant that the major original contributions to the theory were made in the nineteenth century, before the creative period of modern tragedy, and have since been systematised by men deeply conditioned, by their academic training, to a valuation of the past against the present, and to a separation between critical theory and creative practice.

It is in any case necessary to break the theory if we are to value the art: in the simple sense, to see it as a major period of tragic writing, directly comparable in importance with the great periods of the past; and, more crucially, to see its controlling structure of feeling, the variations within this and their connections with actual dramatic structures, and to be able to respond to them critically, in the full sense. [...] Following the historical analysis already outlined it is worth trying to engage, critically, the major points of the theory. These are, as I see them: order and accident;* the destruction of the hero; the irreparable action and its connections with death; and the emphasis of evil. [...]

THE DESTRUCTION OF THE HERO

The most common interpretation of tragedy is that it is an action in which the hero is destroyed. This fact is seen as irreparable. At a simple level this is so obviously true that the formula usually gets little further examination. But it is of course still an interpretation, and a partial one. If attention is concentrated on the hero alone, such an interpretation naturally follows. We have been very aware of the kind of reading which we can describe as *Hamlet* without the Prince, but we have been almost totally unaware of the opposite and equally erroneous reading of the Prince of Denmark without the State of Denmark. It is this unity that we must now restore.

Not many works that we call tragedies in fact end with the destruction of the hero. Outside the undeveloped mediaeval form, most of the examples that we could offer come, significantly, from modern tragedy. Certainly in almost all tragedies the hero is destroyed, but that is not normally the end of the action. Some new distribution of forces, physical or spiritual, normally succeeds the death. In Greek tragedy this is ordinarily a religious affirmation, but in the words or presence of the chorus, which is then the ground of its social continuity. In Elizabethan tragedy it is ordinarily a change of power in the state, with the arrival of a new, uncommitted or restored Prince. There are many factual variations of this reintegrative action, but their general function is common. Of course these endings are now normally read as merely valedictory or as a kind of tidying-up. To our consciousness, the

---

* Not discussed in this extract.

important action has ended, and the affirmation, settlement, restoration or new arrival are comparatively minor. We read the last chapters of Victorian novels, which bring the characters together and settle their future directions, with a comparable indifference or even impatience. This kind of reparation is not particularly interesting to us, because not really credible. Indeed it looks much too like a solution, which twentieth-century critics agree is a vulgar and intrusive element in any art. (It is not the business of the artist, or even the thinker, to provide answers and solutions, but simply to describe experiences and to raise questions.) Yet of course it is no more and no less a solution than its commonplace twentieth-century alternative. To conclude that there is no solution is also an answer.

When we now say that the tragic experience is of the irreparable, because the action is followed right through until the hero is dead, we are taking a part for the whole, a hero for an action. We think of tragedy as what happens to the hero, but the ordinary tragic action is what happens through the hero. When we confine our attention to the hero, we are unconsciously confining ourselves to one kind of experience which in our own culture we tend to take as the whole. We are unconsciously confining ourselves to the individual. Yet over a very wide range we see this transcended in tragedy. Life does come back, life ends the play, again and again. And the fact that life does come back, that its meanings are reaffirmed and restored, after so much suffering and after so important a death, has been, quite commonly, the tragic action.

What is involved, of course, is not a simple forgetting, or a picking-up for the new day. The life that is continued is informed by the death; has indeed, in a sense, been created by it. But in a culture theoretically limited to individual experience, there is no more to say, when a man has died, but that others also will die. Tragedy can then be generalised not as the response to death but as the bare irreparable fact.

'THE IRREPARABLE ACTION'

Human death is often the form of the deepest meanings of a culture. When we see death, it is natural that we should draw together — in grief, in memory, in the social duties of burial — our sense of the values of living, as individuals and as a society. But then, in some cultures or in their breakdown, life is regularly read back from the fact of death, which can seem not only the focus but also the source of our values. Death, then, is absolute, and all our living simply relative. Death is necessary, and all other human ends are contingent. Within this emphasis, suffering and disorder of any kind are interpreted by reference to what is seen as the controlling reality. Such an interpretation is now commonly described as a tragic sense of life.

What is not usually noticed, in this familiar and now formal procession, is precisely the element of convention. To read back life from the fact of death is a cultural and sometimes a personal choice. But that it is a choice, and a· variable choice, is very easily forgotten. The powerful association of a particular rhetoric and a persistent human fact can give the appearance of permanence to a local and temporary and even sectional response. To tie any meaning to death is to give it a powerful emotional charge which can at times obliterate all other experience in its range. Death is universal, and the meaning tied to it quickly claims universality, as it were in its shadow. Other readings of life, other interpretations of suffering and disorder, can be assimilated to it with great apparent conviction. The burden of proof shifts continually from the controversial meaning to the inescapable experience, and we are easily exposed, by fear and loss, to the most conventional and arbitrary conclusions.

The connection between tragedy and death is of course quite evident, but in reality the connection is variable, as the response to death is variable. What has happened in our own century is that a particular post-liberal and post-Christian interpretation of death has been imposed as an absolute meaning, and as identical with all tragedy. What is generalised is the loneliness of man, facing a blind fate, and this is the fundamental isolation of the tragic hero. The currency of this experience is of course sufficiently wide to make it relevant to much modern tragedy. But the structure of the meaning still needs analysis. To say that man dies alone is not to state a fact but to offer an interpretation. For indeed men die in so many ways: in the arms and presence of family and neighbours; in the blindness of pain, or the blankness of sedation; in the violent disintegration of machines and in the calm of sleep. To insist on a single meaning is already rhetorical, but to insist on the meaning of loneliness is to interpret life as much as death. However men die, the experience is not only the physical dissolution and ending; it is also a change in the lives and relationships of others, for we know death as much in the experience of others as in our own expectations and endings. And just as death enters, continually, our common life, so any statement about death is in a common language and depends on common experience. The paradox of 'we die alone' or 'man dies alone' is then important and remarkable: the maximum substance that can be given to the plural 'we', or to the group-name 'man', is the singular loneliness. The common fact, in a common language, is offered as a proof of the loss of connection.

But then, as we become aware of this structure of feeling, we can look through it at the experience which it has offered to interpret. It is using the names of death and tragedy, but it has very little really to do with the tragedies of the past, or with death as a universal experience. Rather, it has correctly identified, and then blurred, the crisis around which one main kind of contemporary tragic experience moves. It blurs it because it offers as absolutes the very experiences which are now most unresolved and most moving. Our most common received interpretations of life put the highest value and significance on the individual and his development, but it is indeed inescapable that the individual dies. What is most valuable and what is most irreparable are then set in an inevitable relation and tension. But to generalise this particular contradiction as an absolute fact of human existence is to fix and finally suppress the relation and tension, so that tragedy becomes not an action but a deadlock. And then to claim this deadlock as the whole meaning of tragedy is to project into history a local structure that is both culturally and historically determined.

It is characteristic of such structures that they cannot even recognise as possible any experience beyond their own structural limits; that such varying and possible statements as 'I die but I shall live', 'I die but we shall live', or 'I die but we do not die' become meaningless, and can even be contemptuously dismissed as evasions. The whole fact of community is reduced to the singular recognition, and it is angrily denied that there can be any other. Yet what seems to me most significant about the current isolation of death, is not what it has to say about tragedy or about dying, but what it is saying, through this, about loneliness and the loss of human connection, and about the consequent blindness of human destiny. It is, that is to say, a theoretical formulation of liberal tragedy, rather than any kind of universal principle.

The tragic action is about death, but it need not end in death, unless this is enforced by a particular structure of feeling. Death, once again, is a necessary actor but not the necessary action. We encounter this alteration of pattern again and again in contemporary tragic argument. The most spectacular example, perhaps, is the resurgence of the concept of evil.

THE EMPHASIS OF EVIL

Evil, of course, is a traditional name, but, like other names, it has been appropriated by a particular ideology which then offers itself as the whole tragic tradition. In recent years especially, we have been continually rebuked by what is called the fact of transcendent evil, and the immense social crisis of our century is specifically interpreted in this light or darkness. The true nature of man, it is argued, is now dramatically revealed, against all the former illusions of civilisation and progress. The concentration camp, especially, is used as an image of an absolute condition, in which man is reduced, by men, to a thing. The record of the camps is indeed black enough, and many other examples could be added. But to use the camp as an image of an absolute condition is, in its turn, a blasphemy. For while men created the camps, other men died, at conscious risk, to destroy them. While some men imprisoned, other men liberated. There is no evil which men have created, of this or any other kind, which other men have not struggled to end. To take one part of this action, and call it absolute or transcendent, is in its turn a suppression of other facts of human life on so vast a scale that its indifference can only be explained by its role in an ideology.

The appropriation of evil to the theory of tragedy is then especially significant. What tragedy shows us, it is argued, is the fact of evil as inescapable and irreparable. Mere optimists and humanists deny the fact of transcendent evil, and so are incapable of tragic experience. Tragedy is then a salutary reminder, indeed a theory, against the illusions of humanism.

But this can only be maintained if the tragic action can be reduced and simplified, in ways very similar to the simplifications of tragic order and the tragic individual and the irreparable death. Evil, as it is now widely used, is a deeply complacent idea. For it ends, and is meant to end, any actual experience. It ends, among other things, the normal action of tragedy. It is not that any of us can deny, or wish to deny, the description, as evil, of particular actions. But when we abstract and generalise it, we remove ourselves from any continuing action, and deliberately break both response and connection.

The current emphasis of Evil is not, we must remind ourselves, the Christian emphasis. Within that structure, evil was certainly generalised, but so also was good, and the struggle of good and evil in our souls and in the world could be seen as a real action. Evil was the common disorder which was yet overcome in Christ. As such, for all the magnitude of its name, it has commonly operated within the terms of the tragic action.

Culturally, evil is a name for many kinds of disorder which corrode or destroy actual life. As such, it is common in tragedy, though in many particular and variable forms: vengeance or ambition or pride or coldness or lust or jealousy or disobedience or rebellion. In every case it is only fully comprehensible within the valuations of a particular culture or tradition. It may indeed be possible, in any particular ideology, to generalise it until it appears as an absolute and even singular force. As a common name, also, it appears to take on a general character. But we cannot then say that tragedy is the recognition of transcendent evil. Tragedy commonly dramatises evil, in many particular forms. We move away from actual tragedies, and not towards them, when we abstract and generalise the very specific forces that are so variously dramatised. We move away, even more decisively, from a common tragic action, when we interpret tragedy as only the dramatisation and recognition of evil. A particular evil, in a tragic action, can be at once experienced and lived through. In the process of living through it, and in a real action seeing its moving relations with other capacities and other men, we come not so much to the recognition of evil as transcendent but to its recognition as actual and indeed negotiable.

This is of course far from its simple abolition, which is the opposite and yet complementary error to its recognition as transcendent, just as the proposition that man is naturally good is the complementary error to the proposition that man is naturally evil. Within a religious culture, man is seen as naturally limited, but within a liberal culture man is seen as naturally absolute, and good and evil are then alternative absolute names. They are not, however, the only alternatives. It is equally possible to say that man is not 'naturally' anything: that we both create and transcend our limits, and that we are good or evil in particular ways and in particular situations, defined by pressures we at once receive and can alter and can create again. This continuing and varying activity is the real source of the names, which can only in fantasy be abstracted to explain the activity itself.

Tragedy, as such, teaches nothing about evil, because it teaches many things about many kinds of action. Yet it can at least be said, against the modern emphasis on transcendent evil, that most of the great tragedies of the world end not with evil absolute, but with evil both experienced and lived through. A particular tragic hero may put out his eyes when he sees the evil that he has committed, but we see him do this, in a continuing action. Yet that blindness, which was part of the action, is now abstracted and generalised, as an absolute blindness: a rejection of particulars, a refusal to look into sources and causes and versions of consequence. The affirmation of absolute Evil, which is now so current, is, under pressure, a self-blinding; the self-blinding of a culture which, lacking the nerve to inquire into its own nature, would have not only actors but also spectators put out their eyes. What is offered as tragic significance is here, as elsewhere, a significant denial of the possibility of *any* meaning.

If I am right in seeing this fundamental pattern in the orthodox modern idea of tragedy, both negative and positive conclusions follow. Negatively, we must say that what is now offered as a total meaning of tragedy is in fact a particular meaning, to be understood and valued historically. Some would go further and dispense with tragedy as an idea at all. There is a certain attraction in accepting the consequences of historical criticism, and cutting out all general considerations because they have been shown to be variable. A sophisticated and mainly technical criticism will then supervene: the meanings do not matter, but we can look at how they are expressed, in particular arrangements of words. It is in fact doubtful if in any case this can be done. If the words matter, the meanings will matter, and to ignore them formally is usually to accept some of them informally.

I believe that the meanings matter as such; in tragedy especially, because the experience is so central and we can hardly avoid thinking about it. If we find a particular idea of tragedy, in our own time, we find also a way of interpreting a very wide area of our experience; relevant certainly to literary criticism but relevant also to very much else. And then the negative analysis is only part of our need. We must try also, positively, to understand and describe not only the tragic theory but also the tragic experience of our own time.

11 *Religion and Literature*

● T. S. Eliot

What I have to say is largely in support of the following propositions: literary criticism should be completed by criticism from a definite ethical and theological standpoint. In so far as in any age there is common agreement on ethical and theological matters, so far can literary criticism be substantive. In ages like our own, in which there is no such common agreement, it is the more necessary for Christian readers to scrutinize their reading, especially of works of imagination, with explicit ethical and theological standards. The 'greatness' of literature cannot be determined solely by literary standards; though we must remember that whether it is literature or not can be determined only by literary standards.[1] [...]

The fact that what we read does not concern merely something called our *literary taste*, but that it affects directly, though only amongst many other influences, the whole of what we are, is best elicited, I think, by a conscientious examination of the history of our individual literary education. Consider the adolescent reading of any person with some literary sensibility. Everyone, I believe, who is at all sensible to the seductions of poetry, can remember some moment in youth when he or she was completely carried away by the work of one poet. Very likely he was carried away by several poets, one after the other. The reason for this passing infatuation is not merely that our sensibility to poetry is keener in adolescence than in maturity. What happens is a kind of inundation, of invasion of the undeveloped personality by the stronger personality of the poet. The same thing may happen at a later age to persons who have not done much reading. One author takes complete possession of us for a time; then another; and finally they begin to affect each other in our mind. We weigh one against another; we see that each has qualities absent from others, and qualities incompatible with the qualities of others: we begin to be, in fact, critical; and it is our growing critical power which protects us from excessive possession by any one literary personality. The good critic — and we should all try to be critics, and not leave criticism to the fellows who write reviews in the papers — is the man who, to a keen and abiding sensibility, joins wide and increasingly discriminating reading. Wide reading is not valuable as a kind of hoarding, an accumulation of knowledge, or what sometimes is meant by the term 'a well-stocked mind'. It is valuable because in the process of being affected by one powerful personality after another, we cease to be dominated by any one, or by any small number. The very different views of life, cohabiting in our minds, affect each other, and own own personality asserts itself and gives each a place in some arrangement peculiar to ourself.

It is simply not true that works of fiction, prose or verse, that is to say works depicting the actions, thoughts and words and passions of imaginary human beings, *directly* extend our knowledge of life. Direct knowledge of life is knowledge directly in relation to ourselves, it is our knowledge of *how* people behave in general, of *what* they are like in general, in so far as that part of life in which we ourselves have participated gives us material for generalization. Knowledge of life obtained through fiction is only possible by another stage of self-consciousness. That is to say, it can only be a knowledge of other people's knowledge of life, not of life itself. So far as we are taken up with the happenings in any novel in the same way in which we are taken up with what happens under our eyes, we are acquiring at least as much falsehood as truth. But when we are developed enough to say: 'This is the view of life of a person who was a good observer within his limits, Dickens, or Thackeray, or George Eliot, or Balzac; but he looked at it in a different way from me, because he was a different man; he even selected rather different things to look at, or the same things in a different order of importance, because he was a different man; so what I am looking at is the world as seen by a particular mind' — then we are in a position to gain something from reading fiction. We are learning *something* about life from these authors direct, just as we learn something from the reading of history direct; but these authors are only really helping us when we can see, and allow for, their differences from ourselves.

Now what we get, as we gradually grow up and read more and more, and read a greater diversity of authors, is a variety of views of life. But what people commonly assume, I suspect, is that we gain this experience of other men's views of life only by 'improving reading'. This, it is supposed, is a reward we get by applying ourselves to Shakespeare, and Dante, and Goethe, and Emerson, and Carlyle, and dozens of other respectable writers. The rest of our reading for amusement is merely killing time. But I incline to come to the alarming conclusion that it is just the literature that we read for 'amusement', or 'purely for pleasure' that may have the greatest and least suspected influence upon us. It is the literature which we read with the least effort that can have the easiest and most insidious influence upon us. Hence it is that the influence of popular novelists, and of popular plays of contemporary life, requires to be scrutinized most closely. And it is chiefly *contemporary* literature that the majority of people ever read in this attitude of 'purely for pleasure', of pure passivity.

The relation to my subject of what I have been saying should now be a little more apparent. Though we may read literature merely for pleasure, of 'entertainment' or of 'aesthetic enjoyment', this reading never affects simply a sort of special sense: it affects us as entire human beings; it affects our moral and religious existence. And I say that while individual modern writers of eminence can be improving, contemporary literature as a whole tends to be degrading. And that even the effect of the better writers, in an age like ours, may be degrading to some readers; for we must remember that what a writer does to people is not necessarily what he intends to do. It may be only what people are capable of having done to them. People exercise an unconscious selection in being influenced. A writer like D. H. Lawrence may be in his effect either beneficial or pernicious. I am not sure that I have not had some pernicious influence myself.

At this point I anticipate a rejoinder from the liberal-minded, from all those who are convinced that if everybody says what he thinks, and does what he likes, things will somehow, by some automatic compensation and adjustment, come right in the end. 'Let everything be tried', they say, 'and if it is a mistake, then we shall learn by experience.' This argument might have some value, if we were always the same generation upon earth; or if, as we know to be not the case, people ever learned much from the experience of their elders. These liberals are convinced that only by what is called unrestrained individualism will truth ever emerge. Ideas, views of life, they think, issue distinct from independent heads, and in consequence of their knocking violently against each other, the fittest survive, and truth rises triumphant. Anyone who dissents from this view must be either a mediaevalist, wishful only to set back the clock, or else a fascist, and probably both.

If the mass of contemporary authors were really individualists, every one of them inspired Blakes, each with his separate vision, and if the mass of the contemporary public were really a mass of *individuals* there might be something to be said for this attitude. But this is not, and never has been, and never will be. It is not only that the reading individual today (or at any day) is not enough an individual to be able to absorb all the 'views of life' of all the authors pressed upon us by the publishers' advertisements and the reviewers, and to be able to arrive at wisdom by considering one against another. It is that the contemporary authors are not individuals enough either. It is not that the world of separate individuals of the liberal democrat is undesirable; it is simply that this world does not exist. For the reader of contemporary literature is not, like the reader of the established great literature of all time, exposing himself to the influence of divers and contradictory personalities; he is exposing himself to a mass movement of writers who, each of them, think that they have something individually to offer, but are really all working together in the same direction. And there never was a time, I believe, when the reading public was so large, or so helplessly exposed to the influences of its own time. There never was a time, I believe, when those who read at all, read so many more books by living authors than books by dead authors; there never was a time so completely parochial, so shut off from the past. There may be too many publishers; there are certainly too many books published; and the journals ever incite the reader to 'keep up' with what is being published. Individualistic democracy has come to high tide: and it is more difficult today to be an individual than it ever was before.

Within itself, modern literature has perfectly valid distinctions of good and bad, better and worse: and I do not wish to suggest that I confound Mr Bernard Shaw with Mr Noel Coward, Mrs Woolf with Miss Mannin. On the other hand, I should like it to be clear that I am not defending a 'high'-brow against a 'low'-brow literature. What I do wish to affirm is that the whole of modern literature is corrupted by what I call Secularism, that it is simply unaware of, simply cannot understand the meaning of, the primacy of the supernatural over the natural life: of something which I assume to be our primary concern.

I do not want to give the impression that I have delivered a mere fretful jeremiad against contemporary literature. Assuming a common attitude between my readers, or some of my readers, and myself, the question is not so much, what is to be done about it? as, how should we behave towards it?

I have suggested that the liberal attitude towards literature will not work. Even if the writers who make an attempt to impose their 'view of life' upon us were really distinct individuals, even if we as readers were distinct individuals, what would be the result? It would be, surely, that each reader would be impressed, in his reading, merely by what he was previously prepared to be impressed by; he would follow the 'line of least resistance', and there would be no assurance that he would be made a better man. For literary judgement we need to be acutely aware of two things at once: of 'what we like', and of 'what we *ought* to like'. Few people are honest enough to know either. The first means knowing what we really feel: very few know that. The second involves understanding our shortcomings; for we do not really know what we ought to like unless we also know why we ought to like it, which involves knowing why we do not yet like it. It is not enough to understand what we ought to be, unless we know what we are; and we do not understand what we are, unless we know what we ought to be. The two forms of self-consciousness, knowing what we are and what we ought to be, must go together.

It is our business, as readers of literature, to know what we like. It is our business, as Christians, *as well* as readers of literature, to know what we ought to like. It is our business as honest men not to assume that whatever we like is what we ought to like; and it is our business as honest Christians not to assume that we do like what we ought to like. And the last thing I would wish for would be the existence of two literatures, one for Christian consumption and the other for the pagan world. What I believe to be incumbent upon all Christians is the duty of maintaining consciously certain standards and criteria of criticism over and above those applied by the rest of the world; and that by these criteria and standards everything that we read must be tested. We must remember that the greater part of our current reading matter is written for us by people who have no real belief in a supernatural order, though some of it may be written by people with individual notions of a supernatural order which are not ours. And the greater part of our reading matter is coming to be written by people who not only have no such belief, but are even ignorant of the fact that there are still people in the world so 'backward' or so 'eccentric' as to continue to believe. So long as we are conscious of the gulf fixed between ourselves and the greater part of contemporary literature, we are more or less protected from being harmed by it, and are in a position to extract from it what good it has to offer us.

There are a very large number of people in the world today who believe that all ills are fundamentally economic. Some believe that various specific economic changes alone would be enough to set the world right; others demand more or less drastic changes in the social as well, changes chiefly of two opposed types. These changes demanded, and in some places carried out, are alike in one respect, that they hold the assumptions of what I call Secularism: they concern themselves only with changes of a temporal, material, and external nature; they concern themselves with morals only of a collective nature. In an exposition of one such new faith I read the following words:

'In our morality the one single test of any moral question is whether it impedes or destroys in any way the power of the individual to serve the State. [The individual] must answer the questions: "Does this action injure the nation? Does it injure other members of the nation? Does it injure my ability to serve the nation?" And if the answer is clear on all those questions, the individual has absolute liberty to do as he will.'

Now I do not deny that this is a kind of morality, and that it is capable of great good within limits; but I think that we should all repudiate a morality which had no higher ideal to set before us than that. It represents, of course, one of the violent reactions we are witnessing, against the view that the community is solely for the benefit of the individual; but it is equally a gospel of this world, and of this world alone. My complaint against modern literature is of the same kind. It is not that modern literature is in the ordinary sense 'immoral' or even 'amoral'; and in any case to prefer that charge would not be enough. It is simply that it repudiates, or is wholly ignorant of, our most fundamental and important beliefs; and that in consequence its tendency is to encourage its readers to get what they can out of life while it lasts, to miss no 'experience' that presents itself, and to sacrifice themselves, if they make any sacrifice at all, only for the sake of tangible benefits to others in this world either now or in the future. We shall certainly continue to read the best of its kind, of what our time provides; but we must tirelessly criticize it according to our own principles, and not merely according to the principles admitted by the writers and by the critics who discuss it in the public press.

NOTES

1. As an example of literary criticism given greater significance by theological interests, I would call attention to Theodor Haecker: *Virgil* (Sheed and Ward).

12 *False Populisms, False Elitisms*

● Richard Hoggart

The outstanding, the inescapable, starting point for any discussion on the arts and social class in Britain today must be this fact: that there is a very high correlation between on the one hand social class of birth and the education likely to go with it, and on the other hand the practice and appreciation of the arts.

Why should this be so? One can imagine three possible reasons.

First, some people would argue that a steady process of social filtration, up and down, during the last few decades has brought it about that, by and large, the people in socio-economic groups A, B and upper C are more intelligent and sensitive than the rest; and their children are presumably, and again more or less, like them.

For the tidy-minded that can be a comfortable assumption. But it ignores, among much else, the fact that these differences in taste and practice long predate the last few decades; and that many in social groups A, B and upper C (and not only the stupid up there) show not the slightest interest in the arts. We are more sensitive to such disturbing correlations nowadays, since we have had over a century of universal public education which has paid a fair amount of attention to the arts. More generally, we tend to feel that, whatever the up-and-down movements, an educated democracy should promote roughly equal access to and practice of the arts. That has not happened and is not happening.

There may be a grain of truth in the 'filtration' assumption. Presumably stupid people born into groups lower C down to E tend to stay there. On the other hand, stupid people born into the more comfortably off groups tend to be held by the groups' safety nets, so that they do not usually sink. And really bright people born into the poorer classes are quite likely to move out of them. But all in all — no, overwhelmingly — our systems of selection are not so refined as to explain on the grounds of the flow of talent the close class/profession/education relationship to the practice and appreciation of the arts. No society is, can be, so fluidly open. The idea is misguided, silly. Nevertheless, many more people than we like to think seem to have the 'filtration' notion at the backs of their heads, available to justify great disparities not only in access to the arts but in entry to higher education, the major professions and much else.

The second way in which some people skirt around what I have called the inescapable starting point for a discussion on the arts and class is cleverer than the first; well, cuter if not cleverer. It argues that what are called 'the high arts' are merely certain activities which certain social groups have chosen to call 'high arts'. They have no special status and are not inherently more valuable than any other kind of artistic expression, whether labelled middlebrow, lowbrow, popular art, folk art or even mass art. The 'high arts' are a bourgeois confidence trick, a way of freezing other people out and making those who claim a good acquaintance with such arts feel superior.

We all know there is a degree of truth in the last charge, even if we have never seen the boredom settle on some of the occupants of the corporate seats at Covent Garden, for whom any work later than Boris Godunov seems outlandish. For some comfortable 'consumers' of the arts (the ugly word fits here), an acquaintance with the chosen arts may not be close or detailed, attendance at artistic occasions being more of a social gesture than an imaginative challenge.

The third explanation for the arts/class correlation is more persuasive. It rejects the simplicity of 'the clever ones have been winnowed out; the stupid are left at the bottom of the heap'. It rejects the smarter foolishness of 'art is no more than a cultural and ideological construct'. You cannot adequately dismiss centuries of drama, music, poetry by discovering that some people see the arts as posh cosmetics. To some degree, they always have had that rôle, at any rate since the emergence of a prosperous bourgeoisie. But there may well be relatively less of that attitude today than there used to be.

The main reason for the startling class/arts correlation, explanation number three begins, is to be found in the social structure itself, and above all in the thrust of sub-cultures to recreate themselves. It is also to do with the fact that, whatever our democratic hopes and no matter how great the devotion of some teachers, educational opportunities are still very unevenly spread among the different social groups. Unless you are very lucky you are likely to have a poorer education, a poorer introduction to the intellectual and imaginative life, in a big, urban, local authority school than you would get in a middle-of-the-range independent school. And the chief reason for this may be the hold of your sub-culture. In saying that, I do not discount the beefy sub-cultures of some independent schools. I leave others to write about the unintellectual and unartistic strata in better-off groups. This third explanation does not grossly oversimplify like explanation number one, nor crudely schematize like explanation number two. It is based on a reasonably complex sense of the way societies and their sub-cultures work to perpetuate themselves, and on a realistic sense of the gap between assertion and achievement in this still greatly divided — perhaps latterly increasingly divided — educational system.

I have written elsewhere about the compensations of a working-class childhood. It is also the case that to be brought up in a solidly working-class area is still to be offered a complete system of yeas and nays: yea to the popular press, mass sports, bingo, quiz shows, ITV, to a bookless world, to this attitude to sex, that to the unions, to a total, wraparound frame for living; nay to an interest in the intellectual life, to abstract ideas, to anything to do with the arts. That is for cissies, poofs, snobs. Our kinds of people do not play around with things like that: they are not manly enough.

Only the strongest, best endowed, most awkward are likely, especially up to early adulthood, to break out of this mould. They may be lucky enough to have an older woman to help them, a mother, aunt, grandmother, or a schoolmaster patron. It is always very much easier, in any social group, to stay with the gang. And the gang's packaged sets of assumptions, of dos and don'ts, are as complete in the life of a working-class teenager as in that of a Guards officer. Some handed-on cultural assumptions are valuable aids to growth in any social groups; others enclose and stultify. The child born into a comfortably off family and to a fair education will have some useless cultural baggage — snobberies, jobberies, futile protocols — which, to the extent that he or she becomes critically alive, can be discarded later.

Thus the cosmetic shell of attitudes towards the arts *can* be discarded; but the kernel is good, and access to that has been made easier for such people. It is harder to break out of the restricting moulds if you are from a less well-educated, less articulate part of society. And as to the arts, if you are born into the poorer social groups everything conspires to tell you they are of no value.

Yet so far I have myself done no more than assert or, more often, simply imply that the arts are a good thing and that there are indeed achievements which can fairly be called the 'high arts'. Certainly, those who dismiss them as an entirely snobbish, 'elitist', culture-vulture form of fencing-off of territory can produce plenty of physical evidence. The point is harder to make if you start by looking carefully at the works themselves.

Passing through Atlanta recently I called in at their large and grand new art museum, a monument to the idea of art as conspicuous consumption by the twentieth-century self-made bourgeoisie if ever there was one. The architect, no modest wallflower, offers the building as a work of art in itself — perhaps just as well, since the collection is not very large, not a patch on those of Melbourne and one or two other Australian cities which I had just visited.

But they were determined to have it, this great, white, startling building, and this not-so-bad collection of precious pieces, chiefly from Europe. So what do they call it? Impossible to refer to High Art, though that is conspicuously what the collection is. So they call it the Atlanta High Museum of Art. What a cop-out, and how characteristic of the double-talking times.

Yet to be concerned at all about this argument you have to believe that some works of art are better than others, that some music is better than other music, some novels better than others and some paintings better than others. Even if such a view can never be incontrovertibly proved, there is no refuge in the 'good of its kind' fog which invites you to settle for saying that a best-selling crime novel is *in its own way* as good as *Middlemarch*, and the Beatles in their own way as good as Beethoven. One has to recognise, against all today's force of levelling, that some products of the human imagination deserve to be called 'high art', or be given some other description which indicates that they have qualities which lift them way above the rest.

Many kinds of artistic expression may have some value. We do not have to mark them down so as to hoist good art up. But we can mark them off, whilst noting their aspirations. If you try to write yourself, seriously and honestly, you will soon know your limits (and may discover some gifts). If, as you come away from each effort, you pick up almost any 'classic', from Shakespeare to Lawrence, you are likely to recognise that there are huge variations in gifts and insight; and that you are not at first base.

You read with more pleasure after that, and with a better sense of your own limits; and that could be the start of progress. No doubt much the same can happen if you seek to paint or compose. We are hagridden by that half-truth: 'the artist is not a special kind of man. Every man . . . etc'. There is a due modesty to be gained here. Time does have a way of separating merely culturally constrained and time-defined art from that which breaks out, whatever the cultural or time-conditionings.

Such facts seem unevadable; and one wishes they were. But some people are able to ignore self-evident truths, so that in the end one wonders whether they have ever disinterestedly read a good novel or play or poem.

With writers at least, two key qualities are needed: a gift with language and a depth of insight. First, without a gift for handling one's medium, whatever the medium, none of us will get far, no matter what our hopes or however exciting the themes we propose or the lives we have led and wish to recreate. We might just as well have lived in a nunnery. All these considerations have nothing to do with a feeling that we would like to become a writer, or with the decency of our emotions. The shock on going back to Shakespeare after years is the realisation yet again of his panoramic, apparently inexhaustible verbal gifts. The gift falls, wantonly and gratuitously, on the just and the unjust.

Second, and in literature most obviously and directly of all the arts, is penetration, insight. Try to sum up a character, a relationship, a landscape, and then go back to those others in the wings. Unless your conceit is impregnable you will, as ever, recognise when you are bested, outclassed. That need not stop us from going on trying; or we can turn to some other activity just as worthwhile. Again, those who have these qualities in high degree (developed by hard application in most instances) are not necessarily nice or 'worthwhile' as people, as some of the best modern writers — Thomas Mann, for instance — have pointed out. They just happen to be gifted; and we may not be.

This part of the argument always reminds me of the Case of the Ungifted Taxi Driver. If you serve on the Arts Council you are sometimes presented with requests for funds from Worker Writers groups. The Council usually seeks to help. It is aware of the social and educational constraints I have described above. But the taxi driver instance threw into relief a muddle at the heart of some Worker Writer groups.

A taxi driver of many years' experience had come along to a group and been encouraged to write his memoirs. They were proudly offered: 'Look . . . a taxi driver writing his memoirs'; as though some important artistic and social case had been proved. But at that level of generality this attitude can reveal itself as a form of external patronising. Like Dr Johnson on the woman preacher — but then he knew he was being insulting.

Even if all allowances are made for social and other limitations, it does not matter in principle whether a writer is a taxi driver or a belted earl or a spinster recluse. The words and insights on the page are all that matter. Is there any sign of some verbal gift, no matter how underdeveloped; or of some insight and observation, no matter how partially expressed? A West Indian cleaner at Goldsmiths', virtually illiterate, asked her daughter to start taking down her memoirs. They were vigorous and observant. Things had happened to her, in a large family in Jamaica; not melodramatic things; rather, she had seen the comedy and the sadness under the habitual routines and the evasions of the common tongue; and she had an eye for the telling detail and incident, and for the metaphor that was more than a dead cliché.

Judging by the memoirs he wrote, the taxi driver was a man to whom nothing had happened. Maybe it had; maybe it was all there underneath, desperate to get out. There was no evidence that the way out would ever be through writing; the keys were dead. He had no evident sense of language, of image or incident. Of course, he has a right to try, and one never knows. But on this evidence there was no hidden literary talent, and nothing of value to him or to others would come from the mistaken pursuit. Perhaps there were other hidden talents whose development would lie elsewhere. I am not at all criticising him. I believe that the Worker Writer people who were encouraging him were muddled in both their attitudes to individual potentialities and to the nature of artistic expression.

We are all and always at liberty to reject what I have said in the last few paragraphs and in particular to reject the concept of different levels of gifts. None of it, as I have also said, is provable. Even if we accept these arguments we should not also assume that to experience great art is to be made better as persons, as a natural by-product. The weight of free will is not so easily shucked off; we must have the freedom to be bastards and to know it. But good art stands available, its penetrations, illuminations, explorations, harmonies stand ready to persuade us that the world is wider and more varied than we always want to think, to enhance our sense of moral dimensions, weights, perspectives.

But if these main propositions are accepted, and if they are set against the social distortion in access to the arts with which I started, it follows that we should try to do a great deal, should do very much more than we now do, to reduce those educational limitations and cultural restraints.

One particularly obvious and strident example of the cultural pressures on people thus deprived is the popular press, which is habitually anti-intellectual and anti-art. Do those newspapers represent the views of those who buy them? Much earlier I suggested that to some extent they do. But there is evidence the other way. That suggests that the majority of people are likely to be *un-* rather than *anti-* in their attitudes to intellectual and artistic things. They have been conditioned to assume that such things are not for them. Opera, for example, is always good for a dismissive giggle from popular journalists. A fairly recent survey of attitudes towards the public funding of opera suggested that most people are not antagonistic; they often have a sort of respect for opera and are willing to accept that those who do enjoy it should be helped to do so.

Even more interesting — and English. The doubt about the value of education in the high arts, which is so widespread among both populists and ideologues, is also to be found among many of those whom the populists and ideologues would call 'elitists', using that word in its current, restricted and false sense. There are many people who are extremely knowledgeable in the arts, and at any one time a number of such people are to be found on the Arts Council and among the Council's staff. They are likely to back away nervously and fastidiously if it is suggested that the urge to practise and to appreciate the arts should, given the social facts I have outlined, be encouraged by direct educational activity at all levels.

That seems a very dreary thought . . . studying T. S. Eliot at night with other adults whilst sitting at small classroom desks, courtesy of the local education authority. And a dangerous occupation, like rubbing the bloom from a butterfly's wings. This was the reaction of a sizeable number of Arts Council members and officers when four or five years ago Roy Shaw suggested that the Council was not properly fulfilling its brief if it did not move directly into educational activities.

Luckily there is evidence the other way and also at all levels. Some schools have a tough time, swimming against the subcultural tides, especially when interest and unself-consciousness evaporate after the age of nine or ten. But there is a long and good tradition of education in the arts at school level and it is neither ineffective nor dead yet, just having a particularly hard time at present.

Among adults seeking continuing education the evidence runs the other way. Many already seek education of that kind, and we know from surveys that many more would take it up if it were more accessible. Even more striking: the majority of those who would like greater access to continuing education do not seek further technical or professional training (as this government would certainly assume and hope). They seek a liberal further education and for good, old-fashioned liberal reasons expressed in good, old-fashioned liberal language: 'it will broaden my mind'; 'it will enrich my experience'; 'it will help me to have a fuller life'. Phrases such as these should bring blushes to the cheeks of those who, out of populism, ideology or elitism (again, in the misused sense) are consistently rejecting that moving call.

There is still in Britain, in some people from all classes and all regions, more respect for the life of the mind and so for the arts, no matter how hidden it may be, than you would guess from reading the popular press, or from listening to most radio anchor-men as they put on their 'this won't hurt a bit' voices when they introduce an intellectual or artistic item, or than you would guess from the nervousness of the Guardians at the Arts Council, or from the aggression of the ideologically anti-art. A plague on all your houses, you feel like saying. There is more virtue in the old liberal, humane, humanist tradition as it still survives in some unfashionable corners than in all the false populisms and false elitisms.

13 The Role of Literature in a Multicultural Society

● Carol MacDougall

> It may show the horrors of the Slave Trade, but it does so in such a way that no young reader would be left with respect for Black people
>
> (Albert Schwartz)

> It is a novel of great horror and as great humanity. It seems to me it approaches perfection as a work of art.
>
> (Bob Dixon, *Catching Them Young* No. I.)

It is difficult to believe that the above comments were made about the same children's book, *The Slave Dancer* by Paula Fox. What is even more surprising is that the writers of these statements are both advocates of a new approach to racial attitudes in children's literature; both believe that in the past much children's literature presented black people in an unfavourable light and that there is now a need for children's literature which reflects authentically the experience of black people.

Why is it then that they show such divergence of views about the same book? I think the most significant reason lies in the very nature of the subject matter with which they are dealing. After a lengthy period of neglect, racially prejudiced attitudes in children's literature have been brought under critical scrutiny. This issue is now capable of rousing such strong feelings that even those campaigning for change can take such an extreme attitude to a particular book that they seem poles apart. Bob Dixon admires *The Slave Dancer* because it highlights the injustice and inhumanity of the slave trade and this seems to have blinded him to any flaws in the book; Albert Schwartz focuses on the inadequate way in which black people are depicted and feels this destroys the book's value.

My own stance would be somewhere between these two extremes; the black characters in the story are not established as individuals with names and personalities and the white characters do play a much more significant part in events; on the other hand, the appalling treatment of black people on slave ships is vividly portrayed and in a narrative style which has the power to grip the reader. This is, therefore, a book I would want to encourage children to read and talk about.

But why all this furore about racial attitudes in children's literature? Why has children's literature become the source of such ardent controversy? It seems that those who campaign for change are suspected of having ulterior political motives unrelated to the literary merit of children's books. They are accused of being interested in children's literature only in so far as it can be used for didactic purposes.

It is true, though, that we are living in a multicultural society; the children entering our classrooms today draw on a wide range of different cultures. If children's literature reflects only certain aspects of the dominant white culture, children are being given an unbalanced impression of our society because this society comprises many different cultures and traditions including Asian, West Indian, Jewish, Polish, Italian, Celtic and Romany. For most adults educated in Britain, personal experience will confirm that, even in the fairly recent past, children's literature has focused on a narrow range of cultural experience. Popular children's writers have, rarely, depicted characters from minority ethnic groups. An obvious example is Enid Blyton, whose Famous Five and Secret Seven stories, devoted to the rather improbable adventures of a group of middle-class white children, continue to enjoy considerable popularity.

There is then a need to redress the balance, to promote literature which reflects the experience of people from a range of different cultures. An increasing awareness of this need has led to the creation of a new genre in children's literature, conveniently labelled 'multicultural'. Multicultural literature has become an umbrella term which covers a variety of types of literature. It is most often used to refer to stories which include characters from minority ethnic groups, but also refer to stories which derive from other cultures such as folk tales.

Inherent in this free-ranging use of the term 'multicultural' are dangers of abuse. There is, for example, the assumption that the recipe for 'good' multicultural literature lies in the inclusion of a few characters from minority ethnic groups. *There Ain't No Angels No More* by Godfrey Goodwin illustrates the fallacy of this assumption. This story, told through the eyes of a young black boy, is about a decaying inner city street and the families it houses. The families belong to a variety of different ethnic groups and are constantly feuding until the arrival of Joe, a black painter/poet. With brush and paint, Joe transforms not only the appearance of the street, but also people's attitudes, so that where there was discord, harmony reigns. The idea is attractive enough, but the trouble is that the story is not rooted in authentic experience. In reality, people from the same ethnic minorities tend to group together, but the book ignores this and has representative members of each ethnic minority living in the same street. Little effort is made to explore the experience, thoughts and feelings of particular individuals. Everything is dealt with at a superficial level and the attempt at the end to turn the story into a dream allegory, only serves to make it seem more confusing and unrelated to anything in the real world.

Very much in contrast to this is *Basketball Game* by Julius Lester. The story is set in America in the 1950s; a black minister and his family move into a white area of Nashville. The story focuses on Allen, the fourteen-year-old son of the family. Allen's thoughts and feelings are revealed in convincing detail and the development of his relationship with Rebecca, a white girl, is depicted with tenderness and sensitivity. The book becomes a powerful indictment of racial segregation because of the way in which it rouses sympathy for the character of Allen. *Basketball Game* succeeds where *There Ain't No Angels No More* fails because its strength of characterisation together with location in a specific time and place make it a convincing representation of human experience.

The point is that the creation of 'good' multicultural literature requires more than a smattering of characters from ethnic minorities; the story must also convey an aspect of life in such a way that it is capable of interesting and involving the reader. No matter how much I admired the sentiments expressed in *There Ain't No Angels No More*, I did not find it convincing or engrossing, but felt it was written to a prescribed formula which sought to pander to the demand for 'multicultural' literature. Because the story seemed contrived in this way, it also laid itself open to the accusation of being didactic; the story became simply a veneer for a set of ideas. All literature embodies values and attitudes in some shape or form, but these can be incorporated into a novel in such a way that they are part of its overall conception. For example, at the end of *Basketball Game*, Rebecca's refusal to recognise Allen and the hurt he suffers as a result, both suggest powerfully the inhumanity of racial segregation. This effect is achieved through the authenticity of the experience, not through an explicit statement of a point of view. This is, of course, a characteristic of all literature; it is different only in so far as it reflects the experience and cultural heritage of people who have hitherto been excluded from representation.

Attempts to produce literature which reflects the multicultural nature of Britain today are inevitably rather self-conscious. They are consciously grappling with social circumstances which have not been represented in literature before. For example, Jan Needle in *My Mate Shofiq* seeks to give an insight into what it is like to be a Pakistani boy growing up in a Lancashire town. The setting and characters in the book are, for the most part, vividly drawn, but in emphasising the injustice and prejudice confronting the boy's family, the writer tends to depict the Asian community as too passive and incapable of self-help. Similarly Farrukh Dhondy in his collections of short stories, *East End at Your Feet* and *Come to Mecca*, strives to convey something of the experience of ethnic minorities living in the East End of London. He tends to dwell excessively on some of the rather sordid aspects of life and his characters' reactions are not always convincing, but he gives an impression of what it feels like to belong to a minority group in Britain.

Books like *My Mate Shofiq* and *Come to Mecca* represent a stage in the evolution of more effective multicultural literature. Such books might be described as being at an intermediate stage between writing which is simply attempting to fit a prescribed formula and writing which effectively depicts authentic experience. They are not contrived in the way I have suggested *There Ain't No Angels No More* is, but are seeking to portray an aspect of our society in a form accessible to young people. Their faults lie partly in their authors' inexperience as writers and I believe it would be a mistake to be destructively critical of such books because writers need the experience of writing in order to improve. Destructive criticism might stem the flow towards the creation of better multicultural literature.

As far as I am aware, the only writers who go beyond this stage of development are American. They are drawing on a longer tradition of thinking and writing about ethnic minorities than is available to most British writers. As a result, the writing of the American authors seems to have a greater self-assurance. I have already referred to Julius Lester who, in addition to *Basketball Game*, has written other books including *Long Journey Home*, a collection of short stories based on the history of black Americans. Again in these stories, Julius Lester is able to depict characters and situations with moving realism. Louise Fitzhugh is another writer worthy of attention. Her book, *Nobody's Family is Going to Change*, is unique in that it deals with relationships within a black American family and is not primarily concerned with injustice arising from racial prejudice.

If we wish to create an atmosphere in Britain in which multicultural literature evolves and flourishes, then, as teachers and librarians, we must be prepared to promote the best of the multicultural literature already available. I believe it is important that we make a conscious effort to redress the balance in this way because literature has a significant part to play in shaping attitudes. It is inevitable that a writer should attempt to shape a reader's response and perhaps even influence attitudes, but this is not the same as didacticism because of the active role of the reader. The reader is not merely a passive recipient of the writer's words, but an active participant in making meaning out of those words; in other words the reader is not actually told what to think, but left to make deductions.

Rather like the potter takes a lump of clay and shapes it into a bowl, the writer takes thoughts and feelings, an impression of life and forms these into a literary creation such as a novel. If the writing is effective, the reader will respond to the writer's vision of the world. For example, if a character in a novel is unjustly treated we may be roused to anger. However, because we are responding to a representation of life rather than a real life situation, we will not be required to act upon our emotion. In real life we might feel compelled to intervene to change the course of events; in reading literature, we may respond emotionally to a 'virtual experience', but cannot influence events. This means the reader has scope for evaluation and contemplation; readers have time to think why they responded in a certain way, why the treatment of a character provoked anger or roused sympathy. The reader may then accept or reject the writer's view of the world, but in doing so the reader's views will almost certainly have been modified through contact with another person's interpretation of life. It may be that the reader's view of the human condition corresponds so closely to the writer's, that the reader's own view is simply reinforced; on the other hand, a writer may be so skilful in presenting a different and unfamiliar view of human experience that the reader's own views are changed or modified in some way. The possibility of a person's outlook being modified through reading gives literature a vital role in a multicultural society.

Through reading about the experience of someone from another culture, children's sympathies can be roused and they can come to understand something of what it means to be part of that culture. Children from ethnic minorities may, in addition, be helped to feel confidence in and increased respect for their own culture, if they experience it represented in literature. I have certainly observed this process at work. I gave *Basketball Game* to four adolescent white girls to read and afterwards we talked about it. All felt strong sympathies with the character of Allen; the most telling comment came when one of the girls explained that before reading the story, she had not realised racial segregation meant that even white people who wished to associate with black people were prevented from doing so, because of pressures put on them by the rest of the white community. The comment revealed an insight into the way racial segregation distorts and dehumanises people's behaviour, which the girl did not have before reading the book.

I gave the same book to a fourteen-year-old black boy who, in terms of the school, would be labelled 'average ability'. From the moment he picked up the book, he read it avidly and completed it by the following lesson. When I asked him what he thought of it, he said it was good apart from the ending which was 'rubbish'. From the way he said the word 'rubbish', it was obvious that he really meant he had found the ending hurtful. I explained that given the circumstances in that part of America at that time, it would have been difficult for the story to have had a different ending. I also commented that I had found the ending very sad. Several weeks later, the boy wrote a poignant story of his own in which the central character, a black boy, has a white girl friend whom he is eventually forced to give up as a result of pressure from her parents. *Basketball Game* had provided a springboard which enabled the boy to present some of his own thoughts and feelings in narrative form.

These examples illustrate children's ability to interpret and evaluate literature. Teachers have a crucial role to play in developing these abilities so that children read with increasing critical awareness. Rather than discouraging children from reading books like *My Mate Shofiq* and *Come to Mecca*, it would seem better to encourage them to read critically, so that they can learn to identify what is of value. My own experience would suggest that two of the most effective ways of developing critical awareness are firstly through talk, sometimes with teacher involvement and guidance, but sometimes just with children talking to each other about a book, because this allows them to draw on their own experiences in evaluating the book: and secondly, through children writing for themselves, so that they learn from firsthand experience something of what it means to be 'a writer' and can in this way share aspects of their lives with others.

My hope is that teachers might use the shared experience of literature to help children enjoy the richness and variety of living in a multicultural society.

RECOMMENDED BOOKS

This book list is geared toward young people of secondary school age.

Ash, Ranjana (ed.), *Short Stories from India, Pakistan and Bangladesh* (Harrap). Stories, in translation, covering a range of experiences.
Craven, Margaret, *I Heard The Owl Call My Name* (Heineman New Windmill). A young priest goes to live with North American Indians. Suitable for more mature readers.
Darke, Marjorie, *The First of Midnight* (Penguin). An historical novel set in eighteenth-century Bristol about a romance between a pauper girl and a slave.
Dhondy, Farrukh, *East End at Your Feet* and *Come to Mecca* (Fontana Lions). Collections of short stories about Asians and West Indians in London.
Dhondy, Farrukh, *Poona Company* (Gollancz). Short stories about an Indian boyhood.
Fitzhugh, Louise, *Nobody's Family is Going to Change* (Fontana Lions). The story focuses on the daughter of a Black American family and her desire to be a lawyer.
Fox, Paula, *The Slave Dancer* (Piccolo). Boy pressganged to serve on slave-ship learns the horrors of the middle passage.
Jacobson, Dan, *A Way of Life and other stories* (Longman Imprint). Short stories about life in South Africa. Suitable for more mature readers.
Leeson, Robert, *Maroon Boy* (Collins). Historical novel about slave-trade to West Indies.

Leeson, Robert, *The Third Glass Genie* (Armada Lions). Racial issues introduced through story of a schoolboy who discovers a genie in a tin can.

Lester, Julius, *Long Journey Home* (Penguin and Longman Knockouts). Stories taken from the history of black Americans.

Lester, Julius, *Basketball Game* (Penguin). Story of black boy's friendship with white girl in racially segregated Nashville in 1950s.

MacGibben, Jean, *Hal* (Puffin). Set in London, an ill and nervous boy is helped to health and confidence by his friendship with a West Indian girl.

Needle, Jan, *My Mate Shofiq* (Fontana Lions). Set in Lancashire, story tells of friendship between white boy and a boy from a Pakistani family.

Palmer, Everard, *Baba and Mr Big* (Fontana Lions). Story from the West Indies about relationship between a boy and an old man.

Salkey, Andrew (ed.), *West Indian Stories* (Faber). Stories written by West Indians, set in the West Indies and London, not written specifically for children, but suitable for 15+.

Sherman, D. R., *Old Mali and the Boy* (Heineman). Set in Northern India, story of fatherless twelve-year old white boy and his mother's gardener.

Taylor, Mildred, *Roll of Thunder, Hear My Cry* (Gollancz). A black family, faced with the Klan riding the night, faces its world with courage and dignity.

14 *The Unmanning of the Mayor of Casterbridge*

● Elaine Showalter

To the feminist critic, Hardy presents an irresistible paradox. He is one of the few Victorian male novelists who wrote in what may be called a female tradition; at the beginning of his career, Hardy was greeted with the same uncertainty that had been engendered by the pseudonymous publication of *Jane Eyre* and *Adam Bede*: was the author man or woman? *Far from the Madding Crowd*, serialised in the *Cornhill* in 1874, was widely attributed to George Eliot, and Leslie Stephen wrote reassuringly to Hardy about the comparisons: 'As for the supposed affinity to George Eliot, it consists, I think, simply in this that you have both treated rustics of the farming class in a humorous manner — Mrs. Poyser would be home I think, in Weatherbury — but you need not be afraid of such criticisms. You are original and can stand on your own legs.'[1]

It hardly needs to be said that Stephen's assessment of Hardy's originality was correct; but on the other hand, the relationship to Eliot went beyond similarities in content to similarities in psychological portraits, especially of women. Hardy's remarkable heroines, even in the earlier novels, evoked comparisons with Charlotte Brontë, Jane Austen and George Eliot, indicating a recognition (as Havelock Ellis pointed out in his 1883 review-essay) that 'the most serious work in modern English fiction . . . has been done by women.'[2] Later, Hardy's heroines spoke even more directly to women readers; after the publication of *Tess of the d'Urbervilles*, for example, Hardy received letters from wives who had not dared to tell their husbands about their premarital experience; sometimes these women requested meetings which he turned down on his barrister's advice.[3] Twentieth-century criticism has often focused on the heroines of the novels; judging from the annual *Dissertation Abstracts* (Ann Arbor, Michigan) this perennial favourite of dissertation topics has received new incentive from the women's movement. Recent feminist criticism, most notably the distinguished essays of Mary Jacobus on Tess and Sue, has done much to unfold the complexities of Hardy's imaginative response to the 'woman question' of the 1890s.[4] Hardy knew and respected many of the minor women novelists of his day: Katherine Macquoid, Rhoda Broughton, Mary Braddon, Sarah Grand, Mona Caird, Evelyn Sharp, Charlotte Mew. He actually collaborated on a short story with the novelist Florence Henniker, and possibly revised the work of other female protegées; his knowledge of the themes of feminist writing in the 1880s and 1890s was extensive.[5]

Yet other aspects of Hardy's work reveal a much more distanced and divided attitude towards women, a sense of an irreconcilable split between male and female values and possibilities. If some Victorian women recognised themselves in his heroines, others were shocked and indignant. In 1890, Hardy's friend Edmund Gosse wrote: 'The unpopularity of Mr Hardy's novels among women is a curious phenomenon. If he had no male admirers, he could almost cease to exist . . . Even educated women approach him with hesitation and prejudice.'[6] Hardy hoped that *Tess of the d'Urbervilles* would redeem him; he wrote to Edmund Yates in 1891 that 'many of my novels have suffered so much from misrepresentation as being attacks on womankind.'[7] He took heart from letters from mothers who were 'putting "Tess" into their daughters' hands to safeguard their future', and from 'women of society' who said his courage had 'done the whole sex a service.'[8] Gosse, however, read the hostile and uncomprehending reviews of such women as Margaret Oliphant as evidence of a continuing division between feminist critics, who were 'shrivelled spinsters', and the 'serious male public'.[9] There were indeed real and important ideological differences between Hardy and even advanced women of the 1890s, differences which Gosse wished to reduce to questions of sexual prudery. Hardy's emphasis on the biological determinism of childbearing, rather than on the economic determinants of female dependency, put him more in the camp of Grant Allen than in the women's party. In 1892 he declined membership in the Women's Progressive Society because he had not 'as yet been converted to a belief in the desirability of the Society's first object' — women's suffrage.[10] By 1906 his conversion had taken place; but his support of the suffrage campaign was based on his hope (as he wrote to Millicent Garrett Fawcett) that 'the tendency of the women's vote will be to break up the present pernicious conventions in respect of manners, customs, religion, illegitimacy, the stereotyped household (that it must be the unit of society), the father of a woman's child (that it is anybody's business but the woman's own except in cases of disease or insanity)'.[11]

Looking at the novels of the 1890s, and at Hardy's treatment of his heroines as they encounter pernicious conventions, A. O. J. Cockshut has concluded that there were unbridgeable gaps between Hardy's position and that of *fin-de-siècle* feminism:

> Hardy decisively rejects the whole feminist argument of the preceding generation, which was the soil for the growth of the idea of the 'New Woman' à la Havelock Ellis and Grant Allen; and this is his final word on

the matter. The feminists saw the natural disabilities as trivial compared with those caused by bad traditions and false theories. Hardy reversed this, and he did so feelingly. The phrase 'inexorable laws of nature' was no cliché for him. It represented the slowly-garnered fruits of his deepest meditations on life. It was an epitome of what found full imaginative expression in memorable descriptions, like that of Egdon Heath. The attempt to turn Hardy into a feminist is altogether vain.[12]

But the traditional attention to Hardy's heroines has obscured other themes of equal significance to a feminist critique. Through the heroes of his novels and short stories, Hardy also investigated the Victorian codes of manliness, the man's experience of marriage, the problem of paternity. For the heroes of the tragic novels — Michael Henchard, Jude Fawley, Angel Clare — maturity involves a kind of assimilation of female suffering, an identification with a woman which is also an effort to come to terms with their own deepest selves. In Hardy's career too there is a consistent element of self-expression through women; he uses them as narrators, as secretaries, as collaborators, and finally, in the (auto) biography he wrote in the persona of his second wife, as screens or ghosts of himself. Hardy not only commented upon, and in a sense, infiltrated, feminine fictions; he also understood the feminine self as the estranged and essential complement of the male self. In *The Mayor of Casterbridge* (1886), Hardy gives the fullest nineteenth-century portrait of a man's inner life — his rebellion and his suffering, his loneliness and jealousy, his paranoia and despair, his uncontrollable unconscious. Henchard's efforts, first to deny and divorce his passional self, and ultimately to accept and educate it, involve him in a pilgrimage of 'unmanning' which is a movement towards both self-discovery and tragic vulnerability. It is in the analysis of this New Man, rather than in the evaluation of Hardy's New Woman, that the case for Hardy's feminist sympathies may be argued.

The Mayor of Casterbridge begins with a scene that dramatises the analysis of female subjugation as a function of capitalism which Engels had recently set out in *The Origins of the Family, Private Property and the State* (1884): the auction of Michael Henchard's wife Susan at the fair at Weydon-Priors. Henchard's drunken declaration that Susan is his 'goods' is matched by her simple acceptance of a new 'owner', and her belief that in paying five guineas in cash for her Richard Newson has legitimised their relationship. Hardy never intended the wife-sale to seem natural or even probable, although he assembled in his Commonplace Book factual accounts of such occurrences from the *Dorset County Chronicle* and the *Brighton Gazette*.[13] The auction is clearly an extraordinary event, which violates the moral sense of the Casterbridge community when it is discovered twenty years later. But there is a sense in which Hardy recognised the psychological temptation of such a sale, the male longing to exercise his property rights over women, to free himself from their burden with virile decision, to simplify his own conflicts by reducing them to 'the ruin of good men by bad wives' (I; p. 7).

This element in the novel could never have been articulated by Hardy's Victorian readers, but it has been most spiritedly expressed in our century by Irving Howe:

> To shake loose from one's wife; to discard that drooping rag of a woman, with her mute complaints and maddening passivity; to escape not by a slinking abandonment but through the public sale of her body to a stranger, as horses are sold at a fair; and thus to wrest, through sheer amoral willfulness, a second chance out of life — it is with this stroke, so insidiously attractive to male fantasy, that *The Mayor of Casterbridge* begins.[14]

The scene, Howe goes on, speaks to 'the depths of common fantasy, it summons blocked desires and transforms us into secret sharers. No matter what judgements one may make of Henchard's conduct, it is hard, after the first chapter, simply to abandon him; for through his boldness we have been drawn into complicity with the forbidden.'

Howe brings an enthusiasm and an authority to his exposition of Henchard's motives that sweeps us along, although we need to be aware both that he invents a prehistory for the novel that Hardy withholds, and that in speaking of 'our' common fantasies, he quietly transforms the novel into a male document. A woman's experience of this scene must be very different; indeed, there were many sensation novels of the 1870s and 1880s which presented the sale of women into marriage from the point of view of the bought wife. In Howe's reading, Hardy's novel becomes a kind of sensation-fiction, playing on the suppressed longings of its male audience, evoking sympathy for Henchard because of his crime, and not in spite of it.

In this exclusive concentration on the sale of the wife, however, Howe, like most of Hardy's critics, overlooks the simultaneous event which more profoundly determines Henchard's fate: the sale of the child. Paternity is a central subject of the book, far more important than conjugal love. Perhaps one reason why the sale of the child has been so consistently ignored by generations of Hardy critics is that the child is female. For Henchard to sell his son would be so drastic a violation of patriarchal culture that it would wrench the entire novel out of shape; but the sale of a daughter — in this case only a 'tiny girl' — seems almost natural. There may even be a suggestion that this too is an act insidiously attractive to male fantasy, the rejection of the wife who has only borne female offspring.

It is the combined, premeditated sale of wife and child which launches Henchard into his second chance. Orphaned, divorced, without mother or sisters, wife or daughter, he has effectively severed all his bonds with the community of women, and re-enters society alone — the new Adam, reborn, self-created, unencumbered, journeying southward without pause until he reaches Casterbridge. Henchard commits his life entirely to the male community, defining his human relationships by the male codes of money, paternity, honour and legal contract. By his act Henchard sells out or divorces his own 'feminine' self, his own need for passion, tenderness, and loyalty. The return of Susan and Elizabeth-Jane which precipitates the main phase of the novel is indeed a return of the repressed, which forces Henchard gradually to confront the tragic inadequacy of his codes, the arid limits of partriarchal power. The fantasy that women hold men back, drag them down, drain their energy, divert their strength, is nowhere so bleakly rebuked as in Hardy's tale of the 'man of character'. Stripped of his mayor's chain, his master's authority, his father's rights, Henchard is in a sense unmanned; but it is in moving from romantic male individualism to a more complete humanity that he becomes capable of tragic experience. Thus sex-role patterns and tragic patterns in the novel connect.

According to Christine Winfield's study of the manuscript of *The Mayor of Casterbridge*, Hardy made extensive revisions in Chapter 1. The most striking detail of the early drafts was that the Henchard family was originally composed of two daughters, the elder of whom was old enough to try to dissuade Susan from going along with the sale: ' ''Don't mother!'' whispered the girl who sat on the woman's side. ''Father don't know what he's saying.'' ' On being sold to the sailor Newson, however, Susan takes the younger girl ('her favourite one') with her; Henchard keeps the other. Hardy apparently took this detail from the notice of a wife-sale in the *Brighton Gazette* for 25 May 1826: 'We understand they were country people, and that the woman has had two children by her husband, one of whom he consents to keep, and the other he throws in as a makeweight to the bargain.'[15]

Hardy quickly discarded this cruel opening, and in the final text he emphasises the presence and the sale of a single infant daughter. From the beginning, she and her mother form an intimate unit, as close to each other as Henchard and his wife are separate. Susan speaks not to her husband, but to her baby, who babbles in reply; her face becomes alive when she talks to the girl. In a psychoanalytic study of Hardy, Charles K. Hofling has taken this bond between mother and daughter as the source of Henchard's jealous estrangement,[16] but all the signs in the text point to Henchard's dissociation from the family as his own choice. The personalities of husband and wife are evidenced in all the nuances of this scene, one which they will both obsessively recall and relive. Hardy takes pains to show us Henchard's rigid unapproachability, his body-language eloquent of rejection. In Henchard's very footsteps there is a 'dogged and cynical indifference personal to himself' (I; p. 1); he avoids Susan's eyes and possible conversation by 'reading, or pretending to read' (I; p. 2) a ballad sheet, which he must hold awkwardly with the hand thrust through the strap of his basket. The scene is in marked contrast to Mrs Gaskell's opening in *Mary Barton*, for example, where fathers and brothers help to carry the infants; Hardy plays consciously against the reader's expectation of affectionate closeness. When Susan and Elizabeth-Jane retrace the journey many years later, they are holding hands, 'the act of simple affection' (III; p. 21).

Henchard's refusal of his family antedates the passionate declaration of the auction, and it is important to note that such a sale has been premeditated or at least discussed between husband and wife. There are several references to previous threats: 'On a previous occasion when he had declared during a fuddle that he would dispose of her as he had done, she had replied that she would not hear him say that many times more before it happened, in the resigned tones of a fatalist' (II; p. 17). When Newson asks whether Susan is willing to go with him, Henchard answers for her: 'She is willing, provided she can have the child. She said so only the other day when I talked o't!' (I; p. 12). After the sale, Henchard tries to evade the full responsibility for his act by blaming it on an evening's drunkenness, a temporary breakdown in reason and control; he even blames his lost wife's 'simplicity' for allowing him to go through with the act: 'Seize her, why didn't she know better than bring me into this disgrace! . . . She wasn't queer if I was. 'Tis like Susan to show such idiotic simplicity' (II; p. 17: ellipsis mine). His anger and humiliation, none the less, cannot undo the fact that the bargain that was struck, and the 'goods' that were divided (Susan takes the girl, Henchard the tools) had been long contemplated. When it is too late, Henchard chiefly regrets his over-hasty division of property: 'She'd no business to take the maid — 'tis my maid; and if it were the doing again she shouldn't have her!' (I; p. 14).

In later scenes, Hardy gives Henchard more elaborated motives for the sale: contempt for Susan's ignorance and naiveté; and, as Henchard recalls on his first pilgrimage to Weydon-Priors, twenty-five years after the fair, his 'cursed pride and mortification at being poor' (XLIV; p. 367). Financial success, in the mythology of Victorian manliness, requires the subjugation of competing passions. If it is marriage that has threatened the youthful Henchard with 'the extinction of his energies' (I; p. 7), a chaste life will rekindle them. Henchard's public auction and his private oath of temperance are thus consecutive stages of the same rite of passage. Henchard's oath is both an atonement for his drunken surrender to his fantasies, and a bargain with success. In Rudyard Kipling's *The Man Who Would Be King* (1899), a similar 'contrack' is made, whereby Peachey Carnehan and Daniel Dravot swear to abjure liquor and women. When Dravot breaks his promise, they are exiled from their kingdom; so too will Henchard be expelled from Casterbridge when he breaks his vows. Save for the romance with Lucetta, in which he appears to play a passive role, Henchard is chaste during his long separation from his wife; he enjoys the local legend he has created of himself as the 'celebrated abstaining worthy' (v; p. 38); the man whose 'haughty indifference to the society of womankind, his silent avoidance of converse with the sex' (XIII; p. 94) is well known. His prominence in Casterbridge is produced by the commercialised energies of sexual sublimation, and he boasts to Farfrae that 'being by nature something of a woman-hater, I have found it no hardship to keep mostly at a distance from the sex' (XII; p. 89). There is nothing in Henchard's consciousness which corresponds to the aching melancholy of Hardy's poem 'He abjures love' (1883):

> At last I put off love,
>   For twice ten years
> The daysman of my thought,
>   And hope, and doing.

Indeed, in marrying Susan for the second time, Henchard forfeits something of his personal magic, and begins to lose power in the eyes of the townspeople; it is whispered that he has been 'captured and enervated by the genteel widow' (XIII; p. 94).

Henchard's emotional life is difficult to define; in the first half of the novel, Hardy gives us few direct glimpses of his psyche, and soberly refrains from the kind of romantic symbolism employed as psychological notation by the Brontës and by Dickens — dreams, doubles, hallucinatory illnesses. But the very absence of emotion, the 'void' which Hardy mentions, suggests that Henchard has divorced himself from feeling, and that it is feeling itself which obstinately retreats from him as he doggedly pursues it. When J. Hillis Miller describes Henchard as a man 'driven by a passionate desire for full possession of some other person' and calls the novel 'a nightmare of frustrated desire',[17] he misleadingly suggests that the nature and intensity of Henchard's need is sexual. It is an absence of feeling which Henchard looks to others to supply, a craving unfocused loneliness rather than a desire towards another person. Henchard does not seek possession in the sense that he desires the confidences of others; such reciprocity as he requires, he coerces. What he wants is a 'greedy exclusiveness' (XLI; p. 338), a title; and this feeling is stimulated by male competition.

Given Henchard's misogyny, we cannot be surprised to see that his deepest feelings are reserved for another man, a surrogate brother with whom he quickly contracts a business relationship that has the emotional overtones of a marriage. Henchard thinks of giving Farfrae a third share in his business to compel him to stay; he urges that they should share a house and meals. Elizabeth-Jane is the frequent observer of the manly friendship between Henchard and Farfrae, which she idealises:

> She looked from the window and saw Henchard and Farfrae in the hay-yard talking, with that impetuous cordiality on the Mayor's part, and

genial modesty on the younger man's, that was now so generally observable in their intercourse. Friendship between man and man; what a rugged strength there was in it, as evinced by these two. (XV; p. 110)

Yet Elizabeth-Jane is also an 'accurate observer' who sees that Henchard's 'tigerish affection . . . now and then resulted in a tendency to domineer' (XIV; p. 104). It is a tigerish affection that does not respect that other's separateness, that sets its own terms of love and hate. Farfrae's passivity in this relationship is feminine at first, when he is constrained by his economic dependence on Henchard. There is nothing homosexual in their intimacy; but there is certainly on Henchard's side an open, and, he later feels, incautious embrace of homosocial friendship, an insistent male bonding.[18] Success, for Henchard, precludes relationships with women; male cameraderie and, later, contests of manliness must take their place. He precipitately confides in Farfrae, telling him all the secrets of his past, at a point when he is determined to withhold this information from Elizabeth-Jane: 'I am not going to let her know the truth' (XII; p. 92). Despite Henchard's sincerity, the one-sidedness of the exchange, his indifference to Farfrae's feelings if he can have his company, leads the younger man to experience their closeness as artificial, and to resist 'the pressure of mechanized friendship' (XVI; p. 117).

The community of Casterbridge itself has affinities with its Mayor when it is first infiltrated by Farfrae and the women. Like Henchard, it pulls itself in, refuses contact with its surroundings. 'It is huddled all together', remarks Elizabeth-Jane when she sees it for the first time. The narrator goes on: 'Its squareness was, indeed, the characteristic which most struck the eye in this antiquated borough . . . at that time, recent as it was, untouched by the faintest sprinkle of modernism. It was compact as a box of dominoes. It had no suburbs — in the ordinary sense. Country and town met at a mathematical line' (IV; pp. 29–30: ellipsis mine). The 'rectangular frame' of the town recalls Hardy's descriptions of the perpendicularity of Henchard's face; entering Casterbridge Susan and Elizabeth-Jane encounter the 'stockade of gnarled trees', the town wall, part of its 'ancient defences', the 'grizzled church' whose bell tolls the curfew with a 'peremptory clang' (IV; pp. 30–2). All these details suggest Henchard, who is barricaded, authoritarian, coercive. He has become, as Christopher Coney tells the women, 'a pillar of the town' (V; p. 39).

Deeply defended against intimacy and converse with women, Henchard is vulnerable only when he has been symbolically unmanned by a fit of illness and depression; his susceptibility to these emotional cycles (the more integrated Farfrae is immune to them) is evidence of his divided consciousness. His romance with Lucetta takes place during such an episode: 'In my illness I sank into one of those gloomy fits I sometimes suffer from, on account o' the loneliness of my domestic life, when the world seems to have the blackness of hell, and, like Job, I could curse the day that gave me birth' (XII; p. 90). Again, when Henchard is living with Jopp, and becomes ill, Elizabeth-Jane is able to penetrate his solitude, and reach his affections. At these moments, his proud independence is overwhelmed by the woman's warmth; he is forced into an emotionally receptive passivity. Yet affection given in such circumstances humiliates him; he needs to demand or even coerce affection in order to feel manly and esteemed.

In health, Henchard determines the conditions of his relationships to women with minimal attention to their feelings. His remarriage to Susan is the product of 'strict mechanical rightness' (XIII; p. 93); his effort to substantiate the union, to give it the appearance of some deeper emotion, is typical of his withholding of self:

> Lest she should pine for deeper affection than he could give he made a point of showing some semblance of it in external action. Among other things he had the iron railings, that had smiled sadly in dull rust for the last eighty years, painted a bright green, and the heavily-barred, small-paned Georgian sash windows enlivened with three coats of white. He was as kind to her as a man, mayor, and churchwarden could possibly be. (XIV; p. 99)

To Susan, his kindness is an official function, and although he promises her that he will earn his forgiveness by his future works, Henchard's behaviour to women continues to be manipulative and proprietary. He deceives Elizabeth-Jane in the uncomfortable masquerade of the second courtship; he has not sufficient respect for Susan to follow her instructions on the letter about her daughter's true parentage. When he wants Lucetta to marry him, he threatens to blackmail her; when he wants to get rid of Elizabeth-Jane he makes her a small allowance. He trades in women, with dictatorial letters to Farfrae, and lies to Newson, with an ego that is alive only to its own excited claims.

Having established Henchard's character in this way, Hardy introduces an overlapping series of incidents in the second half of the novel which reverses and negates the pattern of manly power and self-possession. These incidents become inexorable stages in Henchard's unmanning, forcing him to acknowledge his own human dependency and to discover his own suppressed or estranged capacity to love. The first of these episodes is the reappearance of the furmity-woman at Petty Sessions, and her public denunciation of Henchard. Placed centrally in the novel (in Chapter XXVIII), this encounter seems at first reading to have the arbitrary and fatal timing of myth; the furmity-woman simply appears in Casterbridge to commit her 'nuisance' and to be arraigned. But the scene in fact follows Henchard's merciless coercion of Lucetta into a marriage she no longer desires. This violation, carried out from rivalry with Farfrae rather than disappointed love, repeats his older act of aggression against human feeling. Thus the declaration of the furmity-woman, the public humbling of Henchard by a woman, seems appropriate. It is for drunk and disorderly behaviour, for disrespect to the church and for profanity that she is accused; and her revelation of Henchard's greater disorder is an effective challenge to the authority of patriarchal law. Hardy's narrative underlines the scene explicitly as forming the 'edge or turn in the incline of Henchard's fortunes. On that day — almost at that minute — he passed the ridge of prosperity and honour, and began to descend rapidly on the other side. It was strange how soon he sank in esteem. Socially he had received a startling fillip downwards; and, having already lost commercial buoyancy from rash transactions, the velocity of his descent in both aspects became accelerated every hour' (XXXI; p. 251). The emphasis at this point is very much on Henchard's fortunes and his bankruptcy; although the furmity-woman's story spreads so fast that within twenty-four hours everyone in Casterbridge knows what happened at Weydon-Priors fair, the one person from whom Henchard has most assiduously kept the secret — Elizabeth-Jane — unaccountably fails to confront him with it. Indeed, Hardy seems to have forgotten to show her reaction; when she seeks him out it is only to forgive his harshness to her. Retribution for the auction thus comes as a public rather than a private shaming; and Henchard responds publicly with his dignified withdrawal as magistrate, and later, his generous performance in bankruptcy.

The next phase of Henchard's unmanning moves into the private sphere. Hearing of Lucetta's marriage to Farfrae, he puts his former threat of blackmail into action, tormenting her by reading her letters to her husband. Henchard cannot actually bring himself to reveal her name, to cold-bloodedly destroy her happiness; but Lucetta, investing him with a more implacable will than he possesses, determines to dissuade him, and so arranges a secret morning meeting at the Roman amphitheatre, which is far more successful than even she had dared to hope:

> Her figure in the midst of the huge enclosure, the unusual plainness of her dress, her attitude of hope and appeal, so strongly revived in his soul the memory of another ill-used woman who had stood there and thus in bygone days, had now passed away into her rest, that he was unmanned, and his breast smote him for having attempted reprisals on one of a sex so weak. (XXXV; p. 288)

'Unmanning' here carries the significance of enervation, of a failure of nerve and resolve; and also the intimation of sympathy with the woman's position. The scene is carefully constructed to repeat the earlier meeting in the arena, when the wronged Susan came to Henchard in all her weakness; Henchard's 'old feeling of supercilious pity for womankind in general was intensified by this suppliant appearing here as the double of the first' (XXXV; p. 289). But Hardy does not allow us such simple sentiments; he intensifies the ironic complexities that make this meeting different. There is certainly a sense in which Lucetta is both touchingly reckless of her reputation, and weak in her womanhood; these elements will come together in the fatal outcome of the skimmington-ride, when her wrecked honour and her miscarriage provide the emotional and physical shocks that kill her. While the Victorian belief in the delicacy of pregnant women, and also the statistical realities of the maternal death rate, are behind this incident (no contemporary reader of *The Mayor of Casterbridge* found it difficult to believe), Hardy obviously intends it symbolically as a demonstration of female vulnerability.

But, in another sense, Henchard is stil deceiving himself about women's weakness, and flattering himself about men's strength; his 'supercilious pity' for womankind is obtuse and misplaced. Lucetta's pathetic appearance, her plea of loss of attractiveness, is deliberately and desperately calculated to win his pity and to pacify his competitiveness. She is employing 'the only practicable weapon left her as a woman' in this meeting with her enemy. She makes her toilette with the intention of making herself look plain; having missed a night's sleep and being pregnant ('a natural reason for her slightly drawn look'), she manages to look prematurely aged. Skilled at self-production and self-promotion, Lucetta thus turns her hand successfully to this negative strategy, with the result that Henchard ceases to find her desirable, and 'no longer envied Farfrae his bargain'. She has transformed herself into a drooping rag; and Henchard is again eager to get away. Lucetta's cleverest stroke is to remove the stimulus to Henchard's sense of rivalry by telling him that 'neither my husband nor any other man will regard me with interest long' (XXXV; pp. 287–9). Although he is defeated by a woman, Henchard's understanding of women is still constituted by a kind of patriarchal innocence; he is ashamed of himself but for all the wrong reasons.

It is out of this unmanning, out of his disturbed self-esteem which has been deprived of an enemy, that Henchard tries to reassert his legitimate authority, and rebuild his diminished stature, by invading the welcoming ceremonies for the Royal Personage. Defiantly clad in 'the fretted and weather-beaten garments of bygone years', Henchard indeed stands out upon the occasion, and makes himself as prominent and distinctive as Farfrae, who wears 'the official gold chain with great square links, like that round the Royal unicorn' (XXXVII; p. 306). The scene is the necessary preamble to the fight between the two men; Henchard's flag-waving salute to Royalty is really a challenge to Farfrae, the lion against the unicorn. He puts himself in the young mayor's path precisely in order to be snubbed and driven back, to be inflamed so that he can take his revenge in 'the heat of action'. The wrestling-match with Farfrae is the central male contest of the novel — rivalries over business and women resolved by hand-to-hand combat. But in mastering Farfrae, even with one hand tied behind his back, Henchard is again paradoxically unmanned, shamed, and enervated. The sense of Farfrae's indifference to him, the younger man's resistance to even this ultimate and violent coercion of passion, robs Henchard of the thrill of his victory. Again, it is the apparently weaker antagonist who prevails; and in the emotional crisis, roles are reversed so that Farfrae is the winner. As for Henchard,

> The scenes of his first acquaintance with Farfrae rushed back upon him — that time when the curious mixture of romance and thrift in the young man's composition so commanded his heart that Farfrae could play upon him as on an instrument. So thoroughly subdued was he that he remained on the sacks in a crouching attitude, unusual for a man, and for such a man. Its womanliness sat tragically on the figure of so stern a piece of virility. (XXXVIII; p. 316)

The rugged friendship between man and man, so impressive when seen from a distance by Elizabeth-Jane, comes down to this regressive, almost foetal, scene in the loft. Henchard has finally crossed over psychically and strategically to the long-repressed 'feminine' side of himself — has declared love for the first time to another person, and accepted the meaning of that victory of the weak over the strong. Thus, as Dale Kramer points out, 'In relation to the pattern of tragedy, the "feminine" Henchard is by his own definition a weakened man.'[19] But again, Henchard's surrender opens him for the first time to an understanding of human need measured in terms of feeling rather than property. In his hasty and desperate lie to Newson, Henchard reveals finally how dependent he has become on ties of love.

Thus the effigy which Henchard sees floating in Ten Hatches Hole, whence he has fled in suicidal despair after the encounter with Newson, is in fact the symbolic shell of a discarded male self, like a chrysalis. It is the completion of his unmanning — a casting-off of the attitudes, the empty garments, the façades of dominance and authority, now perceived by the quiet eye of Elizabeth-Jane to be no more than 'a bundle of old clothes' (XLI; p. 343). Returning home, Henchard is at last able to give up the tattered and defiant garments of his 'primal days', to put on clean linen. Dedicating himself to the love and protection of Elizabeth-Jane, he is humanly reborn.

The final section of the novel fulfils the implications of Henchard's unmanning in a series of scenes which are reversals of scenes in the first part of the book. It is Elizabeth-Jane who assumes ascendancy: 'In going and coming, in buying and selling, her word was law' (XLII; p. 349). He makes her tea with 'housewifely care' (XLI; p. 334). As the 'netted lion' (XLII; p. 349), Henchard is forced into psychological indirection, to feminine psychological manoeuvres, because he does not dare to risk a confrontation: 'He would often weigh and consider for hours together the meaning of such and such a deed or phrase of hers, when a blunt settling question would formerly have been his first instinct' (XLII; p. 351). It is a humbling, and yet educative and ennobling apprenticeship in human sensitivity, a dependence, Hardy writes, into which he had 'declined (or, in another sense, to which he had advanced)' (XLII; p. 351).

In his final self-imposed exile, Henchard carries with him mementoes of Elizabeth-Jane: 'gloves, shoes, a scrap of her handwriting, . . . a curl of her hair' (XLIV; p. 366: ellipsis mine). Retracing his past, he has chosen to burden himself with reminders of womanhood, and to plot his journey in relation to a female centre. Even the circle he traces around the 'centripetal influence' (XLIV; p. 368) of his stepdaughter contrasts with the defended squareness of the Casterbridge he has left behind, the straight grain of masculine direction. Henchard's final pilgrimage, to Elizabeth-Jane's wedding, is, detail by detail, a reliving of the journey made by the women at the beginning of the novel. He enters the town for the last time as they entered at the first: the poor relation, the suppliant, the outsider. 'As a Samson shorn' (XLIV; p. 373) he timidly presents himself at the kitchen-door, and from the empty back-parlour awaits Elizabeth-Jane's arrival. As Susan and Elizabeth-Jane watched him preside over the meeting of the Council, so he now must watch his stepdaughter preside over her wedding-party. As Susan was overpowered by the sight of her former husband's glory, and wished only 'to go — pass away — die' (V; p. 37), so is Henchard shamed and overwhelmed by Elizabeth-Jane's moral ascendancy. What is threatened and forgotten in the first instance comes to pass in the second — the rejected guest departs, and neither Elizabeth-Jane nor the reader sees him more.

In a sense which Hardy fully allows, the moral as well as the temporal victory of the novel is Elizabeth-Jane's. It is she to whom the concluding paragraphs are given, with their message of domestic serenity, their Victorian feminine wisdom of 'making limited opportunities endurable', albeit in 'a general drama of pain' (XLV; p. 386). Casterbridge, under the combined leadership of Elizabeth-Jane and Farfrae, is a gentled community, its old rough ways made civil, its rough edges softened. We might read the story of Henchard as a tragic taming of the heroic will, the bending and breaking of his savage male defiance in contest with a stoic female endurance. In such a reading, Henchard becomes a second Heathcliff, who is also overcome by the domestic power of a daughter-figure; like Heathcliff, Henchard is subdued first to the placidities of the grange, then to the grave.[20]

Yet this romantic and nostalgic reading would underestimate Hardy's generosity of imagination. Virginia Woolf, one of Hardy's earliest feminist critics, attributed the 'tragic power' of his characters to 'a force within them which cannot be defined, a force of love or of hate, a force which in the men is the cause of rebellion against life, and in the women implies an illimitable capacity for suffering'.[21] In Henchard the forces of male rebellion and female suffering ultimately conjoin; and in this unmanning Hardy achieves a tragic power unequalled in Victorian fiction. It may indeed be true that Hardy could not be accounted a feminist in the political terms of the 1880s, or the 1970s; but in *The Mayor of Casterbridge* the feminist critic can see Hardy's swerving from the bluff virility of the Rabelais Club, and the misogyny of Gosse, towards his own insistent and original exploration of human motivation. The skills which Henchard struggles finally to learn, skills of observation, attention, sensitivity, and compassion, are also those of the novelist; and they are feminine perhaps, if one contrasts them to the skills of the architect or the statesman. But it is because Hardy dares so fully to acknowledge this side of his own art, to pursue the feminine spirit in his man of character, that his hero, like the great heroines he would create in the 1890s, is more Shakespearean than Victorian.

NOTES

1. Letter of February 1874, given in Richard Little Purdy, *Thomas Hardy: A Bibliographical Study* (London: Oxford University Press, 1954) p. 338.
2. Havelock Ellis, 'Thomas Hardy's Novels', *Westminster Review*, LXIII n.s. (1883) 334.
3. See Florence Emily Hardy, *The Later Years of Thomas Hardy, 1892–1928* (London and New York: Macmillan, 1930) p. 5.
4. Mary Jacobus, 'Sue the Obscure', *EIC*, XXV (1975) 304–28; and 'Tess's Purity', *EIC, XXVI (1976) 318–38.*
5. For Hardy's personal need to have a 'literary lady — not his wife — whom he could mastermind, and who would appreciate him in return', see Robert Gittings, *The Older Hardy* (London: Heinemann; Boston: Little, Brown, 1978) pp. 77–81. Hardy had recommended Mona Caird's essay on 'The Evolution of Marriage' (eventually published in her *The Morality of Marriage* [1897]) to the *Contemporary Review* in 1890; he wrote to Florence Henniker about Sarah Grand's best-selling feminist novel, *The Heavenly Twins* (1893).
6. Edmund Gosse, 'Thomas Hardy', *The Speaker*, II (1890) 295. Gosse attributed this unpopularity to Hardy's unconventional conception of feminine character.
7. Letter of 31 December 1891, in *The Collected Letters of Thomas Hardy*, Vol. I: *1840–1892*, ed. Richard Little Purdy and Michael Millgate (Oxford: Clarendon Press, 1978) 250.
8. Letter to Edmund Gosse, 20 January 1892, in *Collected Letters*, I, 255.
9. Letter to Hardy of 19 January 1892, in Evan Charteris, *The Life and Letters of Sir Edmund Gosse* (London: Heinemann, 1931) pp. 225–6.
10. Letter to Alice Grenfell, 23 April 1892, in *Collected Letters*, I, 266.
11. Letter of November 1906, in the Fawcett Library (London); quoted in Elaine Showalter, *A Literature of Their Own: British Women Novelists from Brontë to Lessing* (Princeton: Princeton University Press, 1977) p. 185.

12. A. O. J. Cockshut, *Man and Woman: A Study of Love and the Novel 1740–1940* (London: Collins, 1977; New York: Oxford University Press, 1978) pp. 128–9.

13. See Christine Winfield, 'Factual Sources of Two Episodes in *The Mayor of Casterbridge*', *NCF*, XXV (1970), 224–31.

14. Irving Howe, *Thomas Hardy* (London: Weidenfeld & Nicolson, 1968; New York: Macmillan, 1967) p. 84.

15. Quoted by Winfield, p. 226.

16. Charles K. Hofling, 'Thomas Hardy and the Mayor of Casterbridge', *Comprehensive Psychiatry*, IX (1968) 431.

17. J. Hillis Miller, *Thomas Hardy: Distance and Desire* (London: Oxford University Press; Cambridge, Mass.: Harvard University Press, 1970) pp. 147, 148.

18. For a discussion of the homosexual implications of the relationship, see Dale Kramer, *Thomas Hardy: The Forms of Tragedy* (London: Macmillan; Detroit: Wayne State University Press, 1975) pp. 86–87. Kramer concludes that 'to stress the potentially sensational aspect of Henchard's character in this manner is to misunderstand seriously the reasons for the success of the novel as tragedy.'

19. Kramer, p. 87.

20. Frederick R. Karl has suggested that Henchard's domination of the novel is equivalent to the 'all-powerful Heathcliff' in *Wuthering Heights*; 'The Mayor of Casterbridge: A New Fiction Defined', *MFS*, VI (1960) 211.

21. Virginia Woolf, 'The Novels of Thomas Hardy', *The Common Reader*, Second Series (London: The Hogarth Press, 1932) p. 253.

III LITERATURE AND THE MEDIA

Marshall McLuhan's axiom, 'The medium is the message', has become almost a household phrase, but its implications are not always clearly realized. This section opens with a brief discussion of its meaning and implications, and then goes on to examine the view that television is essentially a dramatic medium.

In the second chapter, Ellis briefly treats some of the problems of translating literary works into film and television. This is followed by Simpson's sparkling case-study of the BBC's production of Malcolm Bradbury's *The History Man*, a fine cutting-edge to illustrate some of the issues involved in adaptation. Of course, television does not confine itself to high-status literature. David Lusted looks at *Grange Hill* both as school fiction and as a television event.

Beja shifts the focus to the relationships between film and literature. David Lodge then analyses some of the different strengths and different experiences film and drama offer as different media, while in the last chapter in this section, Drakakis is concerned with the relationship between radio and theoretical productions of some of Shakespeare's plays.

15 *The Medium and the Messages*

● Martin Esslin

Of the attempts made to evaluate the impact of television from the broadest possible point of view, none has been more daring and intriguing than that undertaken by the late Canadian critic and media scholar Marshall McLuhan, whose pronouncements are usually encapsulated in the slogan from his book *Understanding Media*: 'The medium is the message'.

What does this axiom mean? Essentially this: television and radio have brought about a fundamental change in the way we perceive the world; they have extended the range of our sensual apparatus by enabling us to see and hear things happening at the other end of the world. Whereas most of the information we received hitherto came to us via the printed page, in words and still pictures, we now hear our leaders discuss their political agenda and see their faces while they do so. Listening to a speech in the presence of the orator gives us a completely different feeling than does a solitary reading of the same text, when we are locked into our own private consciousness. In the spiral of historic development, McLuhan says, we have returned — on a different and higher level — to a situation similar to that of tribal societies whose members could all congregate in the centre of the village to listen to their leaders, priests or shamans. In that respect we are now members of what he calls the 'global village'. The age of civilization based on reading, on a written literature, is over. In our new era of oral communication, the linear, discursive mode of thought is going to be replaced, McLuhan maintains, by a primarily image-oriented type of perception and thinking.

Undoubtedly this is an insight of the utmost importance. At the same time it is sweepingly overstated in the understandable excitement of its author's prophetic fervor and, because it is so generalized, is too lofty to have had a practical impact on our everyday attitudes and practices. Hence, nothing seems to have been done to translate this important insight into any kind of concrete social action. The medium is indeed the message, but only in the widest possible sense, on a long-term secular time scale, from the perspective of a historian whose eye spans the millennia. The coming of television *has* deeply changed a culture based on the concentrated, solitary, attentive habit of reading and has largely replaced it with a new way of perceiving reality, a new mode of thought — more relaxed, diffuse, multidimensional, and immediate. This change in the structure of human perception and modes of thought will lead to fundamentally different attitudes toward the world, society, and culture. An understanding of this development on its long-term, macroscopic scale is essential. But by implying that the innumerable subsidiary influences, the multiple localized messages carried by the medium — the news, the stories of daytime serials, the product information in the commericals — are of negligible importance compared to the 'basic,' universal message, McLuhan discourages further thought about how to deal with the effects of television on a more mundane level.

An awareness of McLuhan's insight must underlie all attempts to adjust our ways of thinking, our institutions, and our social habits to the television age. But just as our awareness that the telephone has radically affected our lives does not diminish the importance of the details of a particular telephone call — a change in the arrival time of an expected visitor, for instance — it is not sufficient simply to accept the credo 'The medium is the message' and ignore the innumerable other 'messages' that are carried by television.

In the operation of any communications medium there is always a hierarchy of message conveyors. For example, in telegraphy there is the wire or wavelength, the Morse code (or some other code that might be used), the language in which the message is conveyed, and only then the explicit meaning of the message. On top of that, there are still a multitude of implicit messages, including the symbolic meaning and the emotional impact of the communication.

The hierarchy of messages and message conveyors in television requires a similar sort of analysis. At one end is TV's most generalized aspect, the nature of the process of communication itself. That is the end of the spectrum McLuhan is concerned with. For him the main message is: time and space have been abolished; we can all be present at the same event; our eyes and ears have immensely increased their powers; we have to see the world differently — think in a new way! At the other end we have the specific data imparted at the level of, say, a news report or commercial — an announcement that a certain make of car is now available at reduced prices. But between the most general and the most particular messages and message conveyors is an intermediate level of communication of the utmost importance, namely the 'language' in which the message is conveyed (the word *language* here is used in the vocabulary of modern linguistics, in its sense of *langue* as opposed to *parole*) — more precisely, the nature, structure, and grammar of that language.

THE LANGUAGE OF TELEVISION

It is my contention that we can gain considerable insight into the nature of the television medium, and a better understanding of its operation, if we recognize that the 'language' in question is in fact one that has a tradition as old as civilization itself; that a great deal of thought has already been invested in the unraveling of the intricacies of its grammar and syntax; that we already possess something like a valid terminology and tested critical strategies to approach it, as well as effective tools to analyze its psychology and impact. It is, in fact, my contention that the language of television is none other than that of *drama*; that television — as indeed the cinema, with which it has much in common — is, in its essence, a *dramatic medium*; and that looking at TV from the point of view and with the analytical tools of dramatic criticism and theory might contribute to a better understanding of its nature and many aspects of its psychological, social, and cultural impact, both in the short term and on a long-term, macroscopic time scale.

On the most obvious level television is a dramatic medium simply because a large proportion of the material it transmits is in the form of traditional drama, consisting of fictional material mimetically represented by actors and employing plot, dialogue, character, gesture, costume — the whole panoply of dramatic means of expression. According to one of the leading statistical summaries of the television market in the United States, *The Media Book*, no less than 59 per cent of the average American adult male's viewing time in 1976–77 was devoted to material in explicitly dramatic form — serials, movies and prime-time network shows. The corresponding figure for the average American female was even higher: at least 63 per cent of the time she spent watching television was devoted to shows in explicitly dramatic form. According to the 1980 edition of *The Media Book*, in the spring of 1979 American men on the average watched television for over 21 hours each week, while the average American woman's viewing time reached just over 25 hours a week. The time devoted by the average American adult male to watching dramatic material on television thus amounts to over 12 hours per week, while the average American woman sees almost 16 hours of drama on television each week. That means that the average American adult sees the equivalent of *five to six full-length stage plays a week!*

A hundred years ago even the most assiduous theatregoer would not have seen more than one play a week over a given year, and only a small proportion of the population of the Western world lived in cities that had permanent theatres. Most people lived in areas visited only sporadically, if at all, by touring companies and thus hardly ever saw a play. Today the average American is exposed to as much drama *in a week* as the most zealous theatre buff of the past century would have seen in several months!

The sheer volume of material broadcast in explicitly and traditionally dramatic form is in itself sufficient to establish television as a dramatic medium. But that, to me, is only the most obvious and superficial aspect of the matter. It is my contention that whatever else it might present to its viewers, television as such displays the basic characteristics of the dramatic mode of communication — and *thought*, for drama is also a method of thinking, of experiencing the world and reasoning about it. After all, much of our thinking consists in devising scenarios for different situations and decisions — which is using drama as a form of thought.

But, one might object, drama is fiction, and much that is seen on television is real — the transmission of actual events. Well, yes and no. The dividing line between reality and art, between nature and its artistic representation, has ever been a tenuous one. When in 1917 the French avant-garde painter Marcel Duchamp submitted a urinal to be displayed in an art exhibition in New York, he drew attention to a phenomenon of basic importance: once an object, man-made or natural, is taken out of its ordinary context and put onto a pedestal or into a frame, it is made to say, 'Look at me; I am here to be observed!' and immediately that object acquires some characteristics of a work of art. In its new context the urinal is seen as a form, a three-dimensional shape rather than as an object of daily use. Its significance is transformed by the act of showing it off.

The function of the stage in the theatre is analogous to that of the pedestal or the frame in an art museum. If a cat walks onto the stage by accident during a performance, it automatically becomes a performer and will be perceived by the audience as having some sort of significance in the play — it may get laughs or even applause — for anything that appears on a stage proclaims that it is on display, meant to be seen, meant to fill some role or have some function within a fictional context. An ordinary chair on a stage, used in a performance of *Hamlet*, becomes an object of fiction; it plays the part of a chair in medieval, fictional Elsinore. In the same manner the man who plays Hamlet becomes the fictional prince of medieval Denmark while also remaining his real self and being observed and admired by the audience as himself, the star. And, likewise, the newscaster who reads the evening news becomes, simply by appearing in the framed square of the television screen, a performer on a stage, an actor.

The TV screen is both a frame, like Duchamp's pedestal, and a stage. Even when the news an announcer reads has been forgotten, the character he creates, his TV personality, will remain in the viewer's memory. The news changes from night to night, but the character of the newscaster persists in the public eye and the public imagination.

The information the newscaster transmits would appear to be the least fictional, least dramatized element on television, and yet most events that can be reported on the news are to some degree *staged*. Whatever reality they possess, in the sense that they actually happened, is most likely to have been filtered through various stages of a process of presentation. Moreover, the version of such events that an audience views on TV news is rarely transmitted live; it is first selectively framed, then filmed or videotaped, and finally edited in a manner that tends once more to emphasize the event's dramatic qualities. Similar considerations apply to other 'real' events broadcast on television. The politician's speech and the interview or press conference with a public figure are also, inevitably, framed, stage-managed, and manipulated The face of the great man or woman has been made up, the background chosen or designed, the clothes carefully selected, and what is televised will have been either edited on film or videotape or, if live, dramatically structured by the use of close-ups, long-shots and reaction shots of the guest and interviewers. The final result is a dramatic performance, which moreover, filmed or videotaped, is infinitely repeatable.

This *repeatability* is a no less fundamental aspect of the theatre — and all drama. Real events happen only once and are irreversible and unrepeatable; drama looks like a real event but can be repeated at will. Plays can have long runs or can be revived from a script. As most of television is recorded, most things seen on TV can be rerun. By the time a news event has been taped, edited and shown several times, it has acquired the characteristics of a dramatic performance: it has become a dramatic artifact. Thus even the relatively rare unrehearsed events captured on TV turn into drama. Consider the televised murder of Lee Harvey Oswald by Jack Ruby. Cameras had been put into position to observe an expected event, the transfer of Oswald from police headquarters in Dallas to the Dallas County Jail. But an unexpected event occurred. The confusion on the screen at the instant when Jack Ruby fired point-blank into Oswald's abdomen, and the fact that the TV viewer could hardly make out what was happening, is a memorable demonstration of the importance of planning and stage management in the filming of news events. Because Oswald's shooting was unforeseen, it was filmed out of focus and was hardly discernable. Nevertheless, the moment it had been recorded, the event became endlessly repeatable and now, when viewed again, can be regarded as a piece of high drama — albeit poorly produced, because unplanned.

The great event that *can* be prepared for becomes a full-scale dramatic production. The first landing of a man on the moon — one of the most spectacular of human events — was thus meticulously stage-managed for television. Cameras were installed in a manner designed to provide the best and most dramatic pictures, and the event itself unfolded in a sequence of preliminaries, explanations and emotion-charged commentaries building to a cleverly calculated, super-dramatic climax to a grand performance when the chief astronaut, the star of the play, spoke his carefully prepared text. The framing of everything that is seen on television and the repeatability of most of its material inevitably turn all of television into a 'show'. It is no wonder that the medium is perceived overwhelmingly as an instrument of entertainment and a purveyor of fiction.

16 *The Literary Adaptation*

● John Ellis

About 30 per cent of narrative films made in Hollywood's classic period were adapted from novels and short stories. Popular literature was the principal source, the novels of James M. Cain or Olive Higgins Prouty, the short stories in the *Saturday Evening Post* or *Ladies' Home Journal*. Culturally respectable sources were rather more rare. The opposite is the case with British television. It specialises in adapting the culturally accredited nineteenth-century novel for the twentieth-century world television market. In each case the actual processes of adaptation are remarkably similar; the reasons are rather less so. Hollywood was principally interested in the tried and tested, narratives that had already been polished and presented to an audience before conversion into a film. British television prefers the tried and trusted, novels which guarantee a substantial audience at home and abroad, drawn by the cultural circulation of an idea of 'Dickens' or 'Waugh'.

In each case, it is not the novel that is adapted, it is the illusion of reality that the novel claims to produce. Adaptation is a process of reducing a pre-existent piece of writing to a series of functions: characters, locations, costumes, actions and strings of narrative events. Adaptation for cinema assumes a concentration of narratives into a short length whereas television adaptation thrives on the multiplication of incidents that characterises the classic novel. Yet in each case the assumed aim of the process of adaptation is the same, to reproduce the contents of the novel on the screen. Hence the habitual reaction of conventional criticism to a literary adaptation: a judgement as to whether the adaptation has kept faith with the novel. The whole marketing strategy of adaptations from literary classics or from 'bestsellers' encourages such an assessment.

The real aim of an adaptation is rather different. The adaptation trades upon the memory of the novel, a memory that can derive from actual reading, or, as is more likely with a classic of literature, a generally circulated cultural memory. The adaptation consumes this memory, aiming to efface it with the presence of its own images. The successful adaptation is one that is able to replace the memory of the novel with the process of a filmic or televisual representation. Thus Malcolm Bradbury's response to the adaptation of his character Howard Kirk, confessed to Phillip Simpson: Bradbury has forgotten his own image of Kirk in favour of the figure of Anthony Sher playing the part for television. The adaptation has repeated even Bradbury's own conception and memory of the character, and in doing so has effaced it. The faithfulness of the adaptation is the degree to which it can rework and replace a memory. This process is always likely to fail to some degree, as the generation of a memory from a reading of a text will involve associations of a contingent and personal nature as well as more culturally pervasive ones.

The form of the narrative novel resists re-reading in our culture: the vast majority of novels are designed to be read once and once only, just as the narrative film is intelligible at one viewing. Re-reading or re-viewing the same text always threatens to disappoint: the process of production of the illusion becomes too obvious, the memory interferes. Adaptation into another medium becomes a means of prolonging the pleasure of the original representation, and repeating the production of a memory. The process of adaptation should thus be seen as a massive investment (financial and psychic) in the desire to repeat particular acts of consumption within a form of representation that discourages such a repetition. From this point of view there is no difference between the filming of a pre-existent novel or the novelisation of a pre-existent film. Certainly the effects upon the institution of book publishing are remarkably similar: television transmission develops sales of Waugh's *Brideshead Revisited* as a mass paperback just as it does of Wilfred Greatorix's spin-off novel from his TV series, *Airline*.

However, the mass paperback market is not the only cultural institution to be interested in the adaptation. Education seizes upon the adaptation from the literary classic to serve rather more dubious ends. Showing recalcitrant students the film or the television serial is regarded as a way to encourage them to read the original novel. In its most extreme form this approach would regard the adaptation as transmitting the values of the original: such was the attitude to David Lean's films of Dickens in some areas of British secondary education. Nowadays, the literary adaptation is taken up in American education as a serious question because it combines elements of a general education with an induction into middle-brow culture for a conveniently large group of students. As Morris Beja writes to introduce his *Film and Literature* (Longmans, 1979):

> The focus is neither on film nor on written literature, but on understanding and appreciating each form on its own and in relation to the other. The premise behind the entire book — like that of most of the courses for which it is intended — is that there is a great value in looking at the two genres [sic] together; such a pairing enables us to get a sense of all

that they share, to be sure, but also of all the traits that they do not, so that one may grasp as well what is unique about each form . . . At such times the 'book addict' or the 'movie fan' — either one a fine thing to be — becomes as well a student of literature, or of film, or of both. Surely at least as fine a thing to be.

Such an approach elides the institutional differences between the novelistic, the cinematic and the televisual every bit as much as it elides the different historical moments into which novel and adaptation are produced and consumed.

17   *'Presentness Precise': Notes on* The History Man

● Phillip Simpson

The television adaptation of a novel about university life led to that
flurry of letters to newspapers, quotation on other television shows,
interviews and photo-articles which are the signs in British public life of
a media event. This reaction was evoked by the adaptation of Malcolm
Bradbury's *The History Man* into a four-part television serial. When it
appeared in 1975 the novel had received excellent reviews from the
critics but none of the public notice accorded to the serial. To say why
the adaptation was so popular with viewing figures rising for each
episode, and why the media took it up, would demand some analysis of
the way both texts were distributed, the cultural and political climate
into which they were inserted, the nature of the response, and the
hundred and one other elements which add up to conjunctural analysis.
In the meantime, I would like to make some speculative points in an effort
to see what happens when a cultural product is 'adapted' from one
medium to another: how the two *kinds* of texts operate differently; how
these two *particular* texts operate; and how the writer of the novel, the
director of the television version[1] and the mainstream critics saw the
adaptation process.

The first and most obvious point is that both book and tele-adaptation
need to be seen within the context of expectations set up by the
conventions they inhabit — the campus novel and the BBC serialisation.
Like his two previous novels[2], Bradbury's *The History Man* provides a
university setting to explore the politics of academic life, the
conventional assumption being that universities are locations where
theories of value, held values and actions immanent with value interact
in laboratory-like conditions: one moment characters pronounce about
morals or politics, the next they act accordingly — or not. Campus
novels rely upon a readership alert to the fact that the titles of both
Howard Kirk, the History Man's, first book, *The Coming of the New Sex*
and his doctoral thesis, *Christadelphianism in Wakefield*, are perfectly

feasible yet, at the same time, satirical thrusts at fashion-mongering in sociology. Comic novels like Kingsley Amis's *Lucky Jim* (1954) or David Lodge's *Changing Places* (1978) suggest the persistence of the comic campus novel, but less amusing writers within the convention include Snow, Powell, Malamud and McCarthy.

Unlike these novels, however, and unlike Bradbury's first two books, *The History Man* has some of the features of the modernist novel. It is not aleatory or heavily self-reflexive but the text does draw attention to itself and organises its narrative in ways which any adaptation would have to come to terms with. Instead of painterly or photographic realism of the conventional novel, tesserae of details are built into a mosaic: Bradbury says he used current Biba catalogues and copies of the *Guardian* 'to keep its presentness precise' and the book often employs synecdochal lists of goods or guests or activities to stand for a greater whole. The author himself appears in the book[3] as:

> a lecturer in the English department, a man who, ten years earlier, had produced two tolerably well-known and acceptably reviewed novels, filled, as novels then were, with moral scruple and concern.[4]

Characters in *The History Man* are presented allusively rather than through the detailed description of appearance or motivation which are the typical strategies of the nineteenth-century realist novel. Behaviour is described very carefully, but no evaluation is conducted through a moralising discourse of the narrator; rather, ironic juxtapositions of event or detail pose moral or political questions about the major characters. Howard Kirk's work-in-progress, *The Defeat of Privacy*, argues that 'the attempt to privatise life is a phenomenon of narrow historical significance' but he tells the student reading the manuscript 'You'd no business to do that . . . It's private.'[5] Professor Marvin chooses to go to Edinburgh to lecture on messianism rather than act as host to the controversial Professor Mangel. Indeed, the satiric tone of the novel and the fact that so much of its action is discussed or reported by the characters themselves have the effect of creating not a model of 'everyday' society but an obliquely-related universe of obsessives like that of Ben Jonson's plays. With the telling exception of Barbara Kirk, we learn little directly about the psychic states of the characters, and so it becomes difficult to locate that narrative discourse which might provide the reader with an assigned, unitary position from which a consistent reading of the novel can be constructed or an uncontradictory knowledge of political meaning of the text produced. It is actually very difficult to predict or declare what the final outcome of the novel is. Great care is taken to deny the reader a sympathetic figure with whom she or he can identify, and it is only after a number of readings that I have come to see Barbara Kirk as the central figure because her pain is much more than liberal 'angst'.

But the latter is a conclusion one has to work towards, it is not the dominant discourse of the novel. Rather, the novel provides two perspectives on the happenings within it, perspectives which the characters explicitly acknowledge. As the man of history, Howard Kirk judges or rationalises his behaviour from a political standpoint, whereas all the other major characters act, or often fail to act, from a moral one. Because this is a satirical novel, it is pointless to expect that either perspective will be presented with any complexity and Howard's vicious energy is seen as no more culpable than Henry Beamish's ineffectual tolerance. The two perspectives are reworked in minor ways throughout: Kirk's Marxism explains as much about Henry's behaviour as Flora Beniform's Freudianism; accident as an explanation is set against inevitability, and the novel speculates continually about plot and contingency. All these equivocations imply the pluralism which informs the narrative and value systems of the book, down to the ambiguity of its ostensible ending: 'there is a lot that is, indeed, happening, and all the people are fully occupied.'[6] One could argue that pluralism is the position of intelligibility constructed by the discourses of the novel, but the pluralist position is, if the word means anything, a contradictory one.

I got excited by the radicalism of the period up to about 1970, and then I got tired or sceptical or doubtful, and the book acquired increasing irony. And the irony was depressing to live with; the irony enriched the book but it left me in a position where I didn't know where my values were. It's a book by a writer whose values are in disarray.

Malcolm Bradbury

Aspects of narrative and character, then, indicate the modernist tendency in Bradbury's fiction, and his treatment of time is another feature marking The History Man off from the conventional campus novel and presenting problems for its adaptation. Except for two important chapters the novel is presented in a tense which Bradbury calls the 'historical present'. The effect of this is to make events seem more immediate to our perception, inviting comparison with the experience of watching a film (although the absolute and substantial differences between verbal and visual images are such that the iconicity of photographic images and the 'photo-effect' sense of objects or people being present and absent at the same time point to the crucial differences between the media[7]). The book's present is fixed precisely between Saturday October 7 and Friday December 15. Events on both days are located historically ('McGovern campaigns ineffectually against Nixon'[8]) but the present tense over-rides the date which is, significantly, given great prominence in the tele-adaptation — '1972'. This temporal ambiguity seems to be an attempt 'to collapse discourse into history, and to naturalise events so that they seem to exist in a space defined from nowhere' as Geoffrey Nowell-Smith says, in arguing that certain novels from Flaubert onwards have been characterisable by such attempts, even when the effect has been the reverse.[9]

I'm not sure the television programme could have been made self-reflexive in the way the book is. The self-consciousness of the novel is self-consciousness about being a novel. How do you get that over into television?

Malcolm Bradbury

Having argued that *The History Man* deviates from the more conventional campus genre, I want to examine how the modernist properties mentioned were accommodated by one of television's more conservative slots, that of the classic serial. Here the dominant convention is that famous novels by long-dead writers are 'faithfully' translated to the screen, and then given extensive critical attention and consequent world sales: a prestige exercise. The critics' reception of the tele-adaptation of *The History Man* certainly seemed to perceive it as such a venture, and the serial's position in the schedules reinforced this view: it appeared in the standard four parts on Sunday night opposite crypto-religious documentaries and Melvyn Bragg's arts magazine, *The South Bank Show*. The classic serial slot encouraged the newspaper columnists to take the adaptation 'literally' — as a hatchet-job on radical academics. (Critics from the left often repeated the argument in aggrieved terms, as the serial coincided with unprecedented cuts in central government funding to the universities.) Even the moribund current affairs programme *Newsnight* managed to join in with an item which linked the adaptation to the sacking of a little-known academic and an obscure debate about literature then taking place in a British university. The response so ignored the modernist properties of the novel as to suggest their absence within the tele-adaptation. But I would argue that this is true only to a limited extent. The critics were able to read the adaptation as a transposition into the form of the classic serial only by ignoring or rejecting some aspects of the programmes themselves.

I was aware of how easy it was for the Right wing to grab it and say, 'At last, somebody is putting down the Left!' And I tried to spike their guns insofar as I could. But it is a slightly rightist view, and it may be that Malcolm is trying to have it both ways when he argues that Howard is not just dangerous, but actually does things.

Robert Knights

The adaptation does indeed dispense with some of the novel's strategies. From the first images, it deliberately rejects the ambiguity about time and tense in the novel. The opening credits exactly capture a moment in the past where political, sexual and domestic changes all seemed possible: a sub-Lichtenstein montage of images show a fist clenched in salute which suddenly holds a corkscrew. The screwing provokes tears, and women are shown as victims and observers; red wine flows and late '60s guitar chords echo: an image for George Melly's epithet about the period — 'Revolt into Style'. Sustained behind the ironic disclaimer about the University of Watermouth, the date 1972 is given great prominence. The images and sounds also signify a break with the conventional opening of the classic adaptation. Compare them, for instance, with the discreet titles and 'Nunc dimittis' opening of another less naturalistic adaption, *Tinker, Tailor, Soldier, Spy*, or the Burgon-baroque overture for that varsity serial, *Brideshead Revisited*.

Though the break is only from Art to Pop-Art, this evocation of a past time is important and is sustained. The adaptation's director, Robert Knights, also made some episodes of *The Glittering Prizes* whose period was earlier, and more evident; but the costumes budget was just as much for *The History Man*. Knights was also responsible for the use of music within the serial — Rolling Stones and sitar to suggest the late '60s, Kirk's formative years, and Mozart's *Don Giovanni* to indicate sexual pursuit. Conversely, Bradbury's novel contains no mention of specific music, a lack of period reference typical of its equivocal treatment of time.

I hoped that when *The History Man* came out it would make a number of people think: 'My god, it can only be eight years ago, and it looks like light years away. It feels like a real period piece.' I wanted people to have the feeling that even so short a time ago we had that strong clear sense that got lost in the '70s, of fun and things being able to be changed. We suddenly realised we weren't able to change things by ourselves.

Robert Knights

In comparing novel and tele-adaptation, the critics usually ignored their different dealings with time. If, after almost ten years in the writing, the novel's publication in 1975 was a bit late for an anatomy of the counter-culture, the 1981 serial took a different tack. Its deliberate periodicisation was intended to show how the optimism about social change which inaugurated one decade seemed naive at the beginning of the next. Not, in itself, a particularly radical theme, but nevertheless ignored resolutely by both critics and viewers, who managed to appropriate both texts into an exposé of *contemporary* British universities.

In this they may have been assisted by the serial's exclusion of the two chapters in the novel written in the conventional past tense. These deal with the Kirks' emergence as bright, hard-working grammar-school pupils from a working-class background who are politicised by their personal experiences with 1968, '*the* year when self-revolutions like the Kirks' turned into a public matter'. Dropping these chapters disturbs the balance, for Barbara Kirk is never seen in the adaptation as Howard's rival and equal whose self-revolution peters out into domestic responsibilities and escapist affairs while he finds a public political stage. Paradoxically, these chapters were omitted because Knights wanted to break with the convention beloved in British drama whereby a character's past has to be brought to the attention of the viewer either through arty flashback or a 'meaningful' conversation about the past. Classic Hollywood avoided these devices and provided a functional past for characters through gesture and telling detail. The adaptation tries this through the Kirks' accents and Howard's occasional gestures, but, generally, the dropping of the chapters from the past produces a History Man without a history.

> By the time (the television adaptation) appeared in 1981, instead of being a needling critique of what exists, it is a satirical attack on what has already passed — and therefore can be misused by people who want to take it over from the Right, in order to turn it into an attack on sociology, universities, radicalism, in ways I deeply resented and disapproved of. If I'd known where 1981 was leading I might have doubted whether it should be turned into a television series.
>
> Malcolm Bradbury

One of Knights' counter-conventional strategies did cut across the consensus which greeted the serial. Malcolm Bradbury remains doubtful about it, and the *Spectator's* critic called it pornographic. In the novel sexual encounters serve as an extension of the interrogative mode that dominates personal relationships; our attention is kept on the verbal exchanges because of their narrative importance, though we are kept aware of what else is going on. The differences between the encounters are signalled more by the questions asked and answered than by the kind of sex taking place. By contrast, the adaptation emphasised the sex in the sex scenes. The variousness of the sexual relations is foregrounded to develop the women characters: Barbara is shown as passive and uninvolved with Howard; Felicity Phee, his student, is presented as subservient, comic and absurd; and his colleague Flora Beniform offers a cool and elegant matter of factness, the mood of which is caught by the David Hockney tones and compositions cued in by the print on her wall. The final encounter, with English lecturer Annie Callender, has the protagonists adopting the postures of *Last Tango in Paris*, as Howard Kirk's poster reminds us. In some of these scenes the characters are naked.

Knights deliberately went against the convention, no longer operated in cinema, that intercourse should not be indicated but implied, with the discreet fade and careful angle used if possible. *The History Man's* use of (non-genital) nudity, and the actors' miming of sexual processes like rhythmic penetration and fellatio, underscored '1972' as an era of experiment and explicitness in sexual matters, one in which the 'personal' was indeed regarded as 'political', and inseparable from other social activities. When Flora Beniform resumes her glasses and notebook but not her clothes, the effect is a bit like that of Manet's *Dejeuner sur l'herbe*; the sensational nature of nudity on television is superseded by the sense that a number of meanings are in play and that the picture is more than the spectacle. Eventually, the blood will stop rushing in (male?) ears (the auditory metaphor is Knights') and the sense of hearing will return.

> TV critics still tend to review after one episode; they wouldn't do it on the basis of, say, a quarter of *Apocalypse Now*. I moved from a light comedy into a bleaker, harsher, crueller story at the end. I was conscious of doing that over four hours.
>
> Robert Knights

But did it work that way? Most of the reviewers treated these scenes without any reference to their context or to the other social changes implied in the adaptation. Reputedly, some scenes from the BBC's *Sons and Lovers* adaptation which followed soon after *The History Man* row were cut as a result, and the latter programme was not reshown, despite its popularity, in the period when the BBC's licence was under review. Certainly the then *New Statesman* critic, Julian Barnes, seemed to believe that sex on television makes you deaf.

> I don't imagine I was the only viewer who found that when (the producer's) high class artistes were grinding their breasts into that nasty little moustachioed mush, it became quite hard to concentrate on the accompanying dialogue.[10]

If it worked like this for the *New Statesman*'s Naked Ape, it seems likely that the attempt to defuse the erotic spectacle through the contrast of encounters and their deliberate placing within the concerns of the serial was a miscalculation.

As I have already suggested, the elusive narrative structure of the novel was likely to cause difficulties for a television adaptation. Page of dialogue follows page of dialogue because what matters is less what is done than the characters' self-conscious analysis of it. ('You're a kind of self-made fictional character who's got the whole story on his side just because he happens to be writing it.') And it is through these discussions that the balance between the two world views at issue is attempted and the dominant discourse of pluralism maintained. But unlike novels, television narratives serialised over several episodes tend to subordinate such elements to narrative action or enigmas. (In Barthesian terms, the differences between novel and tele-adaptation are most marked when we see how much emphasis the latter places on hermeneutic and proairetic elements.)

There is the great thing about inheriting from the previous show until one's got the public from reviews or word of mouth. The audiences went up and up for *The History Man*.

Robert Knights

Two features of the adaptation support this contention. A series of narrative riddles centres on Carmody, the anti-Kirk student, Professor Mangel, the geneticist whose visit to the University is engineered by Howard Kirk to provoke confrontation, and Barbara Kirk. None of the events is unfolded in a tantalising way in the novel, but in the adaptation we see a Renault mysteriously following Howard's movements; a figure we know to be Mangel out jogging, at home and at work in a laboratory; and Barbara doggedly studying commercial French in order to read Simone de Beauvoir. We anticipate, correctly, that these enigmas will be resolved in the final episode, and two of them are brought together in an event which is entirely a contribution of the adaptation: after Carmody attempts to blackmail Kirk by filming his sexual activities from the mysterious Renault, Kirk negotiates a deal which results in the student's expulsion from Watermouth in exchange for an invitation to Mangel to lecture there. The two meet at the railway station, where Professor Mangel, in avoiding the awkward Carmody's luggage trolley, suffers a fatal heart attack. An accident or the conjunction of two inevitable histories?

Barbara's enigma has a double function. The shots of her alone are unreadable initially, though we are sure that their meaning will emerge and their enigma be resolved, and it is this concern that pulls us through the narrative, as it were, until the final episode. At the same time, because the chapters dealing with the Kirks' earlier life have been dropped, these shots are meant to recover some of the psychological intensity with which she and her tragedy are invested in the novel. In my view, they fail to do this and that failure is a loss attributable more to the demands of television serialisation than to simple misjudgement on the adaptor's or director's part.

The second feature tells us something of the nature of the proairetic or 'action' code in relation to television. In the second episode, Annie Callender says to Howard, 'You're very interesting characters, but I haven't discovered the plot.' I do not think television viewers would have noticed this lack of plot which the novel correctly draws attention to because of the way our view is focused on Howard as constantly in action, literally plotting. We see him from high angles crossing the campus directly, with only the slightest of deviations; we see him prepare, with swiftness and economy of movement, for the party; we see him at the centre of small groups; and, when scenes are changed through the unusual (for TV) use of wipes, it is usually Howard who is driving or pushing the frame on to the next scene. Although he appears in most of the scenes in the novel, it is as a voice among other voices, constantly elaborating or explaining; on television words become actions.

Every character is supposed to be an uneasy place of reference.

Malcolm Bradbury

Considering Kirk in this light, however, forces upon us the complex problems of performance and characterisation: what follows when the characters of a highly stylised satire are re-presented as recognisable likenesses of men and women? Both Bradbury and Knights tried to deny readers and viewers secure identification figures who would provide a consistent reference point for the moral and political value structures of their texts. Michael Hordern is cast as the older Oxbridge liberal Professor Marvin, for example, in a considered attempt to offer a character with whom viewers of his generation would initially sympathise. (Hordern, unlike the rest of the cast, was also a famous actor prior to the serial — notably as the liberal philosopher in Tom Stoppard's *Jumpers*.) But in order to criticise his position, Bradbury suggested to script writer Christopher Hampton and Robert Knights that they include in the adaptation a second meeting in the Durkheim Room which Bradbury had rejected from the final version of the novel. In this additional scene the liberals cravenly agree to Howard's blatantly self-serving plan, and Marvin is revealed as the most evasive in a manner that not even Michael Hordern's ingratiating performance can rescue.

Some people see the characters in the novel as slightly two-dimensional. Some critics have picked up that when you see an actress very much there in three dimensions, it's a different sort of weight. My taste is towards a humanist line rather than a stylised production; I wanted to round out the characters more. It's not naturalism; there are slight jokes like the scene between Howard and Flora out of Hockney. They are gestures and self-reflexive in that way, but I wanted the people and not the style to be right up front.

Robert Knights

The meanings constructed by Hordern's performance, then, do not trouble the balance of the narrative discourses. But Laura Davenport's Annie Callendar seems less susceptible to the strategy. Her function in the narrative structure is to represent liberal, literary values, aware of the challenge of new political ideas and academic disciplines but seeking to evade rather than contradict them. These abstractions are clearly signalled; and, when we see her in bed with Howard in the final scenes, in contrast with Barbara and Felicity who are also shown, she is scarcely a victim. The abstraction embodied here is that mentioned in Bradbury's *Stepping Westward*: 'Someone once defined liberals as people who embrace their destroyers.' But this is only *one* of the meanings generated by the adaptation. When Howard dashes the tea things from Annie's hands and verbally assaults her for the life she had made for herself, my sympathies are engaged by Laura Davenport's performance as a male-oppressed woman, and the sight deafens me to the intellectual argument offered in the other scenes in which she appears. And if the shot were held longer, I think I would forget it altogether.

Sher's performance, which bears no relation to my image of Howard Kirk, has become compulsive and is now my image.

Malcolm Bradbury

Similar arguments might be constructed about the serial's characterisation of Henry Beamish and about Howard, for Bradbury has himself recognised that Anthony Sher's performance has obliterated his own image of Howard Kirk. The excess of meanings created by performance is probably greater when the adaptation is not from a realist novel or a screenplay written for television: in such a screenplay what a character means is defined *by* performance, and in the realist novel there is already abundant detail which needs to be omitted so that meanings are clear. But questions about visual representation of verbal style will need to be pursued a great deal more before we are anywhere near a clear understanding of the adaptation of a novel for a visual medium.

Thanks to the Classic Serial Seminar Group at the 1981 BFI Summer School and to John Ellis for their help on this article.

NOTES

1. The views of Malcolm Bradbury as quoted and summarised here are taken from his August 1981 Guardian Lecture at the National Film Theatre. The author was the interviewer on that occasion. Those of Robert Knights are from a discussion with him at the Education Department of the British Film Institute, for which I am extremely grateful.

2. Malcolm Bradbury, *Eating People Is Wrong*, 1959, and *Stepping Westward*, 1965.

3. The original script for the television adaptation also included a cameo of Bradbury playing Bradbury, but this idea was later dropped.

4. Malcolm Bradbury, *The History Man*, London, Arrow Books, 1977, p. 204. First publication by Secker and Warburg, 1975.

5. *ibid.*, pp. 91–92.

6. *ibid.*, p. 230.

7. John Ellis, 'Stars/Industry/Image', to be published in a forthcoming BFI dossier, distinguishes television's conventional immediacy and direct address from the cinema's more ambiguous 'photo-effect'. However, as he usefully observed during the writing of these notes, one of the features of television's literary adaptations is their cinematic aspirations, if only for reasons of cultural prestige. This point may also apply to *The History Man's* cinematic, rather than televisual, treatment of sex.

8. *The History Man*, *op. cit.*, p. 1.

9. Geoffrey Nowell-Smith, 'A Note on History/Discourse', *Edinburgh '76 Magazine*, p. 28.

10. Julian Barnes, 'As For The Sex . . .', *The New Statesman*, February 20, 1981.

18   *Grange Hill*

● David Lusted

First, *Grange Hill* is drama offered to a child audience within a special category the broadcast companies themselves maintain — that of children's television. Audience figures for children's television are rarely enough to allow any programme to enter the ratings, a product not only of the 'minority' audience (30 per cent) such programmes are aimed at, but also of scheduling policies which determine that the programmes are seen at unsocial times: weekdays between 4.15 and 5.15, and Saturday mornings, most centrally. The first series of nine weekly programmes in 1978 was said to rate an average audience figure of 7 million, the second series of 18 programmes a year later had audiences of 9 million and the third series in 1980 attracted audiences over 10 million to its 18-part bi-weekly transmission. These figures are astonishingly high for a programme in children's TV, to be compared with overall ratings which guarantee a place in the 'Top 20' for programmes with ratings in double figures.

Second, the popularity of *Grange Hill* has spawned a subindustry of its own. Its child stars are recognised in the street, invited to open fêtes, sign photographs of themselves and offer anecdotes for media transmission; they have become 'personalities' established by, but now distinct from, the characters they play. Similarly, deviser and main scriptwriter of *Grange Hill*, Phil Redmond, is responsible for a number of *Grange Hill* novels and articles spinning off from the TV serial.

Third, popularity with an audience has also been matched by favour from the television establishment. *Grange Hill* was given a BAFTA award for the best children's programme in 1979 and Phil Redmond a Pye award for best writer for children.

Fourth, acclaim from peers on 'artistic' terms make *Grange Hill* akin to the plays of Dennis Potter and Ken Loach/Tony Garnett in that they have also been the subject of minor moral panics which, for *Grange Hill*, took the form of a vast catalogue of letters and 'phone calls to the BBC complaining of certain programmes in the second series. The strength of *organised* complaint was overwhelming — from teacher's organisations (including a letter to *The Times* from the NUT Head Office) to women's institutes. As Anna Home, executive producer of *Grange Hill* has said; 'There has never been a more powerful reaction to a programme in the history of children's TV.'

POPULAR — AND CONTROVERSIAL

What is it then about *Grange Hill* which has attracted a phenomenally large child audience and aroused to fury organised adult and especially teacher opposition? The ostensible object of popularity and disapproval alike is the *subject* of *Grange Hill*, a subject constituted of setting, characters and plot. Phil Redmond talks of *Grange Hill* as a comprehensive school although there is no internal evidence of this from the serial itself beyond a social mix from roughly executive middle-class to unemployed working-class represented by child-accent and parent-occupation. Within the setting of a probable comprehensive school, *Grange Hill* has characters and relations in interweaving plots in which *their* interactions take precedence over those of adults/teachers. The subjects of the plots are therefore determined by representations of children (centrally) and in school. These representations appear within a particular play between three social agencies: the bearing of 'home' on child attitudes and life in school, the activities of child-relations especially pair-and-group-friendships, and the products of negotiating the school as system. That is, a play between the *social constructions* of home/child/school. One example, necessarily detailed, may suffice to illustrate this play.

In the first twelve programmes of the second series, a relationship between two third-year girls is established. Much of their interaction concerns the worries of one of the pair, Penny, over her responsibility as representative of her year on the School's Council. The second of the pair, Sue, acts as sympathetic listener but she too seems to be suffering from an unnamed stress. This relationship exemplifies a central arm in the play between home/child/school. At the end of the thirteenth programme we meet Sue's mother for the first time at the school play; she is a snob, openly declaring the inadequacy of her daughter's intellectual ability and despairing of the school's mixed-ability policy. This moment shifts attention from the child relationship to that of Sue and *home*, a moment then abandoned in the next programme. I have not seen programmes 15 and 16, but in programme 17 Sue's drama becomes the central topic. Scenes at home reveal that Sue's anxiety derives from constant parental pressure — her brother is an academic but Sue, they believe, is not; they criticise the school for its lack of 'standards'. The rest of the programme is then centrally concerned with the playing through of Sue's anxiety and despondent feeling of inadequacy into the school, the third arm of the play between home/child/school. Sue feels she cannot 'keep up' with classwork; we see her failing to understand in classes (incidentally, the only programme in all the series to represent *formal* learning) and being reassured of her abilities by her tutor, Miss Somers.

In the final programme in the second series, Sue's drama is resolved by bringing the three arms together but, interestingly, in a displaced relation to the central action of the programme, a 'Top of the Form'-type of inter-school quiz competition. Sue is picked to represent the school, has her fears calmed by Penny and Miss Somers and demonstrates academic facility during the quiz, to the surprise of Sue's mother who is further disarmed by the Head's oblique demand that she take the pressure off. The resolution signals to the audience that Sue's relation to school is the secure one; that her relation to home, though a struggle, will change; and that her relation to Penny is now more 'equal'.

'Sue's drama' is *structurally* typical (though not necessarily representative in other ways) of how *Grange Hill* sequences its multi-character dramas through the individual programmes and the series as they develop. The quiz, for instance not only resolves the sub-plot around Sue, but sub-plots featuring other characters, too. More of this narrative patterning later. The function of describing this schematic example of the play between home/child/school at this stage, is to illustrate how child characters and their social relations take precedence in *Grange Hill* and, hence, why this subject of *Grange Hill* appeals to a child audience witnessing the representation of child-centred dramas.

I hope that for readers unfamiliar with *Grange Hill*, this account of Sue's drama also gives something of the flavour of the series. However, it can give no insight into grounds for disapproval of the series and this I turn to next.

There is a discernible and perhaps predictable pattern of child acclaim for the subject's authenticity — 'schools are like that' — and adult condemnation because *Grange Hill* shows only 'the seamy side of school life'. One set of adult condemnations comes from an essentially pro-comprehensive school lobby which reads *Grange Hill*'s representation of child behaviour as an attack on the comprehensive principle. Another lobby also condemns the same child representations but reads them not so much as an attack on (any type of) school but as an attack on received notions of 'good' child behaviour, fearing child imitation in the home and school of the representations on the screen. For the first lobby, then, the subject of *Grange Hill* is children, a subject so represented as to lead, through behavioural reasoning, to offensive child imitation. What both groups of adults share is a negative judgement about *Grange Hill*'s representation of children. Where they are distinguished is in terms of where those representations will have 'effects': the first in adult debate, the second in child behaviour.

BEHIND THE CONTROVERSY

Pursuing the controversy further, it is interesting to reflect on the terms used in attacking or proposing the authenticity of *Grange Hill*'s representation of school life. For Phil Redmond, *Grange Hill* is both the reality of school life and yet contradictorily 'TV that a working class kid would recognise'. Behind this contradiction lie the terms and misrecognitions involved in the controversy and the appeal of *Grange Hill*. The controversy is fundamentally over fidelity to an observable world, a reality which is assumed capable of an unmediated reflection in any cultural product, any 'message' about that reality. It can only make sense, however, to see *Grange Hill* as a drama which constructs certain aspects of school life and represents certain child behaviour. Constructions and representations are active processes, messages *about* a reality incapable of communicating reality itself. Messages have points of origin; they come from individuals or groups situated in society. What *Grange Hill* can and does offer is *points of view* about children in school which attract children and offend adult social groups.

The issue then is not, as dominantly formulated, 'is *Grange Hill* an authentic representation of school life?' but rather 'what points of view does *Grange Hill* represent?' and, perhaps more importantly if we wish to *understand* rather than judge the phenomenon that is *Grange Hill*, 'how does *Grange Hill* represent those points of view?'

For the pro-comprehensive element in the controversy, *Grange Hill* primarily represented certain ideas about such schools that it saw as reactionary. *Grange Hill* therefore found itself in a system of debate about the institutional structure of schooling at the time of its transmission. For the bourgeois moralists in the controversy *and* for the child audience it appealed to, *Grange Hill* represented points of view about children which fiction and children's TV generally had ignored or under-represented. So, what representations of children and school that oppose the conventional does *Grange Hill* offer? And, do those representations constitute an attack on comprehensive schools?

OUTLINING A STUDY

These questions are explored in the following analysis of the tradition of fiction about schools, of *Grange Hill* in the context of children's TV, of the educational context it is transmitted in and of the narrative and form of the second series of *Grange Hill*.

At its broadest, the conclusion is that the representation of children is central to the popular appeal of *Grange Hill* to children. Such representations are distinct from others available but only in the sense that they recognise forms of child experience otherwise repressed or ignored. They can be. considered radical only in this sense of identification as they disturb little of the consensual attitudes to the system of schooling or the child's social position within and without school. However, schooling is qualified insofar as the serial contains certain disturbances or 'shocks' in recognizing familiar child experience in novel ways but not to the extent of framing critical questions of the social relations within school, of the purpose of education or of the school system itself. Such questions are raised only indirectly through the inclusion of the politics of schooling and child relations — issues which are then closed by narrative resolutions favouring acceptance of the status quo.

Grange Hill represents a child's point of view but, most importantly, in certain specific *formal* ways and in the context of other children's TV and other fiction about schools. In short, the child's point of view in *Grange Hill* exists at least as much in relation to other cultural constructions *about* children and *for* children as it does in relation to lived experience of school life and ideological constructions of the child and schooling. It needs to be made clear that these two points in relation — messages from cultural constructions about school and attitudes and experiences within school — are bound together. Within that field, *Grange Hill* finds a place that could be termed progressive in that it disturbs and opens up for questioning received notions of what school 'means' at the same time as representing the interests of a repressed social group in a way that group can identify if not articulate. What follows is an attempt to explore the qualifications and uncertainties in this formulation; to find out in what terms *Grange Hill* can be said to be progressive and how progressive that is.

THE TRADITION OF SCHOOL FICTION

Much of the attack on *Grange Hill* is expression of shock from contact with representations of children other than those conventionally on offer from an adult culture. The tradition of fiction which takes school as its subject is just such an area of conventional representation. It is the fictional area which *Grange Hill* most closely relates to and from which it marks off its distinctive and progressive nature.

Much of school fiction — regardless of medium or mode; from *The Prime of Miss Jean Brodie* to *Blackboard Jungle* and to *Please Sir!* — is a humanistic critique of the wasteland of everyday schooling and a celebration of the skilled teacher. For example, the liberal black teacher Braithwaite, hero of *To Sir With Love*, promises by the novel's resolution not only his own successful future as a teacher but that of the pupils who will pass through his classroom — arriving as disruptive illiterates and leaving as socialised citizens. As in all romantic fiction, the hero is an individual who triumphs over an inert system, so inert indeed that it is paradoxically validated by the demonstration that individual success *is* possible within it *as it is*.

The ostensible critique of schooling in this tradition of school fiction is displaced, then, through the agency of the hero (or, less frequently, the heroine) who, inevitably, is the *teacher*. Schooling as a subject objectively concerns all the social groups involved in it but for school fiction schooling is essentially about *teaching*. There is a hierarchy of concerns at the top of which are adult-determined relations. Children (pupils, students) the primary *consumers* of school (and, no doubt, school fiction) are represented centrally in order to define the progress of the central teacher character; at best they are obstacles, at worst diversions, in the progress of the narrative towards the teacher's ultimate triumph (e.g. *To Sir With Love*) and/or self-awareness (e.g. *Jean Brodie*).

The centrality of the teacher is confirmed by the disposition of school space. For most school fiction, the main spaces in and around the school in which the action of the narratives take place is determined by the presence of teachers. In *Grange Hill*, however, there is an altogether more extensive use of school space: cloakrooms, changing rooms, canteen, playground, playing fields, the school gate and the 'back wall'. The school is also placed in a surrounding context and is not treated as if sealed off from its community and society; streets, corners, homes, the shopping precinct — not just the more familiar and 'safe' places for school outings. What is important about this catalogue of unfamiliar school spaces is that they represent places where pupils hold domain, unsupervised and less determined by teachers and other adults. In places more controlled by adults and more familiar to school fiction such as the classroom, the corridor and the staffroom, only the first two feature in any way as significantly in *Grange Hill* as the previous catalogue of what can now be termed 'repressed spaces'.

It is the presence of children that determines the action, then, but also more than this. The traditional spaces in school fiction, the classroom and the corridor, are centrally represented at the beginning and end and in between lessons. Conventionally, lesson time determines the action of school fiction as it allows for teacher-display but, with the exception of the programme centring on the academic pressure on Suzie, *Grange Hill* represents classrooms (like corridors and other school spaces) mainly *in between* lessons, at their beginning and end. This use of time and space in *Grange Hill* points to the determining role that pupils play on the action of the narrative throughout the series. Cloakrooms and corridors, the times around and in between lessons, are as important a part of the experience and meaning of school for children but these are almost wholly absent from school fiction elsewhere. This sense of space and time which is more the life of school for children goes some way to explaining the 'new' experience in school fiction, the 'feel' that *Grange Hill* has for schoolchildren and adults for whom it matters.

SCHOOL FICTION FOR CHILDREN

Most, if not all, of the school fiction considered so far is intended, if not exclusively so, for an *adult* audience, even if its subject allows its study in the secondary school curriculum. There is also, however, a strand of school fiction consumed almost exclusively by children, a 'despised literature' from Enid Blyton's 'Malory Towers' novels to the comic strips of the Beano's 'Bash Street Kids' and to which it might be considered *Grange Hill* more appropriately relates — the opening titles of the series take the form of comic strip, for instance. With Blyton's school tales, I would want to argue that this kind of school fiction relates more to the tradition just described than to *Grange Hill*. As evidence, I would cite its central heroine through whom the narratives are driven as distinct from the numerous character-relations featured in *Grange Hill*, of which no one assumes such centrality. The 'Malory Towers' novels develop 'personal' stories as a consequence, whereas the personal in *Grange Hill* always relates to social context. A crucial distinction then would be between Gwendoline in *First Term at Malory Towers*, whose behaviour requires no further explication than the invocation of 'a spoilt child', and Penny in *Grange Hill* whose slightly distant, earnest demeanour is related constantly to the stress on her social relationships with those she 'represents' on the School Council. There is no equivalence between 'Malory Towers' and *Grange Hill* in terms of the disposition of characters in their narratives but what may account for their common *popularity* is another kind of equivalence. 'Malory Towers' is structured in un-indexed 'chapters', each constituting a regular and predictable segment of narrative moments which is formally attractive and allows for readers with different reading capacities and periods of time to read in. The formal equivalent in *Grange Hill* is the mini-plots that interweave like those in soap-opera throughout the series.

The comic strip is a different case but I would want to argue that the constant replay of conflict between teacher and taught in *The Bash Street Kids* is too limited a framework for much to be said within or about it and that the limited tolerance of its form amongst adults renders it, like the 'despised' school fiction that 'Malory Towers' represents, unproblematic. Such school fiction *for* children, in their different ways and unlike *Grange Hill*, attract child readers without disturbing the category of fiction.

FORM AND THE CENTRALITY OF CHILDREN

Children's television is a major category in the broadcasting companies' structures, and yet in spite of a putative audience of children, they rarely *feature* children and, where they do, children invariably play subordinate roles to adults. In this context, the mere fact that the central representations in *Grange Hill* are those of children, is notable. But what is distinctive about *Grange Hill* is that in the construction of a narrative across individual programmes, the series and all the series cumulatively, it:

a) foregrounds a heterogeneity of children's points-of-view (simply shows that children are not 'all the same') by integrating multiple child-relations and multiple plots;

b) foregrounds an homogeneity of *a* child point-of-view (simply, shows that children in relation to adults have common interests) through its unusual dominant formal use of camera.

A child point-of-view, constructing that of a social group with common interests distinct from and defined against that of an adult world, can be discerned at the formal level of camera-use in the series.

Most visual narratives are dominantly recorded by a camera at *eye-level* with the performers, whether actors in drama or the famed 'talking heads' of newscast and documentary. Eye-level in most drama and documentary, regardless of age of audience and not only in TV means *adult* eye-level. Even in those children's television programmes that exceptionally do represent children, the camera views them (and hence so do a viewing audience at home) from a higher position. The mere act of 'looking down' on a subject suggests not just a physical distinction but also a social and psychological one. It gives the viewer a position of mastery (how patriarchal is language!), of seniority over the viewee; it encourages the objectification of the viewee so that the 'he' or 'she', a potential subject, becomes the *object viewed*. This formal objectification of children is conventional within visual forms but *Grange Hill* solidly subverts the conventional, opening up another formal space, by consistently (though not, it must be said, exclusively) placing the camera at *child* eye-level. This strategy is employed not only during scenes in which children talk to children (in an otherwise conventional shot/reverse/shot sequence) but also when children talk to adults. For example, in classroom scenes where the camera views a teacher talking, the camera will be placed behind children sitting and looking at the teacher and from child-eye height. If the camera moves in or cuts to close-up, the same camera-height is maintained. Moreover, when a reverse-shot occurs, the camera will be placed behind the teacher but, crucially, still at child-eye level, effectively cutting off the head of the teacher and maintaining the viewer's gaze on the eyes of the children. This disruption of conventional camerawork constructs a formal 'shock' to the viewer, shifting attention from any possible 'neutral' viewpoint towards identification with the drama as it affects whichever child subject is centrally represented. Importantly, *Grange Hill* does this whatever the overt *content* of the programme or, indeed, the series itself, underlining the different 'feel' of the programme and explaining more of its attraction for, and hence its popularity amongst, children.

NARRATIVE AND IDEOLOGIES OF EDUCATION

Before turning now to the narrative of *Grange Hill*, in the sense of the concerns that the series dramatically expresses through the drive of its stories and character relationships, it is interesting to consider the ideologies about education in the social formation at the time of the second series, when the controversy peaked. In the 1950s *Blackboard Jungle* negotiated ideologies about *youth cultures* (as violent and socially disruptive, requiring either a return to an imaginary earlier period of discipline or remedial attention — depending on your politics) prevalent in debates in the U.S. about education. Similarly *To Sir With Love* negotiated more social democratic debates about *educational equality* that underwrote expansion of the comprehensive system in Britain in the 60s. *Grange Hill* entered a 70s social formation in which the social democratic thesis had been broken by the Black Paperites on the back of a 'progressive education' reconstructed as monolithic and laissez-faire by conservative forces. *Grange Hill*'s reassertion of the social democratic/liberal thesis (and I hope to show later how it is no more than that) was a timely TV intervention, opposing programmes like Angela Pope's *Best Days* for Panorama — a demolition job on Faraday Comprehensive School in West London. But expression of the thesis exists in *Grange Hill* only vestigially. At the opening of series 2, there is a brief exchange between a liberal English teacher and the more autocratic, 'traditional' PE teacher, nicknamed 'Bullet'. The exchange concerns 'how you teach' and draws upon the terms of educational debate of the time, informal versus formal, discipline versus self-regulation, and so forth. Nowhere else in the series is a distinctly *educational* debate expressed at this overt level. Such 'differences' are expressed implicitly in the series in terms of teaching *styles*, of teacher personalities and relations of greater or lesser *concern* for pupils. Overwhelmed by any such representation at all, however, *Grange Hill* is centrally concerned with child-relations and educational issues find representation only *through them*, expressed as 'personal'. These are nonetheless as 'political' as the more overt politics (for instance, concerning the School's Action Group and its demonstrations) by dint of the narrative strategy by which *Grange Hill* represents child relations.

The controversy over *Grange Hill* concerned its 'realism', but that is a misnomer. Although agreement with or doubt about *Grange Hill*'s realism is the overt conflict in the controversy, what it is actually about is the degree to which *Grange Hill accurately* represents school life. That argument is one about *fidelity* to an observable reality which is assumed as being capable of unmediated reflection in drama, rather than about *realism* which is a question of form and about which there can be no doubt concerning *Grange Hill*. *Grange Hill* is a drama series presented in a *narrative* realist form. It bears all the marks and mechanisms of that form — it tells stories (in individual programmes, over a series and over all the series in the form of a serial) which are established in turn, merged into others and finally resolved to be superseded by others. The multiplicity of stories are bound into one continuing narrative in 'the life of a comprehensive school'; there are identifiable characters, individuals and groups in conflict, who remain psychologically consistent throughout and act 'in character' without self-conscious reflections on the fact that they *are* characters being performed by actors. The formal construction of the serial is conventional and thus 'invisible' in editing, lighting and composition within the frame. In sum, *Grange Hill* 'tells stories' without attempting to reflect on the fact of their being told — a working definition of realism. Nonetheless, the particular *form* of narrative realism in *Grange Hill* is one that interweaves plots, shifting space and time inconsequentially, privileging first this group of individuals, then that. By this strategy, 'personal' relations have more overtly political ramifications insofar as they appear representative not of individual or psychological dynamics (cf *Malory Towers*) but of general and social ones.

CHILDREN AS SUBJECTS

Tucker Jenkins is a failed academic but succeeds on his own terms in creative activity both constructive for the school (he makes props for the school play, etc.) and socially (he is the ideasperson behind the Tremblers gang); Pogo enters into an elementary entrepreneurial activity of making cakes at his mum's expense and selling them in a school without a Tuck Shop; Andrew and Simon cement an unlikely friendship by resolving bullying their own way, and so on. Where school intrudes, it is to test friendships and alliances by pressures not always academic — Penny survives the burden of accountability to those she represents on the School Council; Doyle gets his come-uppance over blackmail attempts, etc. Throughout, school is seen as setting the agenda for the action of life but in no way determining its progress. Teachers are neither friends nor enemies but just *teachers*, some more sympathetic than others, but essentially *other*, obstacles to manoeuvre and avoid where possible. All the most important action and decisions take place amongst the peer group — other school children. Thus far, then, *Grange Hill* operates simply to *reverse* the familiar balance of representations of teacher and child in school fiction; the children's point-of-view determines the action rather than the other way round. *Children, perhaps for the first time in school fiction and TV drama, are the subjects rather than the objects of representation.* This perhaps contributes to the positive reaction to the serial by children who experience a form of fiction in a 'new' way through central representations of their own social group. The importance of this as an experience cannot be underestimated. It offers validation of child experience by entering into a struggle to counteract the dominant notions of school as a place determined by adults and defined by notions of education.

But since schools *are* determined by adults and defined by notions of education, it is important to ask of *Grange Hill* if it is merely offering a 'new' misrecognition (schools are for children) in place of an 'old' one (schools are for adults and education).

The task, then, is to ask if in the process of constructing child identification *Grange Hill* tables and explores the structures of power in which teachers/adults control children. Further, is this exploration done in such a way as to enable child viewers to engage in strategies of struggle to change those power relations in their own interests? My answer to this is that *Grange Hill* does do the exploratory work but, by the favouring of certain narrative closures, not in the interests of changing but re-affirming present power relations. For instance, overall, *Grange Hill* dramatically introduces subjects conventionally the prerogative of adult association but in *Grange Hill* seen as appropriate subjects for child action. Thus, there are issues of school democracy which transcend the ostensible concerns of school uniform, canteen organisation, working for a tuck shop, etc., to table concerns about (the absence of and struggle for) child power. The School Council, a reformist organisation, is tested against the Action Group, 'led' by a splendidly androgynous sixth-former named Jessica Samuels; a new Headteacher is seen to be deliberately constructing an unworkable timetable manically to 'test' the quality of his staff; a dyslexic has travelled through a school system undiagnosed until Tricia (a child and a *girl*) instigates revelation. Other subjects include the taboos of sexuality in which stories around the onset of puberty, the first 'boyfriend', the first bra, etc., are negotiated by children without the well-intentioned but patronising intrusion of adults.

Such subjects are explored, some over periods of weeks or a whole series, but — crucially — they are continually resolved by a narrative structure in which social democratic ideologies, or their human agencies, are ultimately victorious. The issue of school democracy is resolved by the *ultimate* representation of the leaders of the SAG, beforehand represented as 'committed' and 'rational' ('They have a point' says the Head), as 'militants' and 'wreckers' and therefore requiring expulsion from the school and the series ('Jessica, this time you've gone too far', says the Head, obviously speaking in loco parentis for the BBC). Other subjects are similarly resolved — the Head's 'timetable test' does its work and is forgotten; the dyslexic boy is assigned to the appropriate school, never to return to *Grange Hill*; Tricia's rejection of a boyfriend proves final — another opportunity never arrives; Sue's pubescent revelations in the bra episode are resolved in an unlikely riverside pact, after which post-pubescence is assumed. What I am arguing, then, is that it matters little whether adult *or* child figures resolve the drama over subjects that trouble conventional definitions of school and children in *Grange Hill*, for a social democratic *form* of resolution is ultimately and consistently asserted which re-asserts the status quo. It is the structure of the narrative that does this active work, regardless of the critical *intention* of *Grange Hill*'s various authors. Conventional definitions of schooling and childhood are exposed as 'troubles', tested and put at risk but only to be reasserted as the only way forward, both for the narrative and, crucially, for *schools*. The narrative structure forecloses on a critique of schooling. The role of narrative in fiction is as crucial as that!

THE LAST JUDGEMENT

That the narrative of *Grange Hill* works to return school and children to safe definitions will obviously please both sets of its detractors, though perhaps not quite by the route they think. But does this form of closure reduce the value of *Grange Hill* as a challenging television text? My argument would be that this is so only if the 'test' of any particular text is its overt iconoclasm. *Grange Hill*, by its controversy, has opened up some sores but not in such a way or to such an extent that it has forced it off the screen. The importance of *Grange Hill* is that it is a text that begs for educational and cultural work upon it. In various characteristics of its form, in its relation to a tradition of school fiction and TV drama for kids, in its status as a 'text' *critically* re-asserting the comprehensive principle at a time when it is under attack — in all these ways — *Grange Hill* offers an opportunity for us to engage children in issues vital to that concern, their education and how adult society represents them.

19   *Film and Literature*

● Morris Beja

Ever since film arose as a story-telling art, there has been a tendency by filmmakers, writers, critics, and audiences alike to associate it with literature, as well as an insistence by many people that the association is false or perhaps deceptive; not the least fascinating aspect of making such a connection is that it is so controversial. The assumption that there are fundamental relationships between narrative film and written narrative literature that are worth pursuing is not one that everyone shares, certainly not every filmmaker or writer. Ingmar Bergman, for example, claims that 'film has nothing to do with literature; the character and substance of the two art forms are usually in conflict,' while according to Norman Mailer, 'film and literature are as far apart as, say, cave painting and a song.' Yet numerous filmmakers from Griffith and Eisenstein to Resnais and Fellini have talked about the literary ramifications of their films, and many writers have either openly acknowledged their attempts to adapt cinematic approaches or techniques to their own work or have agreed with the novelist Graham Greene that 'there is no need to regard the cinema as a completely new art; in its fictional form it has the same purpose as the novel, just as the novel has the same purpose as the drama.' And the influential media critic Marshall McLuhan asserts that 'the close relation . . . between the reel world of film and the private fantasy experience of the printed word is indispensable to our Western acceptance of the film form . . . Film, both in its reel form and in its scenario or script form, is completely involved with book culture.'

Both print and film surround us every day of our lives and can hardly be avoided in modern society; as a result, they are tremendously important forces in our culture. Their role can indeed be dangerous, since they can communicate lies and distortions as easily as truth and wisdom. But while print, for example, can be a potentially malign force, it can also be a major liberating one, for literacy and the popularity of literature have been among the most significant democratic and egalitarian forces in the history of humanity in the last five or six centuries. Film, which does not even demand that its audience have so complex a skill as the ability to read, is even more anti-elitist.

Of course many filmmakers and writers have wanted little more than to *be* popular (and thereby financially successful), a goal which in itself is obviously not reprehensible, and in the pursuit of which many works of genuine and enduring value have been created. But artists have also had less tangible goals. Among the most famous words ever uttered about the aims of art are those of Joseph Conrad, in the Preface to *The Nigger of 'the 'Narcissus,'* a novel he published in 1897: 'To arrest, for the space of a breath, the hands busy about the work of the earth, and compel men entranced by the sight of distant goals to glance for a moment at the surrounding vision of form and color, of sunshine and shadows; to make them pause for a look, for a sigh, for a smile — such is the aim, difficult and evanescent, and reserved only for a very few to achieve.'* The visual stress of Conrad's terms makes the aims he cites seem as appropriate to a filmmaker as a novelist, and in fact a passage earlier in his essay is one that is often quoted in comparisons of film and literature: 'My task which I am trying to achieve is, by the power of the written word, to make you hear, to make you feel — it is, before all, to make you *see*. That — and no more, and it is everything.' This passage is cited in studies of film and literature because it closely — if, apparently, coincidentally — parallels a remark made almost two decades later by D. W. Griffith: 'The task I'm trying to achieve is above all to make you see.'

Obviously, Griffith's sense of what it would be to make us see — truly see — encompasses more than showing us pretty pictures on a screen; Sergei M. Eisenstein made the same point in an essay in his *Film Form* comparing Griffith's techniques to those of Charles Dickens:

> Let Dickens and the whole ancestral array, going back as far as the Greeks and Shakespeare, be superfluous reminders that both Griffith and our cinema prove our origins to be not solely as of Edison and his fellow inventors, but as based on an enormous cultured past; each part of this past in its own moment of world history has moved forward the great art of cinematography. Let this past be a reproach to those thoughtless people who have displayed arrogance in reference to literature, which has contributed so much to this apparently unprecedented art and is, in the first and most important place: the art of viewing — not only the *eye*, but *viewing* — both meanings being embraced in this term.

Yet it is important to remember that, in talking about film hardly less than in talking about literature, to speak of making you 'see' is to be metaphorical, and such metaphors should not be used to make identifications between art forms that cannot hold up.

FILM AS LITERATURE

Still, terminology — and labels — can help us to arrive at a greater understanding of substance. For example, asking whether film *is*

---

* See p. 5; see p. 3 for the following Conrad quotation.

literature, or a form of it, entails asking some basic questions and raising some fundamental issues. The title of the present chapter, 'Film *and* Literature,' should not be taken as necessarily assuming that two entirely different entities are being referred to — anymore than would be the case in a title like 'Painting and Art,' or 'Automobiles and Transportation'. In a book with a reverse title, *Literature and Film*, Robert Richardson makes the interesting and valid point that when we think of a historical period such as the Renaissance, we generally agree that its 'literature' includes 'works on theology, philosophy, education, science, history, biography, journalism, manners, morals and navigation, in addition to poems, plays, and works of fiction,' yet for some reason we act as if 'twentieth-century literature is inexplicably confined to poems, plays and novels'. Moreover, if we go further back than Richardson does, we will include works that are not written or printed: everyone agrees that the Homeric epics are literature, yet it was not until centuries after they were composed that anyone ever wrote them down. Had movies somehow existed in ancient Greece — or during the Renaissance — we would surely now be studying them as works of literature.

If, instead of stressing writing or print, we were to argue that it is best to regard literature as a purely linguistic art, one that uses words alone, then no doubt we would have to exclude film — along with the plays of Shakespeare, Sophocles, Shaw and O'Neill, to be sure. Like drama, film is not exclusively a linguistic art; indeed it is not even primarily so. But when some critics argue that it is exclusively a 'visual' art and not *at all* an art of words, one can only wonder when was the last time they went to a movie.

The 'literary' art with which film is most often associated, by far, is not the drama, as one might at first expect, but the novel; and the reason for this near universal tendency is above all that both are forms of telling stories, and their modes of telling those stories are comparably open. So basic indeed are these similarities that they overshadow many of the differences. The French film critic Christian Metz even claims, in his discussion of what he calls 'the total invasion of the cinema by novelesque fiction,' that 'the rule of the "story" is so powerful that the image, which is said to be the major constituent of film, vanishes behind the plot it has woven . . . so that the cinema is only in theory the art of images.'

VERBAL AND CINEMATIC 'LANGUAGE'

But if narrative literature and film share, indeed by definition, the basic element of the story, they do not 'tell' the story in the same way or in the same 'language'. Many critics have got round that fact by in a sense denying it, through elaborate comparisons of verbal and cinematic

language. They point out that the basic components of verbal language
— that is, of course, what most people think of as language — are words
(vocabulary) and the ways in which they are put together (grammar and
syntax). The comparable elements in film, say these critics, are the frame
or the photographed image (which is parallel to the word) and the
editing of the images (parallel to grammar and syntax). Sometimes, just
as the word is seen as the equivalent of the frame, so the sentence is
compared to the shot, the paragraph to the scene, and the chapter to the
sequence.

Such one-to-one analogies, at first glance perhaps intriguing, are in
fact basically misleading. If editing is syntax, how do we know when a
particular example of a 'sentence' (or shot) is 'ungrammatical' or
'nonstandard'? If frames are words, how can a dictionary be compiled
which will 'define' each image? Moreover, a fundamental problem in
such analogies is that by describing film in terminology which is suitable
to verbal language, they inevitably make film seen cruder by
comparison; film is not being examined on its *own* terms.

A more fruitful approach has been the newer one associated with
semiotics, the study of systems of signs and meanings, which has
sought to describe *cinematic* language. According to this approach, film
is a language, but it is one that is quite different from verbal language.
Film is language in the most general sense — it is a mode of
communication — not in the more particular sense by which we mean
'language' to refer to such highly systematized codes as 'the English
language,' or Italian, or German. Christian Metz, who has been doing
important work in this field, has pursued numerous associations and
distinctions between film language and verbal language. For example,
he points out that the total number of *words* is large but finite, while the
number of possible *statements* using those words is infinite; a film image
or frame is in that sense like a statement and unlike a word, since the
number of possible images is also infinite. Each visual image is
comparable to a full sentence in other ways as well. An image of a man
and woman kissing each other is the equivalent not of any single word
— for example, 'kiss' — but, even at the crudest level, of a full sentence,
'The man and woman are kissing each other.' In addition, words
already exist, but at least theoretically each writer creates a statement for
the first time. (The words *whose, woods, these, are*, and so on are part of
the vocabulary for all of us; the statement 'Whose woods these are I
think I know' is the creation of Robert Frost.) Each film image is also,
again at least theoretically, a new invention.

Moreover, the relationship between each 'signifier' (the word or
statement on the one hand and the visual image or shot on the other)
and what is 'signified' is very different. A photograph of a bird has a
relationship to the 'real' bird which seems closer or more direct than
does the word *bird*. Yet the photograph is *not* a bird; it is a picture (a
sign, a symbol, a representation of birdness). It is unlike the word in that

it is universally recognizable as signifying a bird and because it is *specifically* representational (of a cardinal rather than an eagle, say). Still, neither the word nor the picture will fly, so to speak.

WORDS AND MOVIES

The fact that the relation between signifier and signified in a picture seems undeniably more direct than in the case of a word may remind us that, as everyone knows, one picture is worth a thousand words. But what everyone knows need not always be true. In this case, sometimes it is (indeed, if anything, it is often an understatement), but sometimes it is not. It *is* true when the given conception is best comprehended in visual terms. We shall explore this question of which realms may seem more ideally suited to each art, but first it is important to recognize the possibility of a hidden assumption in asking whether one picture is worth a thousand words in the context of a discussion of film and literature. It is in fact an assumption made by numerous critics: that film employs one rather than the other, pictures rather than words. The problem with the assumption is that it is false. Film today is not a 'purely' visual medium, but an *audio-visual* one. If one doubts that, one can ask a number of people to name some of the most memorable film moments they can think of. Even excluding musical numbers — indeed, even those not in musicals as such, like Jeanne Moreau singing 'Le Tourbillon' in *Jules and Jim* — or such nonverbal moments as the devastating one in *The Blue Angel* when Emil Jannings crows like a rooster, an extraordinary number will centre on famous lines: Peter Sellers at the end of *Dr Strangelove* exulting, 'Mein Führer, I can walk!'; Al Pacino and Marlon Brando in *The Godfather* referring to offers that cannot be refused, or an earlier Brando in *On the Waterfront* claiming to Rod Steiger that he could have been a contender; Lauren Bacall telling Humphrey Bogart in *To Have and Have Not* that if he needs her, he can just whistle; or Bogart himself assuring us in several films that he sticks his neck out for nobody (sometimes the line need not be one actually uttered: 'Play it again, Sam'); James Cagney at the end of *White Heat* shouting 'Top of the world, Ma!'; or Paul Muni at the end of *I Am a Fugitive from a Chain Gang* whispering 'I steal!'

The lines are all short, and they do not come from long speeches, and even as one feels that there is no need to exclude words from the tools at a filmmaker's disposal, one can recognize the artistic dangers in being *too* reliant on words alone, or on too many of them. The novelist Virginia Woolf argued in her essay 'The Cinema' that although film 'has within its grasp innumerable symbols for emotions that have so far failed to find expression,' all 'which is accessible to words and to words alone, the cinema must avoid.'

THE LIMITS OF GENRE

Woolf's essay was written in 1926, before the advent of the sound film, but one could still agree that there is little point in a film attempting what can *only* be done in words; however, there will be less universal agreement about what we are thinking of when we talk that way, or about which areas are in fact 'accessible to words and to words alone'. To put the question in more general terms, can we determine which realms in the artistic depiction of human existence are more or less suited to the genre of film than to other genres? Are there aspects of human experience that are better or worse served by written literature than by film?

In practice, attempts to answer these questions seem invariably to talk about the limitations of film, and about what is either 'cinematic' or 'uncinematic': one rarely hears claims that a given topic is unsuited to print, or that it is either 'literary' or 'unliterary'. Probably the most common distinction is one that sees the novel as more appropriate to the presentation of *inner* mental states, while the film is seen as being better able to show what people do and say than what they think or imagine. The reason is that film depicts what is external and visible, physical and material. In the essay from which we have already quoted, Virginia Woolf contemplates a film adaptation of Tolstoy: 'The eye says ''Here is Anna Karenina.'' A voluptuous lady in black velvet wearing pearls comes before us. But the brain says, ''That is no more Anna Karenina than it is Queen Victoria.'' For the brain knows Anna almost entirely by the inside of her mind — her charm, her passion, her despair. All the emphasis is laid by the cinema upon her teeth, her pearls, and her velvet.'

George Bluestone begins his *Novels into Film* by saying that 'between the percept of the visual image and the concept of the mental image lies the root difference between the two media', and throughout his valuable book he stresses his conviction that 'the rendition of mental states — memory, dream, imagination — cannot be as adequately represented by film as by language', since 'the film, having only arrangements of space to work with, cannot render thought, for the moment thought is externalized it is no longer thought'. But it could be countered that written literature itself has only words on pages to work with, and that putting them there is also an act of externalization — and that, in any case, thought is less exclusively 'verbal' than Bluestone's distinction seems to imply.

As a matter of fact, a number of major filmmakers have not been willing to yield their right to the depiction of psychological states so easily. In an essay called 'Words and Movies', Stanley Kubrick explains his preference for adapting novels concentrating on a character's inner life by saying that it is easier to invent external action which will be —

and here he borrows T. S. Eliot's term — an 'objective correlative of the book's psychological content' than it is to invent a character and a motivation for action plots lacking them. Much earlier, in 1930, Sergei M. Eisenstein sought out James Joyce, whose *Ulysses* he greatly admired. The two men discussed what Joyce had done in his novel to represent inner thought processes by means of the *interior monologue*, a device or technique used to record the *stream of consciousness* — that is, the current of associations going on uninterruptedly in our minds, the flux of thoughts, sensations, and feelings that we all experience, the direction of which is determined by associative rather than 'logical' channels. Contrary to the usual assumption, Eisenstein believed that film, even more forcefully than literature, could make such mental processes accessible, comprehensible, and vivid. Joyce was sufficiently impressed by Eisenstein's ideas to remark to a friend that he could imagine Eisenstein succeeding in his wish to adapt *Ulysses* into film.

When Joseph Strick adapted that novel more than thirty years later, in 1966, his chief device for depicting inner thoughts was the *voice-over*, a term for the use of an off-screen voice heard 'over' the scene we are seeing; the voice may be that of a narrator, or that of a character who is in the scene but not talking aloud. Laurence Olivier's *Hamlet* presents a number of soliloquies in this way, and Robert Bresson uses a voice-over to give us the journal entries of the protagonist in *Diary of a Country Priest*. But of course films can also use visual as well as verbal correlatives for mental states: Bergman's *Wild Strawberries* makes extensive use of the voice-over, but we *see* the flashbacks and silent dreams of its protagonist, Isak Borg; the visual world of Wiene's *The Cabinet of Dr. Caligari* seems entirely controlled by the intensely subjective mental perspective of its ambiguously disturbed hero.

Often, verbal means such as the voice-over, narration, and dialogue are used to get round a fundamental limitation within the visual image: it cannot easily and immediately convey abstract concepts. It can show a person in pain, but not the general notion of pain. It can show a woman and a child, but there is no single visual image equivalent to the word 'mother'. Nor are there specific yet general visual signs for love, or hatred, or sex, or violence, or religion. Such abstractions are of course not completely beyond the capabilities of film so long as film uses words; nevertheless, it does seem true that ideas are more economically treated in written literature than in film.

So much is widely acknowledged; many people believe the corollary that while literature is a more 'intellectual' medium, film is the more emotional; according to Ingmar Bergman, the reason film has more in common with music than with literature is that both film and music 'affect our emotions directly, not via the intellect'.

Sometimes a similar but actually quite different generalization says that film is a simple rather than a complex medium (in content, not execution). Such a view is expressed with special frequency by people who have worked as both novelists and screenwriters, such as Budd Schulberg, who says that the film

> . . . has no time for what I call the essential digression. The 'digression' of complicated, contradictory character. The 'digression' of social background. The film must go from significant episode to more significant episode in a constantly mounting pattern. It's an exciting form. But it pays a price for this excitement. It cannot wander as life wanders, or pause as life always pauses, to contemplate the incidental or the unexpected.

Perhaps the most important if obvious source of this difference is in length; the film of two or three or even four hours simply does not have the time to go into all the details which are possible and ordinary in a novel of two or three or four hundred pages. That is one of the reasons for Alfred Hitchcock's conviction that 'the nearest art form to the motion picture is . . . the short story. It's the only form where you ask the audience to sit down and read it in one sitting.' The drama is also experienced in a single sitting, of course, and it is worth observing that playwrights such as Shakespeare, Chekhov, Shaw, and Beckett have managed to be quite inclusive, subtle, and complex within works encompassing only a few hours.

It is coming to seem, then, as if all the distinctions we have considered between film and other forms of literature are valid, certainly, and yet are not completely so either; they are both revealing and potentially misleading. Pauline Kael speaks for many others in their response to much film criticism and theory when she asks, in regard to Siegfried Kracauer's discussion in *Theory of Film* of subjects that are either 'cinematic' or more suitable to the theatre: 'Who started this divide and conquer game of aesthetics in which the different media are assigned their special domains like salesmen staking out their territories — you stick to the Midwest and I'll take Florida?' It is surely true that, as Kael goes on to say, 'what motion picture art shares with other arts is perhaps even more important than what it may, or may *not*, have exclusively.' But the key word, perhaps, is *perhaps*. For the differences among art forms can also be extremely revealing, and no doubt the best stance is to be aware of both comparisons and contrasts.

20 *Drama and Film*

● David Lodge

When Jakobson says that drama is essentially 'metaphoric' he is clearly thinking of the generic character of dramatic art as it has manifested itself throughout the history of culture. Arising out of religious ritual (in which a symbolic sacrifice was *substituted* for a real one) drama is correctly interpreted by its audience as being analogous to rather than directly imitative of reality, and has attained its highest achievements (in classical Greece, in Elizabethan England, in neoclassical France) by being poetic, using a language with a built-in emphasis on patterns of similarity and contrast (contrast being a kind of negative similarity). The 'unities' of classical tragedy are not means of producing a realistic illusion, but of bringing into a single frame of reference a constellation of events (say, Oedipus's birth, his killing of an old man, solving of a riddle, marriage) that were not contiguous in space or time but combine on the level of similarity (the old man is the same as the father, the wife is the same as the mother, the son is the same as the husband) to form a message of tragic import. Elizabethan drama is more obviously narrative than Greek tragedy (that is, more linear or syntagmatic in its construction) but its most distinctive formal feature, the double plot, is a device of similarity and contrast. The two plots of *King Lear* and the complex pairing and contrasting and disguising of characters in that play is a classic example of such dramatic structure, which generally has the effect of retarding, or distracting attention from, the chronological sequence of events. In the storm scene of *Lear*, for instance — one of the peaks of Shakespeare's dramatic achievement — there is no linear progress: nothing happens, really, except that the characters juggle with similarities and contrasts: between the weather and human life, between appearances and realities. And it is not only in *Lear* that the chain of sequentiality and causality in Shakespearean tragedy proves under scrutiny to be curiously insubstantial. Stephen Booth has convincingly demonstrated how the opening of *Hamlet* plunges us immediately into a field of paradoxes and non-sequiturs which we struggle in vain to unite into a coherent pattern of cause and effect[1] (hence, perhaps, the ease with which Tom Stoppard grafted on to it his more explicitly absurdist and metaphorical *Rosencrantz and Guildenstern*

Are Dead). It is demonstrable that the plot of *Othello* allows no time in which Desdemona could have committed adultery with Cassio — but that anomaly does not matter, and is indeed rarely noticed in the theatre: the play is built on contrasts — Othello's blackness with Desdemona's whiteness, his jealousy against her innocence, his naivety against Iago's cunning — not cause-and-effect. Othello's self-justifying soliloquy, 'It is the cause, it is the cause, my soul' (V, ii, 1) carries a bitter irony, for there is no cause: not only is Desdemona innocent, but Iago's malice has no real motive (that is why it is so effective).

The naturalistic 'fourth wall' plays which have dominated the commercial stage in our era must be seen as a 'metonymic' deviation from the metaphoric norm which the drama displays when viewed in deep historical perspective. In naturalistic drama every action is realistically motivated, dramatic time is almost indistinguishable from real time, ('deletions' from the chronological sequence being marked by act or scene divisions) and the characters are set in a contextual space bounded and filled with real (or *trompe l'oeil* imitations of) objects — doors, windows, curtains, sofas, rugs — all arranged in the same relations of contiguity with each other and with the actors as they would be in reality. Such naturalism is, arguably, unnatural in the theatre. In reaction against it, many modern playwrights have put an extreme stress on the metaphoric dimension of drama. In Beckett's plays for instance, there is no progress through time, no logic of cause and effect, and the chintz and upholstery of drawing-rooms has given way to bare, stark acting spaces, with perhaps a chair, a row of dustbins and a high window from which nothing is visible (*End Game*). These plays offer themselves overtly as metaphors for the human condition, for on the literal level they are scarcely intelligible. Yet arguably *any* play, however naturalistic in style, is essentially metaphorical in that it is recognized as a *performance*: i.e. our pleasure in the play depends on our continuous and conscious awareness that we are spectators not of reality but of a conventionalized model of reality, constructed before us by actors who speak words not their own but provided by an invisible dramatist. The curtain call at which the actor who died in the last act takes his smiling bow is the conventional sign of this separation between the actors and their roles, between life and art.

The experience of watching a film is entirely different, notwithstanding the superficial similarity of modern theatre and cinema auditoria. There is, for example, no cinematic curtain call. Credits scarcely serve the same function: being written signs in an essentially non-literary medium their impact is comparatively weak, and often considerable ingenuity is used to make it even weaker, distracting our attention from the information the credits convey and integrating them into the film 'discourse' itself (by, for instance, delaying their introduction and/or by superimposing the words on scenic establishing shots or even action shots). Some films do attempt something like a curtain call at the end when they present a series of stills of the main actors with their real names superimposed, but these are invariably stills taken from the film itself, portraying the actor 'in character' — in other words the gap between performance and reality is not exposed.

Of course it is always possible for the filmmaker to expose the artificiality of his production — Lindsay Anderson's *O Lucky Man*, for instance, ends with a celebration party on the set for actors and technicians, and Fellini likes to incorporate his cameras and other equipment into his pictures — but this is a highly deviant gesture in film. It is a commonplace that film creates an 'illusion of life' much more readily than drama. We are more likely to feel strong physical symptoms of pity, fear, etc., in the cinema than in the theatre, and this has little to do with aesthetic values. Whereas the play is created before us at every performance, the film is more like a record of something that happened, or is happening, only once. The camera and the microphone are voyeuristic instruments: they spy on, eavesdrop on experience and they can in effect follow the characters anywhere — out into the wilderness or into bed — without betraying their presence, so that nothing is easier for the filmmaker than to create the illusion of reality. Of course film is still a system of signs, a conventional language that has to be learned (films are more or less unintelligible to primitive people never exposed to them before).[2] The oblong frame around the image does not correspond to the field of human vision, and the repertoire of cinematic shots — long-shot, close-up, wide-angle, etc. — bears only a schematic resemblance to human optics. Nevertheless, once the language of film has been acquired it *seems* natural: hence the thudding hearts, the moist eyes, in the stalls. We tend to take the camera eye for granted, and to accept the 'truth' of what it shows us even though its perspective is never exactly the same as human vision.

This verisimilitude can be explained as a function of the metonymic character of the film medium. We move through time and space lineally and our sensory experience is a succession of contiguities. The basic units of the film, the shot and the scene, are composed along the same line of contiguity and combination, and the devices by which the one-damn-thing-after-another of experience is rendered more dramatic and meaningful are characteristically metonymic devices that operate along the same axis: the synecdochic close-up that represents the whole by the part, the slow-motion sequence that retards without rupturing the natural tempo of successiveness, the high or low angle shot that 'defamiliarizes', without departing from, the action it is focused on. Consciousness is not, of course, bound to the line of spatio-temporal contiguity, in the way that sensory experience is, but then film does not deal very much or very effectively with consciousness except insofar as it is manifested in behaviour and speech, or can be reflected in landscape through the pathetic fallacy, or suggested by music on the sound track.

This does not mean that film has no metaphoric devices, or that it may not be pushed in the direction of metaphorical structure. Jakobson categorizes montage as metaphoric, presumably because it juxtaposes images on the basis of their similarity (or contrast) rather than their contiguity in space-time. However, the fact that the techniques of cutting and splicing by which montage is achieved are also the techniques of all film editing, by which any film of the least degree of sophistication is composed, creates the possibility of confusion here. John Harrington, for example, in his *The Rhetoric of Film*, defines montage as

> a rhetorical arrangement of juxtaposed shots. The combination, or gestalt, produces an idea by combining the visual elements of two dissimilar images. A longing face, for instance, juxtaposed to a turkey dinner suggests hunger. Or the image of a fox following that of a man making a business deal would indicate slyness. Segments of film working together to create a single idea have no counterpart in nature; their juxtaposition occurs through the editor's imaginative yoke.[3]

The main drift of this definition confirms Jakobson's classification of montage as metaphorical, but the first of Harrington's examples is in fact metonymic or synecdochic in Jakobson's sense: longing faces and turkey dinners *are* found together in nature (i.e. real contexts) and all that has been done in this hypothetical montage is to delete some of the links (*e.g.* a window) in a chain of contiguities that would link the face with the turkey. The fox and the businessman, on the other hand, are not contiguous in nature, but are connected in the montage through a suggested similarity of behaviour, as in the verbal metaphor 'a foxy businessman'. Context is all-important. If the montage of longing face and turkey dinner described by Harrington were in a film adaptation of *A Christmas Carol*, we should interpret it metonymically; if it were interpolated in a documentary about starving animals, it would be metaphoric. Those favourite filmic metaphors for sexual intercourse in the pre-permissive cinema, skyrockets and waves pounding on the shore, could be disguised as metonymic background if the consummation were taking place on a beach on Independence Day, but would be perceived as overtly metaphorical if it were taking place on Christmas Eve in a city penthouse.

Eisenstein himself included in the concept of montage juxtapositions that are metonymic as well as metaphoric:

> The juxtaposition of two separate shots by splicing them together resembles not so much a simple sum of one shot plus another shot — as it does a *creation* . . . each montage piece exists no longer as something unrelated, but as a given *particular representation* of the general theme that in equal measure penetrates all the shot-pieces. The juxtaposition of these partial details in a given montage construction calls to life and forces into the light that *general* quality in which each detail has participated and which binds together all the details into a whole, namely, into that generalized *image*, wherein the creator, followed by the spectator,

experiences the theme. . . . What exactly is this process? A given order of hands on the dial of a clock invokes a host of representations associated with the time that corresponds to the given order. Suppose, for example, the given figure be five. Our imagination is trained to respond to this figure by calling to mind pictures of all sorts of events that occur at that hour. Perhaps tea, the end of the day's work, the beginning of rush hour on the subway, perhaps shops closing, or the peculiar late afternoon light. . . . In any case we will automatically recall a series of pictures (representations) of what happens at five o'clock. The image of five o'clock is compounded of all these individual pictures.[4]

Translated into film such a montage of 'five o'clock' would be metonymic or synecdochic rather than metaphorical, representing the whole by parts, parts which are contiguous (because they belong to a larger complex of phenomena taking place at the same time) rather than similar. This is confirmed by Eisenstein's use of the word 'condensation' a few lines later: 'There occurs "condensation" within the process above described: the chain of intervening links falls away, and there is produced instantaneous connection between the figure and our perception of the time to which it corresponds.'[5] Condensation, it will be recalled, belongs to the metonymic axis in Jakobson's scheme.

Eisenstein was not so much concerned with the difference between metaphoric and metonymic montage as with the difference between montage in general, and what he calls 'representation' — the photographing of an action from a single set-up by a simple accumulation of 'one shot plus another shot' — the cinematic equivalent of non-rhetorical, referential language in verbal discourse. Though celebrated for his daring use of the overtly metaphorical montage (e.g. soldiers being gunned down juxtaposed to cattle being slaughtered, Kerensky juxtaposed with a peacock) Eisenstein was comparatively sparing in his use of the device[6] (*Battleship Potemkin*, for instance, has no fully metaphorical montage though, as Roy Armes points out, the juxtaposition of shots of the three lions, one lying, one sitting and one roaring in the Odessa Steps sequence, creates the impression of a lion coming to life and 'conveyed the idea of protest — with an emotional meaning something like "Even the very stones cried out" '[7]) for the simple reason that if it becomes the main principle of composition in a film, narrative is more or less impossible to sustain. 'Underground' movies define themselves as deviant by deliberately resisting the natural metonymic tendency of the medium, either by a total commitment to montage, bombarding us with images between which there are only paradigmatic relations of similarity and contrast, or by parodying and frustrating the syntagm, setting the naturally linear and 'moving' medium against an unmoving object — the Empire State Building, for instance, or a man sleeping. Poetic drama is also in a paradoxical sense unmoving, nonprogressive, more concerned with paradigmatic similarities and contrasts than with syntagmatic sequence and cause-and-effect. The peculiar resistance of Shakespearean drama to successful translation into film, despite its superficial abundance of cinematic assets (exotic settings, duels, battles, pageantry etc.) is notorious; and one may confidently assert that the same difficulty would be still more acutely felt in any attempt to film Beckett's plays.* Even modern naturalistic drama (e.g. Albee's *Who's Afraid of Virginia Woolf* or Neil Simon's *The Odd Couple*) seems slightly ill-at-ease in the film medium, and most obviously so when it deserts the economical single setting for which it was originally designed, to take advantage of the freedom of location afforded by film. The two media seem to pull against each other. The realistic novel, on the other hand, converts very easily into film — and novelists were in fact presenting action cinematically long before the invention of the moving-picture camera. Consider this passage from George Eliot's first published work of fiction, *The Sad Misfortunes of Amos Barton*:

> Look at him as he winds through the little churchyard! The silver light that falls aslant on church and tomb, enables you to see his slim, black figure, made all the slimmer by tight pantaloons, as it flits past the pale gravestones. He walks with a quick step, and is now rapping with sharp decision at the vicarage door. It is opened without delay by the nurse, cook and housemaid, all at once — that is to say by the robust maid of all work, Nanny; and as Mr Barton hangs up his hat in the passage, you see that a narrow face of no particular complexion — even the smallpox that has attacked it seems to have been of a mongrel, indefinite kind — with features of no particular shape, and an eye of no particular expression, is surmounted by a slope of baldness gently rising from brow to crown. You judge him, rightly, to be about forty. . . .[8]

The passage continues in the same style: Barton opens the sittingroom door and, looking over his shoulder as it were, we see his wife Milly pacing up and down by the light of the fire, comforting the baby. Change George Eliot's 'you' to 'we' and the passage would read not unlike a film scenario. The action certainly breaks down very readily into a sequence of 'shots': *high-angle crane shot of Barton walking through churchyard; cut to door of vicarage opened by Nanny; close-up of Barton's face as he hangs up his hat* . . . and so on. In one respect the passage requires the cinema for its full realization: the charmless, yet human, ordinariness of Barton's physiognomy — the ordinariness which is unloveable yet which (George Eliot insists) we must learn to love — is a

---

*It is noteworthy that Beckett's one screenplay, for a short film entitled *Film*, made in 1964 with Buster Keaton in the main role, is quite different in structure from his plays, though just as 'experimental' and aesthetically self-conscious. There is plenty of action and no dialogue. Event succeeds event in a logical time/space continuum. The camera follows a man along a street and up some stairs to a room; whenever the camera eye threatens to get a view of the man's face he displays anxiety and takes evasive action. In the room he banishes or covers all objects with eyes — animals, pictures, etc. But while he is dozing the camera eye stealthily moves round to view his face. The man wakes and registers horror at being observed. A cinematic 'cut' identifies the observer as the man himself 'but with a very different expression, impossible to describe, neither severity nor benignity, but rather acute *intentness*'. (Samuel Beckett, *Film* (1972) p. 47.)

quality the cinema can convey very powerfully and immediately, whereas George Eliot can only indicate it verbally by means of negations. There is little doubt, I think, that George Eliot would have been deeply interested in the possibilities offered by the motion-picture camera of capturing the human significance of the commonplace: as it was, she had to appeal, as a visual analogy for her art, to the static pictures of the Dutch painters.[9]

NOTES

1. Stephen Booth, 'On the Value of Hamlet', *Reinterpretations of Elizabethan Drama* (New York, 1969) pp. 137–76.

2. Marshall McLuhan describes some of the relevant research in *The Gutenberg Galaxy* (1962) pp. 36ff.

3. John Harrington, *The Rhetoric of Film* (New York, 1973) p. 138.

4. Sergei Eisenstein, *The Film Sense* (1938); reprinted in *The Modern Tradition: Backgrounds of Modern Literature*, ed. R. Ellmann and C. Feidelson Jnr. (New York, 1965) pp. 163–4.

5. *Ibid.* p. 165.

6. Harrington, *op. cit.* p. 139.

7. Roy Armes, *Film and Reality* (Harmondsworth, 1974) p. 51.

8. George Eliot, *Scenes of Clerical Life* (Harmondsworth, 1973) p. 53.

9. See chapter 17 of *Adam Bede*.

21 *The Essence that's not Seen: Radio Adaptations of Stage Plays*

● John Drakakis

It has long been recognised that the dynamics of theatrical performance differ from those of radio broadcasting, even though in terms of creating their audiences each medium seeks to accommodate the *individual* listener and spectator respectively. Even so, there still remain certain fundamental differences. For example, in a theatre an audience is always aware of an actor's presence onstage, whereas on radio reminders of that presence have to be given to the listener from time to time. Very often this is accomplished by means of interjections which take the form either of simple paralinguistic responses such as 'm-m-m' or, particularly in the case of silent servile characters who are acquired to exit at specific points in the action, words such as 'My lord' or 'My lady'. In this way, sound equivalents of visual presences can be established. This creation of a 'sound presence', suggesting to the listener a series of relationships between the characters involved in the action, is a very basic way of solving an obvious problem. Fortunately, in the case of many of Shakespeare's plays, written as they were for a non-naturalistic stage setting, many of the visual gestural responses required of particular actors are described in the dialogue itself. A clear example occurs in *Macbeth*, a play that has proved popular both in the theatre and on radio. At this point in the play Macbeth is suffering from hallucinations intensified by his acute awareness of the horrific murder he is about to commit:

> Is this a dagger which I see before me,
> The handle toward my hand? Come, let me clutch thee.
> I have thee not, and yet I see thee still.
> Art thou not, fatal vision, sensible
> To feeling as to sight? or art thou but
> A dagger of the mind, a false creation,
> Proceeding from the heat-oppressed brain?

I see thee yet, in form as palpable
As this which now I draw.
Thou marshall'st me the way that I was going;
And such an instrument I was to use.
Mine eyes are made the fools o' th' other senses,
Or else worth all the rest. I see thee still;
And on thy blade and dudgeon gouts of blood,
Which was not so before. (II.i.33–47)[1]

This speech enacts, by a kind of reportage, the murder of Duncan, which is not shown on the stage, and it is one of a number of examples in the play where action is reported and not demonstrated. Here, as elsewhere, a theatre audience is placed in the position of a radio listener, as they imagine the physical presence of the object of Macbeth's attention and as they construct in advance a series of mental images of the murder. Moreover, the speech conveys a clear picture of Macbeth's mental processes, his attitude towards the crime he is about to commit, and a general sense of the deepening irony of his position, all of which is focused upon the image of an *absent* dagger. Of course, a theatre audience can *see* the actor and has access to a greater number of comparisons that the combination of dialogue and visual presence forces upon it. But although, for example, the imaginary dagger is compared with a *real* one — 'this which now I draw' — the radio listener is in no way disadvantaged since this articulated stage direction makes possible the very same comparison between the *real* and the *imaginary* to which a theatre audience has access. Equally, the tone and rhythm of the actor's delivery, as dictated by the structure of the soliloquy itself, reinforce the character's own description of his physical gestures: 'Come, let me clutch thee./I have thee not, and yet I see thee still.' Indeed, each pause in this soliloquy is described by the character, so that by the end of it listener and audience alike are given an unusually vivid picture of Macbeth's state of mind.

This particular soliloquy, utilising as it does a mode considered generally well suited to the intimate nature of the radio experience,[2] functions on the basis of a technique that harmonises the rhetoric of dramatic construction with the developing psychology of the character who is the focus of the action. By giving everything a 'voice' on radio (and in the theatre a *persona*) the medium bestows 'character' upon each facet of the play's structure.[3] Macbeth casts his own doubts upon the discrepancy between appearance and reality, and this has the inadvertent effect of making the *means* whereby this process is communicated 'transparent', so to speak. Of course, there are parameters within which the actor works. While in radio the listener is given the task of creating the setting, of deducing a visual essence, as it were, from the spoken dialogue, the actor can control that process without necessarily having access to the kind of photographic verisimilitude involved in, say, a naturalistic stage presentation. For example, the adoption of a conversational rhythm will invariably raise in the mind of the listener certain expectations that will cause him to adjust his mental image of the play's physical setting.[4] Occasionally the two will collide unintentionally, so that a tension is created between a colloquial manner and the more densely expressive idiom of, say, a blank-verse speech.[5] Alternatively, and in a much more complex semiotic way, a declamatory style of delivery, as evidenced for example in Donald Wolfit's 1949 broadcast of Shakespeare's *King Lear*, may as easily carry with it a subtextual component that *signifies* 'theatre' of a rather special, culturally overdetermined sort.

Other Shakespeare plays, such as *Othello, Antony and Cleopatra, The Tempest, King Lear* and, in a more special sense, *Henry V*, provide ample opportunity for naturalising thematic concerns in the way that the text of *Macbeth* allows. In so far as these plays succeed on radio, they all do so by transferring what is basically a deficiency of the medium on to the central characters themselves. For example, Othello is made to create in his own mind an image of both Desdemona and himself; and so careful is Iago's manipulation of his victim that cues for visualisation are extraordinarily dense within the texture of the dialogue. Here the play's themes are reinforced by a kind of *absence* that actually determines physical presence, to the extent that the action always drives towards an essence that is not seen but requires nonetheless to be known. Similarly, and despite the fact that the setting does not transfer easily or well to radio, *Antony and Cleopatra* attempt to imagine a world for themselves, and they seek to create it through a sensuous dramatic poetry whose ultimate veracity the play deliberately leaves open to question. In *The Tempest*, Prospero creates the play for his many audiences, thereby fulfilling the role of personalised narrator; but while in theory the stream-of-consciousness technique often employed in radio seems appropriate here, and does in fact produce a more effective Ariel than is usual onstage, there still remains a certain amount of recalcitrant material that does not withstand the sea change from stage to radio.[6] In *King Lear*, as in a number of original radio plays from Richard Hughes's *Danger* onwards, blindness itself is endowed with a thematic value located in the characters, although again some areas of the play — notably Gloucester's attempt at suicide — require full visualisation in order to be effective.[7] In all these examples, and despite in many cases the spatially panoramic backgrounds, there is ample opportunity for the kind of close focus upon dealings between individual characters that radio can handle so well. However, while it is generally agreed that intimacy is a feature of the medium and that a device such as soliloquy works well on radio, it must be said that the aside (comic or otherwise), which requires rapid spatial adjustment from the listener, is, by contrast, ineffective. Indeed, the creation of a context for dialogue, and the expectations concerning the visual deployment of the participants which flow naturally from it, make it extremely difficult for the listener to accept yet another level of intimacy which is only a momentary violation of the norm he has been persuaded to accept, whereas in the case of soliloquy the sustained context serves to validate the convention.

This problem is, perhaps, another facet of the large difficulty of expansion and contraction that often lies at the heart of the dramatic rhythm of many of Shakespeare's plays. For example, successive radio productions of *Antony and Cleopatra* have found difficulty in coping with the rapid shifts of scenic location without shrinking the world of the play to a series of playfully intimate dialogues between the two central characters. Again, and in theory, the flexibility of the radio medium, and its nominal freedom from the shackles of naturalism, is admirably suited to the business of rapid scene changing, although particular productions of the play have been reluctant to allow its dramatic structure to stand unsupported.[8] In the 1954 radio production of the play by Peter Watts, which was a broadcast of Glen Byam Shaw's Stratford production, the character of Plutarch was introduced as a personalised narrator whose function was obviously to smooth the rapid transitions from one location to another. That such a smoothing has the effect of diluting the dramatic conflict seems to have escaped both directors, as the narrator Plutarch's attempt to 'place' the opening dialogue of the play shows:

> *Music*
> PLUTARCH: Now while Antonius, being this while in Egypt, was
>   delighting in fond pastimes, there came a messenger from
>   Caesar to wait upon his pleasure.
> PHILO: Nay, but this dotage of our general's
>   O'erflows the measure; those his goodly eyes
>   That o'er the files and musters of the war
>   Have glowed like plated Mars, now bend, now turn
>   Their office and devotion of their view
>   Upon a tawny front. His captain's heart,
>   Which in the scuffles of great fights hath burst
>   The buckles on his breast, reneges all temper,
>   And is become the bellows and the fan
>   To cool a gypsy's lust.
>   Look where they come.
> *Laughter off*
>   Take but good note, and you shall see in him
>   The triple pillar of the world transformed
>   Into a strumpet's fool.
> CLEOPATRA: (*approach*) If it be love indeed, tell me how much.[9]

The omission of the character of Demetrius and the consequent elevation of Philo to choric status, combined with Plutarch's overarching narrative presence, establish the strength of the Roman viewpoint from the outset, thus upsetting the delicately balanced dynamics of the play's central conflict. In a play that focuses upon the process of making value judgements, tampering with the mechanism in this way represents a simplification rather than an adaptation. A more recent radio production of the play directed by John Tydeman (30 January 1977), which restricted its adjustments to a fairly judicious cutting of Shakespeare's text and dispensed with the narrator figure in favour of simple musical themes to signify shifts of location, succeeded in reinstating the play's central conflict, thus foregrounding the ambivalent effects of the dramatic poetry and forcing a choice upon the listener. But even here the two worlds of Rome and Egypt receded in terms of their symbolic value as the natural focus of the listener's attention became Antony (played with impressive range and power by Robert Stephens) and Cleopatra (whose seedy beauty was amply conveyed through the faintly cracking voice of Siân Phillips).

Clearly it is the dramatic scope of *Antony and Cleopatra* that creates difficulty for both stage and radio alike. This is not a problem with *Othello*, in which, apart from a few public scenes, the general atmosphere is one of 'a close-shut murderous room',[10] although the black-white symbolism is an important visual effect requiring the attention of the adaptor. John Tydeman's 1972 radio production of the play, with Paul Scofield as Othello, responded well to this close focus. Unlike *Antony and Cleopatra*, in which basic issues such as entries and exits become something of a problem, in *Othello* the listener's attention is so carefully directed that the spatial complications arising in large ensemble scenes are virtually nonexistent. From the point of view of adaptation the most problematical scene appears to have been V.i, where, because of a series of rapid entries and exits involving minor as well as major characters and involving also a series of different perspectives on the action, some attempt had to be made to establish and fix identities clearly from the listener's point of view. Thus the two opening soliloquies of the scene, from Iago and Roderigo respectively, are delivered close to the microphone, while Cassio's entry is marked by Roderigo's ''tis he, Cassio' (V.i.23) as against the unspecific ''tis he' of the text. Also, the absence of an exit line for Iago at V.i.27 in the text is adjusted in the broadcast script by the insertion of a non-Shakespearean interpolation: 'And now depart.' Iago's later re-entry is already catered for in Shakespeare's dialogue, though the radio script makes a minor adjustment at V.i.56 in order to reinforce the listener's impression of the affected nature of his concern for Cassio, 'O my Lieutenant', as opposed to the more distant irony of 'O me, Lieutenant' of the text. The character of Gratiano presents a minor difficulty in this scene since he has a number of lines to speak, but in terms of creating a clear 'sound presence' they offer little assistance to the listener. Thus at the earliest opportunity, and to avoid later confusion as the scene fills, Lodovico's line at V.i.40 is extended from the text's nonspecific monosyllable 'Hark!', which would be self-explanatory in a stage production, to 'Gratiano hark!', which establishes a presence. Similarly at V.i.104, in order to avoid the confusion that might arise with Emilia's entry at

V.i.110, Iago's question, 'What, look you pale?', is extended in the radio script to 'What, Bianca, look you pale?', thus establishing Bianca's presence clearly before the appearance of a second female character.

Virtually all adaptations of Shakespeare's plays require adjustments of this sort, simply as ways of keeping to the fore of the listener's mind distinctions between individual characters. In most cases the objective is to compensate for an absence of visual perspective, thus establishing by implication a framework that has theatrical performance as its reference point. But there are occasions when adjustments in sound alone, at a level below that of the articulated text, can suggest meaning more precisely and economically than is usually possible in the theatre. For example, in a radio production of *The Merchant of Venice* on 3 October 1976 directed by Ian Cotterell, which involved little in the way of explicit adaptation, the use of 'live' sound for Portia's interviews with her three egocentric admirers (II.i and II.vii) effectively underlined the cold formality of her response to their advances, to the extent that the listener could detect a tension between her own wishes and the will of her dead father. Similarly the adjustment to 'dead' sound, without changing the scenic location, for the interview with Bassanio suggested a warmth and a receptiveness that *anticipated* the outcome. Such effects can be used in a sophisticated way to suggest critical perspectives, influencing the listener in a manner not unlike that in which the novelist might influence his reader — by the *style* of presentation as opposed to explicit direction.

NOTES

1. Except where otherwise noted, all quotations from Shakespeare's plays are taken from *The Complete Works*, ed. Peter Alexander. London and Glasgow 1951.

2. Herbert Read, 'Sotto voce — a plea for intimacy'. *BBC Quarterly*, 4(1) (Apr. 1949), p. 4; Mary Crozier, 'Four radio plays', *BBC Quarterly*, 3(3) (Oct. 1948), p. 169.

3. Louis MacNeice, 'General introduction', *The Dark Tower and Other Radio Scripts*. London 1947, p. 10; see my 'Introduction', in Drakakis (ed.), op. cit., pp. 1–36.

4. Raymond Williams, 'Recent English drama', in Boris Ford (ed.), *The Pelican Guide to English Literature*. Vol. 7: *The Modern Age*. Harmondsworth 1961, pp. 496–508.

5. One wonders what listeners might have thought of Hugh Stewart's ultimately abortive suggestion, made in November 1952, for an all-Scottish *Macbeth*, justified in the following terms: 'The Macbeths themselves are really a typical product of the Highlands insofar as they have a tough and dangerous courage but are soft at the core, sentimental and vacillating. Lady Macbeth, played with a West Highland accent, would I think be

extraordinarily effective particularly in the sleep-walking scene . . .' (BBC Written Archives, Accession no. 37622).

6. In Ian Cotterell's recent production of *The Tempest* for Radio 4 (22 May 1977) with Paul Scofield as Prospero, the 'naturalistic' opening sequence was badly handled; some of the group scenes (e.g. II.ii) and some of the entries were also difficult to adapt to radio.

7. In the celebrated 1949 radio production of the play with Donald Wolfit as Lear, there was simply a pause at the point when Gloucester *'casts himself down'*, so that the listener is not certain what to think.

8. See Roy Walker's comments in *Radio Times*, **123**(1588)(18–24 Apr. 1954), p. 7, on Glen Byam Shaw's Stratford Memorial Theatre production of that season, in which he used 'a featherweight permanent setting of which the main feature was the cyclorama. His simple but attractive solution to the problem was that one sky covers all earthly places. So does the air.'

9. Quoted from the script in the BBC Play Library, Broadcasting House, London.

10. A. C. Bradley, *Shakespearean Tragedy*, London 1957, p. 143.

IV ITS PLACE IN EDUCATION

This section has something of a historical focus to it, as it tries to see the teaching of English Literature in the perspective of the years.

It opens with a consideration of *The Newbolt Report* and George Sampson's *English for the English*, two important influences on the teaching of English in schools. It deals with some of the issues raised by Eagleton (8) in Section II, and it is interesting to compare the tone and 'ideology' of the two pieces.

In 1966, a seminar was held in Dartmouth, USA, where a variety of models of English teaching were discussed by American and British teachers of English. In the second chapter Dixon discusses three of the models considered at the seminar: the skills, cultural heritage, and personal growth models. In the third chapter, Allen evaluates some of the effects of the Dartmouth Seminar and of John Dixon's interpretation of it, including the important omissions Dixon chose to make.

The Bullock Report presents the 'official' version of what should happen in schools, emphasizing that increasing the range and amount of reading should be a major aim in secondary schools.

One of the most recent debates in education concerns the position of structuralism. The last chapter is a basic introduction to the nature of structuralism and deconstruction, seen in the light of other approaches to literature. It rounds off the section chronologically, and looks back to the end of Section 1.

22 *The Newbolt Report and* English for the English

● Margaret Mathieson

'. . . literature is not just a subject for academic study, but one of the chief temples of the human spirit, in which all should worship.'

The Newbolt Report (1921)

The Newbolt Report and George Sampson's book, *English for the English*, are landmarks on any survey of the subject's development over the past one hundred and fifty years. They express all the major anxieties about its treatment in universities, schools and teacher-training establishments, as well as all the certainties about the value of English which had been intensified since Arnold's analysis of his 'mechanical' and 'external' society. They reflect, too, the characteristic mood of the period following the First World War, the sharp despair and the faith in the power of education to improve the future. Both documents have greatly influenced later discussion about English in schools; they are still referred to with appreciation today. Most of all, they anticipate future prescriptions about the qualities which seem desirable in the subject's teachers. When their authors were faced with the discoveries of widespread hostility to literature, bad conditions in elementary schools and poorly trained, uncultivated teachers, they responded, in the main, by calling for men and women with exceptional gifts to work in the classrooms. As we shall see, they repeated the Victorian demands for 'apostles' and 'missionaries', thus reinforcing the notion that English was the subject which needed special people as its teachers.

The mood of post-war England was very sympathetic to the need for educational reform. One of the war's results was to produce not only a sense of the military and economic benefits enjoyed by Germany because of her educational system's freedom from irrelevant traditionalism, but also an awareness of our working-class's cultural inferiority. In 1918, at Manchester, Lloyd George voiced his dissatisfaction.

The most formidable institution we had to fight in Germany was not the arsenals of Krupps or the yards in which they turned out submarines, but the schools of Germany. They were our most formidable competitors in business and our most terrible opponents in war. An educated man is a better worker, a more formidable warrior, and a better citizen. That was only half comprehended before the war.[1]

And as one of their many pieces of evidence of the elementary schools' failure in this country to do more than, as H. G. Wells had expressed it, 'educate the lower classes for employment on lower-class lines',[2] the Newbolt Report quotes a chaplain on the personal qualities of the men in the trenches. In support of their case for the improved study of English in schools, the Report quotes him as saying:

The only trouble is that their standard of general education is so low. Put the product of the old elementary schools side by side with the man from overseas, and his mental equipment is pitiful . . .[3]

The war uncovered the old problems of the elementary schools — large classes, poorly qualified staff, physically weak children, children in part-time employment, and continued use of outdated, discredited methods of mechanical rote-learning. Most importantly, the horrors of war produced a yearning for ways of improving the great majority's living conditions. The revelation of the wide differences between rich and poor produced a desire for reform, a response to which was the Report's plea for a more widespread liberal education in schools. H. A. L. Fisher expressed this general feeling when he said, in 1917 at Manchester, in preparation for his Bill to raise the school-leaving age:

I conceive that it is part of the duty of our generation to provide some means for compensating the tragic loss which our nation is enduring, and that one means by which some compensation may be provided is by the creation of a system of education throughout the country which will increase the value of every human unit in the whole of society by giving all our children the best possible opportunity that we can afford to give them, and they can afford to turn to account.[4]

As President of the Board of Education, he expressed also his unease about the division between the public and elementary schools' curricula, between the civilising, humanising subjects and the severely practical. At the above meeting in Manchester, Fisher said on this matter (and it is a plea repeated in more specific terms by the 1921 Report's Committee and by George Sampson):

The proposition for which I am contending is that youth is the period of life specially set apart for education. I venture to plead for a state of society in which learning comes first and earning comes second among the obligations of youth, not for one class only, but for all young people. At present the rich learn and the poor earn.[5]

Expressions of national guilt and the need for greater social justice were now being made publicly at an official level, and it was becoming clear that recommendations for the replacement of the classics by English studies were having implications far beyond practical changes in the curriculum. As we shall see when we look at the Report's emotive language in its chapters on the cultural health of the nation, recommendations for improved English teaching in schools were made with religious passion because, for their supporters, they represented ways in which guilt could be assuaged and greater social justice achieved in a divided nation.

It is useful, first, to look briefly at the background to the 1921 Report. The national sense of inferiority to Europe in education, the rising demand for secondary school places, and the general feeling that reform was necessary, brought about the appointment of a number of committees to inquire into the state of certain subjects in this country's schools. Between 1918 and 1919, four such committees were set up, to report on the teaching of science, modern languages, classics and English. The context against which these investigations were made is clear from the Board of Education's Report for 1917–18, which conveys the national sense of need for improvement, and a vivid impression of the highly emotional sources from which it arose. This context, it can be argued, was particularly important in affecting the kind of Report made upon the teaching of English.

> The tension and suffering of the war have revealed many things which we had forgotten or to which we were indifferent, and we now know that the shattered temple of Peace has to be rebuilt more nobly and the fabric of society has to be reconstructed upon more generous lines.[6]

About his period of office at the Board of Education during this time, Fisher wrote, in 1940:

> The vast expenditure and harrowing anxieties of the time . . . helped to promote a widespread feeling for improvement in the general lot of the people.[7]

It is worth, also, looking at the terms of reference for his inquiry for the insight which they give into what was felt more and more acutely to be an educational crisis. The distinguished Committee, under the chairmanship of Sir Henry Newbolt, and including among its inspectors, principals and heads of schools, Sir Arthur Quiller-Couch, J. H. Fowler and Caroline Spurgeon, was asked:

> To inquire into the position occupied by English [Language and Literature] in the educational system of England, and to advise how its study may best be promoted in schools of all types, including Continuation Schools, and in Universities, and other Institutions of Higher Education, regard being had to:
> (1) the requirements of a liberal education;
> (2) the needs of business, the professions, and the public services; and
> (3) the relation of English to other studies.[8]

In its opening pages, where the Committee refers to the 'wide scope' given by the terms of reference to their 'consideration of English', its members described the breadth of the questions which they consider to have been raised by their assignment. On the first page, they stated:

> The inadequate conception of the teaching of English in this country is not a separate defect which can be separately remedied. It is due to a more far-reaching failure — the failure to conceive the full meaning and possibilities of national education as a whole, and that failure again is due to a misunderstanding of the educational values to be found in the different regions of mental activity, and especially to an underestimate of the importance of English language and literature.[9]

Echoing Fisher's dissatisfaction with the injustice of two different kinds of education designed to prepare pupils for two different ways of life, the Committee deplores the system which has as its object that 'of equipping the young in some vague and little-understood way for the struggle of adult existence in a world of material interests'.[10] It, too, draws attention to the differences between those pupils who receive 'special treatment', the 'superior' education which has been 'the privilege of the minority only' and children in elementary schools, pointing out that 'no source of unity is to be found in the teaching provided by different types of schools'.[11] The existence of such widely differing schools, with differing goals and, hence, differing curricula has, the members claim, 'widened the mental distances between classes in England'.

From the opening, then, members of the Newbolt Committee make it clear that, like Matthew Arnold whose writings they frequently invoke, one of their main goals is the achievement of greater social unity. It is, in fact, the fusion of this Committee's anxiety about the evils of social divisiveness with its conviction about the totally educative value of literature which gives the document its arresting passion. Fundamental changes in society are considered desirable and since, in the Committee's view, improved teaching of English in all our schools is the means of achieving them, it is not surprising that the Report has made an important contribution to the subject's ideology of social and individual improvement.

The committee did not wish to undervalue the study of the classics, but, like the contributors to *Essays on a Liberal Education*, its members thought that their linguistic difficulties would prevent all but a very few from reaching an enjoyment of classical literature. They admitted that the classics, well taught, offered the finest education, but they insisted that the classics were not the means of bridging the all-too-obvious gulfs between social classes. Moreover, transfer of the classical curriculum's teaching methods to the elementary schools had already had disastrous effects upon English. In the Committee's view, the classics, as they had come to be taught in the nineteenth century, had actually held back liberal education in schools. In the historical section on the development of English, the Report states:

> The formalism which so often warped the public school idea of Education is seen setting its stamp upon the Elementary School so soon as it attempts to grow. English, indeed, makes an appearance, but only as a pale reflection of the discipline of classical studies.[12]

Thus, a new approach was needed, one which would provide a truly humanising education for all pupils in public schools, one which would also offer opportunities for greater self-realisation to all pupils in elementary schools. The Report declares its members' convictions very emphatically:

> We have declared the necessity of what must be, in however elementary a form, a liberal education for all English children whatever their position or occupation of life. . . . We believe that in English literature we have a means of Education not less valuable than the classics and decidedly more suited to the necessities of a general and national education. . . . [13]

The introduction of good English teaching into all of the nation's schools would, the Report asserts, do much to promote social unity. If the emphasis in the elementary schools upon memorising, rote-learning and irrelevant, arid composition writing and comprehension were to be replaced by a concentration upon good plain speech and writing, and practice given in talking and listening, a way would have been found of breaking down social barriers. Not only would 'command of his native language' give the working-class child the means of learning other subjects more successfully but it would enable him to be more confident and effective socially. Even more importantly, rich and poor would become united through their involvement in a common culture. The Report suggests that:

> An education of this kind is the greatest benefit which could be conferred upon any citizen of a great state, and that the common right to it, the common discipline and enjoyment of it, the common possession of the tastes and associations connected with it, would form a new element of national unity, linking together the mental life of all classes by experiences which have hitherto been the privileges of a limited section. . . . If we use English literature as a means of contact with great minds, a channel by which to draw upon their experience with profit and delight, and a bond of sympathy between the members of a human society, we shall succeed, as the best teachers of the classics have often succeeded in their more limited field.[14]

The inclusion of literature in the elementary school curriculum would narrow the gap between those who were referred to by Fisher as 'educated to learn' and those 'educated to earn'. Literature in schools could, more than any other study, achieve the education of the whole child because of its deliberate and beneficial irrelevance to him as a future wage-earner. 'The literature lesson', the Committee says, 'is no mechanical matter'; it consists 'not in the imparting of information, but in the introduction of the student to great minds and new forms of experience'.[15] In the Committee's view it was imperative to include the non-vocational in the elementary school curriculum as a matter of social justice, while in George Sampson's view it appeared, in addition, to be politically realistic. In his Preface to the 1925 edition of *English for the English*, he says:

> Deny to working-class children any common share in the immaterial, and presently they will grow into the men who demand with menaces a communism of the material.[16]

George Sampson insists, in a statement frequently quoted by educators in English, that it is the schools' responsibility not to educate children for their occupations, but to prepare children against their environment. He says with a strength of emphasis which was to become characteristic of many recommendations made about the teaching of English:

> I am prepared to maintain, and indeed, do maintain, without reservation and perhapes, that it is the purpose of education, not to prepare children for their occupations, but to prepare children against their occupations.[17]

His argument is that the elementary schools are the most important schools in the country and that English is 'by far the most important subject in the elementary schools'.[18] He repeats the convictions of Fisher and the Newbolt Committee when he describes their goal as being: 'to develop the mind and soul of the children and not merely to provide tame and acquiescent labour fodder'.[19]

With the introduction of English writers for study in all the nation's schools, the Newbolt Report expected a general raising of society's cultural level and its capacity to respond to great works of art. The Committee suggested that what its investigations had uncovered in the way of national philistinism and distrust of art might be counteracted by a changed approach to teaching in schools. It reported that rich and poor in England were inclined to misunderstand, undervalue and be bored by art, and it recommended that serious efforts should be made to substitute imaginatively chosen material in English for the dull routine followed in public and elementary schools. Children's experience of literature as material which is both comprehensible and enjoyable might do much, the Committee felt, to raise the country's level of cultural appreciation.

The powerfully emotional language of both *English for the English* and the Newbolt Report reflects their writers' strong commitment to their views. George Sampson and the contributors to the Report were desperately concerned about the state of the elementary schools. Clearly they believed wholeheartedly in the need for improved English teaching and in the benefits which would result.

George Sampson insisted that the situation in the schools was 'tragic', that 'English cannot wait' since 'the teacher of English is continuously assailed by powerful and almost insuperable hostile forces'.[20] In the closing pages of his book (its introduction refers to it as 'a tract for the times' written 'with the passion of a crusader'),[21] Sampson states that the forces of philistinism, triviality and vulgarity must be opposed in our society. He asks angrily, and his combative language anticipates the tones of Leavis and Thompson, 'but is not the power of the enemy due to the folly that has limited the warriors who might destroy it to the few who could utter the Shibboleth of the classics?'[22] Sampson's, and the Report's, religious imagery is highly suggestive. It obviously helps to convey the strength of these writers' convictions about the need for English studies to replace the classics. It suggests also that a point in the process of secularisation had now been reached where spiritual values were being invested in works of art. Bryan Wilson's discussion of this is illuminating. He says:

> . . . as the arts as such acquired autonomy as craftsmen and artists were employed for purposes not specifically religious, so the arts came to embody values and to evoke emotional responses which were not themselves in the service of religion.[23]

The arts' embodiment of spiritual values, a process hastened during the Victorian period by artists' alienation from their society, meant that they came to be recommended with greater and greater fervour for the majority's well-being. Philanthropic liberals throughout the nineteenth century were deeply disturbed by what they saw as the masses' loss of religion. Although it seems unlikely that the majority of the working classes was much affected by institutionalised religion in the big cities, fear such as Arnold's about its decline sharpened insistence upon the desperate need for literature. Increasing scepticism among educated Victorians gave the impression that the whole population was losing the support of religious faith. The language of the Newbolt Report and *English for the English* certainly suggests that the responsibility for 'uplifting' — the traditional function of the classics and the Church — was, in time of crisis, being transferred to English.

Sampson refers to the 'class of young barbarians whose souls are to be touched by literature'[24] and to the 'pure religion' and 'creative reception'[25] of the literary experience, his tones echoing those of the Newbolt Report in its section on the high responsibilities of the future English teacher. The Report's members expressed their views thus on the university professor of literature:

> He has obligations not merely to the students who come to him to read for a degree, but still more towards the teeming population outside the University walls, most of whom have not so much as 'heard whether there be any Holy Ghost'. The fulfilment of these obligations means propaganda work, organisation and the building up of a staff of assistant

missionaries. But first, and above all, it means a right attitude of mind, a conviction that literature and life are inseparable, that literature is not just a subject for academic study, but one of the chief temples of the human spirit, in which all should worship.[26]

The teaching of literature is often referred to as 'missionary work' in the Report, reminiscent, as D. J. Palmer notes, of the nineteenth-century mood of moral earnestness which caused educators to invoke the Bible and noble poetry as necessary defences against political discontent and the debased attractions of the popular press. The Report states that the teachers of English should have the kind of qualities which are more usually found in the charismatic preacher. For the difficult task of 'humanising the masses', it asks for passion, zeal and creativity, in addition to the humility with which unfamiliar cultural regions should be entered. The Committee acknowledges, with regret, that the working classes are likely to identify superior cultures with privilege. It says, therefore:

> The ambassadors of poetry must be humble, they must learn to call nothing common or unclean — not even the local dialect, the clatter of the factory, or the smoky pall of industrial centres.[27]

The tone of desperation which characterised both the Report and Sampson's book arose from their writers' conviction about the moral and spiritual value of great literature. It becomes increasingly familiar, particularly in the writings of F. R. Leavis and the Cambridge School of English, as the cultural crisis is defined as worsening. Calls will be made in the 1930s and 1940s for 'warriors', for teachers 'who will fight', more aggressive figures than the high-born ambassadors on their good-will missions. Even more depressing than the Newbolt Committee's discovery of mechanical teaching methods and poorly qualified teachers, at a time when so much depended upon the successful diffusion of liberal culture, was the news of working-class hostility to literature. This extract (from the section on 'Literature and the Nation') describes the way in which the Committee responded to the news that the working class, identifying the arts with leisure, viewed literature with distrust.

> We were told that the working classes, especially those belonging to organised labour movements, were antagonistic to, and contemptuous of, literature, that they regarded it 'merely as an ornament, a polite accomplishment, a subject to be despised by really virile men'. Literature, in fact, seems to be classed by a large number of thinking working men with antimacassars, fish knives and other unintelligible and futile trivialities of 'middle-class culture' and, as a subject of instruction, is suspect as an attempt to 'side-track the working-class movement'. We regard the prevalence of such opinions as a serious matter, not merely because it means the alienation of an important section of the population from the 'confort' and 'mirthe' of literature, but chiefly because it points to a morbid condition of the body politic which if not taken in hand may be

followed by lamentable consequences . . . the nation of which a considerable portion rejects this [literature's] means of grace, and despises this great spiritual influence, must assuredly be heading to disaster.[28]

Solution of this problem, in the Committee's view, was to be found in the schools, in the recruitment and education of teachers capable of inspiring pupils with a sense of enjoyment in literature. If the goals of the schools were changed and the teachers could be educated to do more than just impart useful knowledge to their pupils, society, it was suggested, would inevitably improve. Hearts and minds would be changed because of the nature of the literary experience, the power of which was to satisfy 'the love of truth, the love of beauty and the love of righteousness'. The following passage illustrates the Committee members' version of the personal changes effected by literature, and their faith in the teachers' power to bring them about in society as a whole.

> . . . a realisation of what might be accomplished through English literature to 'awaken the mind from the lethargy of custom and direct it to the loveliness and wonders of the world before us' would, if it became general among teachers, transform the face of the schools.[29]

Full consideration has been given to the Newbolt Report and George Sampson's book, *English for the English*, because of their influence upon the teaching of English in schools during the past fifty years, and because of the way in which they illustrate how changes in education and wider society affected the subject's importance in the curriculum. Both works reflect the dissatisfaction with the exclusiveness and aridity of the classical curriculum, dissatisfaction which had its source in nineteenth-century utilitarian and philanthropic discontent. Because of linguistic difficulties, classical studies were 'humanising' only a privileged few; their accessibility to these few perpetuated undesirable social divisiveness; their identification with the leisured class was responsible for the humble status of English and for the wide-spread working-class suspicion of the arts in general. George Sampson added to all this his criticism of our tendency to admire only 'the exotic', and thus to despise the rich heritage of English and neglect ways in which both language and literature could be genuinely 'practical' in pupils' lives.

Both works embody attitudes which, together, have had the effect of strengthening the notion that English has the unique power to improve character and to transform society. The commercial world was viewed with distrust and hostility and, as its 'forces' seemed to be more threatening, men of letters, educated in the nineteenth-century traditions of service and commitment to social improvement, urged the acceptance of a subject which could defend the whole of society against such forces. To English studies they transferred the classics' and religion's traditional responsibilities for character development, their moral seriousness deepened by their desire for social justice.

Moreover, both works illustrated the extent to which progressive theories of education had gained acceptance at official level. Their authors' interest was in the education of the 'whole child', in his participation and creativity, in the 'education of the emotions'. Clearly, these professors, lecturers, principals and teachers had responded warmly to those progressive theories which had been responsible for producing dissatisfaction with a state of affairs in schools where 'faculty' psychology determined content and methods, and for directing attention to the opportunities within English studies for individual development.

The authors of the Newbolt Report and *English for the English* clearly wished to make liberal culture, aesthetic appreciation, and self-realisation through art and the native language available to the whole nation. The following summary, which the Newbolt Committee made of its views about the centrality of English, in the context of the country's educational and social needs, bears an interesting resemblance to recommendations made thirty years later by the Newsom Committee. Both see English studies in schools as the solution to cultural problems produced by mass literacy in an industrial society.

> On the one hand, our national education needs to be perfected by being scientifically refounded as a universal, reasonable and liberal process of development; on the other hand, we find coincidentally that for this purpose, of all the means available, there is only one which fulfils all the conditions of our problems. . . . We recognise fully, on the one side, the moral, practical, educational value of natural science, on the other side the moral, practical value of the arts and of all great literatures ancient and modern. But what we are looking for now is not merely a means of education, one chamber in the structure we are hoping to rebuild, but the true starting-point and foundation from which all the rest must spring. For this special purpose there is but one material. We make no comparison, we state what appears to us to be an incontrovertible primary fact, that for English children no form of knowledge can take precedence of a knowledge of English, no form of literature can take precedence of English literature: and that the two are so inextricably connected as to form the only basis possible for a national education.[30]

NOTES

1. Lloyd George, speech given in Manchester, September 1918; quoted by G. Bernbaum, *Social Change and the Schools* (London, Routledge, 1967), p. 16.
2. H. G. Wells; quoted by G. A. N. Lowndes, *The Silent Social Revolution* (London, Oxford University Press, 1969), p. 4.
3. P. B. Clayton, Chaplain at Poperinghe 1914–18; quoted in *The Teaching of English in England* (London, HMSO, 1921), p. 17.
4. H. A. L. Fisher, speech given in Manchester, 1917.
5. Ibid.

6. Board of Education, *Report* for 1917–18, p. 1.

7. H. A. L. Fisher, *Unfinished Autobiography* (London, Oxford University Press, 1940), p. 94.

8. *The Teaching of English in England* (1921), op. cit., Preface, p. 1.

9. Ibid., pp. 4 f.

10. Ibid., p. 6.

11. Ibid., loc. cit.

12. Ibid., p. 45.

13. Ibid., pp. 14 f.

14. Ibid., pp. 15 f.

15. Ibid., p. 24.

16. George Sampson, *English for the English* (Cambridge, Cambridge University Press, 1952), Preface to 1925 ed., p. xv.

17. Ibid., p. 11.

18. Ibid., p. 18.

19. Ibid., p. 34.

20. Ibid., p. 27.

21. S. C. Roberts, Introduction to *English for the English* (1925) (Cambridge, Cambridge University Press, 1952), p. viii.

22. Sampson, op. cit. (1952), p. 125.

23. Bryan Wilson, *Religion in Secular Society* (London, Watts, 1966), p. 45.

24. Sampson, op. cit. (1952), p. 90.

25. Ibid., p. 89.

26. *The Teaching of English in England*, op. cit., p. 259.

27. Ibid., p. 260.

28. Ibid., pp. 252 f.

29. Ibid., p. 106.

30. Ibid., p. 14.

23   *A Method of Definition*

● John Dixon

With respect to the Master; that he be capable of and diligent in teaching to read, write and cast accounts. . . . With respect to the boys; that they can at least spell well.

(Regulations for the English School, 1704)

The tremendous pressure for a narrow and rigid standard of conformity in spelling, punctuation and usage that has sometimes squeezed nearly everything else out. . . .

(Al Kitzhaber, Dartmouth)

The English curriculum in the average secondary school today is an unhappy combination of old matter unrenewed and new matter that rarely rises above the level of passing concerns.

(Freedom and Discipline in English, 1965)

English is a quicksilver among metals — mobile, living and elusive. Its conflicting emphases challenge us today to look for a new, coherent definition. Its complexity invites the partial and incomplete view, the dangerous simplification that restricts what goes on in the classroom. A map is needed on which the confusing claims and theories can be plotted.

In the map that emerges from the Dartmouth Seminar, one dimension is historical. Among the models or images of English that have been widely accepted in schools on both sides of the Atlantic, three were singled out. The first centred on *skills*: it fitted an era when *initial* literacy was the prime demand. The second stressed the *cultural heritage*, the need for a civilizing and socially unifying content. The third (and current) model focuses on *personal growth*: on the need to re-examine the learning processes and the meaning to the individual of what he is doing in English lessons. Looking back over the history of our subject, we see the limitations in the earlier models and thus the need to reinterpret our conception of 'skills' and 'heritage'.

The idea of a skill, a co-ordination of hand and eye in habitual, controlled action, seems at first sight perfectly suited to the rather narrow field of learning to read and write (to use language in the visual medium, not the oral). The word *skill* is still felt to have literal meaning here, rather than metaphoric. Yet on closer scrutiny it can apply literally only to minor elements of the total process, to the way our eyes scan the line perhaps, or the movements of our hands on the typewriter. The learning of correct spellings, of vocabulary, of punctuation habits, and the comprehending or use of longer and more complex sentences, are only 'skills' in a vaguer, more extended sense; they are far from being exactly similar operations. If we have a persistent sense of their similarity, it arises from a muddled idea of their operation and a clear memory of the common teaching techniques mistakenly applied to some of them.

The first limitation of the skill model, then, is its tendency to assimilate the many different operations we learn in the course of beginning to read and write. Its major limitation, however, lies not in the area of English it chooses to sketch, but in the vast terrain it chooses to ignore. Nearly a century of emphasis on the skills of English has brought almost universal literacy in our countries — a literacy dissipated, for the most part, on the impoverished literature of the popular press (which grew in answer to it). We should not be surprised. Whenever the so-called skill elements of language learning are divorced from the rest of English, the means becomes the end. It has taken the Infant Schools, in their work with five- to seven-year-olds, to prove that a new and complex relationship is possible between the 'skill' elements and the broader processes that prompt a child to use language in the first place. In the secondary schools we still invite defeat by putting the old 'drills' alongside 'imaginative' approaches to English.

The idea of English as a *cultural heritage* was clearly intended to fill the vacuum left by the skills model. Great literature offers, in Arnold's phrase, a criticism of life: what better could the children be reading? Here was a content for English that all could respect, a content moreover that linked the primary schools with the universities (from whom the proposal generally originated). 'The Professor of Literature in a University should be — and sometimes is, as we gladly recognize — a missionary in a more real and active sense than any of his colleagues', said the 1919 Newbolt Report. Through literature all that was best in national thought and feeling could be handed on to a generation that knew largely slums and economic depression. In a happy way, too, the great writers would offer a variety of models on which the pupils' writing could be based.

One might point to the betrayal of this vision in a thousand classrooms today where the 'precious lifeblood of a master-spirit' becomes a series of inky marginal annotations and essay notes; but that would be to miss its real limitations. The central one concerns 'culture'. In the heritage model the stress was on culture as a *given*. There was a constant temptation to ignore culture as the pupil knows it, a network of attitudes to experience and personal evaluations that he develops in a living response to his family and neighbourhood. But this personal culture is what he brings to literature; in the light of it he reads the linguistic symbols (giving his own precious life-blood!). What is vital is the interplay between his personal world and the world of the writer: the teacher of English must acknowledge both sides of the experience, and know both of them intimately if he is to help bring the two into a fruitful relationship.

However, by re-emphasizing the text, the heritage model confirmed the average teacher in his attention to the written word (the point of strength in his training) as against the spoken word (the pupils' strenth). It confirmed him too in presenting experience (in fictions) to his pupils, rather than drawing from them their experience (of reality and self). But in doing so it set up tensions that have brought about its own collapse and a major reinterpretation of its noble aims.

To sum up what we learn from the historical dimension: looking at the first two models from the standpoint of child development, we can see they have exaggerated two areas at the expense of the rest and in so doing have distorted these areas themselves. It is as if the mapping had been done on an elastic sheet. During the skills era this was stretched until the operations specific to the written system of language became the centre of English. The heritage era put 'skills' in their place as means to an end. But it failed to reinterpret the concept of 'skills' and thus left an uneasy dualism in English teaching. Literature itself tended to be treated as a given, a ready-made structure that we imitate and a content that is handed over to us. And this attitude infected composition and all work in language. There was a fatal inattention to the processes involved in such everyday activities as talking and thinking things over, writing a diary cr a letter home, even enjoying a TV play. Discussion was virtually ignored, as we know to our cost today on both sides of the Atlantic. In other words, the part of the map that relates a man's language to his experience was largely unexplored. (Think of the trivial essay topics that still result from this ignorance.) The purposes and pressures that language serves tended to be reduced to a simple formula — a lump sum view of inheritance.

A THIRD MODEL: LANGUAGE AND PERSONAL GROWTH

It is rather easy to be wise after the event; if we are to learn from our past mistakes we need to build English teaching on a second axis, based on our observation of language in operation from day to day.

When we do observe children as they learn to use language for their own purposes, surprising new areas of the map emerge that modify considerably our understanding of the earlier features. Take for instance the following entry in the diary of a ten-year-old boy:

> 1st April. Rainy with sunny periods. After breakfast I went out to get some newts. I got a large jar, washed it and put a stone in it, then went to poplar pond with a stone and a tin.

It was cold and very windy. After about an hour I had caught one femail newt. I was frozzen. I could hardly feel my hands they were so cold. I half filled the jar with water and a few water weeds and put the newt in. In the afternoon I tride to get another. I saw one just out of my reach. I waded out abit and foregot that I had a hole in one of my wellington boots. The water just flowd in. I didn't catch any more newts, and went home with a boot full of water. I'm going to try and get some more tomorrow and I hope I have better luck.

2nd. Very rainy dull and wet. To-day I made a fishing net, not to catch fish but newts. I caught six. I picked out the ones I thought best. I kept three and let the others go. There were lots of newts in the pond t-day I daresay they like this kind of weather.

The three newts I caught, two were a bright orange on the belly with big black round spots all over, the other one was smaller and was a muddy colour and its belly was a bright orange with very small spots on it. I mean, the spots on this one were only on the belly not all over. The one I got yesterday was a dark yellow ochre.

All afternoon I sat watching them, I think they are very interesting things.[1]

It is difficult to remain indifferent to what the boy is saying: the language invites a listener and speaks directly to him. (As he writes, it is as if the boy has that sympathetic listener built imaginatively into his mind.) In sharing the experience with the imaginary listener, he brings it to life again, realizes it for himself. There are places where he has worked to make something exact: 'I mean the spots on this one were only on the belly' . . . 'a dark yellow ochre.' It is as if he is listening and scanning what he has just said. At other places he has wanted a different kind of communion with the listener — has stood in a different relationship to his experience. 'All afternoon I sat watching them, I think they are very interesting things.' It is an open invitation to join him in feeling that life is good. (Complex-sentence hunters might agree that these two plain sentences are the sign not of a failure in expression but of a rather fine type of control.) As an English teacher one can see here a path that connects this writer's intentions with Hemingway's stories of Nick. But earlier there was a different growing point, when the boy chose to say, almost aside: 'There were lots of newts in the pond t-day I daresay they like this kind of weather.' There he was using language to draw observations together and make a tentative hypothesis.

What, as English teachers, can we learn from such an extract? This boy starts writing with a sense of having something worth sharing. We can guess that he is used to having a sympathetic and interested listener. He wants to make his experience real again, and as he does so he makes discoveries. Using language in his case means selecting some things for scrutiny and bringing things into order. So the flux of experiences he encountered that day begin to take on a meaning — a meaning which he treasures. We can be almost sure that the language and the meaning are both *his*, not a product handed over by the teacher. This is language in operation, not a dummy run, and we have to make our classrooms places where pupils want to talk and write from impulses such as these.

This sample reminds us that language serves, and enables us to carry out, certain fundamentally human purposes. Even the private act of writing bears traces of the primary purpose in language, to share experience. The skills model is only indirectly aware of such a purpose: its ideal pupils might well be copy-typists. And that is ironical, since the insistence on correct spelling, etc., is avowedly in the interests of better communication, of unimpeded sharing! A heritage model, with its stress on adult literature, turns language into a one-way process: pupils are readers, receivers of the master's voice. How, we may ask, do these private activities of writing and reading relate to the stream of public interaction through language in which we are all involved every day, teachers as much as pupils? The heritage model offers no help in answering, because it neglects the most fundamental aim of language — to promote interaction between people. As a result drama, the literary form that directly embodies this interaction, has been interpreted as the study of texts, not acting them out. Current accounts of language as 'communication' share the same weakness. They deal only in pre-formulated messages and ignore the discoveries we make in the process of talking and writing from experience, or in re-enacting an experience dramatically.

The fact is that in sharing experience with others man is using language to make that experience real to himself. The selection and shaping that language involves, the choices between alternative expressions so that the language shall fit the experience and bring it to life 'as it really was' — these activities imply imaginative work. If we could observe all the occasions when a child uses language in this way, and put them together, we should have caught a glimpse of a representational world that the child has built up to fit reality as he knows it.

There is, then, a central paradox about language. It belongs to the public world, and an English classroom is a place where pupils meet to share experience of some importance, to talk about people and situations in the world as they know it, gathering experience into new wholes and enjoying the satisfaction and power that this gives. But in so doing each individual takes what he can from the shared store of experience and builds it into a world of his own.

When sceptical teachers ask, 'Isn't that diary an example of the work of the rare few: aren't drills the only thing for the rest?' they must look again at our human purposes in using language. Recalling experience, getting it clear, giving it shape and making connections, speculating and building theories, celebrating (or exorcizing) particular moments of our lives — these are some of the broad purposes that language serves and enables. For days we may not work much beyond the level of gossip in fulfilling these purposes, but inevitably the time comes when we need to invest a good deal of ourselves and our energy in them. It is the English teacher's responsibility to prepare for and work towards such times. If instead of being *more* alert and sensitive to average pupils — more concerned with what they have to say, if only they can realize it — he neglects their day-to-day encounters with people and situations, then they will indeed be unlikely to turn to him when they are struggling to say something of importance.

It was for this reason that members of the Seminar moved from an attempt to define '*What* English is' — a question that throws the emphasis on nouns like *skills*, and *proficiencies*, set *books*, and the *heritage* — to a definition by process, a description of the activities we engage in through language.

How important these activities may be to us personally, how deeply they may affect our attitude to experience, is suggested by much of the best writing, drama and talk that goes on in English lessons. Here we see not only the intellectual organizing of experience that goes on in many other subjects, but also a parallel ordering of the feelings and attitudes with which pupils encounter life around them. For example, after an excited visit to a fine park, a class of eight-year-olds talked over their experiences. The wind in the trees, the lake, the swans, the boy who got mud up to his knees — these and many other things found their way into one or other of the pieces that the class wrote later. Janice wrote this short poem:

> The wind wiseled passed the trees.
> Pushing and puling the trees.
> The water triying to rech it.
> But still the trees remain.
> The wind stops but still the trees remain.
> Pepol diey but still the trees grow biger and biger.
> Flower diey but still the trees remain.[2]

Here simple elements are drawn together into a vision of transience and permanence: of things like the trees that persist, and of things like man that wither; of the forces whose stress and strain we want to withstand. Writing like this is an important moment of personal growth.

The poem sharply reminds us of the power, always available in language, to give meaning and order to the flux and fragments of reality. Thus we make use of the system and order of language to express the order we partly recognize in things. Until, like Janice, we have written (or spoken), our recognitions and perceptions are less articulate, less explicit. Once we have written, they become not merely personal but shared, related to the socially made systems of thought and feeling that our language expresses.

Of course, much of what pupils say and write and enact will be less convincing in its insight than, say, Janice's work here. So will much of our own work, for that matter. How can a teacher help pupils engaged in so personal a task to weigh up what has been achieved? All of us test the validity of what we have said by sensing how far others that we trust have shared our response. An English teacher tries to be a person to whom pupils turn with that sense of trust. The sensitivity, honesty and tact of his response to what pupils say will confirm their half-formed certainties and doubts in what they have said. A blanket acceptance of 'self-expression' is no help to pupils and may well prove a worse hindrance to their growing self-knowledge than a blunt and limited response from the teacher. The more experienced the teacher is in these matters, the more he is able to draw from the pupil the certainties (first) and later the doubts.

In every lesson where written work is read aloud to the class, or where some pupils sit back while a group presents a piece of drama, there is an opportunity for the teacher to draw from the audience an appreciation of what was enjoyed, of what went home, and thus to confirm in the individual writer or group a sense of shared enjoyment and understanding. With a new class we begin by opening their eyes to all they can achieve. And, as both the individuals and the class become confident in their achievement, there will be moments when with the teacher's help a sense of partial failure can be faced too.

For certainty about language is in a sense certainty about experience. Yet finding that others share our confidence in what we have said is only the foundation for work in language. As we mature we become increasingly aware that success in language is a partial business: as Eliot testifies:

> . . . having had twenty years. . . .
> Trying to learn to use words, and every attempt
> Is a wholly new start, and a different kind of failure
> Because one has only learnt to get the better of words
> For the thing one no longer has to say, or the way in which
> One is no longer disposed to say it. And so each venture
> Is a new beginning, a raid on the inarticulate. . . .
>
> (*East Coker*)

We can look on two levels at the source of our partial success. First, that of everyday experience: changes in oneself, changes in the surrounding world, and changes in one's relationship to others, all interpenetrate in the growing child or student to produce their own kind of serial curriculum. 'World is crazier and more of it than we think, Incorrigibly plural.' And at the level of language we can say this: we make for ourselves a representational world, sense out to the full its ability to stand for experience as we meet it, come up against its limitations, and then shoulder — if we dare — the task of making it afresh, extending, reshaping it, and bringing into new relationships all the old elements. Learning to use language continues so long as we are open to new experience and ready to adapt and modify the linguistic representation (the world) we have made for experience.

KNOWLEDGE AND MASTERY OF LANGUAGE

It is in the nature of language to impose system and order, to offer us sets of choices from which we must choose one way or another of building our inner world. Without that order we should never be able to start building, but there is always the danger of over-acceptance. How many teachers, even today, welcome and enjoy the power of young people to coin new words to set alongside the old order? How often do social pressures prevent us exercising our power to modify the meaning of words by improvising a new context, as in metaphor? Sometimes, it seems, our pupils are more aware than we are of the fact that language is living and changing; we could help them more often to explore and test out its new possibilities. Inevitably, though, the weight of our experience lies in a mature awareness of the possibilities and limitations raised by the more permanent forms of order in language. There has already been an explicit case (at our own level) in this chapter. The question 'What is English?' invites a different form of answer, from, say, 'What at our best are we doing in English classes?' If we wish to describe a process, *composition* for example, the first question will tend to suggest the finished product (the marks on the page even) rather than the activity of bringing together and composing the disorder of our experience. 'What . . . doing' will suggest nominal forms of verbs (bringing, composing) and thus help to keep activities in mind.

At a much simpler level members of the Seminar noted that some of us referred to 'talk' in class, others to 'speech'. In order to see why, one might consider some of the contexts in which the words are used. 'Talk' tends to be used of less formal occasions — 'give a speech/give a talk'. In some contexts 'speech' implies accent or pronunciation — 'good speech, classroom speech'; 'classroom talk' may then be used as the generic term, even though in normal contexts we use 'spoken and written, speech and writing' and not 'talk'. 'Speech' seems to be rarely used today for verbal interaction, whereas we do say 'we talked about it, talked it over, had a heart to heart talk'. Tentatively, one might assume that those who preferred 'talk' wanted to encourage informal interaction in class; those who preferred 'speech' were perhaps hoping for sustained and organized utterance (rather than 'chat'). Until differences like this are made explicit one may be trapped in a general uneasiness about what the other man means. Equally, in making the difference explicit we may begin to look more acutely at what goes on in class.

There is, then, a kind of knowledge or awareness about language that affects our power to think clearly and 'to some purpose', in Susan Stebbing's words. Whatever the subject in the curriculum, the places where such knowledge can affect language in operation need to be more fully understood than they are at present. But the teacher of English will be particularly concerned with helping pupils, in the terms of one report, to 'conceptualize their awareness of language'. This seemingly cumbersome phrase was chosen with some care. 'Conceptualizing', a verbal form, suggests *activity* on the part of the individual pupil, whereas 'concepts' unfortunately can be thought of as *things*, reified objects to be handed over by the teacher. 'Their awareness' points to a recognition already there in the pupil's thinking, not yet explicit or fully conscious perhaps, but something the alert teacher will notice and draw on.

The notion of gaining a new control over what we think by increasing our conceptual awareness of language in general has an obvious appeal to a gathering of intellectuals, not least when many of them are linguists! However, the final reports were cautious in their claims for such knowledge at the school stage. The first question at issue is when and how the knowledge becomes explicit. There was some agreement that the answer should apply to an individual rather than an age group. For if we teachers encourage a pupil to conceptualize, we should ideally be doing this at the point where the demands at the operational level of language have already given our pupil the sense that conceptualizing is needed. As experienced teachers we should see this demand emerging and be ready to help it on the way. In other words, our knowledge of the route ahead is not something to impose on the student — thus robbing him of the delight of discovery and maybe dissociating such discoveries as he does make from the systematic framework he 'received' from us.

The second question was what knowledge if any *does* increase our mastery of language. As there seems to be little evidence, and some disagreement, one answer was to suggest further experimentation, with a determined effort to increase the teacher's awareness of the times when the demand for language concepts arises from the pupil but goes unrecognized at present. But the response of the majority of the Seminar was to reject the terms of the question and to ask instead for language knowledge that helps the pupil perceive himself, and for that matter Man, as in some sense the organizer of his experience. It was tentatively proposed that insights of this kind would come from a joint literary-linguistic discipline, the one investigating with more detachment the intuitions of the other. In terms of our map this was a healthy reminder that even over the next decade we may well see new territories being defined.

DANGERS INHERENT IN THE THIRD MODEL

Whatever the current model for English, we shall have to recognize and face its weaknesses. Certainly the swing to process has its own dangers. The first is over-rejection. If the conventions and systems of written English do not come in the centre of the map, where do they come at all? The answer is obviously complicated, so there is a temptation to ignore the question. Let the pupils spell or not spell in the orthodox style, punctuate or not, struggle with ambiguities or not, make choices of structure or not . . . it is up to them! But though we can fight to modify conventions and systems, we cannot ignore them. Language remains a social instrument by which we share, fully or imperfectly, our preoccupations and interests. When deviance from the system becomes too great, interference may swamp and blot out the message. This very fact suggests a broad criterion to answer our complicated question. Where the pupil himself gives signs of being puzzled, disturbed or defeated by the forms of the written message which he is receiving or sending, the teacher should judge whether this is not the right moment to call his attention to the problem. We might note that the children's writing in this chapter includes several examples of deviance, but probably not enough to daunt readers experienced enough to take on this book. In class it might be a different matter: only experience can tell, for we put up with more interference when the message seems vital to us than when it is not.

The second danger, as U.S. members pointed out at the Seminar, is the tendency to over-simplification; of faith blundering from dull skills into the simple formula of 'self-expression'. Then the teacher can relax. Why trouble about people and things when the self is all-important? And, anyway, what criteria can — or dare — we use to assess what the self expresses? But this is to save the tree by cutting its roots. As people we exist and assert ourselves in response to our world (our family, neighbourhood, teachers . . .). The sense of our own reality is bound up with our sense of theirs, and both intimately depend on an awareness built up through language. For, of all the representational systems, language is the best fitted to make a running commentary on experience, to 'look at life with all the vulnerability, honesty and penetration [we] can command'. In an English classroom as we envisage it, pupils and teacher combine to keep alert to all that is challenging, new, uncertain and even painful in experience. Refusing to accept the comfortable stereotypes, stock responses and perfunctory arguments that deaden our sensitivity to people and situations, they work together to keep language alive and in so doing to enrich and diversify personal growth.

To sum up: language is learnt in operation, not by dummy runs. In English, pupils meet to share their encounters with life, and to do this effectively they move freely between dialogue and monologue — between talk, drama and writing; and literature, by bringing new voices into the classroom, adds to the store of shared experience. Each pupil takes from the store what he can and what he needs. In so doing he learns to use language to build his own representational world and works to make this fit reality as he experiences it. Problems with the written medium for language raise the need for a different kind of learning. But writing implies a message: the means must be associated with the end, as part of the same lesson. A pupil turns to the teacher he trusts for confirmation of his own doubts and certainties in the validity of what he has said and written; he will also turn to the class, of course, but an adult's experience counts for something. In ordering and composing situations that in some way symbolize life as we know it, we bring order and composure to our inner selves. When a pupil is steeped in language in operation we expect, as he matures, a conceptualizing of his earlier awareness of language, and with this perhaps new insight into himself (as creator of his own world).

SOURCES OF PUPILS' WRITING

1. *English in Education*, ed. Jackson and Thompson (Chatto).
2. Jane Westlake and Diane Wright.

24 *Dartmouth and Growth through English*

● David Allen

> When we mean to build
> We first survey the plot, then draw the model,
> And when we see the figure of the house
> Then must we rate the cost of the erection
> Which if we find outweighs ability
> What do we do then but draw anew the model
> In fewer offices?
>
> *Henry IV pt 2*

To many teaching English today the Dartmouth Seminar of 1966 will seem like ancient rather than recent history; many will perhaps fail to see any point in looking at such a gathering, distant in time and place, because they feel it has had no influence on their own teaching. Why then go back to a conference held so long ago; many of those assembled then would not be known by many now?

There is nevertheless a historical connection. Those assembled were the 'progressive cutting-edge' of English teaching then, virtually all those who were contributing to a search for a coherent, all-embracing account of English and who were therefore going to influence or be involved with any developments at large. Virtually all the major figures influential since then were present and were influential there. The seminar was not revolutionary, but it can be seen now to have had a substantial effect on the drift of change.

The Anglo-American Dartmouth Seminar was brought together in the belief that 'English as a school subject was facing a series of critical problems both in the United States and in the United Kingdom' and that 'an international exchange of experience and opinion would be helpful in arriving at solutions and in suggesting lines of future international collaboration'.[1] Whether the sense of crisis was as strong in this country as it was in America is doubtful, though undoubtedly there was a certain ferment, an energetic formulation of questions. Perhaps the hopes from international perspectives were born of wishful thinking, for it is hard to see just how such a conference could help problems derived from different traditions, different cultures. The mother-tongue is primarily national, not international and the 'sense of frustration and futility' which H. J. Muller observed at Dartmouth demonstrates this hard fact.[2]

Certainly the frequent references in the various accounts of the Seminar testify to real difficulties in agreeing on the meaning of the words, of recognizing common problems, of defining agreed recommendations. Muller 'wearied at times of the continual clashing of half-truths . . . It was difficult at times to isolate areas of common agreement as a starting point for a broad reconciliation of views . . . The British and Americans were deeply divided by a common language; and . . . the entire conference was shattered into myriad pieces by a common subject and discipline.'

On the other hand John Dixon nowhere records such impressions of incomprehension and confusion but rather 'the excitement and intellectual satisfaction of having just seen a major issue resolved'.[3] It seems that there are two incompatible views of what happened, dependent to an extent on the spectator's evaluation of what came out of it. Denys Thompson for example felt 'the seminar seems now to have made little progress because it was too much given to pretentious intellectualizing' and recalled 'the seminar's unwillingness to come to grips with the issues presented by the more relevant papers' and explained that 'conditions and personnel militated against any effective exchange'.[4] Those who felt on the other hand that what emerged was of value, such as James Britton, clearly felt the process was also a stimulating and enlivening one.

[...] What emerged was *Growth through English* by John Dixon (who had been commissioned by N.A.T.E* to write a report) and *The Uses of English* by H. J. Muller. (The latter is almost unknown to British readers, though it provides sometimes a corrective, albeit journalistic, viewpoint to Dixon's.

Growth through English was an avowedly 'partial report' in which Dixon sought to stress 'the consensus that emerged' and thus underplayed 'the dissenting views that tended to become submerged in the excitement of our agreement'. The consensus was clearly one with which he agreed but nevertheless it is true, as he claimed, that his book was 'a tissue of quotations' from the papers of the Seminar. In considering the book, I want to look in particular at three aspects:

— What were the issues selected as important by the conference?
— Was there any significant personal selection in John Dixon's account? (Any omissions, particularly?)
— What, critically, can be made of the particular picture Dixon gave?

[...] The first paper 'What is English?'[6] sought crucially to account for what should be in and what should be out of the subject English. Delivered by an

---

* National Association for the Teaching of English.

American, Albert Kitzhaber, it excluded etiquette and 'social slops' (the U.S. had experienced a more voracious inclusiveness than the U.K.); Kitzhaber quoted a linguist H. L. Gleason on a point of crucial importance: 'English must have a centre about which it can integrate — a centre of such significance that it can overcome the centrifugal forces clearly at work to dismember the field of English.'[7] He then considered literature as the centre, asking whether we could 'accurately define the central or organizing principles of literature, for these will affect not only sequence but content and approach'. However, as the most satisfactory formulation he suggested the following: 'language must be the integrating centre, about which a new curriculum is to be built'.

Muller in his report saw in this part of the conference a choice actively being considered, between the centrality of literature, which many teachers regard as the very heart of the subject, and language, for 'other teachers believe that English should be centred on language — the understanding manipulation and appreciation of language'. This can be seen as a continuation of the debate in the letter columns in the *Use of English*.

[...] James Britton replied to Albert Kitzhaber in a paper which can be seen in retrospect to have effectively persuaded the Seminar to take its offered direction. (It was the pattern to have a 'respondent' to each paper.) Britton doubted the validity of the question 'What is English?' but sought to present an answer in recognition that 'the function of language' is 'something more than is suggested by the skills of communication'.[8] 'We need to ask "What is the function of the mother-tongue in learning?" . . . What we want . . . is an operational view of language, an operational view of the teaching of the mother-tongue.'[9]

And after an account of his scheme for language uses from the 'spectator' to the 'participant' role, he said 'I suggest that the area in which language operates in English lessons is that of personal experience, in other words — the relation between the ego and the environment' and here clearly was the role of literature (or as he designated it 'language in the spectator role') for literature is about 'the relationships in which the human quality of the emotional relationship is a part of what is afoot'.

Here literature was given an importance but it was within a language schema that it got its *raison d'être*. Literature was *part* of language — a point of view which was converted by John Dixon into the 'map'. The 'map' is, essentially, 'language'. James Britton at that time saw English as being concerned with the 'spectator' role — i.e. one important aspect of language — but once the language schema is accepted as valid it will almost inevitably lead to a feeling that the range of language uses in English lessons should be expanded, and literature only one among many. (Such has been the evolving viewpoint of Britton himself.) This schema is of course largely value-free; it does not say which are less important uses. It just shows there are *different* ones — any criterion of value must come from outside it.

In effect, the case for the centrality of literature had been given up and the reason may be that Britton's schema could become a map on which 'all of our different approaches may be placed'. It enabled all the disparate voices, from linguists to professors of English Literature, academics to teachers, to *go on talking to each other*, while yet postponing questions of value, which would lead to disharmony. That is not to say that the schema was considered valuable only for that reason. It was of course a more high-flown categorization of the conceptions of language already available. For example, Frank Whitehead's view of language as the 'medium in which we have evolved our most deeply-ingrained modes of interpreting the universe in which we live; and our capacity for human relationships, our ways of perceiving, understanding and mastering the phenomena of our everyday existence are shaped and coloured by it in countless ways.'[10] The particular character of his view leads to high relative valuation for literature; Britton's in the end to equality *inter pares*.

In a 'Report to seminar' after the discussion, the point was made that 'We wish to reject the idea of literature as a content which can be "handed over" to the pupils, and to emphasize instead the idea of literature as contributing to the sensitivity and responsibility with which they live through language'.

What did John Dixon make of this discussion in his report? He made a map 'on which the confusing claims and theories can be plotted'[11] and placed on the map three 'models' of English — whether 'theory' or 'practice' is not clear and his treatment varied from model to model.

[...] The 'map' of the three 'models' of English teaching was as far as I am aware John Dixon's own, distilled from the assumptions and compromises of the discussion at the Seminar. (He described them as 'singled out' in discussion.) There is no evidence in the papers of their origin. He described them as an 'historical' dimension — 'the first centred on *skills*: it fitted an era when *initial* literacy was the prime demand'. The second model 'stressed the *cultural heritage* , the need for a civilizing and socially unifying content'. And the third model, which he described as 'current', 'focuses on *personal growth*: on the need to re-examine the learning processes and the meaning to the individual of what he is doing in English lessons'. Of these three the earlier ones were 'limited' and needed to be 'reinterpreted'.

Thus far the argument seems simple and acceptable. The first conception of English *is* oversimple, the second leaves many questions unanswered, the third recognizes that education requires a *learner*. However, in following his discussion of the models one by one, grave doubts arise about the weight being placed on these simple structures. The first is the easiest target; the main onslaught being the charge that teaching 'skills' omits so much of value in the use of English that it is restrictive. (It is clear here that what Dixon had in mind is English by exercises, the very beast hunted by Thompson, Heath and others in the years before Dartmouth.) As a conception of English teaching it is inadequate.

Dixon accounted for his model 'historically' as we have seen. It arose to meet a need, he inferred. Yet if it was still alive and kicking perhaps there was some reason, some purpose it served in some small degree. Having cut it down to size Dixon salvaged nothing. He moved on to model number two — 'cultural heritage' — which he claimed 'was clearly intended to fill the vacuum left by the skills model' — a statement of very doubtful historical accuracy. This was a very wayward account indeed of the thinking of Arnold, Sampson, or the many others who have propounded the importance of conveying the riches of our culture to our pupils; their impetus came from a full sense of the worth of the culture, not as a solution to a curriculum problem. He mentioned Arnold and the 1919 Newbolt Report as creators in part of this 'vision', which was not examined at all as a *theory*, a set of intentions, in the way one would expect, given the nature of the enterprise. Instead we were given a very sad and it must be admitted all too accurate account of 'the betrayal of this vision' in 'a series of inky marginal annotations and essay notes'.

His most searching criticism was levelled at the idea of 'culture as a *given*' which he presented as a flaw in the theory, when it might be more true to see it as a flaw in one version. He then made a remark which would be agreed to happily by many who see themselves as 'transmitters of cultural heritage' — 'What is vital is the interplay between his (the child's) personal world and the world of the writer: a teacher must acknowledge both sides of the experience, and know both of them intimately if he is to help to bring the two into a fruitful relationship.'

To which we would say 'amen' and even add that that is exactly the point of 'culture' and 'heritage'. However, the 'average teacher' had betrayed this 'vision' by his emphasis on the written word and the presentation of 'experience (fiction) to his pupils, rather than drawing from them their experience (of reality and the self)'.

Now the 'average teacher' is a dreadful weapon with which to beat any theory; the use of 'rather than' points to a caricature — an either/or argument of dubious merit. What, if that is what 'the average teacher' makes of the theory, are we to make of the contribution of, for example, Denys Thompson, who seems to have spent his life applauding the value of literature as our inheritance, while yet stressing the need for 'a fruitful relationship'. It is as if the *Use of English* had never been published, its consistent attempt to bring together culture and child never made. Within the Seminar there was abundant complex life in the idea of cultural heritage from Thompson himself, Frank Whitehead, Glyn Lewis and others — why this dismissal?

Perhaps John Dixon saw in his 'cultural heritage' model the approach to teaching literature which had been much criticized by Frank Whitehead particularly but largely with the endorsement of the whole English contingent — the teaching of knowledge *about* literature. Literature and reading were discussed in great detail at the Seminar and throughout there was a strong resistance among the British contingent to a codified, ordered instruction *about* literature in favour of a concern with personal response. But that is not at all the same as a rejection of the cultural heritage.

There clearly was a kind of literature teaching which deserved criticism. Unfortunately John Dixon suffered from a too simple theoretical construct, so that teaching literature in such a way that both the book and the child had safeguarded legitimate rights was given no theoretical foundation, no place in the new pantheon. If there is any place where John Dixon was guilty of historical discontinuity it is here. As a result many teachers could find no place in the new thinking and were condemned either to eccentricity or dishonesty.

The influence of this dismissal of model number two has been great, especially under a thoroughgoing concentration on the child as centre as defined in his third model — 'personal growth'. It has indeed been used since then to support a rationalist rejection of the past, as available to us in literature, but which is not felt to be relevant to us here and now. This in spite of the tradition of 'fruitful relationship' between child and culture already available.

The critique of the caricature was justly done, but the caricature missed out so much truth. This was a fundamental flaw in the first chapter, which unhinged the whole book. The inadequacy of treatment was to some extent due of course to his excitement at a more complex, more adequate model elsewhere, to which he is more sympathetic because it stressed the child rather than the culture. The idea of the 'fruitful relationship' was in fact forgotten for a child-centred theory of an unbalanced kind, though it was based largely on conceptions shared widely at the time.

The remarks of John Dewey on the curriculum are useful here.

> The fundamental factors in the educative process are an immature undeveloped being; and certain aims, meanings, values incarnate in the matured experience of the adult. The educative process is the due interaction of these forces. . . .
>
> But here comes the effort of thought. It is easier to see the conditions in their separateness . . . than to discover a reality to which each belongs. . . . When this happens a really serious practical problem — that of interaction — is transformed into an unreal and hence insoluble, theoretic problem. Instead of seeing the educative process steadily and as a whole, we see conflicting terms. We get the case of the child *vs* the curriculum; of the individual nature *vs* social culture.[12]

John Dixon seems to have attempted 'a reality to which each belongs' but largely because of his treatment of the 'cultural heritage model', risked creating an either/or theory. In fact he fell into the very danger he identified earlier — 'over-rejection'.

In outlining his third model, more adequate, more 'current', John Dixon, as we might expect, developed it more fully. He began with 'the need to build English teaching . . . on our observation of language in operation from day to day' and produced for the reader some writing of a ten-year-old boy, as an example of children using language 'for their own purposes'.

The piece of writing convincingly illustrated a writer with 'something worth sharing' with 'a sympathetic and interested listener'. Dixon overstated the freedom from influence of the piece, but showed with conviction that attention to skills alone would not produce writing 'for the primary purpose in language, to share experience'. Nor would the heritage model help 'because it neglects the most fundamental aim of language — to promote interaction between people'. This was a very tendentious remark which he did not stay with throughout his book; nor could he, for there are other claimants for 'the most fundamental' aim, such as 'making meanings for oneself'. (It seems a mistake to seek *one* as crucial.)

D. W. Harding wrote 'language and experience interpenetrate one another. The language available to us influences our experience at intimate levels and if we manage to convey experience precisely, that may be due partly to the fact that available modes of expression were influencing the experience from the start',[13] which I take to be showing expression as the result of the necessary interaction of individual and culture.

Dixon seems to have shot wide of the mark in his eagerness to hit at the use of literature as model for imitation. As a result he failed to understand the interaction that is necessary for meaningful expression (or self-definition). However, he did show that there are many purposes in using language 'recalling experience, getting it clear, giving it shape and making connections, speculating and building theories, celebrating (and exorcising) particular moments'. This wide range was seen to justify the recognition of children's writing *as literature* — his study of the pieces quoted was couched in such terms, an approach taken up later more fully. Nowhere in his account of the third model did he inter-relate the culture and the child — we were presented with an image of a child seeking alongside others to fulfil his own felt needs.

He did recognize dangers in his theorizing (which he would claim to be an account of actual teaching approaches). The first one — over-rejection — he was guilty of. The second was over-simplification to which he had already, it seems, succumbed in his image of 'growth'. 'As people we exist and assert ourselves in response to our world (our family, neighbourhood, teachers). The sense of our own reality is bound up with our sense of theirs, and both intimately depend on an awareness built up through language.'

Literature, for John Dixon 'by bringing new voices into the classroom, adds to the store of shared experience. Each pupil takes from the store what he can and what he needs.' That is, not finer voices, better voices — just new to the pupil. Presumably then, if the voices are not what the pupil needs he does not listen; he uses them as he wishes; he is the sole arbiter of right use. If this is a caricature, it is one *allowed* by the theory put forward.

What in effect John Dixon's first chapter did — it was his intention — was to set at the centre of English the use of language in operation to create our own world. Literature and reading were given a contributory, ancillary role. Talking and writing (expression rather than impression) took their place. Though the case was presented tendentiously (e.g. the 'average teacher' was not allowed to soil his preferred model) it has been influential on teachers. The very shift in theory he made in the first chapter was the shift of the decade, though it did not originate there.

LITERATURE

The Seminar did take a protracted look at literature when it set up a Study Group on the subject 'Response to literature'. [...]

The selection that Dixon made of the voices at Dartmouth is strikingly clear. What he consistently omitted from his 'map' were any that looked to a tradition, a transmission, a developed collection of values, for these were inert, moribund. Growth and life were to be found only in the person. This selection meant not only that the voices of Thompson and Squire were ignored, those of Douglas and Hardy transmuted; the contribution of Glyn Lewis was as if it had never been, in marked contrast to Muller's book, which allows him a voice.

'Glyn Lewis could sound like a voice crying in the wilderness as he alone kept insisting on the claims of our heritage.' Lewis' main contribution was in his paper 'The teaching of English' given to Working Party IV as part of their considerations. (Their subject was 'Knowledge and proficiency in English'.) He sought to balance the personal dimension of education against the public.

'Though education is an individual and personal process it is not simply subjective, but proceeds in certain observable and objective ways.'[14] And as an important example 'A child needs to be induced to want to judge not simply the interest of a point of view or opinion but whether in fact it is reasonably likely to be true and to judge the relevance of an experience for the task of daily living.'

The grounds for this case were that 'The child's development is a process of learning within a particular culture'. Lewis went on:

> Clearly we must recognize the importance of the instinct of origination, but an education based on the training of this instinct is not enough.

Language conveys to a child an already prepared system of values and ideas that form his culture.

Each new generation is not a new people; we are what we are because we are able to share a past, in a common heritage, not simply because of our ability to communicate in the present and share the excitement of innovation.

I believe there can be no adequate theory of the teaching of the mother-tongue without some attempt at a theory of culture (and Lewis was making an attempt). The bizarre aspect of Dixon's book is that he did not present one, leaving his theory rootless, unable to account for any purpose or aim in teaching English.

On a whole series of issues the conference was united, to such an extent that there was little discussion required and no evidence of dissent. Thus, streaming was undesirable; the influence of examinations was probably harmful and should be studied; drama had an important place in English; children should be encouraged to write creatively (though Holbrook's psychotherapy was put onto a side-track). That this agreement was 'achieved' was perhaps due to an underlying agreement that each child is unique but the processes of growth fall into a pattern. The whole Seminar, it appears, was arranged on the American side as a parallel to the Woods Hole Conference of 1959 out of which came the idea of Bruner's 'Spiral' sequential curriculum. Such hopes were demonstrated in the subject of the second Working Party — 'Continuity in English'. The hopes were that some structured sequence would emerge, which could guide the construction of a curriculum. The U.S. delegates sought structure in the *subject* — in the content. The U.K. representatives however, led by Frank Whitehead, looked to the *processes* of maturation and growth to supply the underlying sequence of a curriculum.

He suggested that 'we must look for our source of order in the inherent and inescapable sequence in the acquisition of a man's mother-tongue'.[15] This of course was a repetition of his espousal of 'maturation' in his book *The Disappearing Dais* and although the Americans were at first baffled by the rejection of the example set by Bruner and later hostile to Whitehead's child-centred structure, they never mounted a coherent alternative. The view of English as the learning of the mother-tongue was certainly common ground to teachers and linguistics experts alike and probably provided a basis for continuing discussion.

Whitehead outlined his view of English teaching as fostering improving and refining 'the individual's ability to use his mother-tongue — to use it flexibly, effectively, sensitively and to use it for all the varied purposes which one's native language must serve in a modern civilized community'. Such a description stressed width and variety (the forces for inclusion) and the word 'civilized' meant little more probably than 'advanced'. Nor was any guidance given as to the more important purposes. Rather, coping with the demands of the community was seen as the minimum aim. However, he continued: 'Literature falls within this province because the creative and imaginative uses of language are an integral part of the life-experience of a civilized human being.' 'Civilized' meant much more now, implying some level of culture, some quality of life. As such it implied some uses of the mother-tongue were especially important, while yet remaining 'part' of the whole language development. At the same time it inferred that productive uses of 'creative and imaginative' language (writing and speaking) were valuable, as well as receptive uses (reading and literature).

This made an instructive comparison with John Dixon's final report for nowhere does he offer us a glimpse of the end of the processes of growth. Instead, we were to seek to know more certainly how growth proceeds (research was the hope) that we may enable it, not restrict it. Frank Whitehead in his paper drew upon such evidence as there was available as to the stages of growth in language, most of it concerned with the early years, the initial steps. He warned that 'it may often be peculiarly difficult to distinguish between those aspects of the observable sequence which are tied to a particular environment and those regularities which seem to be inescapable in all the cultures we know of'. This warning would seem to apply most to the secondary school years where we have little coherent evidence of sequence and maturation. Whitehead picked out some 'dimensions of growth' or lines which seemed to indicate development, one of which was the move to a 'capacity for critical assessment', an achievement surely only found in any measure in the secondary years. The *stages* of this growth were not enumerated; there was in any case no evidence from research on which to base such an account.

Of 'those specialized yet centrally important uses of language which we refer to as literature', Whitehead claimed that there is a 'developmental sequence' which we work on instinctively, based on 'the kinds of experience which young readers can take, with benefit to themselves, from their reading of literature at different stages'. The emphasis at first is psychological, 'with benefit to themselves', but there was a problem. How could such a paediatric pattern be 'reconciled with our wholly justifiable concern for quality and literary standards'? This dilemma (ignored by Dixon) between offering and steering, between reliance on the internal processes of growth and leadership from a mature standpoint, *is* difficult to resolve. However, 'whichever conception of the teacher's role is adopted, it is certainly essential that his guidance should be disciplined by a sound and firm sense of values. He cannot pilot his pupil's taste towards 'the good' in literature unless he has succeeded in arranging all the literary works he knows, both past and present in a hierarchical order of value — a hierarchy, moreover, which cannot be taken on trust from any 'authority' and which needs to be continually reconstructed and modified in the light of fresh personal experience'.

This concern with 'values' in literature derived clearly from the parallel aim of 'the civilized human being' offering a direction and an end for growth and guidelines for priorities in teaching. Some such criteria are necessary for the very understanding of the process (a process, to have any meaning at all, must have a product), but John Dixon, in his report, did not echo such preoccupations. No end was envisaged for development. We were encouraged to seek our model in the normal pattern of development, complex and varied as it may be. But 'normality' is to some extent a matter of choice; education is a matter of deliberate selection and emphasis. The Seminar had many voices speaking for some recognition of the importance of the culture. John Dixon did not represent these voices in his construction of the 'map' and so did not take account of the implications for teaching. Only twice in his book does he even acknowledge the existence of cultural influences from outside the classroom (he refers to 'the impoverished literature of the popular press' and later suggests that 'popular culture, depending so strongly on the media for mass-communication, is subject to continual change and some debilitation perhaps').

BIBLIOGRAPHY

Dewey, John, *The School and the Curriculum*, Univ. of Chicago, 1902; *The School and Society*, Univ. of Chicago, 1910; *Democracy in Education*, Macmillan, New York, 1916.

Dixon, J., *Growth through English*, N.A.T.E., Huddersfield, 1967.

Harding, D. W., 'Raids on the inarticulate'. *U.E.*, Winter, Vol. 19/2, 1967.

Muller, H. J., *The Uses of English*, Holt, Rinehart, Winston, 1967.

N.C.T.E., *Dartmouth Seminar Papers*, N.C.T.E, USA., 1969.

Thompson, D., 'Anglo-American exchanges', *U.E.*, Spring, Vol. 18/3, 1967.

Whitehead, F. S., *The Disappearing Dais*, Chatto, 1966.

NOTES

1. Albert Markward, Foreword to Growth through English, N.A.T.E., Huddersfield, 1967.

2. *The Uses of English*, H. J. Muller, New York, 1967.

3. *Growth through English*, Preface to Second Edition.

4. 'Anglo-American exchanges' *Use of English*, Spring 1967, Vol. 18/3.

5. *Growth through English*, p. xi.

6. *Dartmouth Seminar Papers*, N.C.T.E., 1969.

7. This comment is doubly interesting: it suggested an *explicit* role for the centre, unlike most other uses of the term; and it pointed in a timely way to the danger of disintegration by expansion.

8. *Growth through English*, p. 5.

9. Response to 'What is English?', *Dartmouth Seminar Papers*, N.C.T.E., 1969.

10. *The Disappearing Dais*, p. 13.

11. *Growth through English*, p. 1.

12. *The School and the Curriculum*, Chicago, 1902, p. 73.

13. 'Raids on the inarticulate', D. W. Harding, *Use of English*, Winter 1967, Vol. 19/2.

14. 'The teaching of English', p. 2 (Working Party IV), *Dartmouth Seminar Papers*, N.C.T.E., 1969.

15. 'What is continuity in English?', p. 6, *Dartmouth Seminar Papers*, N.C.T.E., 1969.

25　*Literature*

- Department of Education and Science

'I passed English all right because I had all that Beowulf and Lord Randal My Son stuff when I was at Whooton School. I mean I didn't have to do any work in English at all, hardly, except write compositions once in a while.'

J. D. Salinger: 'Catcher in the Rye'.

'(he) . . . arrived at the conclusion, from which he never afterwards departed, that all the fancies of the poets, and lessons of the sages, were a mere collection of words and grammar, and had no other meaning in the world'.

Charles Dickens: 'Dombey and Son'.

'It would have been impossible for me to have told anyone what I derived from these novels, for it was nothing less than a sense of life itself'.

Richard Wright: 'Black Boy'.

To many teachers literature is the most rewarding form of the child's encounter with language. In the main, opinions converge upon the value of literature, even if they take separate ways on the treatment it should receive in school. Much has been claimed for it: that it helps to shape the personality, refine the sensibility, sharpen the critical intelligence; that it is a powerful instrument of empathy, a medium through which the child can acquire his values. Writing in 1917, Nowell Smith[1] saw its purpose as 'the formation of a personality fitted for civilized life'. The Newsom Report[2], some 50 years later, said that 'all pupils, including those of very limited attainments, need the civilizing experience of contact with great literature, and can respond to its universality'. These are spirited credos, only two of many, and they represent a faith that English teaching needs. They have not, of course, gone unchallenged. In recent years it has been questioned whether literature does in fact make the reader a better and more sensitive human being. What was a matter of self-evident truth in the eighteenth and nineteenth centuries is no longer exempt from question. Few would subscribe to the simple view that it offers models for living which the reader lifts from the pages. In fact, Sampson[3] made the point astringently 50 years ago, and few had a more passionate belief than he in the place of literature in school. '. . . let me beg teachers to take a sane view of literature. Let us have no pose or affectation about it. Reading Blake to a class is not going to turn boys into saints'. One American educationist has said bluntly that when it comes down to it there is no evidence that the reading of literature in schools produces in any way the social or emotional effects claimed for it. Another has argued that the teacher of English is not the custodian of ethics and character, and that in these matters he has no more and no less responsibility than his colleagues in other subjects. Many American teachers would accept his proposition that the prime responsibility of the English teacher in teaching literature is to teach literature. Thus it is not uncommon to find American high school pupils examining the generic characteristics of a work of literature and assembling patterns of image and symbol. This is not to say that teachers in the U.S.A. are single-mindedly concerned with the cognitive aspects of literature. It was, in fact, an American who attacked the writers of sequential curricula as 'afraid to go where the feelings, perceptions, and questions of children would take them'. Nevertheless, there is a difference in emphasis between the two countries in this as in other aspects of English teaching. This was apparent at the Dartmouth Seminar of 1966, when British and American teachers of English met to discuss the subject in depth.

In Britain the tradition of literature teaching is one which aims at personal and moral growth, and in the last two decades this emphasis has grown. It is a soundly based tradition, and properly interpreted is a powerful force in English teaching. Literature brings the child into an encounter with language in its most complex and varied forms. Through these complexities are presented the thoughts, experiences and feelings of people who exist outside and beyond the reader's daily awareness. This process of bringing them within that circle of consciousness is where the greatest value of literature lies. It provides imaginative insight into what another person is feeling; it allows the contemplation of possible human experiences which the reader himself has not met. It has the capacity to develop that empathy of which Shelley was speaking when he said: 'A man to be greatly good, must imagine intensively and comprehensively; he must put himself in the place of another and many others; the pains and pleasures of his species must become his own'. Equally, it confronts the reader with problems similar to his own, and does it at the safety of one remove. He draws reassurance from realising that his personal difficulties and his feelings of deficiency are not unique to himself; that they are as likely to be the experience of others. Adolescents need this kind of reassurance, to be found in the sort of relieving awareness summed up in C. S. Lewis's remark: 'Nothing, I suspect, is more astonishing in any man's life than the discovery that there do exist people very, very like himself'. The media which influence their world often put a relentless emphasis on euphoria as the natural state of life. They encourage the inference that not to experience it is somehow to miss out and fall short of the norm. Most young people take a realistic view of this, but we can hardly be surprised that there are some who feel it as a pressure. This is only one uncertainty, and perhaps a minor one, but certainly reassurance is one of the available outcomes of this encounter with a wide range of possible human experience.

It may well be that we lack evidence of the 'civilising' power of literature and that some of the claims made for it have seemed over-ambitious. But we can look to the results of various studies of children's reading as some indication of its value as a personal resource. These have suggested, for example, that children's favourite stories at different ages reflect the particular fantasies and emotional conflicts which are foremost in their experience at that time. The child gets most enjoyment from those stories which say something to his condition and help him to resolve these inner conflicts. Books compensate for the difficulties of growing up. They present the child with a vicarious satisfaction that takes him outside his own world and lets him identify for a time with someone else. They present him with controlled experience, which he can observe from the outside at the same time as being involved within it. Thus, the fulfilling of private wishes, the fabrication of an inner environment, is an important property of children's reading. It accounts for the conclusion that although the names of the most widely-read authors change from one decade to the next the characteristic features of their books remain much the same. The presentation is vivid and dramatic, the characters relatively unsubtle, and virtue triumphs in an ending which places everyone where he should be. As he works his way through the book the reader's sympathies will be engaged, his antipathies aroused. It is, of course, easy to say this, but less easy to escape its implications. Books may offer vicarious satisfaction and little else. Indeed many do, and the sympathies they engage and the antipathies they arouse may be far from what we would hope. The child will not necessarily, and not automatically, progress from books which simply vicariously fulfil his wishes to those where a complexity of relationships enlarges his understanding of the range of human possibilities. One would hope to develop the kind of response which is summed up in W. P. Ker's remark from 'Imagination and Judgment': '. . . dramatic imagination enters into every question of justice. How can you understand other people's motives unless you act out a fragment or two of a play in which they are the characters?' The development of this response presents the teacher with one of his most delicate areas of operation, and one where his skill and knowledge play an extremely important part. One fact which becomes increasingly evident is the very great extent to which success lies in the contribution of the teacher: it is true in the development of the reading habit; it is true in the growth of discernment.

There is no doubt at all in our minds that one of the most important tasks facing the teacher of older juniors and younger secondary pupils is to increase the amount and range of their voluntary reading. We believe that there is a strong association between this and reading attainment, and that private reading can make an important contribution to children's linguistic and experiential development. Before we go on to discuss what the school can and should do to promote it, it will be useful to spend a moment on what is known of children's reading habits. The most recent information on a large scale comes from Whitehead's survey[4] in his Schools Council research project. Almost half the 10 year olds in this survey claimed to have read three or more books during the previous month, the percentage dropping to some two fifths at 12+ and about a third at 14+. There is, however, a substantial minority of children who do not read books at all in their leisure time, and the number increases significantly with age. Thirteen per cent of Whitehead's 10+ sample had not read a book during the previous month, while at 12+ the corresponding figure was 29 per cent and at 14+ 36 per cent. At each age point this category contained a higher proportion of boys than of girls, and at 14+ the number among the former was as high as 40 per cent. When all else has been considered it seems that there is a fairly large group of children in secondary schools who have the reading skills but do not choose to read books outside school time. A great deal is obviously going to depend on the home environment. It hardly needs saying that where reading has no status and books no place the incentives to read will be slight. But it is clear to us that the school can make a very big difference to this situation. Various studies have revealed that teacher influence on a child's choice of book is considerable, particularly in the case of the less able pupil. Another important conclusion is that for the child who is not an habitual reader the simple fact of which book is where will often determine what he reads. These two factors — teacher influence and book provision — hold the key to an improvement in reading standards in the junior and secondary years.

We referred earlier to the damaging notion that once the child has mastered the decoding process he will make his own way. Few teachers would subscribe to it in such blunt terms, but it is nevertheless a notion that is implicit in much classroom procedure. In many junior schools there is a graded reader series to be completed before the child can go to a free choice of 'real books'. Some schools allow these to be read without such a graduation hurdle, but we often met the assumption that mastery of the graded series meant that the child could now read. The teachers were assiduous in their concern that the child should 'learn to read', but when he could decode to their satisfaction they came to see him as self-supporting. In some schools the dependence on supplementary 'readers' was uncomfortably long, and the child had little experience of good children's literature. We found, in fact, that some capable readers almost never read a book in school. They dipped into reference and information books, many of which did not give occasion for sustained reading, but they did not read novels. We also noticed that this was related to the teacher's discontinuance of any kind of record of the child's reading. As long as the child was engaged on the reading scheme, or the graded readers supplementary to it, the teacher would usually keep a note of his progress through it. But we met few teachers who kept a record of what the child read after this. There were only comparatively rare instances of their knowing the pattern and balance of the children's reading, which in our opinion is one of the essential features of a policy of expanding its range.

A feature which ranks equally with this is the teacher's knowledge of what is available, especially in good modern children's literature. In the middle years of schooling in particular the range of emotional and intellectual development within any one class can be extremely wide, and a correspondingly wide range of fiction is needed. The indications are that narrative books are substantially outnumbered by non-fiction in most primary schools. With the increased emphasis on learning through discovery and personal interests schools have tended to acquire collections of information books to support this kind of work. These are to be found in encouraging profusion in book corners, entrance halls, corridors and bays, as well as in rooms designated as a central library. They are often supplemented by subject boxes or project loans from the school library service, and many primary schools still have their sets of class text-books. The result is a commanding majority of non-fiction material in the school at any one time. This profusion is encouraging only if it does not indicate a corresponding neglect of fiction. We have already discussed the value of good imaginative literature in its own right, but we would also suggest that it should be used more widely in association with information books. Suppose, for example, a teacher of older juniors or younger secondary pupils is setting up a study of the Vikings. There are plenty of information books on this topic, but it would be an incomplete experience if the child were to have access only to these. The teacher might therefore cluster about this core a modernised version of the Old English poem 'The Battle of Maldon' and the Icelandic 'Njal's Saga' or 'The Saga of Grettir the Strong'; Madeleine Polland's novel 'Beorn the Proud' and Walter Hodges' 'The Namesake'; Patricia Beer's poem 'Abbey Tomb', and Gael Turnbull's 'Gunnar from his Burial Mound' from his group of poems 'Five from the Sagas'. All these complement one another and throw fresh light on the source books. Patricia Beer's poem, for instance, is about the fate of monks in a pillaged abbey; Madeleine Polland's novel includes an attack on a monastery from the Vikings' viewpoint. An encounter of this kind could be used to lead a child to wider reading of fiction through an awakened interest. To exploit a promising situation in this way the teacher needs to know what is relevant and available.

The third important feature of this process of developing self-initiated reading is ingenuity in 'promoting' books. At its simplest and most effective level this will be a case of the teacher's knowledge and enthusiasm bringing child, book and situation together in a natural interaction. In the course of one visit two members of the Committee were in a primary school library during the lunch hour when a boy came in carrying a tin containing some maggots he had found. The teacher immediately showed a keen interest, talked to him about them, then led him to a shelf where there was a book on the subject. She generated such a curiosity about the book that the boy went off carrying it with his tin of maggots, promising to let her know more about them when he had read it. This is a seemingly obvious procedure, but not as simple as it sounds, and not as common. There was no doubt of the boy's eagerness to read that book, but it was produced by the teacher's genuine interest in what he had to show her, and her knowing that there was just the book to turn the incident to a reading advantage. In short, it revealed an expert ability to bring the right book to the right child at the right time. Opportunities do not always arrive as such happy accidents, but they can be engineered. We came across similar instances in secondary schools, for example where the teacher had found for the pupil a short story which had something in common with one the pupil had written himself. In the teacher's words, 'the imaginative exploration of the pupil's work can provide a way into the more difficult adult work of fiction.'

It is a particularly effective device for a teacher to stir demand by reading out arresting passages from new books. Television programmes likely to arouse a keen interest can be anticipated, and the teacher can have ready and waiting the appropriate books to catch the wave. There is almost no limit to the 'publicity' devices that might be conceived. For instance, in the display of dust jackets of new books arrows can lead off to large illustrations and short offprints of associated material. Pupils can be given a board on which to pin extracts calculated to make the curious want to know more. The teacher might tape trailer passages on cassettes for children to listen to on headsets. Some pupils might produce advertisement posters or design alternative dust jackets from their knowledge of the book. And always the children should be encouraged to talk about what they have read, to the teacher and among themselves. By keeping a note of what children read he could bring three or four together who had common experience of a particular book and let them explore one another's reactions to it. This is so much more productive and so much less forbidding than the obligatory written book review, where the pupil knows that his pleasure has inevitably to be followed by a chore.

All this kind of activity presupposes a wide range of books ready to hand and responsive to the teacher's controlling inventiveness. The acquisition of books and the promotional activities are essentially related, and anything less than a professionally informed policy will not achieve the object. The building up of book resources is often something of a piecemeal process rather than a planned response to defined objectives. School library services are an invaluable resource, but they are a support for the teacher, not a substitute for his control of the total learning situation. [...] Various studies have shown that a large number of contemporary writers of good quality fiction are barely represented in many schools, despite the fact that quantitatively the school may be generally well stocked with books. The survey conducted by Whitehead revealed that at least 77 per cent of all the books read by his sample fell within the category of 'narrative', which included biographical writing as well as fiction. Though there was some evidence of a veering towards informational books among the older boys, the category of 'non-narrative' still accounted for only 14.5 per cent of all book-reading. It was clear that the narrative mode provided for children of all ages by far the strongest motivation towards the reading of books. The potential of this for a general increase in reading needs no elaboration, and the school should have the books both to create and meet the demand. It is a recognition of this fact that underlies the success of those schools which have achieved a remarkably high rate of voluntary reading.

We believe that this recognition cannot take place at too early an age, and that fantasy, fairy-tale and folk-tale should take their place in the repertoire in the earliest stages of reading. J. R. R. Tolkien pointed out that fairy-tales were not evolved for the nursery; they found their way there by historical accident. They contain the strength and simplicity of their origins, as well as their deep significance. The children will have had experience of them in a good pre-reading programme, when a teacher or parent will have read them aloud or will have told the stories. All too often when their own reading begins they lose this world in favour of a circumscribed domestic situation with narrow limits of action and feeling. We accept the argument that its commonest representation in early reading books offers few toe-holds for the working class child. But we do not believe that it should simply be replaced by one that is set in a working class environment. There is obviously an important place for such material, but we have heard the case for 'relevance' carried to the point of excluding fantasy or any stories with settings or characters unfamiliar to the pupils from their first-hand experience. We do not accept this view. Though we consider it important that much of a child's reading matter should offer contact at many points with the life he knows, we believe that true relevance lies in the way a piece of fiction engages with the reader's emotional concerns. A work like 'Billy Liar', for example, has value for the older pupil not because of its environmental setting but because of its evocation of an aspect of adolescence and its exploration of family tensions.

We have emphasised that learning to read is a developmental process which continues over the years. To read intelligently is to read responsively; it is to ask questions of the text and use one's own framework of experience in interpreting it. In working his way through a book the reader imports, projects, anticipates, speculates on alternative outcomes; and nowhere is this process more active than in a work of imaginative literature. We strongly recommend that there should be a major effort to increase voluntary reading, which should be recognised as a powerful instrument for the improvement of standards. And in making this recommendation we recall a particularly telling remark from the evidence: pupils admitted to an adult literacy scheme had been asked to say why, in their opinion, they failed to learn to read at school. 'Only one common factor emerges: they did not learn from the process of learning to read that it was something other people did for *pleasure*'.

Most teachers of English would include among their most important aims a growth of discernment in their pupils. 'Discernment' is a word that begs many questions, and it could be taken to mean that the task of every English teacher is to take every pupil up to a permanent relationship with the great classics. In the last decade this notion has increasingly drawn contention. On the one hand there are those teachers who see literature in terms of a heritage, with which they must endow their pupils. On the other hand there are those who argue that many pupils can never be expected to take literature into their lives in any such sense. There is an equal polarity of view on what should be done with literature in the classroom. To some teachers there is no question but that this should consist of a close and detailed examination of the text, each successive encounter an attempt to sharpen discrimination. For others the text is very little more than a point of departure, a springboard to be barely touched before taking off for the element of personal experience or social issue. Nor is this to be neatly equated with the ability of pupils. In our visits we saw lessons where pupils of modest capacity were being pressed very closely to the text. And we saw able pupils engaged on experience-based programmes where the text was only perfunctorily visited. Nevertheless, the first approach is traditionally thought appropriate for pupils preparing for examinations and, by extension, for pupils whose road will in due course lead there.

The influence of examinations on literature teaching has come in for a good deal of assault, not least from those who could hardly be accused of anti-academic bias. Sampson, writing in 1921, said 'If in any school something called literature is systematically taught, the efforts will usually be found to be directed towards literary history, or 'meanings', or the explanation of difficulties, or summaries of plays and stories, or descriptions of characters . . . all of which are evasions of the real work before the teacher responsible for literature'. And Aldous Huxley in

'The Olive Tree' wrote that examinations in literature encourage pupils to repeat 'mechanically and without reflection other people's judgements'. C. Day Lewis saw the process as a threat to a true and sincere response. He described it as a lamentable practice to equip the students with highly sophisticated instruments of criticism, check that the poet responds positively to their tests, and then say 'O.K. boys, now you may love him'. Such censures gain force when applied to this approach to literature with pupils of lesser capacity. We have seen pupils preparing for 'O' level and C.S.E. with a diet of activities corresponding very closely to those catalogued by George Sampson. The explanations and the summaries have expanded to take-over point; the literature has receded. We must seriously question what is being achieved when pupils are producing chapter summaries in sequence, taking endless notes to prepare model answers and writing stereotyped commentaries which carry no hint of a felt response. Yet this is the standard experience of very large numbers of fourth and fifth formers who spend a term or more on a modest novel which makes no claim to merit such long drawn out attention. We recognise the difficulty facing the teacher, who has the task of talking about a narrative the sequence of which the pupils have not grasped. There are substantial technical problems with which very many teachers have not yet managed to come to terms. These add up to knowing how to help pupils 'through' a novel to the point of being able to respond to its experience without such unreal chores as chapter synopsis. We should like to see more professional discussion of appropriate teaching techniques for class approaches to a full-length novel.

There is no doubt that many secondary school pupils develop unsympathetic attitudes to literature as a result of their experience in preparing for an examination. We saw lessons in which a novel was treated as a hoard of factual information, with the pupils scoring marks for the facts they remembered. How many sheep did Gabriel Oak lose? What was the name of Bathsheba's maid? Where had Fanny Robins been working before she walked to Casterbridge? We saw pupils encountering poems as little more than comprehension passages, on which the teacher's information and interpretations were recorded as marginal notes. Yet in the same breath it must be said that the right relationship between teacher, text and pupil can and does have a strikingly positive effect on attitudes to literature. In one fairly recent study[5] a substantial majority of a large sample of 'O' level candidates of both sexes said they had no intention of reading more poetry after leaving school. But a study of the boys' responses showed that the small minority taking the opposite view came from just six of the twenty-nine classes in ten different schools. It is likely that the positive effect of the teachers of those six classes had been very strong. It is also clear that some of the recent developments in examining have encouraged extensive reading and imaginative teaching. In some of the C.S.E. classes we visited, pupils were responding sensitively to a wide variety of literature and deepening their understanding and enjoyment of it in the course of their study.

In a very real sense a pupil is himself being judged each time he responds in class to a piece of literature, particularly a poem. More is at stake than his knowledge of the text. Is the value-judgement he forms the one the teacher finds acceptable? Is he betraying himself, he may well ask, as one who lacks discrimination? In no other area of classroom operations is there quite the same degree of vulnerability, with poetry the most exposing element of all. Every skilled teacher has his own means of reducing this vulnerability, of balancing the need to explore the text with the need to preserve its appeal. Some of the most successful lessons we have seen have been those in which the teacher has contrived to stand alongside his pupils in this process of exploration. In other words, he has avoided using the text as a repository of answers to which he possesses the key. His curiosity about the work has remained alive and has not been extinguished by layers of acquired judgement. These are the most favourable conditions for any work of literature: when teacher and taught approach it in a common spirit of exploration. Inevitably and naturally the teacher will guide, but he will do this by devising situations which lead the pupils to their own insight. Nothing is served if the pupil simply learns to repeat 'mechanically and without reflection other people's judgements', and if in the process he is lost to what literature has to offer him. As we see it, the main emphasis should be on extending the range of the pupil's reading. True discernment can come only from a breadth of experience. Learning how to appreciate with enthusiasm is more important than learning how to reject.

Over the past ten years or so there has been a growth in secondary schools of the organisation of thematic work. This has been felt to be particularly appropriate in mixed ability classes, since it enables pupils of varying capacity to work alongside one another productively. Sometimes the whole class may read certain poems or short stories together, while at others the material they are handling has been selected to suit their ability. Thematic work has thus provided the pupils with a common purpose, and by its very nature has encouraged an organic treatment of talk, reading, writing and dramatisation. Literature has fared variously in such arrangements. It has certainly escaped what T. S. Eliot called the 'dryness of schematic analysis', but sometimes the encounter has been so brief that the pupil has been denied anything but a fleeting consciousness of it. We have seen lessons where the pupil's acquaintance with literature, other than what he reads privately, has been confined to a passage used to introduce a discussion; not a discussion upon the passage, which has been barely visited, but upon an area of experience to which it is related. There were several occasions on which virtually no attention at all was given to the words on the page. 'Have any of you had an experience like this?' is a tempting question after a first reading; but it becomes valuable only if the experience is then brought back to the text, and if there is a sharpening of response to the detail of the writing. An obvious danger in humanities lessons is for the literature to be selected solely on the ground that it matches the theme, however inappropriate it may be in other ways. Moreover, when a poem or story is enlisted to serve a theme it can become the property of that theme to the extent that its richness is oversimplified, its more rewarding complexities ignored. There is also a natural tendency to use collections of short extracts, so that the pupils' experience of complete books becomes minimal. We have a definite impression that fewer full-length novels are read. Anthologies are certainly a valuable resource, but they should open up opportunities, not constitute an end in themselves. The teacher's aim should always be to extend the range of writing to which the children can respond. Where anthologies are used we commend those that include complete pieces or substantial extracts, virtually artistic units on their own, rather than merely short snippets clipped out of their context.

The success of any innovation turns upon the manner and quality of its interpretation. At its best, thematic work has given to literature a self-proving eminence in the context of photograph, film, television, radio and newspaper accounts which have been associated with it in developing the theme. We have seen excellent examples of work founded on such constellations of media. We have been particularly impressed by those situations, admittedly rarer, where the teacher has carefully chosen a core of poetry and drama and gathered about it prose texts which set up reverberations. By such means the words on the page can be brought into varying degrees of focus, and breadth achieved without loss of a controlled degree of depth. Many schools are successfully extending the range and variety of their pupils' reading with a large number of carefully selected titles from post-war fiction. These speak to the young adult, often on a helpfully simple level, and explore experiences of direct concern to him. In one small secondary modern school in an urban area we saw a fifth year class of moderate ability supporting their C.S.E. set book study with an extensive range of such titles, chosen by the teacher with an excellent eye for their appeal and relevance. There was no doubt of his success in developing his pupils' enjoyment of wide reading while at the same time preparing them for the examination.

These and similar forms of organisation demand not only professional skill but professional knowledge. Whatever the value of his contribution in other ways the teacher without specialist qualifications in English cannot be expected to have the same ready access to a wide range of sources. Where a team of teachers is co-operating on a theme, particularly with a humanities programme, the guidance of an English specialist is essential. It is by no means always the case that he is to be found there. If the child is to meet literature, the extent, relevance and quality of that literature must not be a matter of chance but the informed judgement of one who has a wide and detailed knowledge of suitable texts. He may not actually be teaching the class, but his advice and support should be available to whichever of his colleagues is. In the best of such arrangements this goes without saying. Regular consultation, reviews and synopses of material, joint study of the books to be used: these and many other devices ensure that all the non-specialist teachers of English are fully resourced. But such planning is not universal, and it is still too readily assumed that anyone can turn his hand to English. This assumption all too often results in a narrower experience of literature, and the closing of opportunities that might have been opened up had the teacher only known of particular books that match them.

In recent years there has been a welcome growth in the practice of wide individualised reading within a class. This is a pattern which some teachers have long operated, and its advantages were pressed by Jenkinson[6] in his 1940 survey when he advocated small sets of books as opposed to the collective reading of the class novel. And yet the latter is still to be found in many schools as the standard, indeed the exclusive, procedure. We refer here not to the classes which are preparing for examinations, but lower and middle school groups. Its great disadvantage is that it usually entails a slow plod, in which the pupils' experience of the book is parcelled out over a term or part of a term at weekly intervals. There are likely to be pupils who read fewer books during the whole term in school than they read out of school in one month. Moreover, this pattern is often associated with the allocation to particular classes or year groups of certain novels. These lists are often interpreted quite strictly, so that a pupil has no official access to a book in a higher list. Such grading systems are more often than not quite arbitrary and are not based on anything other than an intuitive 'feel'. The intuition of an experienced teacher is a valuable instrument, but experience shows that assessments of suitability can vary widely. In one group of four comparable secondary schools there was only partial agreement as to where a particular book belonged. Of the following books, each to be found in the first or second years of at least two of the four schools, only three were prescribed for the same age point in every case: 'Treasure Island', 'Kidnapped', 'Tanglewood Tales', 'Jim Davis', 'Tom Sawyer', 'David Copperfield', 'A Christmas Carol', 'A Tale of Two Cities', and 'Great Expectations'. Indeed, certain of the books that appeared in one school's lower school list would be deferred by another until the third or fourth year. Where classes are of mixed ability the logic of such restrictions is further open to question.

At its most extreme the system of class reading at the rate of one or two books a term must put literature in a somewhat artificial light in the mind of the pupil. We have already remarked that children's voluntary reading is not as great in quantity as it should be, but there is no doubt as to its diversity and variety. The 6,000 children in Whitehead's sample who claimed to have read one or more books during the previous four weeks named more than 7,500 separate and distinct titles. In our view the teacher can have a marked effect on his pupils' reading by extending the individualised provision within the classroom and relating it to their reading outside school hours. We have argued that this implies a knowledge on his part of the wide range of good modern fiction available. Some of the book lists we saw in schools were remarkably well-informed on this score, but others contained little beyond the established 'classics', and reflected a stock which had not received an infusion of new (as opposed to replacement) material for some considerable time. It is equally important that the teacher should know something about the pupils' reading habits, and should discover what books they read in their previous school and the nature and extent of the work that has grown out of this reading. We hope he would then keep his own record of their reading in school and would discuss with them the books they read outside it. Perhaps it hardly needs adding that these will often disappoint him. Every survey so far carried out into children's reading reveals that much of it is ephemeral or well below what informed adults would consider to be good material. Nevertheless, the skilled teacher will not reject or denigrate it. The willingness to talk about it and take up the child's enthusiasm is essential to the process of encouraging him to widen his range.

In recommending an expansion of supported individualised reading in schools we see it as a complementary process to group attention to the text, which provides so valuable an opportunity to deepen the reading experience. Some of the best and most lasting effects of English teaching have come from the simultaneous encounter of teacher, pupil and text. We have suggested above that this experience can be more universally enjoyed when it takes the form of a shared exploration. This is clearly not easy. The teacher has a deeper knowledge of literature in general and that work in particular than his pupils can possess. He brings to the situation a wider experience of life and a maturer view of it. To contain these in the process of sharing is a measure of his skill at its highest level. A child derives value from a work of literature in direct proportion to the genuineness of the response he is able to make to it. The teacher's skill lies in developing the subtlety and complexity of this response without catechism or a one-way traffic in apodictic judgements. This is particularly true in the case of poetry, which our visits showed to be receiving a wide range of treatment. At its best it was distinguished, and the children were being given an experience which was enviable and a pleasure to witness. At the other extreme some children rarely encountered poetry of any kind.

It has to be acknowledged that poetry starts at a disadvantage. In the public view it is something rather odd, certainly outside the current of normal life; it is either numinous, and therefore rarely to be invoked, or an object of comic derision. Definitions of poetry are almost limitless, but they always agree upon this central fact: that it is a man speaking to men, of his and their condition, in language which consists of the best words in the best order, language used with the greatest possible inclusiveness and power. Matthew Arnold said of it that it is 'simply the most beautiful, impressive, and widely effective mode of saying things'. To D. H. Lawrence '. . . the essential quality of poetry is that it makes a new effort of attention and "discovers" a new world within the known world'. Definitions can inspirit, but they can also deter. It is a reinforcement of the prejudice against poetry to present it as something precious, arcane, to be revered. This concept, a particularly tenacious one, sees poetry as 'something more or less involuntarily secreted by the author', oozing from the unconscious in a manner quite unlike that of prose, which is consciously controlled. The teacher is often faced with the task of showing that poetry is not some inaccessible form of utterance, but that it speaks directly to children, as to anyone else, and has something to say which is relevant to their living here and now.

We have already referred to the analytical approach to poetry. This has been successively reinforced by every new examination which has been introduced, even where the authors of that examination have intended something quite different. T. S. Eliot once said of practical criticism: 'It cannot be recommended to young people without grave danger of deadening their sensibility . . . and confounding the genuine development of taste with the sham acquisition of it'. But it is to be found, in however skeletal or distorted a form, in some clearly inappropriate situations. We have seen C.S.E. classes working their way almost mechanistically through a set anthology, paraphrasing and answering endless comprehension questions on the way; and this is standard practice for many O level pupils. It is perhaps not surprising that in the survey mentioned earlier (page 221) the pupils' attitude to poetry was a dispiriting one. Of 1,000 O level and A level students only 170 said they would read any more poetry after leaving school; 96 of the 800 O level students, 74 of the 200 A level students. Equally revealing was their attitude towards particular texts. The four O level poetry anthologies were conspicuously disliked, while at A level Milton's poetry, and particularly *Paradise Lost*, was notably unpopular. It is at least possible that his standing was related to the degree of 'external' labour his poetry demands: factual knowledge, annotation, paraphrase, classical and biblical allusions.*

---

* Cf Sir Arthur Quiller-Couch: 'On the Art of Reading' (1920): 'You have (we will say) a class of thirty or forty in front of you . . . you will not (if you are wise) choose a passage from "Paradise Lost": your knowledge telling you that "Paradise Lost" was written, late in his life, by a great virtuoso, and older men (of whom I, sad to say, am one) assuring you that to taste the Milton of "Paradise Lost" a man must have passed his thirtieth year'.

Our argument here must not be construed as an attack on the notion of a close engagement with a poem; we have already expressed our faith in the value of a shared encounter with a work of literature. Eliot's remark about practical criticism can be balanced with his observation that where a poem is concerned understanding and enjoyment are essential to one another. By this reckoning what kind of understanding has the detailed study of poetry given to the large number of pupils who voted so feelingly against it? It is clear to us that this antipathy rests substantially in the *method* of teaching it; and the comprehension approach is by no means confined to the examination years. It is usually associated with the timetabled poetry lesson, which often assumes the shape of the Procrustean bed. Where this is the medium of encounter there is a temptation for the poem to be read, re-read, socratically worried, eviscerated for its figures of speech, even copied into exercise books. Clearly there are occasions when a poem needs a comfortable amount of time to be experienced, but poetry works best when it is wanted, not when the timetable decrees it. There will be times when a particular poem may make its maximum impact by being dropped suddenly, with neither preamble nor question, into a lull which calls out for it. There will be occasions when it seems the most natural thing in the world for a poem to be read at that particular moment. For instance, to read Anthony Hecht's poem 'Tarantula' while discussing the Great Plague would be to give a new dimension to the subject. Edwin Muir's 'The Interrogation' and Edwin Morgan's 'The Suspect' graphically examine an experience of authority at its most unfeeling, each ending on a tempting question mark. The kind of talk that goes on in class always creates at some point the context for a poem that takes up the general feeling. The strength and relevance of the experience within it should engage the pupils' response and thus their willingness to grapple with the language. Some of the best lessons we saw were those where pupils and teacher were enjoying the exchange of opinions on points of vocabulary, attitude, atmosphere and metaphor.

All this leads us back inevitably to the question of the teacher's knowledge of his material. Many schools simply do not have the resources to take this kind of opportunity. The anthologies, thematic source books and collections of extracts are a great help, but they do not go far enough. Many of them are sensitively and intelligently compiled, and the editor has allowed his own good judgement to operate on his own very wide reading. Some, however, are simply anthologies of anthologies, yielding only a few new poems to supplement the very large overlap with collections that have gone before. A particular poem will appear time and again, though in fact it may not be either the most appealing or the most suitable of the very many the author has written. Inevitably, anthologies age, and where a school relies on class sets (sometimes, as we have seen, shared between two or three classes) the range of available material will become relatively narrower as time goes by. It is exceptionally difficult for the individual teacher to keep abreast of all the new poetry that is published. Indeed, except for those with a particular interest in it there is often a time-lag. So that the teacher is not aware of much of the work produced in the last two decades. A good anthology will do a great deal to introduce teacher and pupil alike to new and unfamiliar material, but it should not be a substitute for the extensive reading of poetry by the teacher himself. We know this is an ideal; but if the teacher wants to find material that he knows will be right for his pupils and the context he has created, this is the most rewarding way. There is some very good poetry published that never finds its way into an anthology, and much of it would appeal directly to the pupils. There is certainly everything to be said for teachers in a primary school and members of an English department maintaining a collective knowledge of what is being produced. We found that one of the strengths of the well-qualified groups of specialists in some comprehensive schools was precisely this team approach to reading. Communally, the department had an impressive knowledge, upon which every individual member could draw. This awareness thus becomes a major contributor to the central resource collection a department creates for itself. Such a collection will contain print and non-print materials of all kinds, and one of its essentials should be a wide range of poetry gathered through teachers' first-hand reading of the work of individual poets. A resource point of this kind can be particularly helpful to a young teacher early in his first appointment. To enjoy so wide a choice, to be able to call freely on record, tape or cassette, may make all the difference to his attitude to poetry in the classroom in that first year. Another valuable facility is the Arts Council/D.E.S. 'Writers in Schools' scheme, which enables poets to visit schools to read and talk about their work. Where we have seen this in operation it has been very successful. Some schools have developed the interest it has generated by taking pupils to exhibitions of poetry and public readings.

We have placed some emphasis on contemporary poetry, but this is not to imply that we recommend it at the expense of older poetry. It is simply that much of the work of this half century, and perhaps particularly the last two decades of it, has a voice to which a larger number of young people can more readily respond. Moreover, it is fresh to many teachers themselves and some feel able to read it to their pupils with the pleasure of a new discovery. Poetry of this century and of earlier centuries can be read side by side, to the mutual illumination of both. And what we have said about going beyond anthologies applies with little less force to the latter.

Poetry has great educative power, but in many schools it suffers from lack of commitment, misunderstanding and the wrong kind of orientation; above all it lacks adequate resources. There are few more rewarding experiences in all English teaching than when teacher and pupil meet in the enjoyment of a poem. We are not so unrealistic as to believe that all pupils can take away from school with them a lasting love of poetry. There will always be many people to whom it offers nothing. But we are certain that it does not reach as many as it might, and we believe this can be achieved.

We can sum up by saying that whatever else the pupil takes away from his experience of literature in school he should have learned to see it as a source of pleasure, as something that will continue to be a part of his life. The power to bring this about lies with the teacher, but it cannot be pretended that the task is easy. In outlining some of the difficulties we have inevitably had to be critical of certain approaches which we believe compound them. However, we must conclude with warm appreciation of the work we have seen in many of the schools we visited, which we believe is representative of the imaginative treatment literature is widely receiving. It is an aspect of English which has made some remarkable advances in recent years, and we feel that great credit belongs to the teachers who have done so much to bring these about.

NOTES

1. Nowell Smith: *Cambridge Essays on Education:* Editor A. C. Benson: Cambridge University Press: 1917.

2. *Half our Future*: H.M.S.O.: 1963.

3. G. Sampson: *English for the English:* Cambridge University Press: 1921.

4. F. Whitehead, A. C. Capey and W. Maddren: *Children's Reading Interests:* Schools Council Working Paper No. 52: Evans/Methuen Educational: 1974.

5. G. Yarlott and W. S. Harpin: *1,000 Responses to English Literature:* Educational Research 13.1 and 13.2: 1972/73.

6. A. J. Jenkinson: *What do Boys and Girls Read?:* An investigation into reading habits with some suggestions about the teaching of literature in secondary and senior schools: Methuen: 1940.

26 *Structuralism and Literature*

● Rex Gibson

[...] If structuralism is impenetrable and obscure for teachers, it seems doubly so for pupils and their parents. For many, the requirements of school English are already far removed from their experience and interests. *Coronation Street* or Conan the Barbarian, James Bond or *The Sun* newspaper rarely figure in the school curriculum. If they do, the approach is frequently hostile, designed to show the triviality or worthlessness of such widely viewed, widely read manifestations of popular culture. Against such a background, heated discussions at an ancient university about literary theory hold neither meaning nor significance. If Shakespeare has only a tenuous hold in Scunthorpe, structuralism has no chance at all.

[...] Literature is central to education; reading is crucial to schooling: but structuralism raises fundamental issues. It is about the shaping of consciousness itself: how we come to see the world, in all its aspects, as we do. For most teachers and their pupils there is a 'matter-of-factness', a 'givenness' about all they do, about the world they inhabit. The importance of structuralism is in questioning that givenness, probing as it does the common-sense assumptions which prevail about the naturalness of our activities and perceptions. In this chapter, I will examine the specific case of structuralism and literature, because of literature's centrality in schooling and because structuralist method here offers fruitful analogies for understanding social life itself.

The relations of structuralism and literature need to be understood in the context of different approaches to the study of literature. It is possible to distinguish four major approaches, all practised at university level, but very differently represented in the teaching of literature in schools. The first (with a long history pre-dating the institutionalisation of English studies in universities) is that of scholarship on texts: patient, scrupulous research which attempts to establish what the author originally wrote. Shakespeare is the classic example and a glance at any editor's introduction to a Shakespeare play reveals the scale, difficulties and interdisciplinarity of the enterprise. One well-known example illustrates the problems involved: does Hamlet speak of 'solid', 'sullied', or 'sallied' flesh? This concern to establish the text is an activity for career scholars and researchers. It is not the business of undergraduate students in higher education, and in schools it is no part of the pupil's activities: for them, the text is given.

The second approach, a product of the 1920s, its origin attributed to I. A. Richards, and much associated with F. R. Leavis, is a method of study that has been influential at all levels of education. It can be called the human encounter with literature, the response to the text. Pioneered by Richards' exercises in practical criticism, it concerns itself with how the individual responds when faced with (most typically) a poem, or novel, or play. Here, in closely focused examination of the text, emotion and intelligence uniquely combine to produce a judgement, an evaluation. Key words in such an approach are 'authenticity', 'sincerity', 'critical awareness'. Its assumption is that there is a correlation between the individual's feelings and the quality of the work. Both responses and texts can therefore be ranked in terms of their depth, sincerity, humanity. The 'educated reader's' response is somehow truer, more perceptive, more authentic; the capability for discrimination is increased and the capacity for responding to great works expanded. 'Great works' are, indeed, the central, undisputed focus of such an approach, and the approach itself can identify them. 'Literature' and 'great works' become interchangeable terms as the moral worthiness of text (and responses) are scrupulously, minutely revealed. George Eliot, Henry James are exemplary, and 'revaluation' (significantly, the title of one of F. R. Leavis' books) admits others (notably D. H. Lawrence, T. S. Eliot) to the canon, to the 'great tradition' of English Literature. The encounter between reader and text is a moral one, and one which transcends local, temporal circumstance. In its 'purest' form (for example, in Richards' book *Practical Criticism*) history, context, author all disappear as the student is presented with only a text (with no mention of author, date or other information) and required to respond to that alone. The encounter is uniquely between the poem and the sensibility of the reader: the finer the sensibility the more refined and discriminating the judgement, the truer the assessment. The capital 'L' of 'Literature' marks its membership off from the other coarser, mundane or trivial writings.

The language of this second approach is everyday, conversational, nontechnical; theory is eschewed. More than that, theory is rejected, despised. It is unnecessary and comes between the reader and the text, sullying the response, impeding common sense. 'This is so, isn't it?' was Leavis' practical, down to earth, antitheory method. However, as the approach developed it proved impossible to keep comparison (other poems, possible authors, historical background) out of such responses. Greater acknowledgement was therefore made of the contexts in which any poem or play is embedded. Nonetheless, attention remained squarely upon the text itself: literature was 'foregrounded', history and society 'backgrounded'. Knowledge of society was valuable for the illumination it afforded of the text. Our understanding of Elizabethan England enriched our response to Shakespeare, but the text itself was nonetheless transcendent, accessible to the discriminating intellect and emotion. In this approach the proper study of literature is literature itself, for it is not a means to an end, not a vehicle to understand society, but an end in itself. Much was made of the educational implications of the approach, for it saw reading literature and moral development as intertwined, mutually dependent. The moral qualities present in the work of art (novel, play, poem) revealed by 'true' reading, an appropriate response, became synonymous with education: they *were* the ends of education. At the levels of both higher education and schooling this approach has been the most powerful influence on English studies.[1]

The third approach alters the balance between literature and history, literature and society. If traditional scholarship and the human response approach used historical and social evidence in the service of the text, now the terms of the relationship shift. Literature is studied in order to identify its role and function in society; to discover the correspondences between *its* forms and other societal forms; to find what it can tell us *about* society. The language of this approach draws heavily on the social sciences; in marked contrast to the human response approach it favours theory (often Marxist). In its strongest version, literary study is used as a tool for social analysis; literature loses its privileged status as its 'mystery' and 'art' are stripped away. It becomes a means not simply for understanding but for improving and serving society. Some Marxist approaches (but certainly not all and certainly not Karl Marx himself) take this latter stance, where no longer is 'art for art's sake' acceptable, but rather 'art for society's sake'. Dickens, for example, can be pressed into service primarily as a tool to criticise Victorian capitalism (an activity which the 'human response' school finds insensitive).

However, the relationship between literature and society has long been a major feature of the English critical tradition. Leavis' writing, for example, is typified by moral and social criticism based on a particular view of 'organic' society. Imbued with notions of social health, right relationships, for Leavis literature was indeed social criticism. Jane Austen and George Eliot exposed the hypocrisies of current social practices. But for Leavis, as for the still dominant tradition of literary study, literature is securely foregrounded. In contrast, radical expressions of the changed balance of literature and society can be seen in the work of Terry Eagleton (1978) and Arnold Kettle (1967), and in recent work at the University of Birmingham's Centre for Contemporary Cultural Studies (Hall, 1980). However, the writer who has done most to shift the balance whilst still respecting the integrity and independence of literature is Raymond Williams. His explorations of the relationships between literature and society have been at once delicate, sophisticated, radical and seminal. No other writer has been so influential in opening up fresh fields of enquiry in the relationships between literature and society. His abiding preoccupation with cultural forms and their connection with the material and ideological forms of society represents a distinctively British reworking of the nature of literary studies.[2] In schools there is a well-established tradition (due largely to the influence of F. R. Leavis) of social criticism and of the opposition of literary and certain social values ('getting and spending we lay waste our powers'). Hostility to consumerism, to the mass media, even to science, is characteristic. Nonetheless, more radically critical approaches, Marxist analyses or the study of correspondences in social and literary forms are rarely if at all present. Such approaches are deferred until the stage of higher education where they frequently encounter strong opposition.

The fourth approach to English studies is one concerned with the internal systems and mechanisms of literature; its questions are: 'How does this text work?' 'What sort of text is it?' It analyses the world of literature, identifying conventions, genres, concepts, methods that are distinctively literary. This approach springs from a very long tradition. The study of rhetoric, which loomed so large in the classical and Renaissance worlds and which was for long one of the main strands of the school curriculum, is its ancestor. In one form it survived and flourishes in schools. Generations of examination candidates faced with practical criticism have striven to show how rhythm, rhyme, repetition, imagery, association, verse form and so on all contribute to the poem's effect (or how plot, character, point of view and so on contribute to the novel). In this form it is held to be complementary but subservient to the human response approach. The literary devices identified contribute to the richness of the work, but its moral seriousness, its imaginative power, or our enjoyment of it, transcend such mechanics. Indeed, most textbooks which set out such techniques do so a touch apologetically, nodding as they do to Wordsworth's 'we murder to dissect', acknowledging the superiority of intuitive, 'true' response. Thus, as most school pupils experience it, this approach is the handmaid of the celebratory, deferential stance to great works favoured by the human response school. It has very little to do with theory and in its conventional form it poses no threat to 'literature', accepting it uncritically as a given and narrow canon of works by English authors.[3]

But the alternative form of the fourth approach *is* threatening, radical, subversive even. It is literary structuralism, which, far from celebrating literature, far from making evaluations as to moral worth, questions traditional notions of what *counts* as literature, concerns itself centrally not with response and intuition, not with evaluation, but with the *system* that makes literature possible. Such activities, and the very self-conscious theorising which characterises structuralism, are regarded with great suspicion by the majority of English teachers who have been socialised into what might be called the Leavisian tradition (or, more simply, to a tradition that stresses a common-sense, respectful, closely textually focused, untheoretical approach to a given set of 'great works').

LITERARY STRUCTURALISM

There are many varieties of literary structuralism; indeed it is fashionable (but inappropriate) to speak of 'post-structuralism' as if structuralism itself belonged to a past era. It is an intellectual movement which flourishes in mainland Europe, particularly France, where attitudes to theory are far more positive than in England. Its most influential introduction to Britain and the United States was through Jonathan Culler's *Structuralist Poetics* published in 1975. Until the much-publicised McCabe affair at Cambridge in 1980–81 brought it to the attention of a wider audience, literary structuralism was the active concern of relatively few critics and scholars in higher education. Among these, the best known are probably Frank Kermode, David Lodge and Geoffrey Strickland, all of whom bring particularly English sensibilities to their study of structuralism, demonstrating its limitations and potentialities.[4] The glare of publicity occasioned by the McCabe case came as a surprise and, as Kermode (until 1982 a Professor of English at Cambridge University) remarked at the time, 'literary theory is somewhat bewilderingly in the news'. Readers who desire an entertaining insight into what a mild (that is, English) version of literary structuralism looks like should read David Lodge's essay 'Oedipuss: or the practice and theory of narrative'.[5] Here, Lodge examines one of his own short stories and discovers its structure to be that of the story of Oedipus. A family, going on holiday, must leave its cat behind to be fed by neighbours. The husband, rushing back from buying the catfood, accidentally runs over and kills the cat. Lodge is struck by the similarity of his story to the legend of Oedipus who has left Corinth to avoid killing his father and marrying his mother but, through that action, inevitably commits both crimes. Lodge's husband-father kills the cat in his action (buying food) intended to keep it alive. Lodge is impressed by this correspondence (discovered *after* writing his story) and by other structuralist elements, concluding:

> . . . it is not so much man that speaks language as language that speaks man; not so much the writer who writes narrative as narrative that writes the writer.

Such structuralist claims ('language speaks man'; 'narrative writes the writer') are anathema to followers of Leavis. Structuralism's decentring of the subject is seen here at full force. The centrality of the individual, of genius, of creativity, on which the 'human response' school insists, is frontally challenged. Translated to the realm of schooling it becomes 'society determines the pupil', 'schooling makes the teachers'. However, Lodge's work is of interest because he actually engages in structural analysis of literature, demonstrating, by considering particular works, how the method provides insights. This is in contrast to much structuralist writing which concerns itself more with theorising about structuralism than with actually practising it. Lodge shows that structuralism is primarily a method, not concerned with the meaning, value or interpretation of a work but with the devices that enable it to be written, that is to say with its structural characteristics. What marks him off from more committed (dogmatic?) European structuralists is that his writing is not only accessible, avoiding excess of technical terms, but that in his criticism he finds it impossible to avoid questions of meaning, interpretation and value. A comparison of his writing with that of Roman Jakobson or Jacques Derrida[6] reveals the very wide range of structuralist approaches to literature. For all its variety, literary structuralism is most easily understood by considering the characteristics of structuralism which are present, with changed emphasis, in every type. In what follows I shall identify respectively how literary structuralism employs the notions of wholeness, self-regulation, transformation, relationships, synchronic analysis and decentring of the subject. This last element leads to a discussion of post-structuralism or deconstruction.

WHOLENESS

Structuralism views literature as a system or structure, a totality with its own conventions and traditions, explicable in terms of itself. This whole takes precedence over individual authors or readers or texts. When Lodge remarks 'narrative . . . writes the writer', or when Gabriel Josipovici asserts 'the genre quite as much as John Milton . . . is responsible for Lycidas'[7] they are drawing attention to the whole, the totality, which governs individual (i.e. the author's) action. The task of the literary structuralist is to identify, within this closed world, the conventions, devices, methods that make it work, which enable authors to write, readers to read. The structured elements of the whole may be such familiar ones as plot, character, symbol, or less familiarly, codes or binary oppositions, or the principles of metaphor and metonymy. Such structures underpin a whole range of structuralist activities: classifying within and between literary genres; identifying the fundamental dramatic situations; revealing the structures of fairy-tales and myths; mapping the laws and functions of folk-tales, demonstrating the various ways in which signs or language create an illusion of reality and hence convey meaning (the structuralist concept of *vraisemblance*). The analogy here is with Saussure's *langue*: the whole that makes speech possible.

SELF-REGULATION

It is the Saussurian notion of the *arbitrary character of the sign* which allows the structuralist to search not for meaning, but for method. His pursuit of the rules governing literary expression can be undertaken within the whole that is literature, without reference to an outside world. As Jonathan Culler puts it:

> Rather than a criticism which discovers or assigns meanings it would be a poetics which strives to define the conditions of meaning . . .[8]

Clearly the 'conditions' are to be found in other texts, in the genres and conventions of literature itself:

> . . . the analyst's task is not simply to describe a corpus but to account for the structure and meaning that items of the corpus have for those who have assimilated the rules and norms of the system . . . the basic task is to render as explicit as possible the conventions responsible for the production of attested effects.[9]

Here is clearly the notion of *self-regulation*, for the conventions of literature are 'responsible' for its effect. Structuralism concerns itself with the 'literariness' of literature: significance lies in the literary laws, patterns and devices that make the individual text and the whole system work. Such concern issues in the formal analyses of Roman Jakobson. Here he is on Shakespeare's Sonnet 129, 'Th' expense of Spirit':

> The four strophic units exhibit three kinds of binary correspondences: (1) alternation (abab), which ties together the two *odd* strophes (I, III) and opposes them to the even strophes which are tied in turn to each other (II, IV); (2) framing (abba) which brings together the enclosing *outer* strophes (I, IV) and opposes them to the two enclosed, mutually related *inner* strophes (II, III); (3) neighbourhood (aabb), which builds pairs of anterior (I, II) and posterior (III, IV) strophes opposed to each other.[10]

And his chapter headings arranged as binary oppositions reveal his structuralist preoccupation with theory construction as they claim to identify the underlying structures: 'Odd against even', 'Outer against inner', 'Anterior against posterior', 'Couplets against quatrains'. Any text is subordinate to the structure; it is the outcome of that structure; the enterprise is one of revealing the codes which govern literary discourse. Particular self-regulating structures can also be found which govern an individual author's work. Tzvetan Todorov, for instance, searches for 'the figure in Henry James's Carpet, the primary plan on which everything else depends, as it appears in each one of his works'.

He finds this 'invariant factor' by considering all James' tales and he confidently reveals the structural formula: 'James's tales are based on the quest for an absolute and absent cause.'[11]

TRANSFORMATION

It is in terms of such 'primal plans' for individual authors, and in terms of its internal laws and mechanisms for literature itself, that structuralists explain how *transformations* take place. An individual author is governed by both particular and general structures as his own work develops. Those structures guarantee change. Within the whole that is literature, both practices and conventions are changed, for there is an internal dynamic such that, as literature comments upon itself, so it modifies itself. The dialectic between any work and other works is such that transformation is effected by the system. Literature has a life of its own with its own inbuilt mechanisms for development. For structuralists it is an active sign system achieving its own transformations: Shakespeare is to be explained through existing conventions which are transformed as he draws on them; modernism arises from the nineteenth-century novel. All are subject to the deep structures which govern literary practice and which ensure both continuity and change. The notion of transformation is not confined to the writing of texts, it is central to the act of reading itself. Structuralism maintains that each reader reconstructs the text anew. Rutherford's comment on reading is rich in Piagetian resonances:

> Reading . . . is a confrontation between the possibilities of the text and the expectations and needs of readers . . . it is activity, construction, play, rather than passivity, reception, contemplation.[12]

But for a structuralist those activities take place within, and are the outcome of, structural laws. Transformations take place at both the level of the system and the individual with both being subject to those laws.

RELATIONSHIPS

Throughout all structuralist writing can be seen the emphasis on the *relationships* that exist within the totality that is literature. Structuralist analysis of literature, as of other practices, concerns itself little with individuals or things, but with the relationships of word to language, of text to genre, convention, device: to the whole that is literature. *Lear* and *Look Back in Anger* alike are to be explained by their structural origins. As Todorov puts it: 'Structuralism is a scientific method implying an interest in impersonal laws and forms, of which existing objects are only the realisation.'[13] Following the principle that elements have significance *only* through their relationships, literary structuralism seeks the relationships of a particular text to the forms that make up literature.

To use the ideas of Derrida, it seeks those absences which give meaning to presences. In these 'absent' networks reside the deep structures of literature that enable writers to write and readers to read. Once again, in this stress on relationships we can see the neglect, even dismissal, of meaning and interpretation. It is not difficult to see why English critics and scholars raised in the tradition of F. R. Leavis react so strongly against the priorities directly stated in Culler's task for structuralists:

> . . . to reconstruct the conventions which enable physical objects or events to have meaning . . . to formulate the pertinent distinctions and relations among elements as well as the rules governing their possibility of combination . . . not (to) discover what a sequence means or produce a new interpretation of it but tries to determine the nature of the system underlying the event.[14]

SYNCHRONIC ANALYSIS

This 'system' is to be studied as a *snapshot* (or *synchronically*). The present, rather than the past, is what matters, and a study of how the words on the page relate to each other and how the text is realised through literary devices effectively banishes history. For all its emphasis on transformation, structuralism emphasises that literature, like the Saussurian *langue*, should be conceptualised as wholes that exist at (and as) particular 'moments'. These moments include an entire network of relationships. The operations which enable texts to be written and read become 'present' through synchronic analysis in which the past is incorporated into the present, made manifest in the network that is literature. Such, at least, is the theory. In practice, few structuralists achieve such ideal analyses — and certainly no British practitioner does.

DECENTRING THE SUBJECT

The most radical form of structuralism banishes not only history but also the author and the reader (in spite of all the emphasis put on the latter's recreation of the text at each reading). Julia Kristeva asserts:

> It is no longer 'I' who reads; the impersonal time of regularity, of the grid, of harmony, takes up this 'I' which is in fragments from having read; *one* reads.[15]

The Anglo-Saxon mind finds it difficult to comprehend such a remark; it is far from our experience and our taken-for-granted assumptions. It, and Culler's comment on it, are deeply threatening to our notions of common sense, to our feelings of personal identity:

> The subject who reads is constituted by a series of conventions, the grids of regularity and intersubjectivity. The empirical 'I' is dispersed among these conventions which take over from him in the act of reading.[16]

What we see here is that literary structuralism, like all structuralism, rigidly, necessarily, *decentres the subject*. The price that must be paid in according the priority of the system is the subordination (or even disappearance) of the individual. Author and reader become mere agents of the structures of literature, passive tools of literary codes. As Catherine Belsey notes:

> Roland Barthes has specifically proclaimed the death of the author; and Jacques Lacan, Louis Althusser and Jacques Derrida have all from various positions questioned the humanist assumption that subjectivity, the individual mind or inner being, is the source of meaning and action.[17]

Signs, rather than men, are dominant, as neither the intentions nor the setting of the author are of interest or relevance. For it follows that if a work belongs to a system, the writer, however much a genius, is forced to follow the codes and conventions of that system. His work exists only by permission and creation of the totality of literature itself.

POST-STRUCTURALISM

In the decentring just noted we glimpse the structuralism of the 'deconstructionists',[18] the post-structuralism which clearly goes against the common-sense assumptions of the great majority of readers. I, and almost every reader of this book, assume that an author intends to tell a story or express himself; that he does so in a poem, play, or novel, and so tells the truth in some way about human nature or about the world so that the reader can grasp and share the author's insights, perceptions. Such common-sense simplicities are not acceptable to the post-structuralists who carry their theorising well beyond any earlier limits. (It is interesting to note that even such a structuralist advocate as Professor David Lodge declares himself baffled by much of the current structuralist texts — small hope for the common reader!) This most radical element of structuralist thought does not simply lack interest in the *meaning* of a text as opposed to its internal devices, but denies that any objective meaning is possible. Like all structuralism, post-structuralism is a heterogeneous movement, but we can discern four elements: a stress on closed systems, on plurality of meaning, on the impossibility of truth claims, and on the impossibility of meaning itself.

The self-enclosed nature of systems is by now a familiar idea to us. It can be seen in Barthes' description of fashion and literature as:

> . . . systems whose function is not to communicate an objective, external meaning which exists prior to the system, but only to create a functioning

equilibrium, a movement of signification . . . they signify 'nothing'; their essence is in the process of signification, not in what they signify.[19]

Here, literature will be replaced by semiotics, for writing — any writing, Shakespeare or advertising jingles — is merely different parts of a system of signs which can be studied to discover how they work.

Plurality of meaning might seem a familiar and acceptable idea to English readers who have grown up with the notion that great literature offers a richness, a plenitude of interpretation. We never finish with Shakespeare. But the post-structuralists go well beyond this, for, linking it with the notion of the impossibility of truth claims, all chance of judging the quality of a work disappears:

> Texts can be read in many ways; each text contains within itself the possibility of an infinite set of structures, and to privilege some by setting up a system of rules to generate them is a blatantly prescriptive and ideological move.[20]

Here the door is open to dispense with any notion of a canon of literature, a set of great works, for such a view treats all claims to truth as delusions. Under such a view literature would lose its implicit capital 'L' and teachers could no longer find reasons to defend the study of Shakespeare as against Ian Fleming, or *The Beano*. The human response approach to literature is fundamentally undermined as relativism rules.

Deconstruction's final move to the very impossibility of meaning itself is made as it 'refuses to identify the force of literature with any concept of embodied meaning', and is seen in the work of Derrida whose 'theory of language . . . teaches the dearth of meaning'.[21] Such a view bewilders conventional scholars and readers. It certainly bewilders me but it can be quickly dealt with, for if no meaning can be established and truth has no relevance, there is no reason why any attention should be paid to these deconstructionists themselves. By their own admission, any reading is possible, none more valid than another. So why bother to read them at all? Such a dismissal is perhaps too easy and in making it I am only too aware of the truth of much structuralist theory, for I recognise in it the grip on my own mind of particular ways of thinking: the Anglo-Saxon empirical tradition and the influence of Dr Leavis.

If structuralism is characterised by its preference for grand theory, post-structuralism must be noted for its sweeping assertions, its excitement and inconsistencies. Its association with events in Paris of the late 1960s is significant: stimulation and challenge, a wilful desire to shake and shock, and a fundamental questioning of the most taken for granted assumptions. Like Marxist criticism, its stance is one of irreverence: works of art are not held in awe, but are to be demystified, exposed, explained. It denies the distinction between literature and other forms of writing, arguing that the codes it postulates apply to all language use, to all sign systems. It is this lack of respect for the mystery of creativity that Denis Donoghue inveighed against in his 1982 Reith Lectures. In its preference for modernism, for resistant, fragmented, uncooperative, uninterpretable, 'unreadable' texts, deconstruction echoes its own values, and reveals its cultural diagnosis. It embraces the 'principle of resistance' employed by modern writers:

> For literature is essentially the discourse of doubt rather than of affirmation.[22]

Where structuralism sought literary codes which gave pattern and significance, deconstruction abandons any possibility of coherence in its sheer relativism and its stress on 'the abysm of words' which denies stable, objective or true interpretation as either relevant or possible in literary studies. The self-indulgent excesses of post-structuralism need not delay us, standing as they do as speculative theorising that relishes its self-contradiction. In its determined exclusion through its private language of all but its own small clique of priests and faithful, it seems to be, in Harold Bloom's phrase, no more than a 'serene linguistic nihilism'.

But the whole complex enterprise that is literary structuralism cannot be dismissed or disregarded. It contains powerful insights as well as self-evident flaws. Its demand for the priority of analytic over intuitive approaches to literature requires attention, even if the practical outcome is likely to be some attempt to accommodate the two. The claims made for it are far too large; all too often its analyses of particular texts are remarkably unconvincing although with Kermode and Lodge there are notable successes. Its Achilles' heel is in its too-close adherence to its insistence on the merely arbitrary connection between signified and signifier which results, for many structuralists, in a neglect of reference to any world external to literature. Such a view quite simply is untenable and any structural analysis which insists rigidly upon such a principle lapses into indefensible solipsism. As Benveniste has shown, the relationships between language and the world are never simply contingent.[23] Structuralism's concentration on pattern and symmetry at the expense of truth and meaning is reductive, diminishing, trivialising. There is a constant curious contrast between structuralism's idea of the intrinsic intelligibility of human affairs and the sense of dehumanisation that is so evident in many of its literary investigations. Its predilection for structure and its critical attitude to humanism square awkwardly with any expanded, integrative notion of 'wholeness'.

Literary structuralism's search for systems and structures that have priority, dominance, control over the individual is a gross denial of the self-evident competence of both author and reader. Like all structuralism it lacks a theory of the competent human actor. Any development of structural analysis must accommodate itself to the fact of human capability and knowledgeability. Further, like all structuralism, its rejection of history is a merely theoretical move that can only weaken its contribution to literary studies. Finally, its claim to scientific status is, like the similar claims of all grand theories about human behaviour, mere hubris, an empty assertion that is in reality only a misguided attempt to raise its own status. It is not surprising therefore that structuralism, in almost all forms, has met with opposition and ridicule from the scholars who work in the mainstream tradition of literature. George Watson's account of (and dismissal of) structuralism meets with widespread approval.[24] But whilst there is opposition too from Marxists (to whom the neglect of history or of social reference is anathema) it must be noticed that there are strong moves to accommodate structuralism to Marxism. Lucien Goldmann's *genetic structuralism* is the most influential example as he identifies correspondences (homologies) between text and society, locating literature as an expression of particular social movements.[25] It is such developments, and those elements which can successfully resist criticism, which reveal the power and insightfulness of structuralism and can usefully advance our understanding, not simply of literature, but of schooling and social life itself.

NOTES

1. Three books, widely separated in time and focus, reveal the purposes and range of this human response tradition and its equation with education itself: Richards (1929); Leavis (1972); Mathieson (1975).

2. This 'social' approach to literature is clearly evidenced in Eagleton (1978); Swingewood (1976); Goldmann (1964). Raymond Williams has made a long and distinguished contribution. The best entry to his thought is still *The Long Revolution* (1961); his developing thought can be traced in the essays in *Problems in Materialism and Culture* (1980).

3. A widely influential writer who epitomises such an approach is Marjorie Boulton: *The Anatomy of Poetry* (2nd edition, 1982); *The Anatomy of the Novel* (1975); *The Anatomy of Prose* (1954); *The Anatomy of Drama* (1960); *The Anatomy of Literary Studies* (1980).

   The purpose of this book is to analyse the things that can be analysed and a residue that is wonderful and cannot be explained will always be left (Boulton, 1982, p. 3).

   In sharpest contrast, Terry Eagleton proposes radical revision of what counts as 'literature'; he argues that departments of literature in higher education are Ideological State Apparatuses, and that literary theory is no more than social or political theory, and that it would be far preferable to study 'discursive practices . . . all the way from *Moby Dick* to the Muppet Show' (Eagleton, 1983, pp. 202–7).

4. Different approaches to structuralism and examples of practice can be seen in Culler (1975); Kermode (1979); Lodge (1981); Strickland (1981).

5. David Lodge, 'Oedipuss: or the practice and theory of narrative' in Lodge (1981).

6. The challenge to more familiar approaches to literature — and the intellectual difficulties these alternatives pose can be seen in: Jakobson (1973, pp. 119–29). (David Lodge renders Jakobson more accessible in his *The Modes of Modern Writing*, 1977.) See also Derrida (1978).

7. Josipovici (1979, p. 309).

8. Culler (1975, p. viii).

9. Culler (1975, p. 31).

10. Jakobson and Jones (1970, p. 10).

11. Todorov (1973, pp. 73–103).

12. Rutherford (1977, pp. 43–56).

13. Todorov (1973, p. 73).

14. Culler (1975, p. 31).

15. Julia Kristeva, reported in Culler (1975, p. 258). Kristeva's writing, like much of post-structuralism, is in the French literary journal *Tel Quel*.

16. Culler (1975, p. 258).

17. Belsey (1980, p. 3).

18. Three useful introductions to the deconstruction movement (embracing such writers as Derrida, Foucault, Bloom, de Man, Hartman and Hillis Miller) are Leitch (1983); Norris (1982); Culler (1983).

19. Barthes (1972). Roland Barthes was killed in a motor accident in 1980. His work is exhaustively reviewed and sympathetically assessed in Lavers (1982).

20. Culler (1975, p. 242). Such openness to the possibility of an infinity of legitimate interpretation (anything goes?) has had amusing results, particularly among psychoanalytic studies of literature. My own two favourites are the following:

   Derrida's agonising over a marginal jotting by Nietzsche, 'I have forgotten my umbrella', asking whether it might contain cryptic significance decipherable only by means of a Freudian or Heideggerian reading; and going on to speculate whether it might not be the case that Nietzsche's entire literary production is of the same undecidable status as the sentence 'I have forgotten my umbrella' (Norris, 1983, p. 21); and Green's speculation:

   My hypothesis of Desdemona's love for Cassio as part of the kernel of truth is not complete, however. It must have as its complement another aspect of things, the aspect of which is much more difficult to see and is totally obliterated from the spectator's view. Silent, but effective, the whole mainspring of the tragedy lies here: Othello's desire for Cassio (Green, 1979, p. 107).

21. Bloom (1979, pp. vii and 4) (and note that Roland Barthes claimed that a text 'contains, finally, no heart, no kernel, no secret, no irreducible principle, nothing except the infinity of its own envelopes — which envelop nothing other than the unity of its own surfaces'; quoted in Culler, 1975, p. 259).

22. Rutherford (1977, p. 50).

23. Strickland (1981, pp. 15–26).

24. Watson (1978, Chapter 2). George Watson is a severe, even contemptuous, critic of structuralism:

    The structural interest in human conviction can only be reductive in the end. Nobody who is seriously concerned with the truth and falsehood of religious and other commitments should be *primarily* concerned with the patterns and symmetries they form . . . structuralism was a playground, and in the end nothing better than that (pp. 33–4).

25. Goldmann (1964). Lucien Goldmann traces the structural relationship between the thought of Pascal and Racine and a social group, the *noblesse de robe* of seventeenth-century France.

BIBLIOGRAPHY

Barthes, Roland (1972) *Critical Essays*. Evanston, Ill.: Northwestern University Press.

Belsey, Catherine (1980) *Critical Practice*. London: Methuen.

Bloom, Harold *et al.* *(1979) Deconstruction and Criticism*. London: Routledge and Kegan Paul.

Boulton, Marjorie (1982) *The Anatomy of Poetry* (2nd edition). London: Routledge and Kegan Paul.

Culler, Jonathan (1975) *Structuralist Poetics: Structuralism, Linguistics and the Study of Literature*. London: Routledge and Kegan Paul.

Culler, Jonathan (1983) *On Deconstruction: Theory and Criticism after Structuralism*. London: Routledge and Kegan Paul.

Derrida, Jacques (1978) *Writing and Difference*. London: Routledge and Kegan Paul.

Eagleton, Terry (1978) *Criticism and Ideology: A Study in Marxist Literary Theory*. London: Verso/New Left Books.

Eagleton, Terry (1983) *Literary Theory: An Introduction*. Oxford: Basil Blackwell.

Goldmann, Lucien (1964) *The Hidden God*. London: Routledge and Kegan Paul.

Green, Andre (1979) *The Tragic Effect: The Oedipus Complex in Tragedy*. Cambridge: Cambridge University Press.

Hall, S., Hobson, D., Lowe, A. and Willis, P. (1980) *Culture, Media, Language: Working Papers in Cultural Studies 1972–9*. London: Hutchinson.

Jakobson, Roman (1973) 'Two aspects of language: metaphor and metonymy', in Gras, Vernon W. (ed.) *European Literary Theory and Practice*. New York: Delta (pp. 119–29).

Jakobson, Roman and Jones, L. (1970) *Shakespeare's Verbal Art in 'Th' Expense of Spirit'*. The Hague, Netherlands: Mouton.

Josipovici, Gabriel (1979) *The World and the Book: A Study of Modern Fiction* (2nd edition). London: Macmillan.

Kermode, Frank (1979) *The Genesis of Secrecy: On the Interpretation of Narrative*. Cambridge, Mass.: Harvard University Press.

Kettle, Arnold (1967) *An Introduction to the English Novel* (2nd edition). London: Hutchinson.

Lavers, Annette (1982) *Roland Barthes: Structuralism and After*. London: Methuen.

Leavis, F. R. (1972) *The Great Tradition*. Harmondsworth: Penguin Books.

Leitch, Vincent B. (1983) *Deconstructive Criticism: An Advanced Introduction*. London: Hutchinson.

Lodge, David (1977) *The Modes of Modern Writing*. Ithaca, NY.: Cornell University Press.

Lodge, David (1981) *Working with Structuralism: Essays and Reviews on Nineteenth and Twentieth Century Fiction*. London: Routledge and Kegan Paul.

Mathieson, M. (1975) *The Preachers of Culture*. London: Allen and Unwin.

Norris, Christopher (1982) *Deconstruction*. London: Methuen.

Norris, Christopher (1983) 'Mortal scripts'. *London Review of Books*, 5, 7, pp. 20–1.

Richards, I. A. (1929) *Practical Criticism: A Study of Literary Judgement*. London: Routledge and Kegan Paul.

Rutherford, John (1977) 'Structuralism', in Routh, J. and Wolff, J. (eds) *The Sociology of Literature: Theoretical Approaches. Sociological Review Monograph* 23. Newcastle-under-Lyme: University of Keele (pp. 43–56).

Strickland, Geoffrey (1981) *Structuralism or Criticism? Thoughts on how we read*. Cambridge: Cambridge University Press.

Swingewood, A. (1976) *The Novel and Revolution*. London: Macmillan.

Todorov, Tzvetan (1973) 'The structural analysis of literature', in Robey, David (ed.) *Structuralism: An Introduction*. Oxford: Clarendon Press.

Watson, George (1978) *Modern Literary Thought*. Heidelberg: Carl Winter.

Williams, Raymond (1961) *The Long Revolution*. London: Chatto and Windus; also published in paperback (1965) by Penguin Books.

Williams, Raymond (1980) *Problems in Materialism and Culture*. London: Verso/New Left Books.

V RESPONDING TO LITERATURE

Section V provides a kaleidoscope of views.

The section starts with Harding's consideration of the psychological processes involved in reading fiction. He puts under the microscope important ideas such as identification and the reader as spectator.

Benton and Fox take off on a different, more pragmatic tack. They too consider some of the mental processes concerned, but tie their discussion to the implications for classroom practice and the different ways in which poetry is learnt when compared to stories.

Protherough adds a further dimension: he goes and asks the customers what they make of it all. He analyses his results into five modes which he suggests young adolescents adopt as reading styles: projection into character, projection into the situation, association between book and reader, the distanced viewer, and detached evaluation.

The colours change yet again with Zindel: he adds a cheery, racy sacrilegious note. Zindel, a 'practising' writer of adolescent tales, gives his version of the procedures he follows to capture his reader's interest. Here you will find everything from 'delicious language' to 'transactional pictures'. Not God's plenty, but a revealing and informative romp.

The final, Rosenblatt extract makes an interesting contrast to the Zindel, taking up issues broached earlier in the section, while, at the same time, providing a framework for many of the concerns of Section VI.

27 *Psychological Processes in the Reading of Fiction**

● D. W. Harding

One of the unsatisfactory features of psychology at the present time is the contrast between an attempt at very exact definition of concepts and terms in some directions and a toleration of extreme vagueness and woolliness in others. The effort after precision is seen mostly in the planning and interpreting of experiments that lead farther and farther back into the recesses of methodology and abstract theory; the very high toleration of ambiguity occurs in discussing problems of complex behaviour in civilized societies. If we want to say how a rat learns a maze, we know by now that we shall have to come to grips with exactly defined terms and a meticulously scrutinized conceptual framework. If we are invited to consider the psychological processes that occur in reading a novel, we probably expect some rather vague waffle compounded of psycho-analysis, sociology and literary criticism. If I provide that, I shall have failed in my aim. Although a real precision may at present be far out of reach, an effort in that direction is incumbent on anyone who believes that psychology as a science can have something useful to say about fiction.

An initial question is whether we should try to discuss fiction within a framework of general aesthetics. I agree with those who maintain that the numerous and extremely dissimilar activities conventionally grouped together as the arts do not form a separate psychological category. Very few literal statements that apply to a novel, a landscape painting, a porcelain dish and a piece of music will be at all illuminating about any one of those things. A novel is so distantly related to many other sorts of art, and so closely related to activities that are not included among the arts, that an approach through aesthetic generalizations would be restricting and misleading. It may seem, perhaps, that the form of a novel and the style of a novelist can be discussed in terms

* Read as a Paper to the British Society of Aesthetics on 10th October, 1961.

equally applicable to other arts, but I suspect that it can be done only by substituting metaphor and analogy for literal statement.

Much more important aspects of fiction are illuminated if the reader of a novel is compared with the man who hears about other people and their doings in the course of ordinary gossip. And to give an account of gossip we have to go a step or two farther back and consider the position of the person who looks on at actual events. As a framework, then, within which to discuss fiction, I want to offer some statement of the psychological position of the onlooker (of which I attempted a fuller discussion in 'The Role of the Onlooker', *Scrutiny*, VI, 3, December, 1937), and then to view the reading of a novel as a process of looking on at a representation of imagined events or, rather, of listening to a description of them. This involves examining carefully — and I believe discarding — psychological assumptions about some of the processes, such as identification and vicarious satisfaction, that have been supposed to occur in the reader.

Part of everyone's time is spent in looking on at events, not primarily in order to understand them (though that may come in) and not in preparation for doing something about them, but in a non-participant relation which yet includes an active evaluative attitude. We can say two things of the onlooker: first, that he attends, whether his attention amounts to a passing glance or fascinated absorption; and second, that he evaluates, whether his attitude is one of faint liking or disliking, hardly above indifference, or strong, perhaps intensely emotional, and perhaps differentiated into pity, horror, contempt, respect, amusement, or any other of the shades and kinds of evaluation, most of them unlabelled even in our richly differentiated language. Attentiveness on any particular occasion implies the existence of an interest, if we take that to mean an enduring disposition to respond, in whatever way, to some class of objects or events. The response almost instantaneously becomes (or is from the start) evaluative, welcoming or aversive. And in a complex, experienced organism, an evaluative attitude is usually one expression of a sentiment, if we take that to mean an enduring disposition to evaluate some object or class of objects in a particular way; an event or situation is then assessed in the light of its cognized significance for the object of a sentiment.

To take an example, for most of us a human being is interesting, and conflict is interesting, and a struggle between two groups of people is extremely likely to command our attention. When we observe one of the groups to be policemen a system of sentiments will be activated; according to the way we identify the other group, as men or women, drunk or sober, strike pickets, rowdy students, smash-and-grab thieves, political demonstrators, or what not, so other sentiments will be activated; the apparent brutality or good humour of the contestants will stir yet others; and whether we want to boo or cheer or shrug when the

Black Maria eventually drives off will be the outcome of a complex interaction among many mutually entangled systems of sentiment.

The idea — still occasionally held — that the spectator's link with the scene consists mainly in his recognition that similar things might have happened to him — 'There, but for the grace of God, go I' — depends on far too limited a view of the human mind. Admittedly the man watching a shipwreck from the safety of the shore may realize thankfully that he might have been in it and is not, or more subtly that it symbolizes something that might happen to him; but to suppose that this is his chief link with the scene would be a crude piece of unpsychological rationalism. By far the likeliest response, and one that almost certainly accompanies any others, is simple horror and distress that this thing is happening to living people, whom he values as fellow-beings and whose sufferings he can imagine. We have a vivid description by William Hickey of what he felt when he was actually in the traditional role of watching a shipwreck from the shore:

> At half-past five nine ships that had parted from their anchors drove on shore between Deal and Sandwich, a distance of only eight miles; others, having drifted foul of each other, were obliged to cut away rigging and masts to prevent the dire alternative of going to the bottom together; two were seen actually to founder. A more horrid spectacle I never beheld, yet so interested did I feel on account of the unhappy people on board the different vessels that neither wet nor cold nor want of rest could induce me to quit the beach whilst a ray of light remained. . . .
>
> At eight o'clock I followed the advice of the hostess by drinking some excellent hot punch, and going directly afterwards to bed, where, although anxiety for the sufferings of the many poor drowning wretches kept me awake some time, fatigue at last got the better, and I fell into a profound and deep sleep, which continued uninterrupted for full twelve hours.[1]

It was only by chance that Hickey himself was not in one of the ships, and yet it seems clear that any relief he felt on his own account was a small part of his total state of mind compared with his concern for the victims.

Although the disclosure or reminder of environmental possibilities in a merely cognitive mode is a minor matter, it remains true that the experience of looking on at events does extend and modify, besides reflecting, the spectator's systems of interest and sentiment. A girl who watches a mother caring for an infant is not just reminded of one of the possibilities of her own life; she may also be extending her insight into the sort of satisfaction that a mother gets, perhaps correcting sentimental preconceptions or seeing compensations where she would have anticipated only trouble. In the same way we may learn as onlookers from the panic or the calmness of people faced with a threatening situation, or from the courage or the blind hope with which they meet serious illness, or from the sort of pleasure they show on achieving a success. In ways of this kind the events at which we are 'mere onlookers' come to have, cumulatively, a deep and extensive influence on our systems of value. They may in certain ways be even more formative than events in which we take part. Detached and distanced evaluation is sometimes sharper for avoiding the blurrings and bufferings that participant action brings, and the spectator often sees the event in a broader context than the participant can tolerate. To obliterate the effects on a man of the occasions on which he was only an onlooker would be profoundly to change his outlook and values.

Besides looking on at events in progress we can be spectators in memory or imagination of things past and things anticipated; further, we can release our imaginings from practical limitations and consider what might have been and what might be if the restrictions of reality were suspended. Even in looking on at actual happenings the spectator often grossly distorts what occurs, misleading himself by a variety of unconscious mechanisms; in memory and anticipation the unwitting distortion of fact and probability is even greater; and in fantasy even the intention to control thought by the measure of possibility is largely relinquished. In all the forms of fantasy, whether dreams, day-dreams, private musings or make-believe play, we give expression to perfectly real preoccupations, fears and desires, however bizarre or impossible the imagined events embodying them.

The imaginary spectatorship of fantasy and make-believe play has the special feature of allowing us to look on at ourselves, ourselves as participants in the imagined events — the hero in the rescue fantasy, the victim of the assault, the defendant rebutting injust accusations, the apparent nonentity suddenly called to national responsibility. In spite, however, of seeing himself as a participant in the story, the daydreamer or the child engaged in make-believe remains an onlooker, too; in all his waking fantasy he normally fills the dual role of participant and spectator, and as spectator he can when need be turn away from the fantasy events and attend again to the demands of real life. But although in waking experience we normally never quite lose grip on the role of onlooker, it remains true that every degree of abandonment to the invented occurrences may occur. We may at times give them, as it were, no more than a sceptical glance, perhaps contrasting them immediately with our present situation; we may let them develop very great vividness although we still remain only onlookers, never letting our real situation be far beyond the margins of attention and always being able at the least necessity to switch back to where we really are; or they may reach the extreme vividness, obliterating everything else, that the night dream possesses, and then, whether as daydreamers or psychotics, we have abandoned the role of onlooker and given ourselves up to delusional and perhaps hallucinated participation.

The solitary onlooker and the man engaged in private fantasy are, of course, members of a highly social species and their apparent isolation is unreal; what they see and invent, and what they feel, must be strongly influenced by their culture. In an environment which is highly saturated socially, our experience as spectators forms an important part of our cultural moulding. Everything we look on is tacitly and unintentionally treated as an object lesson by our fellow-spectators; speech and gesture or the mere intake of breath, smiles, pauses, clucks, tuts and glances are constantly at work to sanction or challenge the feelings we have as spectators. Needless to say, we can at least to some extent resist our fellow-onlookers' influence; and we in our turn, of course, are sanctioning and challenging and suggesting modifications of viewpoint to them.

The influence of our fellow-onlookers draws our attention to one aspect of events rather than another, changing the emphasis or bringing to mind what we might have overlooked. From this it is only a step — but a very important step — to telling us about events we missed seeing, as in a vast amount of gossip and narrative. Instead of literally looking on, we now listen to representations of events; and the social influence of our companion is greater than ever because he not only reports selectively but also conveys what he regards as an appropriate attitude to what he saw. The gossip implicitly invites us to agree that what he reports is interesting enough to deserve reporting and that the attitude he adopts, openly or tacitly, is an acceptable evaluation of the events.

From giving an account of what has happened the next step is to suggest things that *might* happen, a process seen at its simplest in the child's 'Suppose . . .' technique: 'Suppose that lion got out . . .' 'Wouldn't it be fun if we found a secret cave?' 'Suppose that man was a spy . . .' Here at one step we pass into the area of make-believe, whether it takes the form of play with companions, of drama, or of fiction. Imaginary spectatorship now occurs in a social setting. The result is a vast extension of the range of possible human experience that can be offered socially for contemplation and assessment. The ends achieved by fiction and drama are not fundamentally different from those of a great deal of gossip and everyday narrative. Between true narrative and fiction there exist, in fact, transitional techniques such as the traveller's tale and the funny anecdote in which the audience's tacit permission is assumed for embellishments and simplifications that enhance the effectiveness of the story. True or fictional, all these forms of narrative invite us to be onlookers joining in the evaluation of some possibility of experience.

Here I must make two digressions. The first is that the possibilities of experience include grief and disaster. Onlookers gather round accidents and funerals, gossips converse about disease, conflict and misery, newspaper readers want to hear of crime and calamity, the daydream is by no means always an invention of pleasures and children's make-believe includes its quota of illness, injury and punishment. In all these simpler forms of onlooking we are familiar with the fact that the unhappy chances of life are at least as interesting as the happy ones. It is not surprising, therefore, to find the same thing when we come to fiction and drama; the fact that tragic events are of intense human interest should not lead us into formulating pseudo-problems as to how the contemplation of something painful can be pleasurable. If there is a problem here, it is not confined to tragedy. The spectator, whether of actual events or representations, is interested in any of the possibilities of human experience, not merely its pleasures.

My second digression is that in saying that fiction represents possibilities of human experience we have to notice that it may be doing so through the medium of physical impossibilities. Tales that deal in the impossible are of two kinds. On the one hand there are tales of wonder which claim that the wonders are real possibilities — like the 'very true' account Autolycus was selling, of 'how a usurer's wife was brought to bed of twenty money-bags at a burthen'. Some of our contemporary tales of ghosts and the supernatural, whether offered as fiction or as true report, come into this category, as do some forms of science fiction. But on the other hand physical impossibilities may be used, both in fairy-tales and in some sophisticated fiction, as vehicles for presenting realities of experience. In many fairy-tales the wonders are of importance chiefly as providing the least laborious, most compressed and vivid means of representing some quite possible human experience. Everyone longs from time to time to have his own way, untrammelled by reality; the three miraculous wishes offer a dramatic compression of that possibility and allow the consequences to be discussed. Any of us might feel downtrodden and hope to have the tables turned by a benign authority who recognized our merit; a fairy godmother is a brief and vivid way of saying how delightful that would be.

In sophisticated fiction it is a question of the author's technique of presentation whether he aims at verisimilitude or avowed fantasy. When he chooses to depart from real possibilities we might say with Coleridge that the reader is called on for a 'willing suspension of disbelief'. But it makes less of a mystery of the process if we say that he is willing to participate in a recognized mode of communication, an accepted technique for discussing the chances of life. Basically we are engaged in the 'Suppose . . .' technique of children's conversation.

Moreover in this respect — to return to the main theme — fantasy only highlights what is true of all fiction, that it is a convention of communication. The full grasp of fiction as fiction is a sophisticated achievement. Children come to it gradually, and although little seems to be known about the steps by which they reach it, we can plausibly suppose that the phase of 'lying' fantasy that many children go through is one stage of the process. There is good reason to think that the less sophisticated adult often has only a precarious hold on the distinction between fiction and narrative; so some of the reactions to popular series in broadcasting have suggested, though here again full investigation seems to be lacking. It would appear, too, that some primitive peoples, though they enjoy story-telling as a pastime, regard all the stories as true narrative (perhaps of a remote ancestral past) and have little conception of avowed fiction. The Samoans of R. L. Stevenson's time, having read a missionary translation of his story, *The Bottle Imp*, assumed that his wealth really came from his command of a magic bottle, and after a convivial evening with him would sometimes feel sufficiently in his confidence to ask if they might see 'the bottle'.[2] Fiction has to be seen, then, as a convention, a convention for enlarging the scope of the discussions we have with each other about what may befall.

The 'discussion' may seem a one-sided affair since the reader is unable to answer back. But he is none the less active in accepting or rejecting what the author asserts. In the first place, the author offers what he claims to be a possibility of experience; the reader may in effect say 'No: that action of the hero is inconsistent with what he has said or done before; that monster of iniquity isn't humanly possible; that sudden repentance could never have happened. . . .' Secondly, the author conveys what he regards as appropriate attitudes towards events, characters and actions. He is constantly — but of course tacitly — saying: 'Isn't this exciting. . . . He's attractive, isn't he. . . . Wasn't that tragic. . . Isn't this moving . . . ?' Again the reader accepts or rejects the implied assessments.

He may not consciously formulate his agreement and disagreement, but these are the underlying processes that show themselves eventually in enthusiasm for an author's work or disappointment with it. The reader discriminates; and this is true even at the low levels of trivial fiction, though there the discriminations may depend on criteria that better educated or more practised readers have discarded.

The view I have been offering of the reader's active part at the receiving end of a conventional mode of communication contrasts with a good deal of pseudo-psychologizing that sees the process of novel-reading as one of identification and vicarious experience. Those ideas, vague and loose as they have always been, have had such currency that they have to be seriously examined.

We may once more begin with the man looking on at actual events. Unless he deliberately adopts the discipline of detached observation for the purposes of science or painting, he soon in some sense 'enters into' the experience of one or more of the participants.

The basic process connecting the onlooker with any event, real or fictional, involving living things, is that of imagining. The fundamental fact is that we can imagine ourselves in a situation very different from the one we are in, we can create images of the sensations we should have, we can become aware, in part, of the meanings we should see in it, what our intentions, attitudes and emotions would be, what satisfactions and frustrations we should experience. Suppose you are looking out of the window at torrents of rain lashing down in the street: you can imagine yourself out in it, rain beating on your face, your shoes squelching, your legs wet below the mackintosh, rain getting down inside your collar, hands in your pockets, shoulders hunched — and you can imagine the emotions you might experience out there. Suppose a man is in the street, the same process can occur, perhaps facilitated by the sight of him; and because you assume a fundamental likeness between yourself and him you take it that you have imaginative or empathic insight into his experience. Suppose that you watch a film of a man walking through pouring rain, or read of him in a book, or dream of him at night, the same basic process of imagining is at work. To say that this process has long been understood in psychology would be to claim too much, but it has long been recognized; and to what extent more recent ideas of identification and vicarious experience really advance our understanding is a matter for cautious discussion.

The great difficulty about the term 'identification' is to know which one of several different processes it refers to. The reader may see resemblances between himself and a fictional *persona* only to regret them (and perhaps hope to become different); is this recognition of resemblances 'identification'? He may long enviously to be like a fictional character so different from himself that he discounts all possibility of approximating to him; is this admiration 'identification'? He may adopt the character as a model for imitation, more or less close and successful, and it may be this process to which 'identification' refers. Or he may be given up, for the duration of the novel or film, to absorbed empathy with one of the characters. The fact is that we can avoid all this uncertainty and describe each of the processes accurately by speaking explicitly of empathy, imitation, admiration, or recognition of similarities. We sacrifice little more with the term 'identification' than a bogus technicality.

With this pseudo-technicality we discard the idea that there is something pathological about the processes we describe, or something to be better understood by examining pathological exaggerations of them. It may well be true that a continuity can be detected between absorbed empathy with a character and — at the pathological extreme — a psychotic delusion of identity with a great man, Napoleon, St. Peter, the President of the U.S.A. There may also be a continuum between the everyday imitation of some feature of an admired person (the handwriting of a favourite teacher or the hair style of a film star) and the pathological forms of imitation in which, for instance, psychosomatic processes produce symptoms similar to those of the illness from which a close relative has just died (though in this case devotion is often fused with fear and self-reproach). Even latah may claim to be on the same continuum. But we have not illuminated the ordinary processes by showing that they pass by gradual stages into the pathological and by giving to them all, healthy and morbid, the term 'identification'. We are still left with the perfectly usual and healthy processes of having empathic insight into other people (or representations of them) and of imitating features of their behaviour that we admire. To suppose that these processes are explained by being called identification is to be taken in by verbal magic.

The onlooker's observation of other people or of *personae* in fiction and drama may be accompanied by a preference for some, by specially sensitive or full insight into some, by awareness of likenesses between himself and some (not necessarily those he admires), and by a wish that he resembled some. These processes, occurring with all degrees of clear awareness or obscurity, form part of the tissue of ordinary social intercourse as well as entering into the enjoyment of fiction. An adequate account of a reader's attitude to a fictional *persona* may have to include a reference to them all, as well as to the subtler shades and complexities of these broad types of response. No good purpose is served by blanketing them all with a term like 'identification'.

The spectator who gives himself up to absorbed sympathy with some character of a novel or play is sometimes said to experience vicariously whatever the character undergoes. Among those who want a simple but psychological-sounding explanation for the enjoyment of fiction this idea of vicarious experience or vicarious satisfaction has long been popular. But it stands up poorly to serious examination.

Jung expressed the prevailing view when he said: 'The cinema . . . , like the detective story, makes it possible to experience without danger all the excitement, passion and desirousness which must be repressed in the humanitarian ordering of life.'[3] Notice that he says 'possible to *experience*', not possible to 'contemplate' or 'imagine'. On this formulation depends any exact meaning that the notion of vicarious experience possesses. Other writers, over a wide range of criticism and journalism, have popularized the idea. It was used, for instance, by the Lynds in *Middletown* and by Q. D. Leavis in *Fiction and the Reading Public*, where she took 'Living at the Novelist's Expense' as one of her leading themes and interpreted much novel reading as the indulgence of wish-fulfilment fantasies. A contributor to *The Adelphi* (March 1934) wrote: 'With the lovely heroine, the laundry worker dons silk underwear . . . an evening cloak with soft furry collar. During the day she has stood with damp feet in badly-fitting high-heeled shoes which took two weeks' savings. But now her well-shaped leg is enclosed in stockings of finest silk, and shod by shoes from the Rue de la Paix. For an hour!' And Rebecca West wrote in *Nash's Pall Mall Magazine* (February 1934):

'George was glad to earn two pounds a week by tedious toil, and for relaxation . . . indulge in remote concupiscence with unknowing film-stars.' (The quotations date from a period when the cultivated could pity wage-earners.)

What can be meant literally by these views? The desires are not in fact satisfied, of course. The implied suggestion is apparently that viewing a film or reading a novel approximates to having a wish-fulfilment dream — as hungry explorers are reported to dream of good meals — and that the spectator temporarily gets a delusive satisfaction through what amounts to hallucination while he reads or watches. That something approaching this may possibly happen to a few rather unusual people would be difficult to prove or disprove. But that it can be at all a usual mechanism is unbelievable. We may in moments of bitterness speak of the cinema or television as a dope, but we do not seriously believe that the spectators are sitting there in the same psychological condition as opium smokers in a dream, supposing themselves actually to be in some world of their fantasy. (They can pass each other sandwiches or stand up to let somebody else get to a seat, all in the real world, though they watch the screen.) It seems to be a case where a vivid metaphor has been taken literally without realization of the extent of pathological disorientation that the supposed psychological process would imply.

We get nearer the truth by starting from the fact that the 'wish-fulfilment' dream is also a *statement* of a pressing need or desire, defining the desire at the same time as it offers hallucinated satisfaction. In expressing interests and affirming desires for which ordinary life provides small scope, fiction and drama may indeed have something a little in common with dreams. They may, for instance, give expression to interests and attitudes that are partially checked (perhaps even repressed) in ordinary social intercourse, such as sexuality, cruelty, arrogance and violence. But it is very doubtful whether plays or novels that do this can rightly be said to give *substitute* satisfaction to the spectators' desires. They give perfectly real, direct satisfaction, but to a muted and incomplete version of the desires. The parallel is with the person who exclaims of someone annoying: 'I'd like to knock his block off' or 'He deserves to be horse-whipped'; exclamations like this offer no vicarious satisfaction for impulses to homicide or assault, but they constitute a real social attack and give direct satisfaction to a permissible degree of hostility (and may thereby give very incomplete but still direct satisfaction to a more moderate degree of hidden rage). They may, if the anger grows or the countervailing impulses weaken, lead on towards actual physical attack, but more commonly they serve in themselves as a safety-valve. So with novels, plays and films, the represented expression of interests and desires usually held in check may in some spectators precipitate overt action to satisfy the desire (for instance, sexual activity or some form of violence), but in other cases the fiction itself will be a sufficient and a direct satisfaction of the slight degree of interest and desire that it elicits or releases.

Interests and attitudes that are repressed or condemned, however, form only a small part of the material of fiction and drama. Entirely acceptable values, too, receive definition and affirmation. The desire for affection (prominent among the desires represented in the films analysed for the Payne Fund Studies of the cinema), the desire for adventure, for achievement, for the courage of one's convictions, for prestige, for cheerful companionship and for endless other things may all be stimulated, defined more concretely and vividly, revived after waning or confirmed after doubt. Although these desires, perhaps thwarted in real life, will not be satisfied in drama or fiction (or through contemplating real people more happily circumstanced), there may still be a highly important gain in having joined with the novelist or dramatist in the psychological act of giving them statement in a social setting. What, after all, is the alternative to defining and expressing our unattained and perhaps unattainable desires? It is to acquiesce in the deprivation and submit to the belief that with our personality or in our circumstances we ought not even to desire such things; and to forfeit the right to the desire is even worse than to be denied the satisfaction.

What is sometimes called wish-fulfilment in novels and plays can, therefore, more plausibly be described as wish-formulation or the definition of desires. The cultural levels at which it works may vary widely; the process is the same. It is the social act of affirming with the author a set of values. They may centre round marble bathrooms, mink coats and big cars, or they may be embodied in the social milieu and *personae* of novels by Jane Austen or Henry James; Cadillacs and their occupants at Las Vegas or carriages and theirs at Pemberley and Poynton. We may lament the values implied in some popular forms of fiction and drama, but we cannot condemn them on the ground of the psychological processes they employ. The finer kinds of literature require the same psychological processes, though putting them to the service of other values.

It seems nearer the truth, therefore, to say that fictions contribute to defining the reader's or spectator's values, and perhaps stimulating his desires, rather than to suppose that they gratify desire by some mechanism of vicarious experience. In this respect they follow the pattern, not of the dream with its hallucinated experiencing, but of waking supposition and imagination — 'Wouldn't it be wonderful if . . .' 'Wouldn't it be sad if . . . .'

Empathic insight allows the spectator to view ways of life beyond his own range. Contemplating exceptional people, he can achieve an imaginary development of human potentialities that have remained rudimentary in himself or been truncated after brief growth; he can believe that he enters into some part of the experience of the interplanetary explorer, the ballerina, the great scientist, the musician or the master-spy, and again this applies at every level from popular entertainment to serious literature. The spectator enters imaginatively, with more or less accuracy and fulness, into some of the multifarious possibilities of life that he has not himself been able to achieve. One of the bonds between ourselves and others, one among our reasons for interest in them, is that they have done things that we have not. A great deal of gossip, newspaper reports, memoirs, fiction and drama, serves to remind us of the human potentialities that for one reason or another we have left to others, but the knowledge of which, in a diversified group with highly developed modes of communication, forms one of our social possessions.

A related source of satisfaction in entering imaginatively into activities far beyond our own range lies in the fact that we can see in very diverse ways of life certain broad types of experience that we know in our own: we view familiar experiences of struggle, disappointment, excitement, moral challenge, companionship, in the heightening context (biographical or fictional) of a more remarkable way of life, and the ordinary possibilities of our own lives may gain an enhanced significance as a result — whether the Saturday night dance takes on a Ruritanian glamour, or the determination of a Pasteur or Cézanne redeems our everyday persistence in face of the usual setbacks, or the commonplace failure of courage reveals the Lord Jim in our own personality.

In all these ways the process of looking on at and entering into other people's activity, or representations of it, does enlarge the range, not of the onlooker's experience but of his quasi-experience and partial understanding. For it has to be remembered that the subtlest and most intense empathic insight into the experience of another person is something far different from having the experience oneself.

I have suggested that the processes that are sometimes labelled 'identification' and 'vicarious experience' need to be described more carefully and in more detail for psychological purposes. But we have to go further. For even when these processes have been accurately defined they are totally insufficient as an account of the reader's response to fiction. An account based on them alone neglects the fact that the onlooker not only enters into the experience of the participants but also contemplates them as fellow-beings. It is an elementary form of onlooking merely to imagine what the situation must seem like and to react *with* the participant. The more complex observer imagines something of what the participant is experiencing and then reacts *to* him, for instance with pity or joy on his account. The spectators who watch Othello as he kills his wife are not feeling simply what they imagine him to be feeling, they are also feeling, as onlookers, pity *for* him.

Nor is this part of the onlooker's role confined to the upper levels of fiction and drama. It figures prominently in the response of the most naïve spectator watching, say, one of the old films of the hero tearing along a dangerous road in a car, to the rescue of the heroine on whom disaster is closing in. Do the spectators experience imaginatively only what the hero is supposed to be experiencing — his determination, his anxiety and hope, his concentration on the road, his exasperation at the fallen tree, his conflict before taking a hair's-breadth chance on the edge of the precipice? Some part of this comes across but the spectators are in addition responding to the situation as a whole: they are hoping *for* the hero as well as with him, they assess his chances in the light of what they see of the heroine's position, they have ups and downs of hope and anxiety as the situation alters (often in ways that the hero knows nothing about), they may think more of the heroine and her danger than of the hero's supposed feelings, and their taking sides with both of them against the villains introduces another social element that forms no part of the supposed experience of any of the participants.

The onlooker's response to the events as a whole goes much beyond identification with any one of the characters, a point so obvious that one would apologize for making it were it not regularly ignored by those who psychologize about fiction and drama. A clear example of response to the situation as a whole is given by K. O. Newman,[4] who describes '. . . the climax of the last act [of the war play that he saw repeatedly], when a stage-character, believed missing or dead, reappears bodily, hale and hearty, though somewhat tired and bedraggled. The delight of the audience at this auspicious dispensation knew no bounds, night after night, matinée after matinée. His appearance, behind the back of the hero and heroine, engaged in conversation, invariably evoked an excited mutter in the audience, which, at some performances, went as far as an outburst of rapturous applause from the more naïve and impressionable playgoers.' The impulse to applaud was clearly not the outcome of feeling what any one of the characters on the stage was feeling. In viewing a situation like this, commonplace enough, the spectator is contemplating the whole social situation, perhaps anticipating what the characters will soon be feeling, but primarily adopting an attitude *towards* them. His attitude is that of a well-wisher who is not merely anticipating the joy that they will feel but enjoys the fact that they will be feeling joy. He feels pleased *for* them as well as *with* them. For the reader to know more about the events than the characters are shown as knowing is a normal and frequent feature of novels and plays. Dramatic irony is entirely dependent on it. And, of course, re-reading or re-witnessing a novel or play extends and emphasizes the audience's superior knowledge of events and outcomes. Whenever the reader or spectator is in this position it becomes still more evidently a mistake to describe his response as 'identification' and 'vicarious experiencing'.

Let me recapitulate my main points. The mode of response made by the reader of a novel can be regarded as an extension of the mode of response made by an onlooker at actual events. One process on which the response depends — apart from the elementary perception and comprehension of the scene — is that of imaginative or empathic insight into other living things, mainly other people. But this would give only imaginative *sharing* of the participants' experience. At least equally important is the onlooker's, or the reader's, evaluation of the participants and what they do and suffer, an evaluation that I would relate in further analysis to his structure of interests and sentiments. But there is a third aspect of the process: the reader knows that the characters of the novel are not real people but only *personae* created by the author for the purpose of communication. Many readers, even educated readers, fail to hold this fact clearly in mind and they retain traces of the naïve view of the *personae* as real people, wanting to speculate for instance about the influences that made them what they are when the story opens or what will become of them after it ends. The more sophisticated reader knows that he is in social communication of a special sort with the author, and he bears in mind that the represented participants are only part of a convention by which the author discusses, and proposes an evaluation of, possible human experience.

NOTES

1. *Memoirs of William Hickey*, ed. Alfred Spencer, 9th edition (London, 1948), Vol. II, pp. 5–6.
2. See J. C. Furnas, *Journey to Windward* (London, 1952).
3. C. G. Jung, *Modern Man in Search of a Soul* (London, 1945).
4. *Two Hundred and Fifty Times I Saw a Play* (Pelagos Press, Oxford, 1944).

28 *What Happens When We Read Poems?*

- Michael Benton and Geoff Fox

Poems work differently from stories, creating their effects and evoking responses in ways that may overlap with the art of story but which are often peculiar to the nature of poetry. First impressions count a lot in our responses to literature, and this is especially so with children and poems. There is no equivalent cliché to 'getting into a story'; perhaps the nearest comment that children frequently make about a poem is whether they 'get it' or not. In short, children sense immediately that there is a riddling quality to poems, something in the way words are used and laid out on the page, as if the words are saying to them 'We're special; we're the chosen few.' The problem of much current methodology is that far too often we imply that poems are riddles with single solutions which we, the teachers, happen to know rather than objects crafted in the medium of riddling word-play, yielding a range of meanings.

Our approach to a poem must be less continuously linear than to a story. The very presentation signals this. Instead of the eye being channelled along regular lines of print, themselves justified left and right and framed in predictable margins, it is suddenly invited into a more or less varied activity where the shape of the text on the page assumes a special significance. The linearity of prose presentation reflects the importance of the passage of time in fiction. Basically, the reader of a story wants to know what will happen next and how it will all end. By contrast, the infinite variety of ways in which poems are presented indicates different emphases where the sense of space is often part of the reader's reponse. The reader of a poem wants to move about within it, discovering what it means to him and enjoying the way it makes that meaning. The spaces around the words on the page indicate this difference of approach where poems are concerned. They are spaces we inhabit mentally as readers to apprehend the form — as it were, from various viewpoints; rather as, when looking at a piece of sculpture, we are impelled to move around the object and, in so doing, acknowledge that part of the meaning we make depends upon the vantage point we adopt and our appreciation of the way spaces have been employed. If poems cannot enjoy such three-dimensional advantages, nevertheless, by comparison with the rectangular blocks of story text, there is much greater significance invested in their two-dimensional shapes. Beyond these surface features of presentation, however, why are poems distinctive?

WHAT POETRY OFFERS: THE EXPERIENCE OF READING A POEM

In order to remind ourselves of why poetry matters and what it does better than any other kind of language use, we want to consider a single poem in detail. From a reading of 'The Stag' by Ted Hughes we can begin to answer the question of what happens when we read poems and identify four attributes of poetry that are uniquely blended to offer children the type of aesthetic experience that they will not find anywhere else: *language, form, observation* and *feeling*. The discussion is conducted under these headings.

First, the poem — please read it aloud.

THE STAG

While the rain fell on the November woodland shoulder of Exmoor
While the traffic jam along the road honked and shouted
Because the farmers were parking wherever they could
And scrambling to the bank-top to stare through the tree-fringe
Which was leafless,
The stag ran through his private forest.

While the rain drummed on the roofs of the parked cars
And the kids inside cried and daubed their chocolate and fought
And mothers and aunts and grandmothers
Were a tangle of undoing sandwiches and screwed-round gossiping heads
Steaming up the windows,
The stag loped through his favourite valley.

While the blue horsemen down in the boggy meadow
Sodden nearly black, on sodden horses,
Spaced as at a military parade,
Moved a few paces to the right and a few to the left and felt rather foolish
Looking at the brown impassable river,
The stag came over the last hill of Exmoor.

While everybody high-kneed it to the bank-top all along the road
Where steady men in oilskins were stationed at binoculars,
And the horsemen by the river galloped anxiously this way and that
And the cry of hounds came tumbling invisibly with their echoes down
    through the draggle of trees,
Swinging across the wall of dark woodland,
The stag dropped into a strange country.

And turned at the river
Hearing the hound-pack smash the undergrowth, hearing the bell-note
Of the voice that carried all the others,
Then while his limbs all cried different directions to his lungs, which only
    wanted to rest,
The blue horsemen on the bank opposite
Pulled aside the camouflage of their terrible planet.

And the stag doubled back weeping and looking for home up a valley and
    down a valley
While the strange trees struck at him and the brambles lashed him,
And the strange earth came galloping after him carrying the loll-tongued
    hounds to fling all over him
And his heart became just a club beating his ribs and his own hooves
    shouted with hounds' voices,
And the crowd on the road got back into their cars
Wet-through and disappointed.[1]

We would suggest that the reader anticipates the pattern of our discussion by pausing to record some reactions to the poem either by jotting freely for some minutes or, if some signposts help, by using the four headings that we have indicated. In this way, the reader's personal response may be set alongside our own idiosyncratic reading.

A) LANGUAGE

The poem is a study in monochrome: a grey, wet, November landscape, scarcely relieved by the dull colours of verse three, the blues, blacks and browns. The depressing West Country rain drips from every line. It is a poem of movement and sounds, not of colour: the running stag and the chasing hounds; people abandoning vehicles to clamber up the bank, others squirming inside their cars, shouting or leaning on the horn; other sounds as varied as kids' crying, hounds' baying, the 'bell-note' of the huntsmen's horn and the thumping beat of the stag's heart. Hughes evokes the Exmoor landscape and all the sensory effects which fill the poem in words that exemplify the two qualities that, above all, poetic language embodies: precision and concreteness. When we read of the families in the traffic jam in verse two, or hear the cry of hounds as they come 'tumbling invisibly with their echoes down through the draggle of trees' in verse four, we cannot but be aware of the close matching of words and things. This matching is achieved in a way unique to poetry. The clutter of conjunctive 'ands' in verse two suggests the claustrophobia of families trapped in their cars just as powerfully as it evokes the confusion of the hunt in verse four and the panic of the trapped stag in the final verse. Or again, as we read of the unseen hounds running through the trees, we experience the sounds and rhythm of their progress in the way Hughes separates 'down' from 'tumbling', placing the stressed word at the end of the line and filling the gap with words as insubstantial as 'invisibly' and 'echoes'. Such words are not suffering from a sort of lexical anaemia through being shut within the pages of a dictionary; they carry no mere referential meaning. These words are alive with meanings from their context, their associations and their sensory qualities; they are alive with what Hughes elsewhere calls 'the goblin in a word'.[2]

Yet, amid all the naturalistic description, one line stands out as different from all others. It signals the climax of the poem as the stag is finally trapped and we are told that the horsemen

Pulled aside the camouflage of their terrible planet.

The precision and concreteness of poetic language are suddenly thrown into a new dimension. The immediate effect of the words 'camouflage' and 'planet' is surrealistic, forcing the reader to shift perspective upon the events as they have unfolded. Yet, at this juncture, the line is finely placed, picking up the military metaphor from verse three and investing it with all the murderous intent that has so far been masked in the camouflage of 'parade'. The evil is exposed with an existential detachment. Momentarily, as the camouflage with which men cover their intentions is pulled aside, the poem reveals this incident as a symbol of man's capacity for evil on this 'terrible planet'. The language is precise and concrete but operating symbolically, challenging the reader to consider this killing as an instance of the inescapable violence with which we all have to live.

B) FORM

The second quality unique to poetry is the evocative role of language to convert feeling into form. The experience of form in this poem lies in the sense of the stag being caught in a clinically-laid, 'military' ambush. How is this achieved? Two examples running through the first four verses will illustrate the point. First, especially when reading the poem aloud, one is made aware of the steady momentum and pressure of all those subordinate clauses. Each verse begins with 'While . . . ' and is held in suspension for five long lines until it arrives at the moving stag and marks his progress from the familiar to the strange. It is a cinematic technique; the reader's eye is invited to 'pan' across the landscape until the hunt, and the poem, are 'turned' by the impassable river. In order to reflect accurately the pace of the long, run-on lines, the reader has to hyperventilate his lungs. This is no accident. It is a remarkable example of form in poetry, for the poem insists that, to be read aloud at all, the reader must experience the *physical* stress of the subject matter. The breathlessness of the reader is the breathlessness of the stag. Secondly, the sense of form is gained through the mounting, impersonal pressure of the onlookers: the urgency of the farmers to get a good view (vs. 1), the spectators high-kneeing it up the bank (vs. 4); the waiting horsemen 'spaced as at a military parade' (vs. 3), and 'the steady men in oilskins . . . stationed at binoculars' (vs. 4). All of them are figures in a landscape, some moving, others still, all waiting, with a rising sense of expectancy for the climax of a drama. Both structurally and rhythmically in the first example, and here in terms of how the human figures are placed in the development of the incident, there is a sense of formal ordering, of the poem as a made object. The form of 'The Stag' has the qualities associated with any well-wrought poem — a special tautness of structure and a sense of contained energy.

C) OBSERVATION

'The essential quality of poetry', claimed D. H. Lawrence, 'is that it makes a new effort of attention and "discovers" a new world within the known world.'[3] 'The Stag' exemplifies this principle with great subtlety in the way the experience is presented. The observational eye that makes this 'effort of attention' is best understood by reflecting upon the 'onlooker role' (in D. W. Harding's phrase) that we adopt during reading. Notice the progress from *looking* to *seeing* to *perceiving* as the poem develops. In the first two verses we are looking at scenes of relative innocence and ordinariness. The stag is on its territory, in 'his private forest' and 'his favourite valley'; most of the people are confined to their territory, a traffic jam on a West Country lane in pouring rain. There is enough to catch our interest in the movements of the local farmers and the stag itself but nothing, as yet, to create unease or insecurity. On the contrary, the reader is deliberately placed in the position of looking in on another's territory. Then, in verse three, the resonances begin. The military trap is laid and, along with the crowd in verse four, we begin to see the significance of the events and to sense the threat to the stag as it moves 'into a strange country'. But it is not until the final two verses that we perceive the nature of the experience that Hughes is sharing with us. We have already noted how the last line of verse five challenges the reader to respond to the meaning of this violence. The final verse is a carefully orchestrated ending. There is no glib moral about blood sports. Instead, we are left to cope with the nature of the whole experience as one that holds in tension a number of elements: the noisy violence of the 'loll-tongued hounds', the silent threat of violence from the horsemen, the exhausted panic of the stag and the strange sense of theatre where the hunt climaxes before the crowd moves away, 'wet-through and disappointed'. Abandoning our onlooker role, we are left with our feelings, thoughts and questions about the whole experience.

D) FEELING

Good poems are places where thinking and feeling remain unified, avoiding the educational apartheid of so much of school that seems intent upon dividing mind and heart. Poems provide opportunities to experience and exercise the interplay of thought and emotion which Robert Witkin has vividly called 'the intelligence of feeling'.[4] How does this operate? Such exercise is gained through the reader's awareness of the sort of dialogue that is taking place between himself and the 'implied author'.[5] By making an 'effort of attention' he becomes alert to the writer's response to the experience, to his reflection upon it and the resolution of it in verbal form; and he complements this awareness with his own reading, reflection and responses. In so doing, the reader discriminates between his feelings for the efficient horsemen, the trapped and 'weeping' stag and the 'disappointed' spectators. And, in considering these two overtly emotional words in the poem, he will very probably ask himself whether 'weeping' sensationalizes the stag's predicament and why the crowd is said to be 'disappointed'. Thus the reader begins to measure his feelings beside those of the writer. Because of the very concentration of the language that the writer and reader share, feelings are *embodied* in verbal form, not merely indicated by verbal reference.

It is for this reason that a child's awareness of what language is and does will become deeper and more subtle through poetry than through any other sort of language use. A poem, as 'The Stag' shows, has the capacity to educate the feelings. To deprive children of poems is to deny them the society of clear, single voices and a range of feeling for which there is no alternative.

Language, form, observation, feeling — these are the qualities that poems uniquely embody and they are the key concepts in understanding the indirect approach to a poem that involves building up a reading from several different perspectives. One implication for teaching is obvious: if we are to enable our children's minds to take a walk around within a poem, as if looking from different perspectives at a sculpture, then the line by line approach can only be an inappropriate, inhibiting bore. Far better that the children explore a poem, respond to the bits that interest them, and slowly piece together the parts into a sense of coherent whole. Poems need to be experienced rather than explained. The main emphasis of the teacher's job is not, in fact, *explication du texte* but the cultivation of individual and shared responses to the text. If the four attributes we have discussed are fundamental to the experience of a poem then this suggests that certain recurrent, 'starter' questions will underpin our work with children. They are open, general questions inviting the reader both to attend to the words and to frame and value the individuality of his own response. We might ask:

On language
> What words, phrases or lines stood out — for whatever reason — when you were reading or listening?

On form
> Can you say anything about the shape of the poem, how the words are laid out on the page?
> Do you notice any patterns?
> What effect does such a shape have on you?

On observation
> What is the writer really looking at, either outside or inside himself?

On feeling
> What feelings are conveyed during the poem at different points?
> Do they change?
> Do you share them?

Of course, these questions will be asked about particular poems and in language which will be readily understood by a particular group of children.

HOW POEMS MEAN: 'A POEM SHOULD NOT MEAN/BUT BE'

The meaning of 'meaning' where poetry is concerned is a plural and ambiguous concept: plural because, as the discussion of 'The Stag' shows, and as you will have experienced if you teased out your own reading of it first, the meanings made in reading the poem are a result of individual exploration, idiosyncratic points of entry into the experience presented, and personal awareness of the way the words are rendering that experience; ambiguous because 'meaning' usually betokens something that can be explained or, at least, described. There *will* be matters that need explanation about many poems; there will be the need for explanatory talking or writing to hold and to represent the gist of a reader's response to a poem; there may even be the need to answer specific questions about this or that aspect of a poem; but to claim that any of these explanations resolves the 'meaning' is fatuous. As with stories, meaning is a compound of what the poem offers and what the reader brings. However, the nature of the art is such that, as we noted earlier, in the apprehension of a poem, the temporal sense of storyreading (what happens next?) gives way to a greater spatial awareness (what does this pattern of words mean to me?); and, further, in our comprehension of a poem, meaning is made as much from the reader's response to the sound, rhythm and formal ordering of the language as it is to its line of thought, syntax and lexical definition. It is these characteristics of the art of poetry that at once provide the challenge to the art of teaching it and the source of many pupils' uncertainties. For, while we may well hear many children ask of a story 'What happens next?', there will be few who ask of a poem 'What does this pattern of words mean to me?' Children have to become familiar with what sort of thing a poem is to a degree that is not necessary when responding to stories. This distinction may seem difficult to sustain at first sight, given the natural affinity children have with rhymes and jingles in their play; but oral chants are very different experiences from printed poems.

A poem by Archibald MacLeish tells the reader about the nature of poetry. It is both an assertion and itself an example of what it states. Read it aloud.

> ARS POETICA
>
> A poem should be palpable and mute
> As a globed fruit,
>
> Dumb
> As old medallions to the thumb,
>
> Silent as the sleeve-worn stone
> Of casement ledges where the moss has grown —
>
> A poem should be wordless
> As the flight of birds.
>   *
>
> A poem should be motionless in time
> As the moon climbs
>
> Leaving, as the moon releases
> Twig by twig the night-entangled trees,
>
> Leaving, as the moon behind the winter leaves,
> Memory by memory the mind —
>
> A poem should be motionless in time
> As the moon climbs.
>   *
>
> A poem should be equal to:
> Not true.
>
> For all the history of grief
> An empty doorway and a maple leaf.
>
> For love
> The leaning grasses and two lights above the sea —
>
> A poem should not mean
> But be.[6]

The poem is a succession of images each trying to catch the essence of poetry through the medium of poetry; images that develop in sequence and lead to a strikingly simple, imageless conclusion, yet images whose essential quality is their ability to symbolize meaning, to stand for what is inexpressible in discursive language; or, as the poem puts its, 'be equal to'.

The spatial sense of poetry is immediately evoked in the 'globed fruit'.

While inviting the reader to handle this tactile object, potentially delicious to taste as well as to hold, the poem is actually saying something about how poems speak to us. A poem becomes a three-dimensional presence in the reader's imagination. It does not tell us about itself, explaining itself away, dissipating its power; instead, it literally 'expresses itself'. The images which follow suggest different sources of power and delight that poems contain: the romance and secret experience of 'medallions', the richness of human lives and histories in the 'sleeve-worn stone', the natural aspirations of the human spirit in the 'flight of birds'. And, as befits the theme of silence that unites these four images, the words that make the images are themselves examples of the principle of *ars poetica* as expressed in the last lines of the whole poem. Hence, their point is made by *how they are*, not by *what they say*. So the fruit is 'palpable' and 'globed' — the words are ripe and sensuous; 'dumb' is displayed alone on its line, its roundness reflected in 'medallions' and echoed in the rhyming 'thumb'; the lines lengthen and the sibilance increases as the slow passage of history is evoked through the sleeves which have worn away the stone over which the moss is growing; there is the flutter of wings in 'wordless'. The sensory qualities of the words are both the medium and the message, the means of expression and the idea being expressed.

The second section moves the poem on from silence to stillness; it enfolds itself by repeating the first statement as the last one, stressing the stillness, inviting us to experience permanence and stasis via the moving moon. It shifts our attention from externalized objects, the moon and the winter trees, to the internal world of the mind and hints at how poems come into being for both writers and readers. A poem becomes lodged in the mind: memory works paradoxically for, as time passes, the experience of the poem changes; it is both 'leaving' and arriving, establishing its own existence. Irrelevant details fall away leaving the symmetry and the still presence of the poem in the writer's and reader's consciousness. Such interpretations are hazardously made for the poem is operating symbolically; and again, how the words are being used is a fundamental aspect of what a poem is. Hence, we experience the enclosed atmosphere created by the repeated lines and the single focus of the moon metaphor; the imperceptible pace of the moon, caught in the alliterative reversal of what is moving and what is still, '. . . as the moon releases/Twig by twig the night-entangled trees . . .'; the cunning play on 'leaving' and 'leaves'. As earlier, the words are relating to each other; they are not looking outside themselves in order to say something about poetry-making, but are contributing the whole of themselves to making a poem about making a poem.

As the last section indicates, therefore, we should not ask of a poem what it means and whether it is true or untrue; rather we experience what Eliot called 'objective correlatives', images that act as the formulae for the emotions, whether of grief or love, on the aesthetic principle that 'A poem should not mean/But be'. However we react to the nostalgic images of the first section and the clichés through which grief and love are conveyed in the last one, this principle remains valid as the point of MacLeish's poem.

There is no more severe a test for such a principle than a 'nonsense poem'. Edwin Morgan introduced the following composition on BBC Radio some years ago as 'a sound poem'. Whatever we choose to call it, it highlights both the plural and ambiguous nature of how poems mean. To make a point we will come to in a moment we have omitted the title. Read the poem aloud!

> Sssnnnwhuffffll?
> Hnwhuffl hhnnwfl hnfl hfl?
> Gdroblboblhobngbl gbl gl g g g g glbgl.
> Drublhaflablhaflubhafgabhaflhafl fl fl-
> gm grawwwww grf grawf awfgm graw gm.
> Hovoplodok-doplodovok-plovodokot-doplodokosh?
> Splgraw fok fok splgrafhatchgabrlgabrl fok splfok!
> Zgra kra gka fok!
> Grof grawff gahf?
> Gombl mbl bl-
> blm plm,
> blm plm,
> blm plm,
> blp.[7]

It is revealing to withold the title of the poem from a class and invite their responses. Denied the language of the dictionary, there are few who can resist the instinct to create meanings. Commonly, someone will remark on the watery sounds, particularly at the beginning and end, and the harder sounds in the middle lines. Differences in line length are noticed and the significance of the punctuation is pointed out: someone or something is making exclamations and asking questions, rhetorical or otherwise; the rhythm of the writing is not that of flat statement. Pictures form in the mind's eye, speculations are made, as the readers acknowledge that there is some sort of development; an event is taking place between the opening question and the final 'blp'. Inexorably, the mind spawns its images and stories and translates them into words. Occasionally, one of the interpretations may come close to Edwin Morgan's title — 'The Loch Ness Monster's Song'.

ELEMENTS OF RESPONSE

What this last exercise reveals is the manner of our apprehending. In order to make the monster, we have to meet the poet rather more than half way and rely upon the fundamental signposts of poetic composition to guide us from nonsense to sense. These may be expressed in terms of four over-lapping qualities of the language of poetry which are present, in differing degrees, in the experiencing of all poems, even ones as dissimilar as 'The Stag', 'Ars Poetica' and 'The Loch Ness Monster's Song'. The four elements of the imaginative experience of responding to a poem are: words as sound, words as rhythm, words as pictures and words as story. All contribute to the meanings we make. The importance of any one element will vary from reader to reader and reading to reading. First impressions of these three poems may well give prominence to the narrative of 'The Stag', the wordpictures of 'Ars Poetica' and the sounds of 'The Loch Ness Monster's Song'. Yet our discussion of Hughes's poem demonstrates how all four elements are at work together; and, even in the other two poems where the sounds, rhythms and pictorial evocations of the words are not employed to tell a formal story *per se*, the narrative imagination is readily detectable in the ordering and development of images towards a conclusion about art, or in the sense we have of the monster coming to the surface, quizzically remarking upon the world about him, deciding that he dislikes what he sees and submerging once more into his underwater world.

These four elements need to be born in mind by every poetry teacher. The appeal of sound and rhythm is fundamental in sharing a poem with a group of children. It is a recurring testimony to the importance of what Eliot called the 'auditory imagination (which) is the feeling for syllable and rhythm, penetrating far below the conscious levels of thought and feeling, invigorating every word . . .'.[8] Teachers know from personal observation as well as from the work of the Opies that children possess this auditory imagination from infancy and develop it in their play. These aspects of a poem's meaning, as we suggested earlier, are the ones with which children have a natural affinity. Repetition of key words, the significance invested in particular word sounds and rhyming patterns are all sound effects that appeal to children. Similarly, children bring an innate sense of rhythm to poetry. Youngsters especially prefer rhythm to be strongly-marked, a clear beat that is regularly accented. Older readers may develop a liking for both the buoyant, rhythmical character of a Causley ballad and the slow down-beat of an introspective lyric by de la Mare and be able to discriminate between their tastes. Just as Eliot's phrase 'auditory imagination' incorporates the elements of sound and rhythm, so the notion of the 'narrative imagination' includes the elements of picture and story. 'Words as pictures' covers a range of visual effects that poet and reader share through the medium of a poem, from the mental imagery that is provoked in the reader's mind to his awareness of the haiku poet's genius for miniature or the concrete poet's sense of fun. In poems our pictorial sense may be exercised in response to form and lay-out or in the picturing that we find the words evoking as we read. Just as we are proliferators of images, so we are of stories. Again, the sense of narrative may be no more than the natural propensity to link pictures into sequences, the ordering of experiences to represent them to ourselves more coherently. Yet the enthralling power of story in poetry can go beyond this. Stories in verse hold children in a double spell: the enchantment of the fiction and the form. It is a power that is felt most richly in the traditional literature of narrative and ballad verse arising directly from the oral heritage. Words as sound, rhythm, picture and story: these verbal elements of the art are the carriers of feelings and ideas in poetry.

IMPLICATIONS FOR THE CLASSROOM

We need a methodology that enables us to translate this plurality of meaning into classroom activities.

A) THREE QUESTIONS TO KEEP IN MIND

The singular nature of poems and the unique way that they convey meaning demand that the teacher of poetry must ask:

> *What is my knowledge of the poetry written for and accessible to children?*
> *What time do I give to poetry?*
> *When the voices of poet, children and teacher are talking about a poem in my classroom, is the discussion based on the primacy of the individual child's response?*

Knowledge of the poetry for children is our fundamental professional commitment. If we are not readers of poems we can scarcely expect to become teachers of poems. The corrective, if one is needed, is easy and pleasurable: it is simply to read as many slim volumes of individual poets' work as possible and not merely to confine ourselves to school anthologies. Such a reading programme is often best carried out along with one or two colleagues: likes and dislikes, stock responses and personal reading habits are usually challenged in this way and strong recommendations are more likely to be followed up, leading to a sharing of 'how things went' in the classroom.

Time is a significant factor in the teaching of poetry. After all, most poems are so short that they take no time at all to read and enjoy by comparison with novels or plays. There ought to be plenty of time for poetry, then, even if the poems only survive in the gaps between other activities. Examine your own practice. How much time per week do we give to poetry? Children (all of us) develop as readers by keeping in continual practice. It follows that, if we and they expect to take this aspect of English seriously, all children should have the chance to hear, and when appropriate talk about, several poems each week. Secondly, what do we do with the time? If poetry lessons repeatedly fall into a 'read-discuss-write' sequence then it is not surprising that the majority of children will lose interest. Poems are unpredictable; we should try to emulate this quality in the patterns of our lessons. The implication for our teaching is to be flexible in the ways we work and, above all, to allow the singular nature of a particular poem to dictate to us how it should be handled.

Responses to poems are often oblique in nature and hesitant in the expression if they are genuine efforts to come to terms. Conversely, they are usually uncompromising, not to say blunt, if they are simply a means of indicating a dislike of the whole business. Enough is known about the operation of all-class lessons and discussions in small groups from two to five pupils to suggest that the latter have a particularly significant role to play in poetry teaching.[9] Again, if the answer to our question about time suggests the need for a change of emphasis, the direction is clear: put the onus more squarely upon the children to explore the poems and talk out their responses in a variety of differently structured tasks. Inevitably there will be more *talk* about matters unconnected with the task in hand but this does not mean that there will be less attention given to a poem than in an all-class lesson directed by the teacher. On the contrary, if groups are given a clear goal to achieve, a physical arrangement conducive to discussion and the urgency of a time limit then, with most classes, the teacher's fears about time-wasting, irrelevance or anarchy largely disappear. When talking about poems, as about anything else in schools, the paradox applies that free speech demands a firm framework. Small group work is not an instant panacea. A class unfamiliar with it will need to be trained, and there are as many dangers in over-use as neglect. Nonetheless, there are clear advantages.

The sorts of benefits that accrue in pair and group discussions of poems and which are much harder to achieve in all-class discussions, are: the willingness to tolerate uncertainty, misunderstanding and ignorance; the sense that whatever they make of the poem it will be uniquely theirs; the awareness that, since they are in control of the talking, they can return to parts of the poem when they like and so fit their sense of the details into a growing appreciation of the whole. Such benefits, of course, are not only to be gained in poetry lessons; but, in view of the nature of poems, the advantages of small group discussions are particularly helpful in eliciting individual responses.

B) MEETING, SHARING AND STUDYING POEMS

Meeting Most children meet most poetry either on sheets of duplicated paper or in anthologies. It is a curious fact that, while we know that if children like a story by Enid Blyton or Robert Leeson they are likely to seek out another by the same author, we deny them the possibility of this social bond with poets by the way we mediate between the writer and the reader. How children meet poems in school is the area of work that requires most attention. It ought to be self-evident, but it often strikes teachers as a novelty, that the single most important resource in poetry teaching is a collection of three or four dozen slim volumes of poems by single authors. This collection can be augmented by anthologies, so that there is a variety of voices and styles and an eye-catching presentation. The main purpose of such a collection is not as a staff room resource but as the basis for classroom activity. For one of the best ways for a class to meet poems is by spending ten minutes regularly set aside to browse through a wide variety of books, dipping and skipping, and finding out what they like and dislike. Individuals may well discover they prefer one person's poems to those of another and the social bond thus begins to develop. Given a wide and varied choice of poetry books, the most reluctant pupils are hard-pressed to claim that there is nothing of interest. After this browsing time, it is generally an easy transition to reading poems aloud as individuals choose them. Discussion may follow some poems but not others: close scrutiny is certainly not required. The purpose, especially in the early weeks with a class, is to put everyone at ease with poems by reading a lot and saying little. Regular exposure to a wide selection of poems in an informal way is the best grounding we can give children if we want to cultivate a liking for poetry.

Sharing The key to a proper sharing of poetry is performance. It is easy to set children to work at 'improper' sharing by sending them on metaphor hunts and simile chases, by exhorting them to collect examples of assonance and alliteration (or, as one of our pupils said with more truth than he knew, 'illiteration'), or by asking them to think about a poem as evidence supporting a project on, say, 'Water' or 'The Wild West', rather than as a totality in itself. This is not to outlaw the use of figurative and technical language or to decry project work. It is simply to plead for activities that are appropriate to the nature of poems. If 'A poem should not mean/But be', then the sharing children do should focus not on worrying out its meaning but on celebrating its being. This is why performance is important. It may imply copying out and illustrating favourite pieces for display purposes, public readings, dramatizations and the like where groups of children concentrate upon presenting poetry in such a way that it may be enjoyed and savoured for its own sake.

A cassette tape-recorder is an indispensable aid in this area of work. A simple demand upon small groups of children might run along these lines: 'You have a ten minute slot to fill for BBC Radio's *Poetry Please* series. Your producer wants you to catch the interest of a young audience and to include a minimum of four poems read by different voices. You must introduce and link the poems in a suitable way. Choose your poems, script your introduction and linking passages and then record your programme.' This activity requires reading and discrimination, the exercise of personal choice, ordering and relating poems in sequence, comment upon the selection and, above all, rehearsal of the presentation with the decisions about voices, pace, intonation and mood that this entails. The tape-recording of such mini-anthologies provides a class with a pleasurable activity in itself, a source of material for future use and the exacting discipline of performance. If a 'real audience' in another class or school can be arranged, so much the better. In this sort of work the art of teaching poetry comes closest to the art of poetry itself, for both are based upon a common principle: playing with words within the discipline of form. This maxim should inform our teaching just as it does the poems themselves.

Studying From time to time, even with young groups, the teacher will want to concentrate upon a poem in some detail. Close study will only work, and can only be justified as an occasional activity, if it is rooted in the pattern of meeting and sharing poems outlined above. By 'close study' we do not mean the formal criticism of a poem: this has no place in poetry lessons with children in the years before public examination courses. But, if children are exploring poetry in an atmosphere that encourages them to develop their own tastes and articulate their own responses, then there will be times when it is right to pause over a particular poem. Three questions may provide a useful framework within which to plan detailed work:

> What does the poem say to you?
> How does it do it?
> Does it work?

The first requires the reader to hold on to his own response, (for example by jotting down his reactions prior to discussion) and to articulate his thoughts and feelings about the poem. Among any group of children these will be varied and the teacher's role here is to collect something from as many as possible, delaying judgement and being content to let the descriptions of mood, idea and atmosphere gather round the reading of the poem. The second question, too, will produce a scatter of reactions and the teacher may well end up with a blackboard-full of all the things the class has noticed about the shape of the poem, its sounds, rhythms, individual words and images — again, details which are to be collected for fun 'to see what we can find', not worried over for judgement. The third question must remain until last. It invites the reader to say whether a poem succeeds for him and to offer a judgement of personal value about his sense of the whole piece. If the question is put prematurely it may invite the rejection of poetry that comes from ill-considered and inaccurate reading or insufficient opportunity for reflection. It is important for the teacher to be receptive to hostile feelings and judgements about a poem that develop from careful reading.

L.A.G. Strong reminds us of the central principle of poetry teaching and provides a challenging conclusion:

> Remember, the object at every stage is to keep and develop the child's liking for the music of words. Explanations and annotations do not matter. A child's misconception may be of much greater value to him than the explanation which destroys it.[10]

NOTES

1. Ted Hughes, 'The Stag' from *Season Songs*, Faber, 1976, pp. 56–57.
2. Ted Hughes, *Poetry in the Making*, Faber, 1967, p. 18.
3. D.H. Lawrence, 'Preface' to *Chariot of the Sun* by Harry Crosby in E.D. Macdonald (ed), *Phoenix*, Heinemann, 1961, p. 255.
4. Robert Witkin, *The Intelligence of Feeling*, Heinemann Educational Books, 1974.
5. The term Wayne Booth uses to distinguish the real author of everyday life from the implied one as revealed in the text. See his *The Rhetoric of Fiction*, University of Chicago Press, 1961, pp. 71–6.
6. Archibald MacLeish, *Collected Poems*, Houghton Mifflin, 1963, pp. 50–51.
7. Edwin Morgan, 'The Loch Ness Monster's Song' from *From Glasgow to Saturn*, Carcanet Press, 1973, p. 35.
8. T.S. Eliot, 'Matthew Arnold' in *The Use of Poetry and The Use of Criticism*, Harvard University Press, 1933, p. 111.
9. See especially: Douglas Barnes, *Language, the Learner and The School*, Penguin, 1969; Douglas Barnes, *From Communication to Curriculum*, Penguin, 1976; Douglas Barnes and Frankie Todd, *Communication and Learning in Small Groups*, Routledge and Kegan Paul, 1977.
10. L.A.G. Strong, 'Poetry in School', in *The Teaching of English in Schools: A Symposium*, edited by V. da Sola Pinto, Macmillan, 1946, p. 1.

29 *How Children Describe Their Reading of Stories*

● Robert Protherough

This article is concerned with the ways in which children themselves see the reading of fiction, the connection between their views and those of some recent theorists, and the implications for teachers.

Critical accounts of reading in general or of the significance of particular texts have normally postulated a theoretical 'ideal' reader or have been concerned with the responses of highly educated adults. Only from the mid-seventies onwards has there been sustained attention in journals and elsewhere to children's perceptions of reading and to the nature of their responses at different ages.

[...] Studies of Hull children suggest that they instinctively see books in terms of what they *do* to them as readers. Young people repeatedly justify their preferences in terms of the effect which a story has had on them. The reactions may be essentially emotional, like these: '*Black Beauty* upset me when the animals were tortured so', 'When I read *Only Time will Tell* I cried my heart out', '*1984* horrified me'. However, response may also be described in terms which suggest a changed attitude or behaviour:

> Kizzy (The Diddakoi) made me look differently at new children in School.

> The *Mallen* novels made me realise more clearly that people who seem happy and unmoved by most things can really be the most sad person in the world. And it has made me tolerate happy people when I'm sad.

> *Lord of the Rings* opened up the world of older stories to me.

Similar responses characterise the way pupils in the Exeter area described their reading. *Bevis* 'altered my whole approach to life'; after reading *The Belstone Fox*, 'I gave up hunting'; when part of *F.67* had been read, 'I felt sick', 'it makes me want to cry . . .'[1] The 15-year-olds in the APU sample who defined the importance of reading in terms of enjoyment also instinctively seemed to validate the process by referring to their responses. Reading 'helps me', 'calms me', 'lets me live a different life' or 'become involved in different times and situations', allows me to 'escape', 'relax', 'forget', 'unwind', 'get away', it 'gives immense pleasure'.[2]

When children themselves describe how they actually read novels, it is almost in terms of a direct relationship between their own lives and the imagined life of the book. The images they use are nearly all spatial ones: they *enter* a character whose experiences become their own, they *move* through a series of events alongside the participants, they *observe* incidents 'there' in front of them, realising them in terms of people and places known to them. In fact, the ability to operate in this way seems to mark off those who get pleasure from reading from those who do not. The responses of several hundred secondary children of all levels of ability in the Hull area suggest that it is those who do not enjoy reading fiction who either do not understand what is meant by questions about how they read, or who reject the implications. Their responses tend to be simply 'I just read it, that's all' or 'If it's interesting I keep reading it and if it's boring I stop'. The assumption is of an automatic decoding process; no significant experience is created by the reader. Some of their replies indicate that these children have been put off reading by being forced to read books they found too dull, difficult or babyish. The great majority of replies, however, can be categorised in terms of the amount of distance they suggest between reader and text. In general, the younger readers are much more likely to 'project' themselves into the text and older ones to be more withdrawn. The widest range of preferred reading styles is to be found at 13–14 and most of the following examples of different modes are therefore taken from this age group:

MODE 1   PROJECTION INTO A CHARACTER

The simplest and commonest way of experiencing what one 16-year-old boy described as being 'immersed . . . *in* the book . . . identifying with some of the characters' is imaginatively to become one of them, to lose yourself in that character's personality and situation. The same idea is repeated over and over again:

I put myself in the person's place I am reading about' (girl 13).

I often imagine I am one of the characters, the hero or heroine (boy 13).
[...]

Sometimes they mention books which they like to read in this way: frequently Enid Blyton's stories for younger girls and James Bond books or other thrillers for boys. An interesting view of the extent of the identification is given by a girl of 14: 'I imagine myself as the character and if I stop reading the book without finishing I find it hard to pick the story up again because I have forgotten my past.' The notion of 'becoming' conveyed in '*my* past' is vivid. This is not an experience limited to younger children. D. H. Russell cites studies which quote older, able students who identified with the protagonists of novels. Reading *The Catcher in the Rye*, one reported that 'after a few pages I found I was not merely reading the book, I was also living it.' Another said of *A Portrait of the Artist as a Young Man* that 'In reading Joyce's novel I *was* the "young man".'[3]

MODE 2   PROJECTION INTO THE SITUATION

Many readers describe the experience as being 'there' in the book with the characters, but not as identifying specifically with any one of them. They see themselves as spectators on the outskirts or margin of events, emotionally involved, but unable to affect the action. They often perceive themselves as 'close' to the characters, their 'friend':

> [...]
> I feel as though I am there, witnessing the events . . . I am the characters' friend (boy 13).

> [...]
> I think that I am there with the characters, listening and seeing everything they do and say. Sometimes I feel that I am one of them (girl 14).

Not infrequently readers conceive themselves as being present but invisible to the characters:

> As I read a book I imagine that I am very close to where the events are happening, but I always remain unseen (girl 14).

> I see myself as an invisible spectator who sees everything that happens (boy 13).

One or two perceive themselves as a kind of 'extra' character, alongside the ones in the book: 'I quite often find myself as a character in that adventure, though the character is never mentioned in the book.'

MODE 3   ASSOCIATING BETWEEN BOOK AND READER

Whereas in the first two modes readers are to differing degrees trying to enter the book and to lose themselves in it, here they are more concerned to establish links between themselves as readers with their own actual experiences and the people and situations of the book. The movement is in both directions: they visualise the book in terms of their own world, and they imagine how they would feel and act if they were people in the story. The first movement is expressed in such terms as these:

> Often part of the scene I read about I imagine to be going on at a place I know and am very familiar with, e.g. my best friend's house (girl 14).
> [...]
>
> When I read about people's emotions, I think to myself, 'Is it like me?' (boy 13).

The second movement is described like this:

> I put myself in their position and see if I would think or do the same as them (boy 13).
> [...]
>
> I always put myself in their place and think about what I'd do in their position (girl 15).

In other words, readers may realise the secondary world of the book by importing into it elements from their first-hand experience, or they may use the book as a testing-ground for their own feelings and ideas, or indeed both.

MODE 4   THE DISTANCED VIEWER

A number of readers described their experience as being somehow above the characters, watching them play out their roles as if on a kind of chess-board. 'I just see it all by looking down', said a 15-year-old girl. Other critics have quoted children who described this mode of reading as being like watching a play on television, or a film, or a football match from the stand. The reader is firmly outside the action, but emotionally involved in what happens and wishing to be able to influence the outcome. One 13-year-old said, 'I sometimes get so close that I start to think of ways of stopping or starting what is happening.' Within this view of reading they may express feelings of empathy or a more distanced awareness of what 'ought' to be happening.

> I feel differently for the characters: if they are unhappy I pity them, if they are mean I hate them, etc. (girl 14).
> [...]
>
> When I read a book, I hope that the baby doesn't get injured and that the villain gets killed and so on (boy 13).
>
> They seem to come real and you feel you know them . . . I keep thinking to tell them to do the right thing (boy 13).
> [...]

Although, as has been suggested, the later modes seem in general to be associated with a later stage of development than the earlier ones, it would be dangerous to suggest that they are necessarily 'better' ways of reading, or that readers all acquire their modes of reading in the same order.

What does seem to be associated with maturity in reading is the ability to operate in an increasing number of modes, according to the work being read and the mood or needs of the moment. Readers at what is called here mode 1 frequently seem to assume that there is no other way of reading; whereas more perceptive readers were aware, as adults are, not only that different people react differently to the same text, but also that individuals respond in varied ways to different works, or even to the same work at different moments. One 14-year-old girl began a lengthy analysis of her own reading habits:

> I feel with the characters, sometimes I am an onlooker watching the adventure, sometimes I am one of the characters. I feel great sympathy with the characters if they die or become blind, crippled etc. I enjoy trying to work out riddles and mysteries if they are written like that . . .

Here she seems fully aware of herself bringing the text alive in a variety of different ways.

There is, of course, another mode of reading that increases still further the distance between reader and text, a mode that we associate particularly with formal literary studies.

MODE 5   DETACHED EVALUATION

This mode of reading is rarely mentioned except by older pupils. A 14-year-old girl is perhaps operating in this way when she says, 'I understand, rather than feel, the emotions of the characters.' She seems neither to be identifying nor to be empathising with the figures in the story, but to be analysing them more coolly. Another says, 'I like to see how the author tells the story, creates a mood . . .' A boy who reads science fiction 'to see how convincing the inventions are' is in a different way, also reading from a stance that is likely to inhibit emotional involvement with the story. Critical reading of this kind seems to be a practice learned in school. Gill Frith quotes a girl of 17:

> What enters my mind when I read a book?
> When I read a book, the things that go through my mind are whether I can understand the characters, the way in which they act and why they act in a certain way. Whether the plot is moving fast enough or whether there is not enough action but too many descriptive passages. I often guess as to what will be the outcome of a certain scene and whether the scene will greatly influence other scenes . . . If I find the book interesting I will tend not to take in what I am reading at the moment but think about what will be happening on the next page or in the next chapter.[4]

The concepts here seem to be those that have grown out of literary studies. One boy was aware of the difference between the ways in which he responded while actually reading a novel and at the end of the process, looking back. He saw the more detached mode as essentially retrospective. While reading, the characters 'are part of you and you of them in the action, and as you are reading you want to help them live for real the life the character has. Afterwards one thinks more carefully and considers what that character considered . . .' (boy 15).

The children's perceptions of how they read all suggest an essential interplay between the world of the reader and the world of the book. There is a huge difference between simply understanding the meanings of words on the page and the experience of a story which brings into play the reader's faculties to create the narrative. Studies like these flesh out the model of the reading process which is being hammered out jointly by psychologists, literary theorists, critics and educationalists.

This model suggests that in the process of reading a story, the narrative is 'constructed' or 'performed' through a series of interactions at any given moment. The information in the text is realised in terms of the reader's actual and second-order experience of the world. The movement of the narrative is also perceived in the light of the reader's awareness of conventions and techniques, and any particular moment in the text is related to the total, accumulated information acquired up to that point in the reading. The values and concepts implied in the book are construed in relationship to the reader's own ideological views. The action is not one-way. Neither the communications image of the reader being passively imprinted by the text nor the building-blocks image of the reader making any self-gratifying meaning out of raw materials in the text will do. The reader simultaneously shapes and is shaped by the story being read. In Horst Ruthrof's phrase, 'The reader is changed by a work which he has partly constructed himself.'[5]

Such a view of the relationship between reader and text points to the unique quality possessed by a book as opposed to the other objects we perceive around us in our world. The book diminishes — or even eliminates — the sense of division between the thinking mind and the objects of thought, between 'in here' and 'out there'. Forty years ago, F. R. Leavis said that the text was only 'there' in terms of the reader's response: we can have it 'only by an inner kind of possession'.[6] In the late sixties, George Poulet termed books 'interior' or 'subjectified' objects. To a degree, the work lives its own life within us, we think the thoughts of another, we and the book 'start having a common consciousness'.

> Thus I often have the impression, while reading, of simply witnessing an action which at the same time concerns and yet does not concern me. This provokes a certain feeling of surprise within me. I am a consciousness astonished by an existence which is not mine, but which I experience as though it were mine.[7]

From a psychiatrist's stance, Norman Holland has related such a 'transformation' model of literary experience to Winnicott's concept of 'potential space': a middle ground which both joins and separates the individual and the person or object cared about, or, in Holland's terms, 'a space which reader and work create together'.

> He no longer feels a distinction between 'in here' and 'out there', and between him and it. Indeed, there is none, and he becomes, as we say, 'absorbed'. He and the work (as he has synthesised it) blend and merge in a potential space between perceiver and perceived where distinctions between inside and outside, self and other, found object and created object, objective reality and created symbol, have ceased to matter.[8]

A third formulation of the special quality of texts is given by Wolfgang Iser:

> We always stand outside the given object, whereas we are situated inside the literary text. The relation between text and reader is therefore quite different from that between object and observer: instead of a subject-object relationship, there is a moving viewpoint which travels along *inside* that which it has to apprehend. This mode of grasping an object is unique to literature.[9]

Although Poulet, Holland and Iser realise the concept in significantly different spatial images (the text is 'in' us, 'thinking' us, in Poulet; we travel 'through' it in Iser; we meet in a mutually created third ground in Holland), they agree on the essential qualities of the model of reading that is being presented.

Why is this important for teachers? Three points need to be made. First, it eliminates the sterile antithesis between the extreme objective and subjective views of reading and evaluation, related to that other damaging antithesis between 'child-centred' and 'subject-centred' education. Secondly, it directs attention to the *development* of reading abilities, and to practices which may be helpful in the classroom. Thirdly, it provides a sound basis for considering variations in interpretation, particularly (though not only) in the upper forms of schools. Each of these points can be briefly developed.

First, the way in which the reading process is seen by the teacher will inevitably colour classroom practice. Two traditional views are still commonly held. The first is the extreme objective model. The text has a 'meaning' which has simply to be conveyed to passive recipients. It is assumed that pupils will or can all receive the same meaning and that they can be tested to see whether this has taken place. The teacher is the arbiter between 'right' and 'wrong' readings. Such a view is clearly a convenient one for a teacher who has to 'take' the same book with a whole class, or who wishes to mark conventional tests of 'comprehension'. The poem or story is seen as representing some kind of ideal reading (sometimes identified with the author's 'intention') to which individual readings will more or less approximate.

The second is the extreme subjective model. Here the work is seen as lifeless or even non-existent until its 'meaning' is supplied by the reader. Since all readers construct their own meanings, which are the only ones valid for them, there are no right or wrong interpretations or judgements. As critics disagree and as psychologists increasingly reveal hidden motives and values both in authors and in critics, pupils may be encouraged to feel that any reactions of their own are as valid as the teacher's or the scholar's.

Teachers in school, and particularly in sixth forms, have been in a good position to see the damaging effects of such critical polarising between two extreme positions. Their students, after all, swing in a relatively unsophisticated way between the notion that literary preference is not unlike supporting a football team ('I know what I like', 'it's all a matter of taste') and the assumption that there is a 'right' interpretation or judgement which must be accepted, however insincerely, and afterwards parroted.

The new model fits between these two extremes. The relationship between a reader and text is variously termed by different scholars a transaction, a re-creation, a performance, an interplay, a participation, a construction or an encounter. The literary work does not have to be seen as either entirely internal, equated with the mental and emotional experience of a reader regardless of its relevance to the text, or entirely external, an entity which exists independently of being read. Reading, that is, is a participatory act; readers re-make the book as they read it, relishing, speculating, questioning, predicting, judging and so on. Indeed, one of the marks of major literature is that it provides the greatest amount of free ground for these activities of the reader. Trivial, undemanding literature spells out everything: it leaves little for the reader to do. The text of a novel as well as of a play demands to be performed; it has to be realised in a particular interpretation.

Secondly, then, we have to ask how it is that we come to develop the ability to read stories. Psychologists have demonstrated that our memory of an event cannot be separated from the way in which we make sense of that event. What is true of real events holds good for fictional ones too. Our sense of pattern, what are sometimes called 'story grammars', dictates the way in which we recall what we have read or seen.

Very young children have only a limited acquaintance with stories, and therefore find them very difficult to repeat. In one set of experiments, young children were asked to retell a favourite story which they knew well. Most of them were reluctant and argued that they did not know how to do so. Direct questioning revealed that they knew all the facts of the story, that it was potentially complete in their heads, that if they were given a lead they could say what step followed next. But they could not unreel the whole story; they were unsure where to begin, and how the incidents were linked. They were insufficiently aware of the conventions which dictate how stories work.[10]

As we grow older and experience hundreds of stories heard or read, we subconsciously establish typical schemes or frameworks, which enable us more easily to sort out and understand any new story which we encounter, predicting likely outcomes, assessing the characters and so on. Applebee has shown how early such awareness begins.[11] Bower's research in the U.S.A. has indicated that if a text violates some of the conventional patterns or 'rules' of story grammar, then that story seems less coherent to readers.[12] Stein and Glenn showed that children who are familiar with the story grammars of their own culture not only use them to make sense of new stories but also tend to add missing conventional elements when they retell those stories.[13]

It would seem to follow that one step in increasing children's ability to read and to discuss their experiences with others is to awaken in them a realisation of how far their own backgrounds, experience and attitudes affect the way in which they read, understand and interpret texts. It is sometimes helpful to consider how far differences in reaction to a book depend on pupils' existing attitudes to the issues found there, and how far attitudes are modified by reading. Much good work goes on in schools examining texts for bias and prejudice: comparing different newspaper accounts of the same event, working on advertisements and political propaganda, analysing racial or class bias in history books, and so on. Developing awareness of the way that values are transmitted in texts, though, needs to be balanced by corresponding awareness of the way in which readers apply their own sets of values to their reading. As teachers we can be too involved in imposing a view of the text — our own, or what we imagine the author's to be — rather than in exploring the variety of response.

The shift of emphasis from the text as object to the text as the occasion for an experience means asking new key questions: What is the reader doing? What is being done to him? Why? As the questions are answered, the particular structure of the reading experience appears as a 'reading', a competing interpretation. Whereas Wimsatt and Beardsley said the Affective Fallacy was 'confusion between the poem and its *results*, what it *is* and what it *does*',[14] reader-response critics maintain that, in fact, a poem *is* what it does.

This leads naturally to the third point, about interpretation. The notion that a text is somehow neutrally read and then interpreted, explained, evaluated, has to be replaced by awareness that readers bring their own stances, assumptions, interpretations, categories with them to the reading, and that reading and interpreting are inseparable processes that go on throughout. 'In written discourse, and especially in fictional narrative . . . the reader is called upon to perform complex tasks of interpretive construction before narrative meaning can be adequately established.'[15] Teachers in school have always been aware of this as they have seen pupils working through a long novel, but the pressure of a university model — where discussion focuses on texts already read — has been dominant. Clearly there are major differences between reading in process, a forward-moving creating of meaning, and the retrospective view of the work as a whole. Teachers have often pretended that 'getting through the text' is somehow a neutral, explicatory process, to be followed by critical activity, despite all the evidence that interpretations and judgements are being individually formulated and revised all the way through the reading. Indeed, in examination forms the thrust of the subsequent work is often to eliminate the personal and subjective responses that have arisen in reading and to establish an 'agreed' norm of interpretation that the teacher believes will be acceptable to an examiner. What is being discussed is response to response. It is still not unknown for students to be told, 'You may feel like that, but it's not safe to put it in an answer'.

If we hold that meaning is something which is constructed in the course of the individual's interaction with the text, then we may perhaps be less puzzled than Thorndike was in 1917, when he found a variety of responses among pupils between 10 and 13 which 'threatened to baffle any explanation'.[16] Once we abandon the assumption that meaning is there in the text, to be pulled out like plums from a pie, then we can go on to the essential, though difficult, issue of what readings are permissible.

To say that interpretations of a work are personal and plural, that there is no one 'right' meaning to a poem or story, does not mean that the situation is simply relative, that all meanings are equal. Try reading Thurber's 'The Secret Life of Walter Mitty' to a group of pupils and pausing at intervals to ask them to jot down where they think the real events of the story are actually happening. The more sophisticated will swiftly understand that everything takes place in a small American town, and that the dramatic adventures are all in Mitty's head. Others will only reach this conclusion at the very end. Some will believe that events shuttle, as in a film, between the town and the hydroplane or the trenches, or that the action scenes are memories of actual occasions described in flashback. Some will believe that the real story takes place in a war, and that it is the scenes with his wife that are dreams or memories.

The fact that some of these readings are unacceptable does not mean that they are necessarily unsatisfying at the time for the readers (we do not normally *choose* to read stories 'wrongly'). Any of us can neglect aspects of a work, misread information or give a wholly personal symbolic stress to certain objects or events. The test is how far the interpretation can convince other readers of its validity. Of Walter Mitty's two styles of speech and behaviour, each appropriate to a different context, which would be more likely to belong to real life and which to fantasy? What expectations do we have of a story of this kind? What seems the most appropriate reading of the ending? Consensus seems the only simple test. Agreement comes about not because different readers have identical responses, but because they all make meaning from the same text and from shared experiences of the real world. When our interpretations are shared by others we feel more strongly that they are somehow 'objective', rather than simply rationalisations of our own feelings.

Literary texts are organised so that readers can feel certain that they are answering 'correctly' some of the implied questions about meaning, but less certain about others. When Dickens begins *Little Dorrit*

> Thirty years ago, Marseilles lay burning in the sun one day. A blazing sun upon a fierce August day was no greater rarity in Southern France than at any other time before or since.

only one correct answer is possible to questions like:

> In what month and how long ago is this opening description said to be?
> In what country and city is it set?

or Was this unusual weather for that place and time of year?

The same answers would be given to the implied questions on the tenth reading as on the first. When, one page later, we read:

> In Marseilles that day there was a villainous prison. Like a well, like a vault, like a tomb, the prison had no knowledge of the brightness outside.

there is more than one answer to questions like:

> Why is the prison described as 'villainous'?
> What is the effect on the reader of the sequence of images used to describe the prison?

A reader encountering these words for the first time is likely to answer in different terms from one who has just finished the whole book, or from one who has also studied what critics say about the theme of imprisonment in *Little Dorrit*.

The practical problem, then, is: Do we permit students to hold *any* view of the text being studied? If there is no authoritative 'meaning', how can we judge (let alone grade) our students' approximations to it? How do we 'teach' them? On what grounds do we claim that our reading of a text is more 'valid' than theirs?

The simple response to doubts about student autonomy is to examine the alternative. If a student *really* holds a view, then what are we asking him/her to do? To pretend *not* to believe it, and to parrot an interpretation he/she does not actually hold? The problem is only real if we believe that interpretations are absolute and unchanging, and literary history or memory should disabuse us of this. Surely we can all remember reading *Emma* or *Mansfield Park* in quite different ways in school, at university and at different times in our teaching career. The fact that I now view *Mansfield Park* or *Little Dorrit* differently from the way I did implies that I may well see them differently again in a few years' time. Of course, the 'I' that did, or will do, the reading is not the same as the 'I' that is writing these words. At the moment, however, I am convinced that my current reading of the novel is the 'correct' one. This does not mean that I cannot entertain interpretations and judgements that differ from my own, but that they will all either seem to some degree mistaken and unconvincing, or they will convince me that in some respect they are more perceptive than my existing view. In the latter case, I modify my own position. In engaging with these other views, my own may shift imperceptibly or dramatically, but this will not be because they are objectively 'right' but because *now* they have become part of 'my' reading.

This is the process, then, in which we are asking our students to engage. We are *not* trying to get them insincerely to take on board, ready-made, a reading which is presented to them either as the 'right' one, or the teacher's, or the one that the examiner will expect. Surely we are trying both in the actual process of shared reading of the text and in subsequent discussion of it to help students articulate their interpretations and judgements, so that they understand more clearly what it is they feel, define more precisely where differences of opinion exist, and engage in the mutual modification of views that suggests progress in learning. The notions that people can be persuaded, that interpretations are developing, not static, are essential if students are to feel that literary criticism has any value.

NOTES

1. Geoff Fox, 'Reading fiction — starting where the kids are' in John L. Foster (ed.), *Reluctant Readers?*, Ward Lock, 1977, pp. 17ff.

2. APU, *Language Performance in Schools*, Secondary Survey Report No. 1, H.M.S.O., 1982, pp. 40–1.

3. David H. Russell, *The Dynamics of Reading*, Ginn-Blaisdell, Waltham, Massachusetts, 1970, p. 207.

4. Gill Frith, 'Reading and Response: some questions and no answers', *English in Education*, vol. 13, no. 1, Spring 1979, p. 31.

5. Horst Ruthrof, *The Reader's Construction of Narrative*, Routledge and Kegan Paul, 1981, p. 77.

6. F. R. Leavis, *Education and the University*, Chatto and Windus, 1943, p. 70.

7. Georges Poulet, 'Phenomenology of Reading', *New Literary History*, vol. 1, no. 1, Fall 1969, pp. 53–68.

8. Norman N. Holland, *Poems in Persons*, Norton, New York, 1973, p. 146.

9. Wolfgang Iser, *The Act of Reading*, Routledge and Kegan Paul, 1978, p. 109.

10. Frank Smith, *Writing and the Writer*, Holt, Rinehart and Winston, New York, 1982, p. 193.

11. A. N. Applebee, *The Child's Concept of Story*, Chicago UP, 1978.

12. Gordon H. Bower, 'Experiments on story understanding and recall', *Quarterly Journal of Experimental Psychology*, vol. 28, 1976, pp. 511–34.

13. N. L. Stein and C. G. Glenn, 'An analysis of story comprehension in elementary school children' in Roy O. Freedle (ed.), *New Directions in Discourse Processing*, Ablex, New Jersey, 1979, pp. 53–120.

14. W. K. Wimsatt Jr. and Monroe C. Beardsley, 'The Intentional Fallacy' in *The Verbal Icon*, University of Kentucky Press, 1954.

15. Horst Ruthrof, *The Reader's Construction of Narrative*, p. 4.

16. E. L. Thorndike continued to use this phrase in a number of works (e.g. *Human Learning*, MIT Press, Cambridge, Mass., 1931, p. 149 and *Man and His Works*, Harvard U.P., Cambridge, Mass., 1943, chapter four) though with increasing belief in a hypothesis that would explain the variations.

30 *Words into Life*

● Paul Zindel

I have been invited to share a few words with you about what's on my mind these days, and I find those few words fall into two categories: (a) is there really any such animal as a novel for young adults? and (b) if there is, what should we do with it? Well, there is such an animal and we should use it to disimprison our youth.

First, I must describe the animal to you as I see it:

It is SCHOOL ORIENTED. Teenagers go to school, and quite naturally are stimulated by academic references and environments in their fiction. In *The Pigman* much of my international fan mail tells of the delight in finding its hero set off a firecracker in the boys' bathroom. Also, young readers love to discover that other school cafeterias exist which serve soup tasting like boiled sneakers. And they absolutely adore hyperbole when applied to teachers and librarians, whether it is the humour of nicknaming one 'The Cricket' or the pathos of one who kept her dying mother in a bed in the living room.

Young people like stories in which the PARENTS HAVE SMALL ROLES. There are exceptions to all these points but let's not quibble. The teen years are the time to break away and define one's Self, and a young reader will sniff suspiciously if he comes across too many paragraphs devoted to how omnipotently competent and deliriously happy the adults are — particularly because he knows there are now about eight thousand self-help books on the market for these older astute folk. In *My Darling, My Hamburger* I deliberately kept the parents in the background because that was the way the story unfolded in real life. Liz, who goes to get an abortion, really couldn't turn to her mother or father because they were (you might as well know here although it isn't in the book) both over six feet tall, loud, domineering, and surrounded their children with the largest appliances in the world, including a General Electric toaster which could pop out eight slices at a clip.

Young people love books written in the FIRST PERSON. This point of view demands that every word of the book be as a kid would see and say it. In my *Confessions of a Teenage Baboon* I found the technique particularly successful because it allowed me to deal with the threats to a boy's sexuality without rapaciously ripping into some of the more ghastly adult opinions I have about that subject — opinions which would bore the pants off any kid. My young narrator never once had to tiptoe through the complexities of transvestism and sexual preference and all those other euphemisms which fairly well keep the lid on what is basically a crippling script.

DELICIOUS LANGUAGE is also important; language which gives the appearance of being contemporary but not so trendy that it will date in ten years. Oxymorons are worshipped here, second only to phrases which combine the sublime with the unexpectedly absurd — for example, a raccoon sandwich. I took my lead here from an article in *The New York Times* on stories written and published by teenagers themselves. One girl called her story 'She Was Nice to Mice'. A boy called his story 'The Cockroach of the 86th Street Crosstown Bus'. Why should adults writing for the young adult be any less creative? Of course, I test-market my titles with the kids. My newest book *The Undertaker's Gone Bananas* was originally called *The Mortician's Gone Nuts*, but when I went into classrooms for advice the pupils asked me 'What's a mortician?' I queried, 'Do you know what an undertaker is?' They all said, 'Oh, yes!' Then I quizzed them on their favourite word for insane and discovered it was the same word that was popular when I was in school thirty years ago. Any word that's around for thirty years is no longer slang except for purists badly in need of a high colonic.

Kids love romance. ROMANCE! No explanation necessary except that it's hard to come by at any age.

HONESTY. H. L. Menchen said 'Youth, though it may lack knowledge, is certainly not devoid of intelligence. It can see through shams with a sharp and terrible eye.' If he didn't say it, he said something like it. In *I Never Loved Your Mind* I had to use a few invectives because that was how those kids spoke. And Yvette, the earth-girl had to go off and leave Dewey the Innocent, and . . . oh, I'm just going to stop this paragraph right here because I think I'm beginning to stretch things a bit just to get in the name of every one of my books. More succinctly, kids like a pancake called a pancake.

And MISCHIEF — this is the one quality I find adults tend to phase out and enjoy more by proxy or through ribald humoresques told by barbers, and women's movement magazines. Mischief is, of course, a form of play, sometimes risky play. In all of my books I make certain the young reader gets his share of off-stage and on-stage mad kids doing things like dropping balloons filled with water from roofs or getting dressed up in costumes for various effects; clerical garb is a favourite. Offering candies at a party and then telling the munchers that they really aren't chocolate-covered Rice Krispies, but indeed ants — runs a close second. TRANSITIONAL PICTURES are greatly appreciated and I used them abundantly in *The Pigman* — a relief from cold hard print, which actually is the way kids write. *Literary graffiti* — they love to put doodles and arrows and other graphics on their compositions and epistles. Letters in *italics* are even appreciated, and considering the escalation of printing costs it's a good thing I chose only such relief for *Pardon Me, You're Stepping On My Eyeball*. Thanks to the letters connected to the character of Marsh Mellow, that book is the most italicized tome in history.

Needless to say, young adults like ACTION AND SUSPENSE. This was made somewhat clear to me when I was a high school sophomore and our English teacher, Miss Kalling, who was a Shakespearean scholar, threatened to jump out of the third floor classroom window and land head-first on the cement below. We, the students, were being particularly inattentive while she was dramatizing one of the more provocative speeches from *All's Well that Ends Well*, when she screamed and rushed to the window, throwing it open and swinging her not terribly unattractive legs over the ledge. 'Stop this or I'll jump!' she ordered, seated, prepared to fly. The class in unison responded swiftly: 'Jump!' A certain Mr Stuart, then the Dean of Boys (he's dead now), darted in the front door and secured Miss Kalling before she could follow through with her temptation and one could sense the disappointment of the youngsters in the room.

What is most vital is that a book for young adults should be SHORT. Short books for short book reports! This may appear to be bathos of a sort, but it is not.

Herewith are halted the ten articulations of the animal known as a novel for young adults. There is probably an eleventh implied in this letter from Kathie Willhite of Tulsa, Oklahoma: *To Mr Paul Zindel* —

> When you feel something very deeply it is often difficult to say exactly what is rattling around in your brain. 'Ah ha!' you say, 'An insane teenager has written to me!' Not far off base really. I just finished *Pardon Me, You're Stepping on my Eyeball*. It pulled part of me out and I want to finish this letter before that part of me goes back in. I am still not quite coherent and usually that means I'm at my best. I wanted to cry so bad that it hurt. Something in me refused to let go and I couldn't. I know a person like Marsh Mellow who hides sometimes from reality and I think that is what held in the tears. I cried too many times for him and I just didn't have any left for Marsh. I don't know why and I won't hazard a guess but I am almost afraid to read any of your other books. I cannot see what makes a person write such a book but it had a part of everyone in it and I can't tell which one was me. I'm moved and I'm almost speechless and I want you to know that.

I think what this girl was telling me was that she understood the emotional investment from my remembered youth and my selfish insistence that each story I write must solve a problem for *me*!

[...] Now on to how these young adult books should be used to improve the lives of our youth. A book is created by a writer who observes life and then freezes it into words. I think here's where we really need the school experience and the inspired teacher and librarian. It's all very nice that a kid can have a good read on his own. It's all very pleasant if a class, miraculously rare, can have their fun at the same time, too. But what I find most exciting is when the words of the book are turned back into life. A book is a departure point from which·kids can take a page, a written event — and turn it into an experience. The actual experience captured in the book is not half as important as a kid *himself* being able to speak out in a class and to say:

> Hey, I understand what these words say, that John Conlan sat across from his girlfriend and they had secrets to share over a candlelit dinner they concocted; And Hey, I think I would have done something else if I was left alone in a house with a girl like that. I would have behaved differently here and the same as John at another point; And Hey, this event reminds me of the time I was alone with a girl in a cemetary and we told each other we heard footsteps and thought we saw a hand reach out of a grave!

What I'm trying to say is that a young adult book in particular offers a grand opportunity to take full advantage of word and phrase configurations as a take-off point from which a boy and girl can enter into the *performance* of life. Jung knew a single alien letter from an unknown alphabet was enough to trigger endless thoughts in the human mind. Imagine the power of a whole book in the hands of a teacher and class. A paragraph would be enough to provoke a balance between sending and receiving which must occur in the learning process. Right now in America we are just beginning to dream of turning away from fact bombardment and opening up our ears to listen to the kids. So many of our pupils are breathtakingly ignorant, and I mean that in the loftiest sense of the word. The rather shocking and horrible part of having created so many dummies is that, precisely as stated, they were *created*. We were so busy sending information we never let the kids speak up for themselves. The scenario went as follows: a lot of kids were made to feel they were not very worthy. The villains were the schools, teachers, parents, peers, and several mogul-dominated electronic devices. Kids who were not fed back a positive image of themselves, mainly due to a lack of opportunity to express themselves, did one of three things: they became as silent as wallpaper; they developed into neurotics floundering in psychosomatic ills; or they committed acts of violence in proportion to the acts of neglect; the refusals to let them contribute or *perform*. There is that word again. So many children in schools are denied expressing their experiences, and hearing of the experiences of others. So many never had a chance to think of goals, success paths, or simply, opportunities to practise showing their emotions.

Gaining confidence and belief that one *could* speak to groups were never our recent priorities for the young. There was little chance to learn that one has a right to talk, or how to vitalize expression, or how to give appreciation to others for sharing. Books in schools could have been used to help each pupil crash through his or her shell of self-consciousness — or for the garrulous few, to help them shut up once in a while. Almost all speech therapists agree the biggest problem they have in improving a person's speech is to get a person to open his mouth. Our schools have been for open books and closed mouths. To hell with that. Let's let our kids lift their books *and* their voices. Maybe, just maybe, the young will no longer hate reading, school, and the world as much. Words should at every age mean a better life for the reader.

31 *Efferent and Aesthetic Transactions*

- Louise M. Rosenblatt

The transactional paradigm applies to all reading-events. The reader actively creates meaning under guidance of the printed symbols, no matter whether in a newspaper or the text of Virginia Woolf's *To the Lighthouse*. From the beginning, I have emphasized the difference between reading, for example, a novel and a social science text, and I have been concerned with the development of an explanation which differentiates the aesthetic transaction — the evocation of a poem, a novel, a play — from other kinds of reading (Rosenblatt, 1938, 1969, 1978). Aestheticians have, of course, expressed this general distinction in a variety of ways, some more acceptable than others, yet the heart of the matter for reading — what the reader *does* in these kinds of reading — seems to have been glossed over or at best only tacitly admitted.

In general, most weight has been placed on the text, the set of verbal symbols. The essence of the poetic or aesthetic is often attributed to the author's 'poetic' or expressive language, to such linguistic details as the deviations from normal syntax, or to imagery. Sometimes the essentially poetic is found in the content, such as Poe's ideal subject, the death of a beautiful woman. Obviously, as I have insisted, the text is important. A Keats text will reward an aesthetic reading more than, say, a legal text. Yet the pop poets have been reminding us that the seemingly most mundane and refractory texts may become materials for poetry. The difficulty in looking only at the text, we must recall, is that any text — no matter what its author's intention — can be read either aesthetically or efferently, to use the term that, as I shall explain below, I apply to the nonaesthetic.

Those who emphasize literature's remoteness from 'real life' (often designated as fictionality or 'aesthetic distance'), also fail to isolate what is special to the verbal work of art. To express the contrast, for example, in terms of an opposition between 'participation' in actual life and the 'spectator role' in literature (Britton, 1970) is to use a metaphor that obscures the directly-experienced, dynamic character of the literary work. Moreover, the contrast with actual life applies to all kinds of reading; a scientific formula or an historical account is as much a way of *looking on* at actual life as is a story or a poem.

The Two Stances. The difference between these kinds of reading lies elsewhere — in what the reader *does*, where he or she turns his or her attention during the transaction with the text.

In *efferent* (nonaesthetic) reading, the reader's attention is centred on what should be retained as a residue *after* the actual reading-event — the information to be acquired, for example, from the label on a medicine bottle; or the operations to be carried out, as in a scientific experiment; the conclusion to be reached, as in a legal brief; or the actions to be performed, as in a recipe. I have sometimes thought of this as 'instrumental' reading, but this criterion of practical purpose also breaks down. Hence I have chosen to call this kind of reading *efferent*, from the Latin *efferre*, to carry away. The reader's attention is focused mainly on what the words refer to, on what is to be taken away from the transaction.

In the *aesthetic transaction*, the reader's attention is focused on *what he is living through during the reading-event*. He is attending *both* to what the verbal signs designate *and* to the qualitative overtones of the ideas, images, situations, and characters that he is evoking under guidance of the text. The literary work of art comes into being through the reader's attention to what the text activates within him.[1]

Any literary transaction will fall somewhere in the continuum between the aesthetic and the efferent poles.

The transaction between a reader and a text involves the reader in a highly complex ongoing process of selection and organization. We need not pause here to deal with the primary level of recognition of the printed signs. As soon as we turn to the matter of their lexical or semantic interpretation as symbols, we find ourselves involved in consideration of 'what the reader brings' to the text — a fund of past linguistic, literary and life experiences. The reader must select out from the multiple meanings and associations activated by the verbal signs. Extrinsic or intrinsic cues suggest the general stance to adopt — whether primarily efferent or aesthetic — since this provides the basic principle for selecting what to pay attention to. Drawing on past experience, the reader must also sense some organizing principle or framework suggested by the opening verbal cues. This will guide interpretation and organization of the further cues as the text unrolls. If elements appear that cannot be synthesized into the earlier framework, there may be revision or even a complete reversal and rereading.

For the efferent reading of, for example, a newspaper or a scientific work, another text, a paraphrase or restatement, or a summary by another reader may serve. But for an aesthetic transaction, no one else can substitute and no other text can serve. The reader must personally select out and synthesize the ideas, feelings and images that have been aroused within by that particular set of verbal signs. Throughout, in the evocation of the poem or novel or play, there is a to-and-fro movement of attention between the words and the experienced, felt, meanings being elicited, organized, and reorganized. The literary work 'happens' during the aesthetic transaction. Recognition of the importance of the reader's stance, or focus of attention, in the aesthetic transaction is unfortunately lacking even in theoretical treatments that seem to emphasize the reader but still seek the aesthetic factor entirely in the text.

The reader, then, is not passively receiving the imprint of an already-formed 'object' encased in the text. Nor is the reader merely a distanced spectator. Readers' feeling that they are looking on at the characters and situations of a novel does not contradict the fact that they themselves called forth those scenes during the transaction with the text. They have had to draw on their individual past experiences of language and of life to provide the raw materials for this new experience. Hence, even when we feel ourselves as onlookers at the characters and situations of a novel we are also *participants*, having ourselves created the scenes that unroll before us. The aesthetic transaction is not vicarious experience, not 'virtual' experience, but a special kind of experience in its own right.

The transactional concept of 'the evocation' should save us from the fallacy of reducing the poem to a set of theoretical categories. The tendency is to turn away from the lived-through experience and to efferently apply a ready-made system of analysis to the reading. The structuralists draw on the analogy with Saussurian linguistics to see the text as manifesting a particular set of codes, for example, social, moral, literary. The linguists analyse the text as a set of phonemic, morphemic, syntactic patterns, as do some analysts of style. The Freudians would reduce the work to particular defense mechanisms or symbols of postulated unconscious drives underlying a reading. The Marxists apply a similarly reductive type of analysis. Such analysts are perhaps psychologists, bibliotherapists, semiologists, social or economic analysts and historians, or linguists. They are doing something different from analysis of response to the poem or story or play *as evocation*.

The literary transaction, as a form of human behaviour, can be fruitfully studied from the point of view of any discipline (Rosenblatt, 1976, Pt. 3; 1978, chap. 7). But from a literary point of view, such analysis is useful only if it illuminates, places in a context, and does not destroy or ignore the lived-through structured evocation which the reader sees as the work of art corresponding to the text and which is the 'object' responded to both during and after the reading. Keeping the reader's active process of evocation of the work central — keeping the aesthetic transaction central — will have important implications for questions raised and methods used in both teaching and research.

Evocation and Response. It is now possible to refine our understanding of 'response to literature'. To what, in fact, do we respond? Often the term is used rather loosely to cover two processes — both the aesthetic relationship to the text and our response to the work that we are evoking. Hence, I prefer to speak of, first, *the evocation* — what we sense as the structured experience corresponding to the text — and second, *the response* to the evocation. In our transaction with Dickens's text, *Great Expectations*, for example, we evoke the characters of Pip and Joe. We participate in their relationship and, at the same time, we respond with approval or disapproval to their words and actions. We see parallels in our own lives; perhaps we savour the vividness of imagery or linguistic exuberance. All of these processes may be going on at the same time. Later reflections on the transaction can be seen as an effort (a) to recapture, to reenact the evocation, and (b) to organize and elaborate our ongoing responses to it.

TRANSACTIONAL CONCEPTS

Concern with research on response to literature and the teaching of literature requires clarification of the underlying theoretical model, since the model influences the questions we ask, the formulation of hypotheses, and the research methods used to test them. It affects the teaching situations we study and the criteria of evaluation we apply. Hence the importance of the[se] distinctions:

- The concept of reading as an event involving a particular reader, a particular text, at a particular time, under particular circumstances.
- The concept of the *transaction* between reader and text as a reciprocal *process*, in contrast to notions of the passive reader acted on by the text, or the passive text acted on by the reader.
- The concept of *stance* or focus of attention, which leads the reader to select from a broader or narrower range of the elements of consciousness activated in transaction with the text.
- The concept of the *efferent transaction* in which the reader's selective attention during the reading is focused mainly on the public referents of the words, on the ideas being developed for retention after the reading.
- The concept of the *aesthetic transaction* in which the reader's attention during the reading is focused on his or her lived-through evocation of the literary work.
- The concept of *the evocation*: the aesthetic transaction with the text is a process in which the reader selects out ideas, sensations, feelings, and images drawn from his past linguistic, literary and life experience, and synthesizes them into a new experience, the evocation — the poem, story, novel, or play.

● The concept of the *response to the evocation*, generated during and after the aesthetic transaction.

NOTE

1. Where I use *efferent*, Britton (1970) uses *transaction* and *transactional*. Britton's association is evidently with practical 'real life' affairs, as in 'commercial transaction'. He obviously is not thinking of the two-way process (a buyer implies a seller, and vice-versa) as the reason for calling it a transaction. When I use transaction or transactional, I am indicating the reciprocal relationship in all reading events.

   Where Britton uses *spectator role*, I use *aesthetic stance*. It is regrettable that in this field, as in others, terminological problems have arisen, especially since in many ways Britton reinforces and supports much that I have been saying since 1938. Britton seems to derive his terminology mainly from the point of view of the *speaker* and *writer*, which is another reason why his terminology does not fully take care of the aesthetic *reading* transaction.

REFERENCES

Britton, J. *Language and learning*. Coral Gables, FL: University of Miami Press, 1970.

Rosenblatt, L. M. *Literature as exploration*. New York: Appleton-Century, 1938; revised ed., New York: Noble & Noble, 1968; London: Heinemann, 1970; 3rd ed. New York: Noble & Noble, 1976; reprinted New York: Modern Language Association, 1983.

Rosenblatt, L. M. Towards a transactional theory of reading. *Journal of Reading Behavior*, 1969, *1*, 31–49.

Rosenblatt, L. M. *The reader, the text, the poem: The transactional theory of the literary work*. Carbondale: Southern Illinois University Press, 1978.

VI HOW IT MAY BE TAUGHT

Here, we are at the heart of the matter.

The opening article (34) acts as a general guide to curriculum planning, dealing with the issues involved in preparing a syllabus.

The Language of Literature deals with aspects of the relationship between theory and practice in a structuralist context, and leads on to a clutch of three articles on teaching poetry. How games can be used to assist in the teaching of poetry is the first of these (34), and it is complemented by Woodhead's more sober evaluation of what good poetry teaching entails. The rather strange and unpromising title of Fox and Merrick's article, *Thirty-six things to do with a poem*, belies the useful and sensitive advice they offer. This contains a wealth of practical positives to balance the rather negative tone of the Woodhead.

The Hayhoe and Parker extract stresses the importance of getting the student to become personally and actively engaged in writing. Personal logs, dossiers and the camera lens are but a few of the ways they suggest to achieve this.

Ashton and Bethell offer a variety of techniques for engaging the student's involvement with *Macbeth*, suggesting activities which should help the student in his/her writing about the play.

Exton's article on *Coronation Street* is out of the same stable as Lusted's article on *Grange Hill* and could happily come in Section III. However, he does use children's knowledge of the television serial as a springboard for teaching, so it is very relevant here. It does emphasize the link with Section III and Section I, as it implicitly raises the question of 'what counts as literature'.

The section ends with an assessment of some of the issues involved in Sixth Form teaching of English. The aim here is to build on what has happened in the middle years of school and not to be restricted, as the authors see it, by the demands of public examinations.

The Syllabus: Five Levels of Questioning

● Mike Raleigh and Michael Simons

The business of making a real and useful syllabus need not mean an intensive slog of full-scale meetings in which the department starts (boldly) with the 1st year and finishes (limply) with the 5th year. It could well be a slow process of accretion which involves department sub-groups looking at aspects of current practice as a prelude to forging an overall direction. The most appropriate starting point and style of working will depend on the department's history, its complexion and the ways in which it operates.

Whatever the starting point and the style of working the department adopts it is as well to be aware of the different levels at which discussion about English teaching needs to take place. What follows is a crude outline of the different levels of questioning which should inform the compilation of the syllabus: roughly, 1) WHY, in broad terms 2) WHY, in terms more specific to English 3) WHAT 4) WHEN 5) HOW. No hierarchy is implied by the order here. The levels of questioning overlap and are intimately linked; in fact the making of the connections between the five levels is the centre of the department's work in agreeing a syllabus in which principles and practice cohere. That is the hard bit. Otherwise principles and practice can easily come adrift from one another.

LEVEL ONE: WHY? (THE NUTRITIONAL VALUE)

What kind of child would we ideally like to see emerge from five years of English teaching?

Answering such a question will involve looking at English teaching in relation to broad educational aims and at the social and political context in which schooling takes place. It means the department articulating the ideas it has at the back of its head about children, culture and learning.

These have to be formed in general terms. A department might identify, for example, a wish to encourage children to:

— take responsibility for their own actions and their own learning;
— develop a critical consciousness about themselves and the society in which they live;
— work co-operatively with others.

It is clear that a department with broad educational aims of this kind could well find their views to be in conflict with the school's current — though perhaps inarticulate — notion of what it is about. The brand of English teaching which identifies aims of this kind has oppositional elements built into its function — and these need to be discussed and thought through.

Questions about children, culture and learning are heavy matters and since they inevitably involve talking about issues of race, sex and class, they are almost bound to be controversial ones. For some departments they will not provide the most sensible *starting point* for syllabus discussions. But they cannot in the end be ignored; nor can agreement about the answers be assumed.

LEVEL TWO: WHY? (THE INGREDIENTS)

What role does English teaching play in the development of children's use of language?

Answering this question involves a focus on the components of English teaching and on the development of the child as a skilled user of language. It means a consideration of ideas about the nature of language and language development and a consideration of the kinds of context which most effectively support it. Among the issues for discussion here are:

— the varieties of function within the modes of talking, reading, writing;
— teachers' attitudes to children's language;
— notions of correctness and appropriateness;
— what children need to know *about* language;
— the relationship between speech and writing;
— what writing is for and how it gets done;
— the nature of the reading process and of comprehension;
— what literature can do for people and how it does it;
— the linguistic demands of adult life.

The answers teachers propose to the first level of questioning (what kind of child?) will obviously have a bearing on their attitudes to issues such as these at this second level. Those teachers who believe, for example, that the major function of schooling is to encourage children to regard themselves and value themselves as active learners are likely to respond to a view of the reading process, for example, as an active business in which readers *make* texts mean something. So in considering attitudes to issues of language and its development we are getting closer to the ground, to the shaping of classroom practice. What discussion might produce here is a series of 'statements of principle' about reading, writing and talking out of which classroom practice should grow.

LEVEL THREE: WHAT? (THE RECIPE)

What is the proper stuff of English?

Answering this question involves consideration of the relationship between *content* and *process* in English teaching. It means looking at what the department sees as its rightful territory in terms of material and as its proper ways of managing that territory — in other words how English teaching goes about its business in ways distinct from other subjects. The agenda at this level will very much be determined by the department's views on issues at the second level, and will look directly at how these views on language and language development should take shape in the material and activities to be used in the classroom. In addition there may be areas of content suggested here by the department's views on issues at level one; a study of how newspapers report the news might be implied, for example, by the belief in the need to develop pupils' critical thinking.

So while the focus here is on 'what to do' in terms of topics, themes, units of work or items of literature, choice of content is not something to be made independently of either language process or value. The department needs to develop criteria for choosing content in terms of what pupils will do with it and what they will get out of it. The department might consider here for example:

— what kinds of literature pupils should be encouraged to read, and whether literature is something pupils should 'know about' or simply experience in quantity;
— the part that simply 'making things' (stories, poems, plays and so on), with no content strings attached, should have in pupils' experience of English;
— whether themes such as 'The Seasons' or 'Old Age' are to be introduced (for their intrinsic importance? for their social relevance? for their interest to pupils? for their power to stimulate talking and writing?);
— the extent to which children's own cultural interests should form the content of English lessons;
— whether the study of language as a topic in its own right should be included in the curriculum and, if so, in what form;
— whether the study of film and TV is rightfully 'English' and, if so, what form that study should take.

OTHER SUBJECTS

The problems involved in deciding on 'what to do' in English can seem particularly sharp in comparison with other subjects which have apparently clear parameters and solid substances. In geography they do glaciers; in biology they do rats; English has only Language and Life, and the problem of where to draw the lines. In fact the proper stuff of geography and biology is almost as elusive as that of English. Teachers of those subjects worry just as much about the quality of their content (is it worthwhile/illuminating/relevant/interesting/appropriate/accessible?) and about whether the content is getting in the way of pupils' understanding of the subject's special processes (however these are defined). Discussion with other subject teachers about how they decide 'what to do' may be helpful in a general way; more directly the English department's decisions about content may be affected by an awareness of the content their pupils meet in subjects like social studies, careers or health education.

LEVEL FOUR: WHEN? (THE DIET)

How is one year's work in English different from the next?

Answering this question involves consideration of sequence, continuity and development in English teaching. It means looking at the logic and coherence of the department's 5-year programme of work, and at the match between (a) what teachers ask pupils to do in particular phases of that programme, and (b) teachers' expectations of the kind of performance pupils should be producing at different ages. It is a matter here of putting the intentions represented in levels 1–3 into an order of events. Discussion of the match between (a) and (b) will necessarily involve articulating some crude hypotheses about general linguistic, emotional and intellectual tendencies shared by most children at a particular age. Linguistic, emotional and intellectual development, as far as any one individual child is concerned, is not a smoothly linear business; we know enough about sudden spurts and odd delays, about uneven and inconsistent progress, about the 'plateau effect' and deterioration before breakthrough, to realize that any simple plotting of growth would be naive. Mixed ability teaching in English is founded on a reaction against naive and confused notions of development which have assumed, for example, that the test of a child's capacity to respond to a 3rd year curriculum which includes Shakespeare could reasonably be his/her ability to paragraph informational prose at the end of the 2nd year.

But however flexibly mixed ability operates teachers still have to make broad decisions about *when* to do *what* with a class. Such decisions are inevitable, since it is impossible to move forward simultaneously on all fronts; they are also practical necessities if teachers are at least to avoid the nuisance of the 4th years complaining that they wrote their life stories last year or that they have already read *Of Mice and Men*.

CONTENT/PROCESS

Bearing the issues of level 3 in mind, sequence in content and development in process need to be considered together here. Coursebook series in which material is designed for no-one in particular and everyone in general tend to assume a conventional movement in terms of appropriate thematic content from, roughly, 'Animals' to 'Adventure' to 'Ghosts' to 'Parents' to 'Work'. This progression is related to a generalized notion of what children of a certain age are interested in as they move towards 'adult interests'. There is of course no reason, considering content independently, why that progression could not be reversed; it depends, as suggested in level 3, on what you want pupils to do with the material and what you hope they will get out of it. The same applies to the order in which items of literature are put. Given five Steinbeck novels (*The Red Pony, The Pearl, Of Mice and Men, The Grapes of Wrath, Cannery Row*), the conventional response would be to present them to children in that order. There is clearly some sense in that order, but we have all had experiences (*The Pardoner's Tale* with a 1st year, *Flat Stanley* with a 5th year) which overturn the conventional order. In other words, what is demanding or interesting is not so much to do with the material (within certain limits of tolerance) as in what pupils do with it: the language and thinking processes they are expected and willing to operate.

What development means in terms of language processes is a difficult issue — and would be even if there were not substantial differences between individuals in rates and patterns of development. One of the problems is to avoid the 'hierarchy trap': assuming that because one particular skill (in reading, for example, 'questioning the author's intention') *seems* more advanced than another ('reading for literal meaning') it must therefore 'come later'. It may be more helpful to think in terms of establishing everything you would like to develop as early as possible in classroom activities. Then it becomes a matter of marking points in the 5-year span at which you say simply 'more of this', 'better at that', 'confident of this', 'getting closer to that'.

(Sorting out hypotheses, however crude, about development in language process is an essential preliminary to an informed departmental policy about the assessment of individual pupils' performance.)

LEVEL FIVE: HOW? (EATING AND DIGESTION)

What happens in practice?

Answering this question involves looking at the materials the department uses, at teaching strategies, at what pupils *do* and what they *learn*. This is the closest encounter, the level of questioning which really makes a syllabus useful; it refers to that stage of discussion which details what happens in the classroom when the department's broad aims, its ideas about language, its ideas about appropriate content and its ideas about sequence and development are translated into reality. It will be concerned, therefore, with such things as:

— ways of getting work going and sustaining it (is this worksheet interesting, demanding and sensible?);
— the kind of activity or activities to be encouraged in a particular unit of work (how much emphasis should there be on redrafting in the unit on 'Writing Stories for Others'?);
— the patterns of communication in the classroom (should small group discussion be the pattern for work on the poetry anthology in the 3rd year?);
— how pupils respond to being asked to work in particular ways (what do they get out of writing a play with other people?).

WORKING TOGETHER

There is an assumption here that it is sensible for teachers within a department to share the materials they use, to pool their experiences of working in particular ways and to devise materials and plan strategies together. Most teachers in most departments would drink to that. For some departments this kind of shared work on what happens in practice does not happen in any systematic way. This may be partly because of the time that working together needs; it may partly arise from the unspoken belief that teaching (and perhaps English teaching in particular) is heavily dependent on individual inspiration and personal style; working together may also be discouraged by the system of pupil grouping and/or the timetabling.

Departments which have systematically worked together on what happens in practice know that it has immediate rewards. It reduces the pressure on each teacher to find, adapt and produce materials from scratch for their own classes every day of the week. It also broadens individual teachers' ideas of what can be done in the classroom. But it would be a mistake to see this level as strictly pragmatic. The syllabus-making process will not be served simply by swopping worksheets or by getting people to turn the handle together to make new ones. When a department works together on shared materials it creates the possibility of common ground for people to examine and evaluate their own practice — which is something very difficult to do on your own. So discussion at this level is a matter of looking analytically at what you do in order to find out why you do it — and in order then to work out how you can do it better.

EVALUATION

Any intentions which teachers formulate on behalf of their pupils are in a sense provisional; there is a need to evaluate continually the effectiveness of the practices which are to make those intentions operative and, by doing so, to re-examine the intentions. If a department decides, for example, that it wants to encourage understanding of the meaning of forms in literature in the 3rd year, and works out how that is to be done, it needs also to assess the effectiveness of the approach, albeit in an impressionistic way (e.g. by interviewing pupils, asking them to write reports, sharing a series of lessons with another teacher). Feedback from this kind of 'testing' could be used to revise the materials and/or the classroom procedures and possibly the intention itself (the idea may be wrong or have the wrong emphasis; the 3rd year may be the wrong time).

Can it happen?

Setting out in this way the levels of questioning to which syllabus discussion can be addressed may make the business seem elaborate. In a sense it is; designing a real and useful syllabus covers more or less the full spectrum of the department's concerns. Getting the thing done needs calm waters — and most departments work in conditions of varying turbulence. So can it be done? A number of points are worth emphasizing here.

HOW MUCH TIME?

Syllabus-building ought to be a slow process if it is to be worth doing. Attempting only a bit at a time is good sense as well as practical necessity. If the department does not have a meeting period built into the timetable already, there is every good reason to press for it if you are embarking on syllabus-building. Even if the time-tabler can only manage to do that for a miserable single period a week, that at least can be used for administrative matters which might otherwise clog up after-school meetings. It may also be useful to plan for a weekend meeting on the syllabus at an appropriate juncture, even if not everyone can make it.

PRACTICE-THEORY-PRACTICE

Part of the reason why any department would feel weak at the knees faced with syllabus-building as outlined here is the sense of the intellectual weight of levels 1–4 bearing down on level 5, classroom practice. There may be some people in a department who, though quite happy to tell you what they did with *Joby* and how it went, tend to find urgent business elsewhere if explicit discussion of the nature and function of literature is suggested at a meeting.

Every one of the issues raised as examples in levels 1–4 (as well as others not raised) is difficult to explore; books have been written about most of them, often with only a low degree of resolution of the issues. But while it is fair to say that many teachers come to a useful understanding of these issues by a pragmatic route, there is a danger in assuming that experience and commonsense will always lead to a useful understanding of them. The 'commonsense tradition', the hearty denial of the value of 'theory', is a strong one in English teaching. But commonsense is a volatile commodity and what it tells us is reasonable to do varies from year to year. Teaching by commonsense is not teaching without theory (since all practice implies a set of theories) but teaching without thinking, without articulating and analysing the assumptions upon which practice is based.

But, that said, it is the development of practice which is the aim — not the perfection of theory. Practice, analysed and examined, comes first and last; if that is established in work on the syllabus by always starting with and coming back to particular agreed problems at level 5, there is a good chance that the discussions will be anchored not only in classroom reality but in department reality.

WHAT WILL IT LOOK LIKE?

We have got used to the idea of a syllabus as a single, continuous, once-and-for-all-time wad of paper, with everything from general aims to the kinds of dictionaries available jostling for space on closely-typed A4 pages which fade with each new generation of photocopy. The single continuous document guarantees its own obsolescence; the feeling that if you change one thing you will have to get the whole thing done again produces a disinclination to make any revisions at all. The single continuous document is also unlikely to meet realistically the information needs of the different groups of interested people outside the department. Parents, for example, will be more interested in a brief and accessible statement of overall aims and in examples of what you do in lessons than in lists of 3rd year class readers.

Both those considerations suggest the syllabus should be (wait for it!)

a ring-binder folder instead of a stapled wad. The folder could have a number of separate sections — for example:

- a *short* statement outlining the department's philosophy for the whole age range;
- detailed statements of policy on particular areas of concern, like encouraging independent reading for pleasure or helping pupils with spelling difficulty;
- descriptions of organizational matters, like the relationship between English and remedial provision, how cover work is arranged, and so on;
- outlines of general plans and agreed curriculum units for particular years, with annotated lists of relevant stock (and perhaps with the pupil materials for one unit included as illustration);
- titles of books and copies of articles on aspects of English teaching which the department has found useful, and which might form 'prescribed reading' for newcomers.

Other items (the special handout for parents on marking; examination syllabuses; minutes of meetings and so on) can be added to the folder at will, so that it becomes the department's reference book/history book/guide to the galaxy. The sections can be done in whatever stages are appropriate; particular pages can be extracted and revised when necessary, without having to unravel the whole thing.

WHO DOES IT?

Thinking of the syllabus as a series of unassuming sections rather than a seamless dissertation means that the H.O.D. can be relieved of sole responsibility for getting the syllabus devised and written. Subgroups can be set to work on a section with a variety of people (and not only the obvious people) responsible for organizing and chairing meetings, editing the section, and taking it back to the whole department.

Getting discussion going

Seeing the syllabus as a developing, re-negotiable manual-and-manifesto, rather than as a once-and-for-all wad, would seem to make the business less intimidating. This model suggests a series of excursions, led by different people in the department, starting from and coming back to problems which the department identifies. But issues at all five levels will be met on each excursion, and, at some point, discussion held on them in order to establish — and then to write down — what the department thinks. Assumptions which emerge in the course of excursions need to become explicit views: the framework of attitudes and principles which makes bits of practice coherent. The suggestions which follow relate to the five levels outlined above; they are examples of ways of focusing discussion which have been used in departmental meetings or on in-service courses.

LEVEL ONE: WHAT KIND OF CHILD

1. Read together an article or an extract from a book which addresses the issues of childhood, culture and learning either in an educational context (like the Schools Council booklet *The Practical Curriculum*) or in a wider context (like Colin Ward's *The Child and the City* (Penguin)).
2. Ask everyone at a meeting to write down five qualities or virtues (self-discipline, confidence etc) that they think schooling should encourage. Start from there.

LEVEL TWO: LANGUAGE ISSUES

1. Collect a series of statements from articles or books on the particular issue on the agenda (the function and value of literature, for example). Ask members of department at the meeting to put them into the order in which the statements have some 'bite' for them. Start by comparing the different orders people have.
2. At a meeting given over to a general consideration of writing, for example, give everyone three small filing cards and ask them to write down three conditions which they think help people to write successfully. Spread the cards out, organize them into categories and go from there.
3. Draw up a series of questions that the department has on a particular issue (like the nature of reading difficulty). Then invite in an outsider (someone from the Remedial department, an English teacher in another school, or an advisory teacher) to open the discussion using the questions as starters.

LEVEL THREE: THE PROPER STUFF OF ENGLISH

1. Ask everyone in the department to describe one unit of work they do which they feel particularly committed to: what kind and range of activity does it encourage? what do pupils get out of it?
2. Invite someone from humanities/social studies to talk to the English department about the kind of work their department does, perhaps focusing on a particular unit of work. Discussion about this may highlight what is considered specifically 'English' material and approach.

LEVEL FOUR: DEVELOPMENT

1. If pupils' exercise books or folders are retained in school at the end of each year it is possible to look at the differences in the nature and the range of the written tasks they are offered over a period of time. By concentrating on a small sample of pupils it may also be possible to look at the ways pupils of different ages take up and respond to written tasks of a similar kind.
2. Try out a particular bit of work (perhaps a short story or a set of poems) with classes of different ages. By documenting in an impressionistic way what goes on it may be possible to use this evidence to start a discussion on the assumptions normally made of what demands are proper to make of pupils in a given year.

LEVEL FIVE: CLASSROOM PRACTICE

The starting point here is whatever currently raises itself as a problem needing solution — preferably something that catches the widest spectrum of departmental practice with a particular year. It may be, for example, that everyone uses a class reader with a 1st year, and that there is some doubt about what kinds of thing are possible and useful after the book has been read. The particular focus here may be an agreement to compile a booklet of activities for pupils based on an agreed book in order to investigate the possibilities. The sequence of events might be:

1. Children who have read the book are asked to tape a discussion about it so that the department can learn something of the way children respond to it without teacher intervention.
2. A department meeting is given over to a discussion of the book 'at adult level' to see what issues in the book and reactions to it are worth pursuing.
3. Activities based on the book are baldly outlined, tried out on a guinea pig group, and then fully formulated in a home-produced booklet.

The department might then on that basis construct a sort of map illustrating generally the kinds of things which can be done with a class reader and then proceed to develop pupil booklets on other agreed class readers; or move sideways to look at the provision it makes for independent reading — which it may agree the use of class reader is primarily intended to stimulate.

33 *The Language of Literature*

● Richard Exton

Much teaching of literature in schools suffers from a double handicap. On the one hand, it exists within an educational framework which is rigidly hierarchical in countless interlocking ways. On the other hand, it operates within that English tradition which penetrates all aspects of cultural life in this country: namely, a firm separation of creation from criticism, of practice from theory. I would like to explore the consequences of this double handicap and the implications of that inheritance, before offering some modest proposals which may point to avenues of escape. It is not only teachers and teaching which suffer, but also the children who are being educated into the 'naturalness' of the situation in which they find themselves. We owe it to these children to find ways of teaching literature which break out of the narrowing confines of the hierarchies, be they institutional or conceptual, and which free them from the culturally imposed separation of theory and practice.

The English education system is a complex amalgam of often contradictory assumptions, and English as a subject has a strange existence within it. In the earliest stages, 'English' is learning to read, and then to write. The verbs tend to be intransitive, though the question of subject-matter *is* raised from time to time. Then 'English' becomes comprehension, stories, poems and projects. Stories and poems are read (or listened to) and stories and poems are written: there is not much connection between the two. At the other end of the system, 'English' becomes English literature and, to a lesser extent, English language. Here, literature is read and written *about* or language is studied and written *about*. Never are stories and poems written. In between these two extremes, lies the secondary school, which contains, in miniature, the features of the whole system. In the lower school, stories and poems are written and read, but rarely studied; in the middle school 'creative writing' and 'study' take place but are rigidly separated. The examination system confirms/imposes/reflects the conceptual and cultural assumptions built into the total educational system, which in itself contains a giant contradiction: 'creativity' is celebrated, valorised, championed, while 'criticism' is at the pinnacle of the educational hierarchy. And, as if our culture is aware of this contradiction, an intellectual sleight-of-hand comes into play. Only sensitive people can be great artists; criticism is about developed sensitivity; therefore, all parts of the education system can unite in a flowering of sensitivity, and somehow theory and all related problems disappear completely.

What follows is an account of two approaches to literature in the second year of secondary education. The approaches challenge the implicit hierarchies and are firmly rooted in theory, while remaining eminently practical. One 'studies' literature — a short story by Graham Greene — yet is language-based and involves 'creative writing'; the other studies a poem, 'teaches' the idea of simile and metaphor and yet demands that poetry be written. Both lessons challenge the tyranny of taste — that other unwritten hierarchy inscribed in Eng. Lit. — and assume that literature teaching is to do with developing understanding and conceptual skills in *all* our pupils, and concerned with exploring the complex relationship between the formal qualities of a text and the producers and consumers of those texts. More than anything the methods used are designed to give children confidence and recognise their creative power when they read and negotiate with poems, stories and novels.

The starting point for teaching *I Spy*, a short story by Graham Greene, was to demonstrate to the class, a 'lower band' second-year form in a mixed comprehensive in Hackney, that language is a rule-governed system and that every pupil present was a highly skilled manipulator of those rules. I began by asking them to 'read my mind', that is, to predict what word I was about to speak. They had no trouble completing the phrases 'bread and . . .', 'apples and . . .', 'cat and . . .', though I cheated by accepting 'jam' when I had 'butter' in mind. As the game developed with 'the old man crossed the . . .' I was able to show that the answer had to be a particular kind of word — in this case a noun — and once this was accepted I complicated matters with 'the woman put on her hat and . . .' in this case 'left the room'. In other words, it was possible to operate a range of rules, and only knowledge of context would permit a 'correct' mind-reading.

The next stage was to assert that just as language could be seen to be rule-governed, so could literature. And just as the pupils had proved themselves skilful in using their knowledge of the rules of language to read my mind, now I wanted them to demonstrate their knowledge of literature by completing a short story whose first half I would give to them. The class worked in pairs, examining the text closely for clues and trying to identify the rules that were in operation in the story. Although not everyone in the class spotted all the features of the story which permitted accurate predictions, the sharing of different possible endings

— all accepted if they developed plausibly from features in the first half — allowed rich discussion to take place about the nature of narrative and literary conventions. Not all the points made were articulated in the terms in which I am presenting them here, but there was no doubt that learning was taking place and that the class were beginning to think about *how* a narrative worked rather than what it meant or how they felt about it. They were all doing this, whatever their 'ability', and without being intimidated by feelings that they lacked sensitivity or were 'not good at literature'. Indeed, this seems to me to be a crucial strength in work of the kind which derives from a structuralist or post-structuralist tradition.

Many of the issues raised by the children were related to what Roland Barthes calls the cultural or reference code. For example, the crucial fact that the story is set in war-time is indicated by passing references in the text to searchlights and to blackouts. Not all the children recognised, or registered, these references, and consequently their predictions existed within totally different frameworks. Similarly, those children who failed to recognise the signifying system in the 'strangers'' clothes, invented a whole range of possibilities which were logical, but within different narrative frameworks.

The crucial role of cultural reference embodied within the language of a text was clearly revealed; but equally important was a recognition of the notion of genre. The children were able to offer satisfactory endings to the story because they recognised elements in the first part which they had seen in other stories or films. And when, after talking from notes about the ending of the story, I asked them to write, as a continuous narrative, their version, they revealed themselves to be highly skilled manipulators of generic conventions, using totally appropriate language registers. They also demonstrated that they had a good understanding of what Barthes calls the hermeneutic code — that code which carries a narrative forward through a series of enigmas and resolutions until the final resolution which ends the story. They clearly identified a series of potential enigmas in the first part of the story for which they offered a variety of resolutions in their versions.

What I would like to stress in this is the way that the 'study' of a text was combined with 'creative' activity and was firmly rooted in a theoretical framework. The class did further work once they had been provided with the complete text. Drawing upon the idea of all narrative being the movement from one state of equilibrium through a disruption to another modified state of equilibrium — a concept deriving from the French structuralist, Todorov — I asked the pupils, again in pairs, so that ideas and hunches could be tested and shared, to note down a list of facts from the beginning and ending of the story which remained unchanged, and another list of things that had changed. What was revealed was most illuminating. As well as making accessible to thirty 'less-able' 13-year-olds the central theme of the boy's feelings towards his father, the exercise also drew attention to the way that the mother in the story is totally marginalised: she is asleep in bed throughout! A whole range of issues could have been pursued with the class at this point, but the one I chose to concentrate on was the construction of the characters of father and son, once more turning to Barthes, but this time using his notion of the semic code — the narrative code which operates as the organising principle for character. The class were asked to list similarities and differences between Charlie and his father, and through this exercise they developed deeper insights into the story, its language, form and structure. They noted what is made obvious in the story, the tugging at the collar and the use of proverbs, but they also explored more fully that other explicit similarity, the 'doing things in the dark which frightened (them)'. They were able to speculate most fruitfully upon the title of the story in relation to all this. It seems clear that structuralist and post-structuralist approaches to narrative can work well in the second form as well as in the postgraduate seminar.

Approaches deriving from the same tradition have been equally valuable in the teaching of poetry. Poetry presents a problem for many English teachers. They feel that it is somehow 'special', yet may fall victim to the contradiction I mentioned earlier in relation to the whole school system. Of all the 'creative' activities, writing poetry is felt to be the most 'creative', and there are teachers who are quite happy to correct spellings and make critical interventions into children's writing of narratives, who say they 'won't mark poetry'. But poetry criticism is a semi-scientific activity, post-I.A. Richards, and therefore demands rigour. However, Leavis asserts that it is response we are after. So what is the poor English teacher to do? Very often the answer is to forget poetry altogether for large stretches of the school year and then guiltily to bring it out as something special, without providing ways of understanding how poetry works.

The lesson I am going to describe uses an approach[1] that was developed in order to find a non-threatening way of reading and developing understanding of poetry in the English classroom. It is appropriate at all levels and abilities in the comprehensive school, but it does assume that in junior school and in the first years of secondary school children will have been given plenty of opportunities to browse through poetry anthologies, to copy out favourite poems, to make their own mini-anthologies and to experiment themselves with writing poetry of all kinds. In particular it assumes that they may have had the chance to explore, through reading and writing, the formal elements of poetry: rhyme, rhythm, typography, 'sound' poems, 'shape' poems, and so forth. It seems to me to be vital to develop in teaching an understanding of what is specific to poetry. I would not argue, as the Russian formalist critics have done, that poetry is about nothing but itself, but most of my approaches derive from work they developed, and I do think it crucial to understand precisely *how* and therefore *what* a text says, and how we make those meanings, before moving on to make statements about 'life' outside the poem.

The lesson was taught to a mixed-ability second-year class in a girls' comprehensive school in Hackney, in response to a request from a teacher who wished to explore new ways of teaching poetry and who also wished the class to learn about simile and metaphor. The poem I chose to use was 'The Locust'.[2] The lesson took the form of a series of steps. Although in this case the teacher took the traditional position at the blackboard with chalk and duster conducting a 'whole-class' lesson, the aim was to provide the class with a methodology which they could operate in small groups on other poems.

Step one was to instruct the pupils that they must not for the rest of the lesson think about meaning, about what the poem is 'about'. Nor would I ask them about what they 'felt', what their 'response' was, arguing that 'feeling' was a complicated matter and would take a lot of thinking about, and in any event was private to them. I also explained that this first step was the most difficult one — after this things would become easier — but only if they did not think too hard! All of this was designed to take away any idea of threat from the lesson and to make it absolutely clear that every single person in the class was going to be able to take part.

Step two, though not particularly appropriate in this case, was to give the class the title of the poem and invite them to speculate in as free a way as possible on what a poem with this title could be about. This did not contradict Step one because they did not yet have the poem. The value of the exercise is to set up a framework where free association can take place, and frequently the metaphorical implications of poems become clear before the poem itself is seen.

Step three was to read the poem itself, with the class following in their own copies, and to invite them to read it through a few times themselves.

Step four became easier as the basic idea was established, namely, that the class would call out, and I would write haphazardly on the board, any word or phrase which — for whatever reason — drew attention to itself. It might do so because it was unusual, because it rhymed, was repeated, was a contrast, was an echo, was on a line of its own, or for any other reason. Very soon the blackboard was filled with words. In some senses what we had on the board was the poem, but jumbled up. And at that point we moved on to *Step five*, which was simply to list on the board as many of the linguistic features of the poem as we could.

What was interesting at this stage was how observant the class were. They noted very quickly that the poem was structured around the basic device of the question followed by answers; that the pronoun 'it' was constantly repeated; that there were very few verbs apart from 'is'; that the whole poem exists in the present tense. They also said that it had lots of description but noted that there were very few adjectives. It was through this last point that the class were able to explore the functioning of simile and metaphor and to lay the basis for their follow-up lesson, which was to write — in groups — their own poem, using the same structure and form as the poem we were studying: creativity and criticism were brought together and were seen to be mutually supportive and illuminating. The following poems are examples of what the class produced:

> What is a human being?
> It's a machine made to do things
> Its brain, a snake coiled up together
> Its head, the figure point of the body
> Its hair, as long as the grass
> Its skin, as smooth as silk.
> The eyes, the image of a camera
> The nose, the air it breathes.
> Its mouth, made to talk
> Its feet, made to walk
> The body, the main production of life.
> Life and death is it.
> (Marian, Androulla, Barbara)

> What is a Person?
> The hair, strands of thread
> The fingers, bendable sticks
> Finger nails like see-through glass
> The eyes, glowing torches reflecting the world
> The feet, a blind person's stick guiding them through the path of life
> The teeth, the human knife and fork
> The tongue, the taster of food
> The brain, the ruler of the body
> The heart, a steady beat of a drum
> The voice, a telephone
> The nose, like a human oxygen tank and also a sniffer
> The toes, a shorter form of fingers
> The skin, the clothing of the body.
> A person is neither man or woman: just a person.
> (Sharon, Corita)

Step six was to return to the blackboard with the jumbled poem on it and to suggest different groupings, or 'boxes', as I called them. What this class suggested included the following: a *sharp* box — which contained 'knife', 'saw', 'scissors' and 'razor'; a *life* box, which contained 'grain', 'corn', 'eggs', 'rain', 'sun' and 'plant' and a *death* box, containing 'knife', 'clothing for the dead' and 'Desolation'.

Step seven was to look for any patterns that were beginning to take shape. Clearly the dominant one which presented itself was the life/death opposition, and when we moved on to *Step eight*, which is to read the poem again and to try out a few hunches about what the poem might possibly be about the class drew attention to the way that Life and Death are inextricably bound up within the figure of the locust and what it is.

Step nine is a series of questions which shifts the work from the 'creative structuralism' of the previous steps and looks at the poem's relation to a particular social and historical formation. To begin with the class were asked who was 'speaking' the poem. Was it the poet or someone or something the poet has invented to speak through? And next, who is the poem 'spoken' to? Is it to a particular person, or to the poet him- or herself, or to the public in general? What is the speaker's attitude to that audience?

The class decided that the poet was speaking in her or his own person but as a member of a community that had direct experience of the locust. They had problems with the other questions and indeed we were under pressure of time, though those questions have proved invaluable in working on poetry further up the school. The final stage is to consider the poem's shape and form and organisation in relation to all the thinking and talking and exploring that has gone on so far, and certainly by the end of this process the question of meaning, which was banished in *Step one*, has taken care of itself. What is most important, as a teacher of English Literature, is not that a class understand the 'meaning' of a particular poem, but that they can read *any* poem, have insight into how it works and how its meanings are produced, and also have a model for their own writing.

The two lessons I have described are examples of a range of approaches to literature which are based in particular theoretical perspectives but are 'practical' and possible in inner-city mixed-ability classrooms. They do not aim to develop sensitivity but, rather, to contribute to a developing understanding of the nature and function of prose and poetry. They attempt to build on knowledge pupils, of any ability, already have and to combat some of the mystifying rhetoric which often surrounds poetry and Eng. Lit. They also start from a position which argues that it is important for pupils to have access to our assumptions about English as a subject: it is not good enough for a pupil to define what goes on in English lessons as 'reading books and writing stories'. We must begin to break down the anti-intellectual, anti-theoretical tradition which informs much of British cultural life, so that pupils have the tools to analyse the world around them, the literature they read, the films and television they watch, and to make their own decisions.

NOTES

1 HOW TO READ A POEM — a guide in ten easy steps

If possible, follow this guide with one or two friends. If you do, talk about all the possibilities before you write anything down.

Step   1.   Forget about what the poem may or may not mean, or what it may be about.

Step   2.   Look at the title and jot down about half a dozen things that it suggests to you. Give literal meanings as well as associations.

Step   3.   Read the poem once quickly and then three times very slowly. Try to hear the poem aloud in your head.

Step   4.   Make a list of all those things which force their attention on you or which catch your interest for one reason or another. You might jot down unusual/odd/striking words
        or striking rhymes
        or striking rhythms
        or repetitions
        or patterns
        or contrasts
        or echoes etc. etc.

Step   5.   Look at and list any features of the language used in the poem, e.g.
        No capital letters
        No full stops at line-ends
        Presence/absence of adverbs/adjectives
        All verbs active/passive
        Tense — all past until last line, etc.

Step   6.   Try to find groups of words (thematic boxes) e.g.
        (a)   All similes make reference to animals/death/plants, etc.
        (b)   All the first words of lines are conjunctions, etc.
        N.B. Don't worry if your groups of words seem silly or improbable.

Step   7.   Look at your lists, notes and groups. Do you see any pattern taking shape? Try out a few.

Step   8.   Read the poem again and then try out a few hunches about what the poem may mean.

Step   9.   Answer the following questions
        (a)   Who is 'speaking' the poem?
            Is it the poet or has s/he invented someone or something to speak through?
        (b)   Who is the poem 'spoken' to?
            Is it to a particular person
            or to the poet him/herself
            or to the public in general?
        (c)   What is the speaker's attitude to that audience?
            Is it angry, sincere, jokey, teasing?
        (d)   What is the poet's attitude to his/her audience?
        (e)   Why is the poem organised in the way it is?
        (f)   What is the effect of all the things you have noted at Steps 2, 4, 5 and 6?

Step 10.   Now, if you wish to, or *have to* (because of an exam) you can write a critical appreciation of that poem.

NOW   Read the poem again. Good, isn't it?

2 The Locust

What is a locust?
Its head, a grain of corn; its neck, the hinge of a knife;
Its horns, a bit of thread; its chest is smooth and burnished;
Its body is like a knife-handle;
Its hock, a saw; its spittle, ink;
Its underwings, clothing for the dead.
On the ground — it is laying eggs;
In flight — it is like the clouds.
Approaching the ground, it is rain glittering in the sun;
Lighting on a plant, it becomes a pair of scissors;
Walking, it becomes a razor;
Desolation walks with it.

> (Translated from a Madagascan language by A. Marre
> and Willard R. Trask, Traditional)

34   *Poetry Games*

● S. Brownjohn

I see the teaching of poetry writing to children as the teaching of skills and techniques almost as much as the use of original ideas — a love of language and the excitement of exploring its possibilities, of making it work for you. Children are capable of writing with a high degree of sophistication and control if they are encouraged to do so, and we should beware of those who say it cannot, or should not, be done — they merely wish to keep children 'childish', or save themselves some effort. We must not underestimate what children can do.

To achieve this takes time and enthusiasm. Haphazard or halfhearted lip service to teaching poetry will lay no foundations. It is a constant building on layers of knowledge and practice that brings the rewards.

I make no apology for mentioning the teaching of grammar in connection with some of the poetry games. I feel it is important; and good writing, in the end, should be correct in grammar and spelling. Teaching it this way is not only more enjoyable, but also more relevant. Reading and writing poetry — being steeped in poetry — incidentally introduces and reinforces many aspects of English teaching. I would almost go as far as to say that most necessary skills in English can be taught through poetry at this level.

The following games represent only a few of the ways that can be used to encourage children to think about the meaning of words and to use them adventurously. They are fun to play and can be considered as 'warm-up' exercises before a lesson or as a lesson in itself. It is not a good idea to play more than one (or perhaps two) games in one session. Some of these games can lead directly into poems as will be seen.

THE EXQUISITE CORPSE

This game is a version of Consequences and was played by the Dadaists and Surrealists; indeed, it is the surreal quality of the sentences produced which particularly appeals to adults and children alike. There are various ways of playing this game, but the result is always of the same kind.

Each child has a piece of paper on which are drawn several columns. The headings of these can be as follows:

Adjective/Adjective/Noun/Verb/Adjective/Adjective/Noun
or Adjective/Adjective/Noun/Verb/Adverb/Adjective/Adjective/Noun

In other words, the column headings stand for the main parts of speech required to make up an interesting sentence. Some work will have to be done to explain the grammatical terms, but the children will soon learn them by playing the game. Because children often have difficulty in understanding each other's handwriting I usually find the following method of play most successful.

Each child writes down five different adjectives in the first column. (It is best to use lined paper as this will help later.) Five seems to be about the right number. The paper is then folded back so that the first column cannot be seen. Now five different adjectives are written in the second column. This is folded back and five nouns are written, and so on until each column has been filled. When completed, the paper is opened out and the resulting sentences are read across the page with definite or indefinite articles inserted where appropriate. Prepositions can also be added and verbs can be put into the required tense and form.

The sentences usually have a bizarre quality which appeals to the children and occasionally produce a phrase or a whole line that is quite remarkable. These can often be used in future poems. It is these fortuitous combinations of words that can help to show children that poetry does not have to be 'long words', but simple words put together in an unusual way.

As will be obvious, the game can also be played, a whole line at a time, with each person writing a word in a column, folding it back, and passing the paper on to the next person (more like the game of Consequences).

ADVERBS

This is a simple game involving some drama work and can be used to give a clearer understanding of what adverbs are and how they work.

The children sit in a circle while one person leaves the room. Those left behind decide on an adverb on which they all agree (e.g. gloomily). The person outside is called in and must try to guess the adverb. Each child in the circle is asked in turn to illustrate an action in the manner of the adverb. The children might be asked to do simple tasks, like doing up a shoelace, dancing, playing football, writing a letter. While acting them out they must attempt to convey the spirit of the adverb. This forces them to think hard about words and their meanings. Equally, the person guessing has to work at understanding the hints offered.
[...]

I should like to . . .

The idea for this came from the poem 'To Paint the Portrait of a Bird' by Jacques Prévert (translated by Lawrence Ferlinghetti) which can be found in the anthology *Touchstones* 3. Briefly, this poem says that you paint a cage with an open door and place the canvas against a tree. Then you must hide and wait for a bird to enter the cage. As soon as it does you paint the door closed and paint out all the bars. Then you must paint certain things to make the bird sing:

> . . . the green foliage and the wind's freshness
> the dust of the sun
> and the noise of the insects in the summer heat.

It was this part of the poem that gave me the idea of asking the children to write about things they would like to do, which could not normally be done — for example, to hear things you could only normally see, touch or taste, and to see sounds, to taste smells, or touch tastes, although it was not confined solely to the senses. They were asked to write for each 'wish' and to expand the description of it to make each picture more vivid.

I find this particularly useful as an exercise in the first few lessons with a class since it acts as a key to open up their fantasy. When I read them the Prévert poem at least two-thirds of the class always says it is not possible. But once they are off their very rational plane and into this more fantastic world they soon begin to enjoy the idea. It opens up marvellous possibilities and paves the way for more interesting writing in the future. With all the barriers down and the constraints of the real world forgotten, the children are free to experiment with words and ideas.

EXAMPLES

I would like to paint the noise of a vulture on the eastern mountains on a
   summer's evening,
The buzz of the dragonflies on the marsh,
The sound of a humming bird's wings as they go up and down in a plant.
I should like to take home the rays of the moon on a frosty night,
The crinkle of the willows on the lake at the bottom of the world.
I should like to touch the magic of the witch in Hell.
I should like to hear dew on the grass on a cold winter's morning,
The painter's brush wipe on the canvas,
The glow in a tiger's eye on a very dark night,
The calling of a painting to an artist.
I should like to understand the ways of the gods of ancient Mexico,
The animals' thoughts of being locked up in a zoo in the Saturday noise,
The mystery of the dark,
And the paint in the tin, waiting to be mixed.

Roddy Mattinson

I should like to paint the snowflakes' hearts which are beating away to the
    second,
The disobedience of a flag that won't flutter in the breeze,
The heat of a candle in the middle of the night,
The happiness of a merry-go-round which has started spinning,
The coldness in an iceberg's fast running blood,
The hyena's hysterical laugh when it howls at night.

Daniel Phillips

[...]

Sonnets

If anyone had suggested to me a few years ago that I might have eleven-
year-old children writing sonnets I should have laughed at the idea.
However, after teaching the same group of children for two years I
found they had progressed so far, and their enthusiasm was so great,
that I decided to try them on sonnets as an experiment.

I felt the lesson required a more lengthy build-up than usual so I wrote
out two of the more accessible Shakespearean sonnets on the board —
'When I do count the clock that tells the time', and 'My mistress' eyes
are nothing like the sun'. We looked at them one at a time.

I read the sonnet and explained any difficulties of meaning, but
principally asked the children to explain what it was about. When this
was done I asked them what they noticed about the form. Since by now
they knew quite a lot about poetry, they were quickly able to spot the
rhyme scheme and the ten syllable lines. I then explained the rhythm of
each line by marking the feet in the usual way — ∪/ ∪/ ∪/ ∪/ ∪/ — and by
tapping the rhythm while speaking the lines. We enjoyed a short period
of time trying to speak to each other solely in iambic pentameters, which
made something of a game out of fixing the rhythm in their minds. They
had to be steeped in the rhythm in order to be able to escape its
constraints and concentrate on what they wanted to say when it came to
writing.

I then told them of some different sonnet rhyme schemes. They were able
to choose which type of sonnet they would write and I gave them a free
choice of subject. This particular group were never short of ideas for their
writing so I did not always prepare a subject. With many groups it may be
necessary to talk around a particular idea.

[Here is an example of a completed sonnet by one of] these top primary
children. All of them used the Shakespearean form. I would say that it
was a valid exercise although some of the spontaneity is missing at times;
but it was a difficult task! All the children enjoyed doing it although, by
the very nature of the work involved, not all managed to complete their
sonnets.

They may never write another sonnet in their lives but I feel this lesson was worth doing. It opened up a further influence on their work and it certainly made them think hard about words, especially rhymes which, at their reasonably advanced state of development in poetry, they were not content to use to the detriment of their poems. A large amount of re-working was constantly going on to try to make the lines right rhythmically; the rhymes worked, and above all the poems said what they wanted to say.

EXAMPLE

Sonnet

Hundreds of people shouting to the world,
Too many speeches to let people breathe,
Too many hopes in vicious flags unfurled.
Eventually for blood they all will seethe
And war and bombs will start to smother us.
And on Death's pillow which will be uplifted
You'll see without regalia or fuss,
How we the nations civilised have drifted
To dust and hell upon this arid plain.
But from this desert new races will grow
And godliness and peace will live again,
Live men not dead machines will reap and sow.
Then they shall learn to love one another
And so to curse the man who hates his brother.

Matthew Festenstein

35 *Getting the Proper Attention*

● Chris Woodhead

It was last lesson in the afternoon. Outside a sunny day had turned to rain, and a cross-country race plodded its way round the playing fields to the amusement of the children in the class I was observing.

A second year group, they were reading Ted Hughes's poem *Pike* with a student teacher. It reminded me of a hundred similar lessons which I have taught myself: the cold classrooms and battered furniture, the kids in their scruffy uniforms, and the poem blue and blurred on the Banda sheet, disturbingly remote from the audience it was meant to reach.

Things began, however, well. 'Shut your eyes', Felicity commanded, 'and listen to me before we read the poem.' The class obeyed, the giggles subsided, and I marvelled at the magic of silence in the comprehensive classroom.

'Imagine' she said, 'huge fish swimming deep down in the water. Fish that are really fierce: so fierce that they eat each other and only the strongest survive. And now, think of a pond in the grounds of an old monastery. It is night and the water is still. You are fishing there and you become more and more aware of the silence, and of the monsters that might be lurking down there at the bottom of the pond, biding their time until they are ready to rise up through the water to see who you are.'

She stopped talking, but for a minute or two the silence continued. The children were caught: the gap between them and the world of the poem had, it seemed, been bridged, and their concentration continued through the actual reading of the poem which followed. I mentally applauded her, for it was an unusually mesmeric performance by anybody's standards.

But as she approached the last verse I found myself becoming increasingly tense. The old, familiar panic which used to accompany my own reading of poems to children was returning. What next? What do you do when the poem ends? By some miracle the children have been listening, genuinely involved in the poem. Then, abruptly, your voice stops and there is a curious silence.

It is a moment worth examining. At home, if you read a poem to yourself or listen to a reading on the radio, and you are moved by what the poet is saying, then you probably sit for a while after the poem has ended to think about the words and images you can remember, and the effect that they have had on you. What happens in the school English lesson? Do teachers allow for this private and silent period of thought?

Far from it: in my experience, we tend rather to open fire immediately with questions about the meaning of difficult bits. Or we will make platitudinous and/or coercive remarks about how 'powerful' or 'vivid' or 'immediate' the poem is. This at least is the kind of thing I used to do, and though I have visited many very different schools in the past four years, I have yet to find much evidence of a more intelligent practice.

There is, of course, another strategy which teachers use, and it was this tactic which Felicity employed. I cannot now remember her exact words, but she asked who in the class went fishing themselves. What followed was animated chat about the one that got away, fascinating enough and certainly enjoyed by the children (or at least by the boys), but not by any stretch of the imagination very relevant to Ted Hughes's poem.

Felicity herself seemed, in fact, to feel this irrelevance, for she began to steer the class back to the text, asking sharper, much more specific questions. The anecdotes consequently ended. Now it was guesses at the meaning of the word 'malevolent' and touchingly hopeful explanations of how the pond could be 'deep as England'.

In writing this I do not want in any way to appear critical of Felicity: I myself have pestered countless children with similarly counter-productive questions. But I am certain that all of us who were in that classroom could sense the earlier magic slipping away as this kind of game continued and the poem became a crossword to be solved.

When I talked to Felicity afterwards she explained how she had felt that the children could not understand the poem as a whole unless they understood all the individual words and images. At first sight it seems a logical enough argument. I have, however, little doubt that the pedagogy it helps inspire goes a long way towards explaining why English lessons are often so boring and poems so little read.

But what happens in classrooms where poetry is taught does not, in the end, have much to do with logic. When I taught literature in schools I no doubt had some more or less conscious understanding of its educative value and of how best I could communicate this value to the children I taught. If I had been asked to explain this understanding I could probably have done so, but such an explanation would inevitably have been a rationalization after the event: it is perhaps more important to consider the nature of the classroom and institutional pressures which define our practice when we work with literature.

To return to the silence which follows the end of the reading: our practice here, I have argued, contradicts the lesson we ought to have learnt from our own experience of reading poems, and so destroys what is an essential stage in any genuinely felt response. Why, then, do we tend to sabotage the very educational end we all want?

One fundamental reason is that we are deeply anxious that the children will take advantage of us and escape our control. Unless we crack the pedagogic whip we fear that the circus animals will desert. Silence is fine if I, the teacher, have commanded it. If the pupils have chosen not to speak, then it threatens because they then have the initiative. In poetry lessons as in every other lesson, questioning is a form of social control. We kid ourselves if we pretend that this is not a major reason why we are always probing our pupils' response.

A second reason is perhaps more peculiar to English teachers. How would we ever know a 'genuinely felt response' to a poem if we were ever to meet one? Teachers like, reasonably enough, to feel that they are teaching something, and once English teachers move beyond concrete issues of spelling and punctuation, then it becomes very difficult for them to know whether or not they are achieving anything. Unless, that is, they treat the enterprise of reading literature as a purely intellectual business, and ask questions which test literal comprehension.

Believe that literature makes its impact in a mysterious and elusive way, and that children are unlikely to be any better than we adults at articulating how they feel in response to a work of art, and you have to tolerate a real burden of anxiety. Life is simply more comfortable if you fill the silence and question the children, guide their response to the poems which are read, and then mark their version of what you have told them: all these are tactics which help maintain a healthy ego. What they contribute to the pupils' enjoyment and appreciation of literature is another matter.

There is finally the point that if the poem has really worked with the class then we are probably a little embarrassed. The clearest example I can give from my own teaching experience of what I mean is a reaction provoked not by a poem but by a film, *Cathy Come Home*. But the point is the same. When the film finished there were 10 minutes to fill with 'discussion'. I found the fact that the class was clearly too upset to talk about what they had seen acutely disturbing. I wanted to defuse the situation, bring it down to a less emotional level where we could talk, sensibly and intelligently, about the social issues involved. Our culture as a whole does not seem to like emotion, and our classrooms are certainly not geared to engage profitably with it.

Taken together these three factors explain something of why not just Felicity but most English teachers fail when they teach poetry. They need, moreover, to be set against the background of a curriculum which is exclusively preoccupied with what Robert Witkin calls 'the public world of fact'. A lesson which aims to relate the words on the page to the experience and feelings of the pupils fits uneasily, if at all, into this kind of framework.

In a sense, too, it is more difficult for the pupils than it is for the teacher. What place does the inner world of feeling — that sense of mystery, awe and fear *Pike*, for instance, conjures up — have in chemistry, French or even history? And if English teachers do avoid in teaching poetry the kind of pedagogy I have criticized above, then the shock to their pupils is going to be all the greater. A lesson where you have to sit and think and feel! A lesson where the teacher is not interested in the speed with which you can grasp the point and articulate your understanding!

Willing as children are to comply with all the different demands made on them as they scuttle from lesson to lesson, they are going to see a teacher who acts like this as a curious beast indeed. 'Tell us the answer, sir, you know what it is.' To reply that you do not, and that your answer might not be theirs, is likely to cause no little upset. It is hardly surprising that in our desire to avoid this upset we tend to conform to a style of teaching nicely calculated to destroy that proper attention to poetry we are supposed to be fostering.

What constitutes a 'proper attention' depends obviously enough on the age of the children being taught; what needs remembering is that there is always both the poem, and the child who reads the poem. If institutional pressures explain something of why teachers depend so heavily on comprehension questions when teaching poetry, nevertheless such questions spring from a desire to develop a finer, more complete appreciation in the pupils of the poem as a carefully wrought verbal construct. The danger is that in emphasizing verbal complexities we forget the child.

Alternatively, it is the children who are focused upon, their reactions and experience, and the poem is used only as a springboard. So Felicity encouraged her children to talk about fishing. To give a more disturbing example — since the book must be one of the most popular poetry anthologies used in schools — the authors of *Touchstones* set writing exercises which tend to ask the children to think not so much about what is uniquely defined in the poem, as about anything which they have done or felt, which might in some ways be relevant to the general theme of the poem.

Whatever the age of the pupil, each of these approaches is an evasion, as is any strategy which does not help each pupil in the class to explore their sense of how *these* words on *this* page engage with and develop their experience and understanding.

This kind of engagement with the text will never be something which is achieved easily. It demands, for a start, that readers escape sufficiently from the bonds of their habitual fantasies to see the poem as an object independent of their own ego. It means attempting to understand why it is that we are moved in the way that we are by the poem. It involves the search for words to articulate what is almost certainly complex, mysterious and elusive.

Each of these things may involve considerable effort. The reward is what R. W. Hepburn has called 'an alert, mobile, exploratory attitude to our emotional life'. But is this what we want, either for ourselves or for the children we teach?

In theory, perhaps. In practice much in our own make-up and almost everything in the institution of school seems to conspire against it.

36 *Thirty-six Things To Do With A Poem*

● Geoff Fox and Brian Merrick

At the 1980 conference of the National Association for the Teaching of English at Warwick University, a group of teachers considered the classroom teaching of literature. It seemed to the group that poetry was rarely popular with pupils in the schools they knew and that a checklist of ideas for teaching poetry might be helpful. The list is introduced here by the group's leaders, Geoff Fox and Brian Merrick, of the School of Education, Exeter University. Specific contributions were also made by Graham Baldwin, Barbara Bleiman, Roz Charlish, Dave Klemm, Colin Padgett and Andrew Stibbs.

The premises which lie behind the suggestions in the list are:

(a) Poetry is to be experienced before it is to be analysed.
(b) The enjoyment of a poem *is* often deepened by analysis, though such close study can be carried out obliquely, not only through line by line study.
(c) Any classroom activity in teaching a poem should bring reader and text closer together, not come between them.
(d) We need to discourage any message, implicit or explicit, that poems are really puzzles in need of solutions.
(e) A poem rarely belongs to its reader on one or two readings, particularly when such readings are immediately followed by an all-class discussion of an evaluative kind; in fact, 'Do you like it?' questions about the whole poem or its diction, rhythm, rhyme, etc., are best deferred as long as possible or not asked at all.
(f) Whether a poem is finally valued or rejected, we need to provide means for reflection upon it, the opportunity for readers and listeners to work in and out of the text.

The contributors to the list make no claims for originality: our hope is that such a checklist might provide a range of possibilities for the inexperienced, two or three new ideas for the experienced, and an *aide memoire* for the frenetically busy.

Ideas are offered not as developed schemes of work, but as starting points, intended to be useful in making poems more accessible to children in the circumstances of most schools. In this rather skeletal form, some suggestions may seem banal or even philistine; but we hope that many of the ideas could be developed and refined for pupils of virtually any school age. Inevitably, some of the ideas would be quite inappropriate to some poems, and we accept that the best teaching of a poem may well arise uniquely from that individual text.

The group at Warwick felt strongly that poetry often needs to have its way prepared. Sometimes, the mood of a class may be such that a particular poem is an appropriate response to that mood; indeed, this way of introducing a poem is surely an essential practice. More frequently, the constraints of a school timetable, especially at the secondary school level, mean that some kind of preparation for a poem is necessary. Talk around and about a topic is perhaps the most common approach. It may be that some preparation through role play is useful: turning the classroom from the moment children come into it that day into a busy railway terminal for Spender's *The Express*; setting up the bar of 'The Red Dragon' as a context for the anecdote of Grave's *Welsh Incident*. More simply, groups could be given only the title of a poem and asked to speculate about the poem's content; or, through concentration exercises and questions, the pupils' store of personal memories can be explored in the silence of their own minds or in a few minutes of private writing.

Some of the Warwick group's more idiosyncratic suggestions have been excluded ('Prepare and deliver a sample of poets' work to houses in streets named after them . . . Keats Way, Chaucer Green, Tennyson Avenue, Betjeman Mews'). We have also deliberately omitted some of the most valuable approaches to reading poetry which stem from pupils writing their own poems. We presuppose that the ideas on the checklist will work most usefully in a climate where children are writing and talking about their own work; to have gone more fully into this area would have doubled the length of the list.

Many of the suggestions imply that children choose poems to work on for themselves. They would need time to browse amongst a range of poetry books — individual copies or small sets — in the classroom; the amount of help they need in this tends to decrease as it becomes a more accustomed practice.

FIRST ENCOUNTERS

1. The pupils listen to a couple of readings of a poem or read it silently, and then jot for five minutes of 'instant reaction' to hold, discover, and begin to develop their own responses.

2. Pupils listen to a taped reading, perhaps with the voices of other staff or pupils from other classes (see 7, below).
3. A poem is read, without discussion, every day for a week (by the teacher and/or by class members who have prepared their readings).
4. A section of a display board in the classroom is reserved for poems (see also 13). These are changed regularly and those that have been on display are put into a file which forms part of the stock available to the class.

SHARING AND PRESENTING POEMS

5. In pairs or groups, children work out ways of presenting different poems in dramatic form to the rest of the class.
6. Pairs or groups prepare their own readings of the same poem; these readings are then heard and compared.
7. Groups make taped versions of poems for their own class, year, or other classes (secondary pupils make tapes for primaries and perhaps vice versa) or exchange anthologies with a 'penfriend' class in another part of the country. Sound effects *et al.* This is a particularly useful activity for a group of enthusiasts — e.g., Poetry Club or Advanced Students.
8. Teacher directs an all-class chorally spoken version, using a tape-recorder in rehearsal to foster the class's own critical refinement. Sound effects.
9. Groups, with the help of specialist colleagues if necessary, prepare some movement work to accompany a reading of the poem.
10. Children choose photographs or slides to project during their reading of a poem.
11. Episodic poems (e.g., ballads) are presented in a frieze to be displayed around the room. Each child is allocated a section of the poem and illustrates it, with the text included in the picture. Alternatively, a looseleaf folder can be compiled.

BECOMING FAMILIAR WITH A POEM

12. Well-liked poems are copied out by individual pupils into an accumulating personal anthology.
13. Pupils make posters, individually or in pairs, with some appropriate artwork to set off the text. Posters are then left for, say, a three-week period in classrooms or other 'safe areas' around the school.
14. Children learn poems by heart — a practice fashionably deplored, but deeply valued by many who had to do it. The choice of poem

could well be personal and lead not so much to a test, as to a contribution in a group performance, perhaps around a theme.

15. Children listen to different taped versions of a poem and determine their preferred version.

EXPLORING A POEM TO INCREASE COMPREHENSION

16. Group discussions, with or without a guiding framework, depending on how familiar the class is with such work.

17. Pupils A and B write brief 'instant reaction' papers and exchange them; add a comment on each other's responses before discussion.

18. Pairs or groups are presented with the poem with particular words omitted and asked to speculate about what might best fit in. If specific words are omitted rather than, say, every seventh word as in standard cloze procedures, groups' attention can be focused on particlar aspects of the poem — its imagery, rhyme, or rhythm, for example, as well as its diction.

19. A poem is given to the class untitled. In pairs, they propose titles, leading possibly to consensus. Compare with the poet's title.

20. Pairs or groups are presented with a poem in segments to be placed in what they judge to be the best order. This is then compared with the full text of the poem.

21. Some 'wrong' words are included in a version of the poem. In pairs or groups, pupils decide which they are and propose alternatives.

22. Pupils attempt parody or imitation: of a whole poem, or of specific techniques (e.g. conceits) or of poetic form (e.g. concrete poetry).

23. Pupils make a picture (without incorporating the text) which illustrates or captures the essence of a poem. Abstract pictures might be feasible with older pupils, and collage is also a possibility. Liaison with specialist colleagues could be helpful.

24. Invent the story behind the poem. What has happened before? What is happening 'off stage'? What will happen later?

25. Pupils play 'Chinese Whispers' (in which whispered messages are passed around the group and the original and final versions are compared). The 'messages' are sometimes prose, sometimes verse — perhaps a few lines from a ballad. The accuracy retained in the verse messages (hopefully) compared to the prose should open up the areas of rhyme, metre, oral tradition, etc.

26. Pupils rework a poem in a different genre (e.g., as a newspaper item). What has been gained, and what lost?

ASKING QUESTIONS

27. Groups prepare factual questions for others in the class or for younger classes, to use as a way in to the poem.

28. Groups prepare open-ended questions on matters of opinion about the poem for other groups to use.
29. Groups prepare a list of their own questions about a poem (matters of fact or of opinion) which they want to ask their teacher.
30. Pupils annotate a poem to meet the possible questions of a foreign student.

COLLECTING POEMS

31. Classes or groups prepare an anthology — written or to be spoken — of remembered children's rhyming games or jokes in verse.
32. Pupils 'find' poems; how many found poems are there around the school, the neighbourhood, today's papers, local graveyards?
33. Groups prepare an anthology of favourite TV jingles to set alongside an anthology of most-loathed TV jingles. Performed either on tape or live.
34. The English Department builds up and uses a stock of cassettes which include readings by poets, actors, teachers or children (see item 7) of a variety of poems arranged in 10- or 15-minute programmes. These might be grouped around a theme or a particular poet's work. The programmes can be heard, and reheard, by individuals or groups and possible modes of response could be suggested at the end of a programme, either on the tape or in an accompanying typed booklet (which might also include the text of the selection).
35. Desert Island Poems — a group or a pair (subject and interviewer) prepares a list of, say, five favourite poems with readings and reasons for selection.

DEMYSTIFYING

36. If money can be found, it seems a Better Buy to bring a poet into several classrooms to read his poems and to be asked any kinds of questions, than to stage large poetry readings.

AND A POSSIBLE THIRTY-SEVENTH

Forget It or Attack It — to persevere with a poem disliked by a class seems entirely counterproductive once it has had a fair hearing and negative responses need to be expressed and respected.

37 *Exploring through Writing*

● Mike Hayhoe and Stephen Parker

Pupils spend a lot of their time in school writing. When it is related to literature, writing is often of a 'practical criticism' kind, expecting a response in cool, measured language supported by evidence from the text. It is not surprising that this kind of assignment takes up a lot of time in English work, particularly with senior forms sitting public examinations, although some boards accept work which shows more evidence of feeling comprehension. 'Practical criticism' is usually a late stage activity, involving maturity and a trained intellect. Its successful development comes about where it is *part* of a wider involvement. A pupil should not only be a critical observer but an active participant in reading a book, using a wide range of abilities of which the intellect is but one. Pushing for immature detachment recalls Dr Johnson's dictum that 'endeavouring to make children prematurely wise is useless labour'.

Free response

SPRINGBOARDS

Free response writing has a long and honourable history. In recent years, there have been some particularly fine games played back at texts, such as Tom Stoppard's using Shakespeare's *Hamlet* as his springboard for *Rosencrantz and Guildenstern are Dead*, Jean Rhys telling the story of the first Mrs Rochester, the mad wife in Charlotte Brontë's *Jane Eyre*, in her novel *The Wide Sargasso Sea*, and Auden's poems in response to Shakespeare's *The Tempest*.

Pupils should certainly be encouraged to regard what they read as springboards for their own responsive writing, for in so doing they are likely to sift out features and issues which strike them and with which they might like to stay for a while. They may also echo features of the author's techniques in their own writing — an unconscious assimilation of authorial skills. Some schools set aside an occasional lesson or homework in which pupils are expected to write on from something they have encountered in their reading. This can range from a naïve retelling to a polished and sophisticated extension from the text. Choice of springboard and technique is the writer's. The only commitment is for the writers — pupils *and* teacher — to write.

This sort of assignment can be valuable, provided that writers see it as their chance to make choices. Some pupils find the opportunity a burden and prefer to be given a specific task in the early days, working towards making their own decision as they grow in confidence. Some possible assignments are outlined later under *Focused writing*.

PERSONAL LOGS

Individual response is important to teacher and pupil alike, whether the pupil is in the reception year or facing the public examination system. Reading a story inevitably involves its remaking within the individual mind, a process which calls upon the reader's abilities and emotions and his or her own life story, including experience of other anecdotes and tales. The process of weaving webs of significance is a complex one, often involving matters which may at first seem relatively small — checking up on the facts of the fiction, such as the names, relationships and attitudes of the characters; checking the values of characters against the values of the reader or of people close to him or her; savouring moments of particular importance to the individual. Sometimes these take place in silence and privacy. Often they follow our usual pattern of coping with the new, the interesting, the puzzling — through shared talk. To devalue the role of such 'gossip' can be a mistake, for it can push pupils into the detached 'law court game' approach of some public examinations far too early and suggest that their natural exploratory responses to a story are not relevant. They need a climate of encouragement over a long period in which to develop not only the social confidence to respond but, deeper than that, the patience and ability to reflect upon their reading.

The keeping of a personal log is one means of providing insight into this response to fiction, whether it is fiction by published authors or by the pupil as author in the making. Personal logs help some pupils at least to see that all writers, including themselves, have problems and opportunities in their work as they provide for their readers.

The ideal personal log is a small notebook. One school chops up cheap exercise books into three, so that pupils have a pocket-size log which they can carry around with them — the pages numbered so that it does not become a source of paper for other purposes! Pupils are encouraged to jot down informally personal reactions to their reading and writing of fiction as they go along. Written 'little and often', such notes help to build up a habit which, ideally, should not be seen as a chore. Some forms may need a couple of ten-minute slots a week set aside in which to jot things down, perhaps at the end of a literature lesson or during a library period. Others may be motivated enough to keep their logs in their own time. A log can relate to one text, running a commentary on reactions and details as the reading progresses; it can be a record of personal reading outside the syllabus; it can be a commentary on problems and experiences the pupil has had in his own writing of fiction; it can include comment on fiction in other media.

The log can be part of an assessment system read by the teacher, but if it is to be a genuinely personal document, its owner should have rights of privacy over its immediate contents. Some pupils find the log useful as a means of externalizing how they feel and think; some find it easier to 'talk' to their teacher by handing in their log from time to time for her or him to read and jot down a couple of 'talking back' comments, rather than having to engage in conversation. The log can be the basis of information which the pupil turns to in group discussion, a device found useful up to and including sixth form work. It can also be a means of reflecting on progress, with the pupil writing an end-of-book or end-of-term review on how reader and reading have got on together.

Such work takes patience and tact to develop. Where it succeeds, readers come to see something of the growth of their skills and awareness and something of the complex of abilities they call upon.

Focused writing — characterization

Practical criticism tends to keep some readers outside a text, especially where there is a priority in extracting and analysing features to do with technique. What is also needed is the means of drawing a reader into a text. Free response writing is one means of promoting this engagement. Focused writing can be another, developing awareness of authorial techniques by trying them out rather than through analytical discussion alone.

THE DOSSIER

The key concept to be grasped is that the author chooses to include — and therefore to omit — certain features of a character, so that he can get the reader to pay attention to significant features. It may be true that senior pupils can quickly produce lists of which features an author has chosen to use in generating a character, but younger pupils may need a more structured approach. One advice is to have each reader or small group *adopt* a character — someone from their own heads or from a picture or story. They then have to produce the dossier for that person.

Name, address, age, sex, marital status, are easy. Categories such as personality; habits; manner and mannerisms; likes and dislikes; roles; other features, prove more demanding. Dossiers can be used in various ways. One is for another pupil or group to take over a dossier, creating one pleasant and one unpleasant character from the data and then discussing which features they adopted, adapted or rejected in order to create their Jekylls and Hydes. Another is to circulate or display dossiers so that groups can work out which characters are sympathetic or otherwise and then use their choices for the starts of stories in which characters get on well or do not. Again, the writers should discuss and jot down what they chose to use and how they chose to use it. Senior pupils can examine how far their characterization was explicit, with authorial advice to the reader, or how far it was implicit and how it was achieved — by action, interaction, dialogue, internal monologue, and so on.

'THOUGHTS IN THE HEAD OF'

This device explores a character by going inside his or her mind. In the case of an existing book, a pupil can write a character's 'inner monologue' at a critical moment in the book when the author has kept outside the character. This can range from setting out the thoughts of the aborigine boy when he meets the white children in James Vance Marshall's *Walkabout* to the thoughts of Frank Churchill as he playfully vies with the heroine at Box Hill in Jane Austen's *Emma*.

ENCOUNTERS

'When I was with X' or 'When I met X' gives a pupil a chance to imagine himself in one of two contexts. In the first, he can engage with a character beyond the book — for instance, he may meet the white children after *Walkabout* has ended and, assuming that they do get back to white civilization, write of their encounter. In the second, he may enter the book, becoming a character and interacting with others, for example as one of the unidentified choirboys in *Lord of the Flies*. Both provide chances to write dialogue as one means of gaining insight into how characters and relationships can be created and grow in a novel.

POINTS OF VIEW

This is an extension of 'When I was with X'. An author can call upon a range of devices to create character — actions, speech, inner thoughts, others' comments and reactions — and this approach calls upon pupils to discuss which they have used. An episode in a novel is assigned to various syndicates in the class, each group adopting a character who is in the episode or affected by it. The siege in *Treasure Island* can be described through the eyes of Long John Silver, Jim Hawkins, the Doctor, Squire Trelawney and so on. Some teachers find this a useful device when handling a text containing multi-cultural issues, for example the attack on the Pakistani children at the start of Jan Needle's *My Mate Shofiq* can be seen through their eyes, helping to gain some idea of their feelings and of some of the issues the book tackles. The resulting mini-yarns can be used for a class 'read in' and comment on which devices were used to create the various kinds of characters.

PROJECTION

Projection uses information in a book to consider a character in a situation beyond the text. Writing a report as a Welfare Officer on Rocky O'Rourke in S. Sherry's *A Pair of Jesus Boots* involves a knowledge of the text and a response to the characters and their circumstances. So would writing the summing-up speech of the defence and prosecution counsels at Magwitch's trial in Dickens's *Great Expectations*. So would the official report of the rescuing officer in Golding's *Lord of the Flies* as he writes of the tattered, smoke-stained children he found on the island.

Focused writing — setting

A novel's setting causes problems for many pupils, especially where the author spends a lot of his and the reader's time on it. It has its importance, whether it is as passive background or, as in the novels of D. H. Lawrence or Dickens, it has its own life and affects characters and events powerfully. Setting can be seen in terms of place, natural or man-made; time, for example evening or autumn or the Middle Ages; weather; the people among whom a character is placed; the culture in which he or she finds him- or herself. Often the setting promotes an atmosphere or mood, sometimes reinforcing it, sometimes contrasting with it.

INTO ACTION

Most pupils like a rapid pace to the plot of their stories and give little attention and reaction to setting. To encourage closer attention to description, pupils can try creating incidents which have a great deal of action in a defined setting but little plot movement — a fight in a western saloon, with blow-by-blow detail; a crisis in a needle match of football; riding a tricksy horse in a high wind; jostling for the star bargain in the first five minutes of a sale. The emphasis is on the eye for detail, with the minimal narrative helping to support the writer who might flounder if there was no sense of time sequence at all.

CAMERA LENS

Descriptive paragraphs of the traditional kind, where the writer has no narrative to help order the detail being described, can be helped by this approach. Because of their familiarity with television and film, many pupils can grasp the techniques of describing scenes and people in camera terms. Younger pupils can cope with *three distance* description, starting with people in long distance, then middle distance and then in close detail, as the characters move in their setting towards the reader or the reader is taken towards them. They can describe a setting from a landing helicopter or a rocket going into orbit.

Quite young pupils enjoy watching a bravura writer create a setting — the railway cutting in Dickens's ghost story *The Signal Man*, for instance, or the stinking alleys of Tom All Alone's in his *Bleak House* or in Leon Garfield's *John Diamond*. After discussing how a setting might be filmed, they go on to write their own. They are likely to start with the dramatic and gloomy. Describing more relaxed or more subtle setting takes maturity. Another device is to work from the macro or micro viewpoint, as in Swift's *Gulliver's Travels* in which the hero finds himself in lands peopled by manikins or giants. F. P. Heide's modern text *The Shrinking of Treehorn* can be a useful book here, with the world seen through the eyes of an increasingly small boy. Such writing helps to see items afresh and sometimes in different detail.

SETTING THE SCENE

George Bernard Shaw wrote very detailed setting notes for the scenes of his plays. Using these as an example, pupils can work out setting notes for a key episode in a novel. Some texts may well be explicit about a setting; some will leave room for informed conjecture. Younger pupils may find it useful to develop their setting notes from preliminary drawings. Older ones can use reference books or visits to enhance detail or capture atmosphere. In one instance, a visit to a stately home of the relevant period helped students to understand something of the 'superior' world which Elizabeth encounters in Jane Austen's *Pride and Prejudice*.

RESPONSES

Characters in novels may react very differently to the same setting. In Betsy Byars's *The Midnight Fox*, Tommy initially finds the country extremely boring, while his cousin leaves signs throughout the house and the novel of his love for it. Pupils can make notes on these different reactions, perhaps writing contrasting 'day in the life' accounts or an imagined episode where the two boys meet. The responses to the urban tyranny in Orwell's *1984* of Winston Smith, of his interrogator, O'Brien, and of the proles are different and complex, can lead to similar comparative note-taking and could lead to further responsive writing. Characters' reactions to settings can be written as diary entries, as letters home to friends, or whatever strikes the reader. They provide a chance to re-narrate, to summarize and to express obliquely the reader's understanding of a character's personality within a setting and his or her response to it. Younger pupils might write the sort of letter that one of the children might have written in Nicholas Fisk's *High Way Home*, before their desperate attempt to escape from the doomed island. Senior pupils might understand much about Lady Dedlock in Dickens's *Bleak House* by writing at least some of her diary entries, for example during her dreary stay in Lincolnshire at the time of the floods. A C.S.E. class reading Solzhenitsyn's *One Day in the Life of Ivan Denisovitch* was asked to work out how to provide advice to new inmates on how to survive in the labour camp without running the risk of being identified. Their bleak and brief lists on staying alive and how to avoid risks appeared scrawled on cheap toilet paper, on old scraps of wrapping paper, even scratched on a flat stone.

ON THE INSIDE LOOKING OUT

Inner monologue has already been discussed as one means of creating characterization. It can also help older pupils to see the interplay between character and place, since the result can be strongly impressionistic, especially if it uses the first person, present tense. A classic example is the opening of Joyce Cary's *The Horse's Mouth*. This is a difficult technique to sustain in an extended story. Careful crafting is often needed if the effort is to be regarded as work 'going public', but it has its place in developing insights into the range of techniques available to an author. Some pupils find the task easier when they are exploring not only a place but a time of day or a type of weather, for example an old street with a fading winter sun, and where they can bear in mind a very defined mood on the part of their character.

POETRY

While it is not a technique to do with writing novels, writing a poem can be one way of evoking a setting. Many poets have done so. Some pupils find that reworking a setting from a novel into a poem of their own making helps them to 'own' it more fully, affectively as well as intellectually.

Focused writing — structure

Many pupils find it hard to realize that a novel's structure is often more than a simple, time-sequenced narrative. Some devices are best understood by trying them out.

PLOT OUTLINES

Some pupils are so involved with a book's detail that they find it difficult to grasp its overall structure, especially when the book is being read over a number of weeks instead of being block read in, say, a week. At an early stage, pupils tend to find their plot as they go along, but they can benefit from sometimes trying to map out the possible general design for their own efforts beforehand. Some schools encourage younger pupils to write a 'long novel', taking up as much space as they like over several weeks. This can involve an initial note-making phase in which character profiles are compiled and an outline diagram of the book's major events is devised. Comparing their original 'maps' with what they have written shows pupils something about how far an author's intentions are realized or affected during the writing.

PLOT VARIATIONS

The linear plot is the basic structure of narrative, but older pupils can try other devices. Using stereotypes, they can play with such ideas as the cliff-hanger and the foreshadowing of crisis so much used by Charles Dickens and soap operas. The flashback is more sophisticated, but most pupils are familiar with it on film and television and can find it interesting to work out how a novel can use the device. Particularly sophisticated are plots where the same event is seen through several different characters' eyes — a chance for writers to adopt a character each and tell their tale and then discuss their treatment of the device as they pool their narratives. While it may seem one of the more obvious devices to a reader, writing a sub-plot causes many problems. It is often worth letting pupils have a brief attempt at writing with these devices, especially with senior pupils, so that they have time to consider their own efforts alongside those of established authors.

CHANGE ROUND

Quite often the plot of a story is affected by the personality of a character or by some aspect of its setting. Rewriting an episode to obtain a different result by changing one of these can help to illustrate this. For instance, in Golding's *Lord of the Flies*, Ralph and Jack have some initial regard for each other. Rewriting an episode in which that friendship remains strong and hence affects the action can help to show how, in the novel, their relationship worsened and affected its subsequent events. Some pupils have found it interesting to rework episodes with girls on the island instead of boys. The less reverent have removed the characters from their idyllic setting to a polar island!

OFF THE SET

This device, already used to explore characterization, can be used to consider plot potential. Pupils are asked to write what is going on with characters offstage during an episode. Younger ones may want to concentrate on dialogue; older ones can try their hand at the offstage setting as well. This work involves knowing preceding and succeeding chapters, in order to make the offstage episode fit the tale. In sum, the pupils are creating a sub-plot episode which can lead to interesting discussion about what they wrote, what information they used and what techniques they found effective.

Focused writing — style

Style is probably the most nebulous of features to explain. Certainly, direct work on it requires patience and often should be seen as a late stage activity. Contrastive reading and many of the activities already suggested should have helped some pupils to catch awareness of how one author is different from another in his choice of approaches and techniques.

I OR HE OR SHE?

Pupils can write two versions of the opening paragraphs of a story, using the first person and then the third. The first gives a sense of involvement and immediacy; it also presents problems ranging from how to tackle tenses to how to carry essential information to the reader. The third person provides room for authorial commentary; it may lack immediacy. Younger pupils may not be able to say much beyond which technique they found the more natural to them; older pupils should be able to start to comment on the problems and opportunities each stance provided.

AUTHOR, NARRATOR OR PROTAGONIST?

The distinction between the viewpoints of the author, the narrator and the protagonist can be subtle and important, for example in understanding the ironies of Jane Austen's work. Author-narrator distinction can be demonstrated by getting pupils to create a character very unlike themselves — of the opposite sex, old, criminal, for example — and then have them write an episode seen through the eyes of that character in which they meet and interact for some reason, using dialogue and expressing views. In many novels, either the author or the protagonist narrates the tale. In some, matters are more complicated. Charlotte Brontë has her heroine narrate much of *Jane Eyre* but she herself is narrator-cum-commentator in several places. Jack Schaeffer creates the boy Bob Starrett as the half-aware narrator of his hero Shane's coming into his family's life, in the novel of that name. Conrad also tells some of his tales and sees characters through the narration of another, as in *Lord Jim*.

This aspect of writing can be followed up as pupils try writing a brief passage about an event with the omniscience of the author, through a character created by the author telling of another's involvement and finally through that person's own telling of the tale. Explicit and implicit comment can be developed through fairly simple devices, with pupils writing a brief, directly critical account of a character or event, trying sarcasm and, finally, employing irony.

SADDER, FUNNIER

Young writers take readily to extremes from pathos to farce, perhaps because these produce the most obvious response from their readership. They should be encouraged to do some writing which has a clear idea of what it wants to do to its audience. One device is to outline a 'consequences' event in neutral, telegraphese language — a man walking on the outside of a ladder being knocked down by a cyclist swerving to avoid a warning cone knocked out of place by a falling window-cleaner. Younger pupils can write contrastive versions, one sad, one funny, using whatever techniques they wish. Older ones can widen the range of effects they practise in manipulating an event, producing pathos, nostalgia, anticipation. They can reminisce over an event with regret at its passing and then with distaste that it ever happened; they can anticipate an event with fear and another with eager excitement, using the third person with authorial comment or inner monologue or whatever devices they wish. Throughout, the writing of contrastive passages will help them to see something of how mood and tone have been generated.

PARODY

This well-known device can be very sophisticated, but there are many models of its use which can illustrate its techniques without the need for complex, abstract description. Television is one rich source. Parody can be attempted at all levels in the secondary school, but initially the style of the book or passage to be parodied must be obvious. This is where genre study is useful, since the stereotypes of the western, ghost story, romance or thriller can easily lead to gross parodies being written. The more subtle discrimination required to see how writers break out of cliché can only come about once pupils have recognized cliché, a stage which might otherwise come late for some pupils. Parody depends on forms of humour, an aspect which again encourages pupils to think not only of themselves but of their readers and how they wish to affect them. Early results often seem embarrassing and unfunny to an adult, but the benefits in terms of greater awareness of the importance of choosing techniques to do something specific may well repay the teacher's patience.

PASTICHE

Encouraging pupils to 'write back' at a text through such devices as 'meanwhile' episodes or seeing events through another character's eyes should cause at least some of them to echo features of an author's style — to engage unawares in pastiche. Pastiche is not parody. With older pupils, trying to write a brief passage on an episode which a particular author might have chosen, using features of his or her techniques and trying to capture his or her attitudes can have particular importance. It can be one way of bringing together the affective and the cognitive, the heart and the head, to find out through conscious imitation features of that author's techniques and, perhaps, something of the effort and achievement of the original writer.

38 *Writing about Macbeth*

- Paul Ashton, Andrew Bethell *et al.*

In this section are suggestions for work on *Macbeth* aimed at increasing your understanding of the play. All of them involve discussing aspects of the play in groups, and many of them have suggestions for writing that could be included in a Literature folder. [...]

PUBLIC . . .

Look like the innocent flower — but be the serpent under it . . . (I.5.64)

This is Lady Macbeth's advice to Macbeth as they prepare to welcome King Duncan to their castle. Already the king has been deceived by someone he trusted, and he has observed that a person's *public* face does not necessarily reveal their *private* thoughts.

> There's no art
> To find the mind's construction in the face:
> He was a gentleman on whom I built
> An absolute trust.
> *(I.4.12)*

This idea that 'things are not what they seem' reappears again and again in *Macbeth*:

— The witches' prophecy *seems* to be good but is really bad.
— Macbeth's castle *seems* to be safe but is really a place of murder.
— What *seems* to be a wood is really an army.

Of course once the plan to murder Duncan takes root, Macbeth and Lady Macbeth have to live the rest of their lives with a public face of innocence and a private feeling of guilt.

Here are some quotations from the play which express the difference between the public face (what seems to be) and the private thoughts (what really is):

> False face must hide what the false heart doth know *(I.7.83)*

> To show an unfelt sorrow is an office
> Which the false man does easy. *(2.3.138)*

> . . . but wail his fall
> Who I myself struck down. *(3.1.122)*

AND PRIVATE

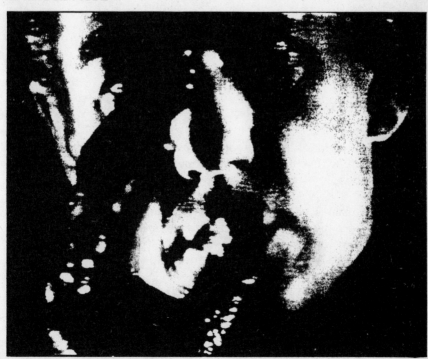

Gentle my lord, sleek o'er your rugged looks,
Be bright and jovial among your guests tonight. *(3.2.28)*

And make our faces vizards to our hearts
Disguising what they are. *(3.2.34)*

What to do

Write a story in which the main character has to: 'Look like the innocent flower, but be the serpent under it'.

It does not have to be a modern version of *Macbeth*, but you could make the story more interesting by relating it to the play.

a) You could use the quotations above as chapter or section headings. For example, the first section, in which the villain meets the victim and has to act innocent, could have the title:
    False face must hide what the false heart doth know.

b) You could base your story on the same structure as the play *Macbeth*:
    1. The False Welcome
    2. The Treacherous Deed
    3. Fake Grief
    4. Acting The Innocent

Some suggestions:
— the star player on the school team
    an accident is arranged by the person who has been kept out of the team . . .
— the well-respected leader of the gang (or oil company?)
    a nasty accident is arranged by the person next in line for leadership
    . . .

[...]

MACBETH ON THE STAGE

As you work through *Macbeth* for your exam it would be easy to forget that this play was written to be performed on stage.

  The person who decides how a play is presented on stage is called the DIRECTOR. He or she will read the play very carefully indeed and decide how each scene is going to work on stage. A director will expect the actors to have their own ideas, but he or she will need to have a picture of the whole play.

  For each scene of the play a director needs to ask several questions, of which the most important one is:

1. How can I make the audience experience this scene in the way I want them to? (By getting them gripped, laughing, crying, horrified, etc.)

The other questions are:

2. What objects will I have on stage for this scene and where will they be placed?

3. Where will the actors come on to the stage from? Where will they move to, and when? (Actors will be given some freedom in this, but the director must have an overall plan.)

4. How will the actors behave during this scene? What are they supposed to be feeling? How will they show these feelings in the way they move and the way they speak their lines?

5. What will the actors who are not speaking be doing in the background?

6. What will the lighting be like? Will there be any extra sounds? (Music, sound effects, etc.)

Before the director begins rehearsals he/she must visualise the scene in his/her mind's eye and then write notes, usually on a copy of the script. These notes will remind the director of the answers to the questions.

On the next page you will find a page taken from a director's script. You can see she has made notes on the script.

MACBETH ON THE STAGE

What about stockings over their heads? They must look threatening and cool to begin with.

Very dim lighting – with shadows on the back wall (perhaps dark clouds?)

Scene III. [*Near the palace.*]

Enter Three Murderers.

First and second come in from E③ ahead. 3rd is stalking behind

Spoken over his shoulder as he enters

First Murderer. But who did bid thee join with us?

Third Murderer. Macbeth.

This surprises the other two – they both stop

Stops in mid movement

Second Murderer. He needs not our mistrust; since he delivers
Our offices and what we have to do
To the direction just.°

We must feel that they are dealing with their suspicions.

First Murderer. Then stand with us.
The west yet glimmers with some streaks of day.
Now spurs the lated° traveler apace
To gain the timely inn, [and near approaches
The subject of our watch.]   5

Moves up onto dais.

Third Murderer. Hark! I hear horses.

Moves into darkness of E⑧.

Banquo. (*Within*) Give us a light there, ho!

Crouches below dais.

Second Murderer. Then 'tis he. [~~The rest
That are within the note of expectation°~~   10
~~Already are i' th' court.~~]

First Murderer. His horses go about.

flattens himself against back wall

Third Murderer. Almost a mile: but he does usually —
So all men do — from hence to th' palace gate
Make it their walk.

Enter Banquo and Fleance, with a torch.

from Ent. A. with bright, single light

1st M follows them round and silently moves onto dais.

Second Murderer. A light, A light!

Third Murderer. 'Tis he.

First Murderer. Stand to 't.   15 *at Z*

Banquo. It will be rain tonight.

First Murderer. Let it come down.

jumps down

LIGHTS DOWN

[*They set upon Banquo.*]

Banquo. O, treachery! Fly, good Fleance, fly, fly, fly!

[*Exit Fleance.*]
Thou mayst revenge. O slave! [*Dies.*]

Moves centre stage – and B. thrashes about with 3 murderers playing about – B killed dropped over dais. Q.

Third Murderer. Who did strike out the light?

First Murderer. Was 't not the way?°

tries Ex B, then makes it back to Ex A.

Third Murderer. There's but one down; the son is fled.   20

Second Murderer. We have lost best half of our affair.

First Murderer. Well, let's away and say how much is done.   *Exeunt.*

sits down on the dais exhausted.

Here is a plan of the theatre:

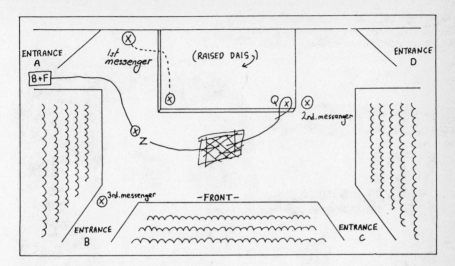

What to do

Here is a list of three scenes in *Macbeth* which a director would need to think about carefully:

ACT II Scene 3. Lines 51 to 125.
The discovery of Duncan's murder and Macbeth and Lady Macbeth's cover-up.

ACT III Scene 4.
The banquet scene in which Macbeth 'sees' the ghost of Banquo. (N.B. an important decision is whether or not to have Banquo's 'ghost' on stage.)

ACT V Scene 1.
The sleep-walking scene.

1. Ask your teacher to photocopy the scene you are interested in directing.
2. Stick your copy of the scene onto a larger sheet of paper so that you have plenty of room to scribble notes.
3. Go through the six questions and decide how you will present the play.
4. You can *either* use the plan of the theatre on this page *or* do a plan of the theatre space in your own school.
5. You will need to include sketches and diagrams to explain the more complicated bits.

Obviously the best way to see how successful you have been as a director is to TRY IT OUT with a group of people in a space. If your ideas work, you might want to go on and put the scene on in front of an audience.

MACBETH: HERO OR VILLAIN?

To help you write an essay about Macbeth, which explores his role in the play:

1. Discuss with someone whether each of these statements is true:
    a) Macbeth is a brave and loyal soldier.
    b) Macbeth is a fool to believe what the witches say.
    c) Macbeth is weak compared to Lady Macbeth.
    d) Macbeth regrets killing Duncan.
    e) Although Banquo's ghost terrifies him, Macbeth does not regret killing Banquo.
    f) Macbeth rules Scotland by murder and terror.
    g) Macbeth admits to himself he is evil, so he is honest, and not a hypocrite.
    h) Macbeth never loses his bravery, even when he realises the witches have tricked him.

APPEARANCE AND REALITY

Macbeth is full of things that are not what they seem to be, and people whose *reality* is different from their *appearance*.

Here are some examples:

1. The weird sisters look like men *and* women. (1,3,46)
2. It is not certain at first whether they really exist, or are just visions. (1,3,82)
3. Macbeth and Lady Macbeth seem to Duncan to be loyal, loving and trustworthy, when he enters their castle.
4. Banquo describes the castle where Duncan is to die as a pleasant and healthy place.
5. Macbeth and Lady Macbeth *seem* horrified at Duncan's murder.

What to do

There are many examples of this kind in the play. Can you continue the list in the same way?

Here are some hints to help you find the examples: In your list, mark which is which with an A or a B.

a dagger   a wood   false promises
a ghost   two guilty grooms   a wicked prince
a 'foul and fair' day

A. Sometimes we, the audience, know that the appearance is different from the reality before some of the characters.
B. Sometimes we are in the dark just like them, and discover later what the truth is.

DARKNESS

The work on these two pages is to help you look more closely at the way Shakespeare's language affects an audience as much as the events in the play.

1. *Macbeth* was first performed indoors, in front of a small audience.

2. In Shakespeare's time there was, of course, no electric light; the play-room would have been lit by candles. If you have ever been in a place lit only by candles, you will know that they give bright spots of light, and deep shadows that move as people move past the candles. (Candle light also affects the way faces appear — half in light, half in shadow.)

3. You remember that some of the most important events in *Macbeth* take place in darkness: the murder of Duncan, the murder of Banquo, Macbeth's visit to the witches, and Lady Macbeth's sleep-walking. Shakespeare chose to do this deliberately — it is not hard to think why.

[Handwritten annotations:]

Notes on Darkness in MACBETH

Indoors – small audience

Candle light – deep shadows spooky!

Important scenes in MACBETH in the dark : Murder of Dunc Murder of Banquo MACB's visit to witches

Shakes. deliberate – it's a dark play!

4. Many of the characters mention darkness as the play goes on. The repetition of word-images of dark and night feeds our imaginations, so that we never forget for long, even while reading the play in broad daylight, that darkness hangs over the play. Here are some examples:

(Macbeth thinking about killing Duncan — Act 1, Scene 5, line 50 —)

> Come, thick night,
> And pall thee in the dimmest
>   smoke of hell,
> That my keen knife see not the
>   wound it makes,
> Nor heaven peep through the
>   blanket of the dark,
> To cry 'Hold, hold!'

(Banquo, just before the murder — Act 2, Scene 1, line 5)

> There's husbandry in heaven.
> Their candles are all out.

5. Shakespeare also gives us word-pictures of darkness *struggling* with light, and darkness winning. When this is repeated, it creates a feeling, or *atmosphere* in the play which we can remember even when we have forgotten the words themselves:

(Macbeth thinking about killing Duncan — Act 1, Scene 4, line 50)

> Stars, hide your fires.
> Let not light see my black and
>   deep desires.

Handwritten margin notes:

Darkness mentioned a lot.

repeated word-images of dark and night - feeds the imagination.

Lady Macb - 1.5.50 "Come, thick night..."

Darkness struggles with light, Light wins.

Atmosphere - because always repeated. "Stars hide your fires." 1.4.5

What to do

Talk about these images together. Do you understand what they mean? For example, what does 'dark night strangles the travelling lamp' mean? What do the words 'Light thickens' mean to you?

When you have discussed them, copy out each quotation and write notes on the meanings you arrive at in your discussion.

"Dark night ~~strangles~~ the ~~traveller's lamp~~" 3.4.46

Sun??

"nights' black agents" – good quote. Could say Macb. & Lady Macb. are ----

AND DISEASE

There is another chain of images in the play which deal this time with disease. They create an atmosphere in which Scotland is like a healthy

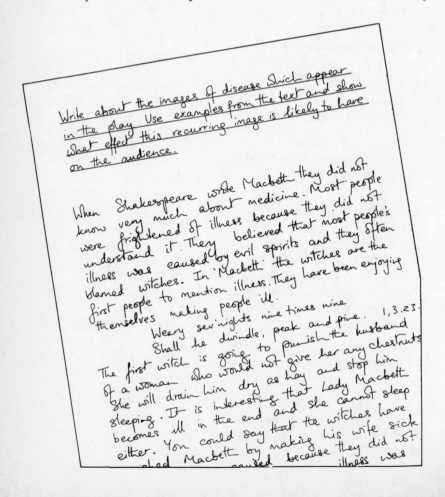

Write about the images of disease which appear in the play. Use examples from the text and show what effect this recurring image is likely to have on the audience.

When Shakespeare wrote Macbeth they did not know very much about medicine. Most people were frightened of illness because they did not understand it. They believed that most people's illness was caused by evil spirits and they often blamed witches. In 'Macbeth' the witches are the first people to mention illness. They have been enjoying themselves making people ill.

Weary sev'nights nine times nine   1,3.23.
Shall he dwindle, peak and pine.

The first witch is going to punish the husband of a woman who would not give her any chestnuts. She will drain him dry as hay and stop him sleeping. It is interesting that Lady Macbeth becomes ill in the end and she cannot sleep either. You could say that the witches have made Macbeth by making his wife sick caused because they did not illness was body which contains a deadly disease — Macbeth — waiting to break out. These are the references for the images:

1,3,23 — Who is causing this sickness?
2,2,45 — Why does Lady Macbeth tell Macbeth his brain is sick?
3,4,87 — Why does Macbeth lie like this?
4,3,214 — How is Macduff's revenge like a medicine?
5,1,62 — Why is this disease beyond the Doctor to cure?
5,2,26 — How will Scotland be cured?

What to do

A. Look up each reference. Copy out the line/s which contain the image of disease.
B. Make sure you understand what each one means, by talking about them. Again write notes on your discussion.
C. You can use your notes as the basis of an essay on imagery in *Macbeth*.

LOOKING CLOSELY AT ONE SCENE

METHOUGHT I HEARD A VOICE CRY, 'SLEEP NO MORE!'

In the course of the play, although Macbeth manages to sleep, we learn that he is afflicted by 'terrible dreams' after he has murdered Duncan. And he is not the only one. Lady Macbeth suffers too; we see her walking in her sleep and going over in her mind what she has done. Even in her sleep, her deeds are not forgotten.

Lady Macbeth's sleepwalking statements are very confusing to the Doctor and Waiting Woman, but we know they refer to various things that have happened in the play, though not in the right order. Lady Macbeth is speaking a nightmare out loud, and these are some of the things she says:

a) One; two; why, then tis time to do't.
b) Fie, my lord, fie! A soldier, and afeard?
c) Who would have thought the old man to have so much blood in him?
d) The Thane of Fife had a wife. Where is she now?
e) No more o' that, my lord, no more o' that! You mar all with this starting.
f) I tell you yet again, Banquo's buried. He cannot come out on's grave.
g) To bed, to bed! There's knocking at the gate.
h) What's done cannot be undone. To bed, to bed, to bed.

What to do

1. Can you remember what earlier incidents each of these statements refer to?
   For example: a) — This refers to the ringing of the bell which was the sign for Macbeth to murder Duncan.
2. Now see if you can find the exact references in the play. Most of the incidents she refers to are in Act 1 Scene 7 and Act 2 Scene 2, but there are some references to other places.
   For example: a) — This refers to the lines: 2,31,32.:
   Go bid thy mistress, when my drink is ready,
   She strike upon the bell.
3. Why does Shakespeare select these particular fragments to repeat in this scene?
   Why do you think Shakespeare has the Doctor and the Waiting Woman in this scene at all?

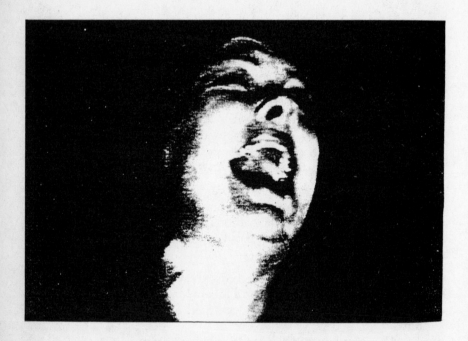

39   *Coronation Street*

● Richard Exton

Children grow up with serials in comics; they change their loyalties, as
they grow older, to adolescent magazines; and all the while they are part
of the mass audience for *Crossroads* or *Coronation Street*. These two British
television serials, together with American counterparts and family
drama series both British and American, are major points of reference in
children's talk. They are a means of contact, a way back into the school
friendship situation after the interruption of home: 'Did you see
Coronation Street last night?' 'Yeah, wasn't it good when . . .' and so
the retellings and comments begin and the individual television viewers
of home are re-established as a group at school.

Although this whole area is clearly important, there has been little
serious work from teachers or theorists on serials. This article is
intended to indicate some possible directions for work in school; it
comprises a summary of an article by Christine Geraghty which forms
part of some research into *Coronation Street* done by the London Women
and Film Group and the Potteries SEFT Group, and an account of some
work with 4th year students in an East London comprehensive school.

AN ANALYSIS OF SERIALS

Christine Geraghty's article attempts to 'provide a definition of the
continuous serial on TV and radio and then to look at the implications of
that definition both in terms of the formal questions of narrative and
character construction and the role of the audience'. She confines
herself to analysis of British serials, and is concerned initially to
distinguish between a serial and a series. She summarizes what she calls
the three marks of a serial as follows: the manipulation of narrative time
to give an impression of the passing of real time; the interweaving of
different plots; and a sense of an 'unwritten' future.

Narrative in serials, she argues, has a number of key characteristics. It
tends to work through the presentation of an enigma and is so
manipulated as to set up a series of cliff-hangers. Unlike the reader of

books, a TV serial viewer *has* to wait. (The exquisite agony provided for
Dallas viewers by the actors' strike which delayed the revelation of JR's
attacker should remind us of the importance of this distinction!)
Another feature of the narrative organisation in serials is the mixture of
long-term problems seen over many episodes and those problems which
are specific to one episode. Similarly, audiences can be kept in the dark
about some aspects of the plot, *or* given knowledge which is denied to
some characters. The overall resolution is not final for as long as the
serial continues.

Turning to the audience's relationship with the serial, Christine
Geraghty points out that there is very little reference in serials to past
events because the makers cannot assume that an audience has seen
every episode. Conversely, though, regular viewers can round out
apparently flat episodes with a wealth of accumulated knowledge. It
seems, also, that lacunae can occur in plots without damaging
involvement.

On the issue of characterization, Christine Geraghty points out that
because of the serial's commitment to both casual and committed
viewers, delineation of character has to be quick and clear, but
audiences gradually build up round characters in the moment of
viewing. A serial has its own scale of characters which can usefully be
split into three sections: a) the Individuated Character (e.g. the stingy
Albert Tatlock); b) the Serial Type (e.g. 'Elsie Tanner type' — warm
hearted, tarty, hot-tempered); c) the Position Holder (e.g. the
Unmarried Man, the Betrayed Wife).

Looking at plots within serials, the article identifies three main types:
a) the Big Event (e.g. birth, marriage, death); b) General Plots (e.g.
parent/child friction); and c) plots specific to certain characters or which
can only involve certain characters (e.g. any story about thieving in
Coronation Street could only involve Eddie Yeats). The interaction
between the three different kinds of characterization and the three
different kinds of plot is designed to give the feeling of endlessness: one
may have the same story but with different characters or have the same
characters involved in different stories.

What this summary fails to indicate is the range of examples used to
support the central argument — drawn from *The Archers, Wagonner's
Walk* and *Crossroads* as well as *Coronation Street*. But I hope that readers
will be able to supply their own illustrations from their own viewing and
listening experience.

CLASSROOM WORK: CREATING A NEW SERIAL

It seemed to me that a number of useful points emerged from this study
of serials, which could be integrated into areas of English work often

explored at 3rd and 4th year level. I had often asked my 4th year class in the past to consider who was telling the story and how the plot was organized in books I read with them, and in their own writing I made point of view, and consequently characterization, important. I had intended to move on to consider genre — particularly as it affected style and plot — and so this work on serials provided a useful bridge between aspects of my ongoing work as well as being of interest and importance in its own right.

As an initial lesson I wanted to establish a framework which drew on the class's collective knowledge of TV and radio serials. I put the class into groups of 4 or 5 and told them that they were a production team whose brief it was to create a new television serial. If it were successful it would run for ever, and initially it would be screened two or three times a week. The location must be British, and by the end of the one hour lesson I wanted a list of some of the characters who would be involved, together with a brief description of them, and an indication of some of the possible initial plots. I discovered that, of the 21 girls present, all but four watched either *Crossroads* or *Coronation Street* on a fairly regular basis, while several watched *Soap* and nearly all also watched British and American series such as *Dallas* or *Fox*.

Broadly speaking, the children organized their characters along the lines described by Christine Geraghty: they are types who are also holders of a position. The following is one group's list of characters:

1. Agnes Trollope — 50s — nosy type
2. Dave Lockwood — 20s — flashy type
3. Rosie Jones — 30s — tarty
4. George Trollope — 50s — weak man, married to Agnes
5. & 6. Jenny & Bill Thomson — 30s — pub owners, helpful
7. Emily Dobson — 70s — lonely old lady, husband died in war
8. Mildred Hughes — 50s — nosy rival of Agnes
9. Stephane — 35–40s — snobby, looks down on everyone
10. Patricia — 17 — unlike mother
11. PC Rodgers — 40s — old-fashioned, law-abiding
12. Barry Jones — 40s — works on oil-rig, tough

Although this particular group did not provide a location for their serial, they clearly assumed a small community. Two of the groups specifically set their serials in seaside boarding houses, and another group chose a small village on the Scottish border with a British Legion club as a focal point. One of the boarding houses had the following list of inhabitants:

STAFF:
Landlord (bachelor) — late 20s — Jack Gaid
Cleaners — Mrs Josephine Johnson, Ethel Smith
Receptionist — Joey Fox

Cooks — Ethel Smith, Patrick O'Leary
PERMANENT GUESTS:
Family — married couple — Gary & Cindy Bailey
Old Man (General)
Landlord's mother
VISITING GUESTS:
2 teenagers (17–19)
Incognito film star
4 filmstars associates

While clearly the locations (small community, but with the potential for variety) and the character lists are influenced by *Crossroads* and *Coronation Street* and by the memories of series such as *Upstairs, Downstairs*, the plots are more influenced by American series such as *Dallas*, and by the parody of *Soap*. The following set of notes from one group illustrates well the way that *Soap* is brought to bear on the British tradition:

Set in Millam, English/Scottish dot on the landscape.
Most people belong to the British Legion Club.
Mr Bulloch (50) is a prominent farmer — a geriatric nymphomaniac — fancies Miss Simms the local 'do-gooder' — arranges things for people who don't want arranged things. Mr Bulloch wants to carry on family line of Bullochs.
Julie Mazda, a teenage (18) tearaway tart — village scandal.
Priest (Rev. Parsons, 64) tries to convert Julie.
Shy boy called Michael Parsons who is 22, son of Rev. Parsons fancies Julie. Mother died.

PLOT: Julie gets to know Michael particularly well.
   Miss Simms and Mr Bulloch get off to a good start too.
   Mr Mazda also has quite a nice time with Rev. Parsons.
   Miss Simms takes OAPs on day trip where one old lady drowns.

The class as a whole were totally absorbed in the work and argued with some sophistication for particular characters or combinations of characters. Although I did not allow enough time for them to develop plots at length, consideration of a potential plot played an important part in their creation of character types. There was considerable understanding of the serial as a form implicit in their discussion.

WHY DO YOU WATCH CORONATION STREET?

Before moving on to an attempt to teach about character in serials in an explicit way, I asked one group of volunteers to discuss *Coronation Street* and *Crossroads* with a tape-recorder running. The only questions posed were: 'Why do you watch *Coronation Street*? What makes you continue to watch it? In what way is it different from *Crossroads*?' They started off apologetically. Although they volunteered because they are regular viewers, in some senses they did not want to give their viewing a seriousness which was implied by my asking them to tape-record a discussion:

— Don't you mind if you miss it?
— No
— You're not really addicted to it?
— No, it's a bit of a laugh. I just watch it more for the sort of fun you know — because it's sort of pathetic acting and Hilda Ogden's stupid
— and everyone making mistakes,
— It's as bad as Blue Peter sometimes.
— I don't watch it like the old people do, 'cos they sort of live in it,
— They sort of get into it, don't they?
— Did you see that interview they had with Ernie Bishop and all these old ladies were crying because he died . . . ?
— Like in Crossroads they used to write letters to Stan telling him his wife had an affair with Anthony and telling him it's all his fault anyway so he shouldn't take it out on her.
— It's just force of habit.
— Yeah
— You get addicted to it and once the story gets going you can't miss it because you want it sort of to end.

Despite the fact that they distance themselves from 'old people' who believe the serials to be true, the girls constantly throughout the discussion tell anecdotes about the characters, reminding each other of events, and making judgements which reveal real involvement on their part.

— I think Coronation Street's better because it's got better characters in it, like Annie Walker.
— But they're not modern, are they?
— But Crossroads ain't exactly 21st Century is it?
— Look at Diane, look at the way she dresses — she's not exactly Hilda Ogden, is she?
— In Coronation Street the actors have got more go in them, haven't they?
— They've got a wider range — it's more involved — there's the whole street — all the shops and everything.
— and nosy neighbours
— whereas in Crossroads they've only got the motel and that.
— Yeah.

They discussed a range of issues — most of them related to character and plot, but also concerned with the future of the serials, the motivation behind particular events and frequently the question of nothing happening. They talk about there being nothing interesting happening at the moment (May 1980) and contrast this with events from the past such as the lorry crashing into 'The Rovers Return'. They clearly have a notion of what would comprise an exciting episode.

— Nothing drastic ever happens on Crossroads.
— It did, when Jill got pregnant by her step-brother.
— But that wasn't a big tragedy, was it?
    . . . .
— I think Coronation Street's got more life in it than Crossroads.
— Yeah, Annie Walker, you can really laugh at her, can't you?
— They've got all different characters, haven't they? They've got the really low ones, then the middle-class ones.
— Annie Walker with her game soup 'It's not pub grub, Fred'.
— The cast, you can actually really picture them being married together and living their everyday lives together.
— Yeah, cos it's all sort of ordinary, isn't it?
— Like in Soap, you wouldn't really imagine a normal family to be like that, would you?
— No, it's meant to be funny.
    . . . .
— I reckon the people in Crossroads, things keep happening to them and it goes on and on — but in Coronation Street you can drop them for ages.
    . . . .
— If Coronation Street was true, they must lead a really boring life.
— The same thing every day, Rovers every day of the week, god!

These comments on the ordinariness of *Coronation Street* are in tension with their expressed desire for excitement; the conflict is again present when they discuss a possible ending for the serial:

— I think the old fogeys are on the way out.
— They're dying!
— Do you remember when Ena had a heart attack?
— I reckon when all the old people have died, I don't think people are going to watch Coronation Street any more because there'll be hardly anyone left.
— All the young people'll take their place.
— It can't go on for ever.
— They can't just suddenly take it off, though, can they? There'd have to be an ending.
— How do you end a programme like Coronation Street?
— I reckon a war.
— Or the street gets knocked down and they have to evict them — that's how they *could* end it.
— Or a bomb.
— It would have to end realistically — you can't just chuck a bomb, can you? That's not how you expect it to end.
— I just can't picture Coronation Street ending.
— No.
— No.
— I'd like to watch the last episode.
— Yeah, I'd like to see how they end it.
— I bet they've attempted to finish it thousands of times.

A MORE COHERENT UNDERSTANDING

I think what this unstructured discussion about television serials shows is that children do have a basic understanding and awareness of the elements which Christine Geraghty discusses in her article. What is lacking is her framework of character types and narrative forms which would permit a more coherent or explicit understanding. The lesson which followed was an attempt to provide just this framework for one aspect of the serial, namely character.

Again working with the class in groups, I gave them the following worksheet which was briefly talked through before the class were asked to begin the task set. They were allowed two one-hour lessons, but once more their involvement was such that more time might have been desirable. This was the worksheet they were given:

Television Serials
1. In all serials there are characters who are made to be individuals different from everyone else, and they each have their own particular characteristics. One example is Albert Tatlock who is always seen as stingy and this gives him his individuality.
TASK: Make a list of as many characters from Coronation Street and Crossroads as you can, saying what it is about each which makes her/him individual.
2. In all serials there are particular 'serial types'. For example, in Coronation Street there is the 'Elsie Tanner type' — sexy, rather tartily dressed, hot-tempered, impulsive — and which would include, as well as Elsie herself, Rita, Suzie, Bet, (and possibly Len Fairclough as a male equivalent).
TASK: Name some other serial-types from Coronation Street and Crossroads, and list the characters which fit each type.
3. As well as individuated characters and serial-types, all characters also exist in serials as holders of a position. For example, in Coronation Street, Ken Barlow, Steve Fisher, Brian Tilsley, Mike Baldwin, Eddie Yeats, Billy Walker and even Albert Tatlock are all unmarried males and therefore available for stories about courtship and marriage.
TASK: List some other ways that characters could be grouped as 'holders of a position' and show what kinds of stories they would therefore fit into. Use examples from past episodes or invent some possibilities.
FOR FURTHER DISCUSSION:
Can you think of any other way of looking at characters in Coronation Street and Crossroads?
Do any characters not fit into any of these three categories (individuals; serial-types; holders of a position)?
FINAL TASK: Imagine you are telling a friend who has never seen

Coronation Street or Crossroads about the characters in one of them. In less than one side of paper, write what you would say to your friend.

As might be expected, the class found Task 1 the easiest to cope with. Each group came up with a list of characters, each one definable within a few words, and the groups were generally agreed about each individual character. Equally, on Task 2, the groups found it possible to group characters into a number of serial types. The talk which accompanied this categorizing, and the choice of label was very lively and involved some sophisticated consideration of characterization. Readers of this article might like to compare their own groupings with the following examples from 4BK:

a) Nosy types: Hilda Ogden, Elsie Tanner, Ena Sharples, Annie Walker.
b) Tarty types: Bet Lynch, Elsie Tanner, Rita Fairclough, Suzie Burchill.
c) Jack-the-lad types: Len Fairclough, Chris Hunter, Mike Baldwin.
d) Pig-headed: Len Fairclough, Ken Barlow, Stan Ogden, Mike Baldwin, Eddie Yeats, Albert Tatlock, Fred Gee.
e) Silly Women: Emily Bishop, Mavis, Ivy Tilsley, Vera Duckworth, Hilda Ogden.
f) Lazy: Stan Ogden, Eddie Yeats, Albert Tatlock, Annie Walker, Rita Fairclough, Audrey Potter.
g) Intelligent; understanding: Bert Tilsley, Alf Roberts, Ken Barlow.
h) Egotists: Mike Baldwin, Bet Lynch, Rita, Elsie, Fred Gee.

It was with Christine Geraghty's third category — character as 'holder of a position' that the class had most difficulty, finding it hard to establish a distinction between this and the serial-type, but some of the groups were clearly moving towards an understanding which I hope to be able to develop. The following 'positions' emerged from the class as a whole: single women; sexists; busybodies; boozers; married couples; old people; respected persons; widows.

Looking back, I now recognize my own nervousness about devoting a long stretch of time to 'something like *Coronation Street*'; that I had had a failure of nerve. In fact, had I allowed more time, and exploited the clear interest that existed from the class, then the insights they were beginning to gain into the way that character is built into particular fictions and narrative forms might have been developed even more effectively into their work on set-books and short stories and plays. Far more than through a complete film, the television serial was able to involve the class and engage its interest on an emotional level while at the same time permitting itself to be analysed objectively. There were none of the usual complaints that the teacher was spoiling the text by dissecting it and I think real advances were being made towards that position which I take to be a key goal for teachers of literature or of film: namely the creation of a person who is both reader and critic, who can weep at the end of *Of Mice and Men* or *King Lear* and yet know precisely why the work in question is organized in that way, how meanings are being generated, and what is the nature of the work in question. The work I began on character I intend to develop into work on narrative organization and constant cross-referencing between the television serial can be made to other aspects of my literature teaching. And if I have any doubts now about studying the serial as a form, I need only remind myself that many of those 'great works' set for A-level, first appeared as, and were experienced as, serials in the 19th century.

40 Creative Responses in the Sixth Form

● John Brown and Terry Gifford

INTRODUCTION

As the summit of English studies in school, why is 'A' level English often so disappointing? It promises well, with major writers at its centre; but the influence of the examination system has promoted narrow forms of assessment which have little, if any, room for students' creativity and which recognise only a severely limited kind of writing. It is a sad irony that on a course which is so art-centred the timed critical essay should have the monopoly.

What kind of influence does that specialised form of writing have on the way students read and respond to books? Is there a danger that analysis and exegesis can function independently of a student's felt response? In the following pages we shall offer practical suggestions for helping to develop a student's responsiveness and understanding, and ways of linking books and other forms of art. The suggestions are largely based on work either completed or in progress in a comprehensive school on a council estate in North Sheffield.

We shall describe ways of working which encourage students to have confidence in their engagement with a book by admitting a wider range of response, including creative work (as in the sections on poetry and documentary). We briefly touch upon the need to consider stages of learning in a course, with ideas for individual and group activities. In a section on *The Grapes of Wrath* we suggest ways in which the cultural context of a work of art can inform judgement and extend the sympathies through other art-forms. Our contention is that the wide range of teaching techniques and creative modes of work used lower down the school should enhance the development of a fully involved, individually critical engagement with a text in the Sixth Form. It is heartening that much of what we describe has been stimulated by now established alternative 'A' level syllabuses which move beyond the conceptions of English underlying the traditional forms of assessment (such new schemes have been developed, for example, by the Associated Examining Board (AEB) and the Joint Matriculation Board (JMB).)

INDUCTION AND BEYOND: GROUP ENGAGEMENTS WITH POETRY

Students need to have time to find their own way into a text, to make the text their own in some sense, before the rigours of a teacher-led class discussion. Small group work can provide the support and questioning necessary for tentative explorations. The degree of structure and the direction of its focus in the activities described below must be seen in relation to the stages of learning for which they were devised, whether it be the teaching or discovering of a particular concept, exploration of an area of experience, coming at a set text through juxtaposition with others, or initiation into the experience of group work itself.

An induction session for Fifth Formers about to join the Sixth Form was arranged, which aimed to indicate something of the range of activities in Sixth Form English, and to begin to forge working relationships through an exploration of the central idea in Ted Hughes' *Crow* poem 'Lineage'. A part of the Genesis creation story, followed by a Biblical lineage, was read to the class. Then, in groups of three, students were given an envelope containing the separate lines of the Hughes poem. Each group was asked to arrange the lines into a sequence, to create stanza spaces as necessary, and to glue this sequence on to a sheet of paper. The groups gave a choral reading of their version to the class. Then each member of the group was asked to select one line from their sequence on to which to add the word 'because' and complete as a sentence on the sheet. The class then listened to a recording of Hughes reading his poem 'Lineage', were given a copy, and again asked to add 'because' to one line each in order to complete a sentence. Next, groups of six were formed and asked to produce a lineage poem of twelve lines, by the process of each member contributing one line and passing the poem on until it had been round the group twice. Finally individuals were asked to tell, in a poem of their own, the lineage story of an object or creature from its earliest form, perhaps through some metamorphosis, to its present condition.

Later work on *Crow* began with groups preparing readings of the following six poems for a ritualised class performance: 'Lineage', 'Examination at the Womb-door', 'Crow's First Lesson', 'Crow Tyrannosauros', 'Crow and the Sea', and 'How Water Began to Play'. This selection provides a narrative framework through some of the best poems in the book. Work progressed to consider two questions: 'Of what story might these songs be the fragments?' and 'Write the anthropologist's report on the tribe which tells the story of *Crow*. What are their qualities?' Whilst striking at the heart of what *Crow* is about through creative work on the first question, the second question requires analysis and judgement.

Similar kinds of activities were devised as preparation for class discussion of earlier Hughes poems which were in the set text. These ranged from open-ended explorations to activities which drew attention to a particular area of experience or way of reading a poem. Three poems concerning death were given to the students: 'Dulce Et Decorum Est' by Owen, 'Vergissmeinnicht' by Keith Douglas, and Hughes' 'The Green Wolf'. Students were asked to place the three poems in an order or sequence before explaining their criteria by quotation. The effect of this is to have some comparative responses to each author's treatment of death brought to a discussion, which can then clarify each individual's readings of the poems from there.

In order to introduce a sense of the writer's stance towards subject matter a more structured and deliberately narrow activity was based on Lawrence's 'Fish' and Hughes' 'Pike'. Students were asked to use a scale in which −10 represented an extreme of 'subjectivity', the author completely identifying with his subject matter, and +10 represented the opposite extreme of 'objectivity', in which the author is a detached observer of his subject matter. Pairs of students were asked to give each poem a score on this scale. The average results of −7 for 'Fish' and +4 for 'Pike' are not in themselves as important as the perception of this dimension in the poems. The importance of the writer's stance to the achievement of each poem needs evaluating in discussion, which is the better for the concept having been used rather than externally produced.

Our last example of group engagement with poetry is not as a starting point for response but provides an opportunity for taking stock in the process of sorting out what is actually going on in the head of Hamlet. We had been reading *Hamlet* with some attempt to sense the dramatic tension in Hamlet's contributions in the early scenes. We had just read the 'To be or not to be' soliloquy, and needed to pause to consider the nature of Hamlet's self-questioning before the turning point of the play scene. Students were given copies of three poems: 'I Am' by John Clare, 'I am Vertical' by Sylvia Plath, and 'Wodwo' by Ted Hughes. In small groups students were asked to find any links between these poems and Hamlet's state of mind at this point in the play. They were given a big sheet of card and felt-tipped pens of two colours, as they were asked to show visually the relationship between these texts for a new reader of them. This card was to act as a guide for such a reader and could utilise arrows, quotations, annotations, and titles. One of the results is shown on p. 373, and although it is shorthand for the results of group discussion it does represent a coherent summary of the essential qualities of the poetry as it relates to Hamlet's state of mind. The placing

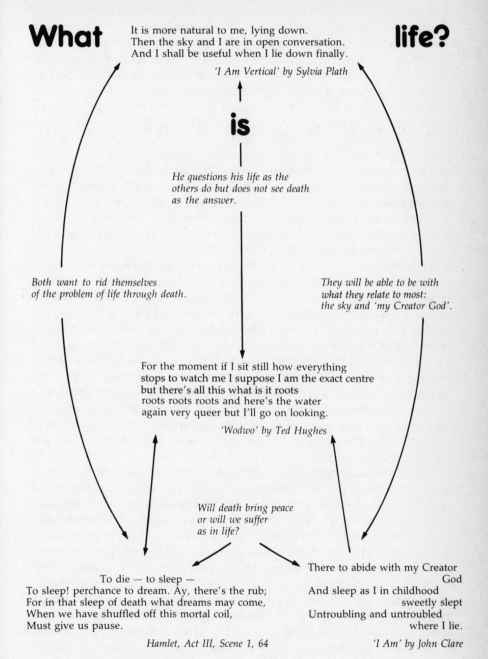

What

It is more natural to me, lying down.
Then the sky and I are in open conversation.
And I shall be useful when I lie down finally.

'I Am Vertical' by Sylvia Plath

life?

is

*He questions his life as the
others do but does not see death
as the answer.*

*Both want to rid themselves
of the problem of life through death.*

*They will be able to be with
what they relate to most:
the sky and 'my Creator God'.*

For the moment if I sit still how everything
stops to watch me I suppose I am the exact centre
but there's all this what is it roots
roots roots roots and here's the water
again very queer but I'll go on looking.

'Wodwo' by Ted Hughes

*Will death bring peace
or will we suffer
as in life?*

To die — to sleep —
To sleep! perchance to dream. Ay, there's the rub;
For in that sleep of death what dreams may come,
When we have shuffled off this mortal coil,
Must give us pause.

Hamlet, Act III, Scene 1, 64

There to abide with my Creator
God
And sleep as I in childhood
sweetly slept
Untroubling and untroubled
where I lie.

'I Am' by John Clare

of Clare's melodious lines beside the frenzied logic of Hamlet provides the material for further discussion of Hamlet's fear of, and flirtation with, self-deception. Isn't Sylvia Plath's 'useful' a false concept as much as the Wodwo's casual assumption that he is 'the exact centre'? Further questions arise out of the student's own consideration, selection and presentation, but can be followed through in the knowledge that an engagement of some quality has already taken place.

EXPLORING THE ART OF DOCUMENTARY

A well-chosen non-fiction book is worth an early place on an 'A' level course because of its likely accessibility, and because it can lead to some simple practical investigations by students. Orwell's *The Road to Wigan Pier* is a seminal choice on a syllabus, both as a key book from the pioneering days of documentary in the 1930s and in raising many of the basic issues about the art of documentary.

At a first reading many students may take Orwell's book as the kind that seems to offer empirical evidence of such a nature as to render dispute unlikely. However, on closer study, the reader will almost certainly want to know to what extent he can trust the artist's integrity.

The film-maker Grierson defined documentary as 'the creative treatment of actuality'; both in the process of gathering the material and in editing and selecting for the final draft the individual writer or maker of documentary will have his own bias and criteria. Moreover, whenever language is used to describe 'actuality', by its very nature it confers a degree of disjunction from reality that offers opportunity for deception. Art ought not to be confused with propaganda; how, then, can students be helped to discover these kinds of problems for themselves?

One obvious starting point is to look at one of the first published documentaries, Defoe's *Journal of the Plague Year*, which was published in 1722 about events in London in 1665, when its author was only four years old. The book claims to record 'observations . . . of the most remarkable occurrences written by a citizen who continued all the while in London', and the growing reading public at the time seems to have accepted this reconstructed eye-witness account. A close look at the *Journal* will offer significant clues as to how a writer captures this trust — by its detailed graphic narrative, its use of statistics, its personal asides and its dramatised dialogues. Students can be invited to say how far they think Defoe is a reliable reporter by comparison with parts of Cobbett's *Rural Rides*. It is important for students to meet committed thinkers from earlier periods, whose treatment of strong social, moral and political purposes may be compared with Orwell.

At this stage, students can be shown some of the photographs from the 1930s, particularly those of Bill Brandt. His book, *The English at Home* appeared in 1936, a year before Orwell's, when Brandt had decided to concentrate on reportage and documentary; it contains photographs of miners, both at work and at home. Another resource is the Mass Observation archives, but these are more selective because the aim of that group was to be more 'scientific'. Compared to Orwell's description of the Lancashire slums, the Mass Observation photographs of Bolton by Humphrey Spender seem to avoid those harsh conditions.

Students can now be asked to make their own short documentaries, in groups, armed ideally with cameras and tape recorders. Their aim is to try to record actuality, with no more specific purpose declared, since the process of editing will then become very revealing. Clearly photographs impose their own limited framework on reality, and when tapes are transcribed and edited then the resulting tape/slide programme will inevitably be a very selective presentation of what students actually witnessed on location, especially if one student in each group has acted as observer during the whole operation. It may be possible using the same basic material, but by selecting different sequences of slides and tape, or by omitted certain images and sounds, to produce two or three different documentaries. The shock of recognition experienced by the students, gained during the process of making, can give an impetus to study of social, moral and political aspects of art; and practical investigations of this kind are well worth giving time to.

On returning to Orwell, two sections of the book can be looked at closely: that which records the author's first visit underground to a pit, and some later pages about scrambling for coal. Earlier drafts of these pages are to be found in 'Diary of the Road to Wigan Pier' (in *Collected Essays, Journals and Letters*, Vol. I, 1968), and it is revealing to make a detailed comparison of tone, presentation and selection of material. The changes in the text show Orwell's awareness of his audience who were, in the first place, members of the Left Book Club.

It is also useful to compare Orwell's attitude to miners, remembering that he was from a middle-class background, to that of D. H. Lawrence in 'Nottingham and the Mining Country' and B. L. Coombes, a Welsh miner, in his autobiography *These Poor Hands*. A photo-narrative about Coombes appeared in *Picture Post* (4 January 1941); Henry Moore's distinguished drawings of miners at work are a further valuable source. There are more recent reports on mining to look at — *Weekend at Dimlock* by C. Sigal (1960), and a collection of reminiscences by miners themselves, *Essays from the Yorkshire Coalfield* (published by the University of Sheffield, 1979). Having a range of attitudes to consider makes it easier for students to judge whether Orwell indulges in a form of hero worship of working men at times.

Essential reading at this stage is Orwell's essay 'Why I Write', since there he declares his political commitment in all his writing since 1936, the year before he wrote *The Road to Wigan Pier*. A comparison with Grierson's classic film *Drifters*, which is still available for hire, offers another perspective, since the dignified images of fishermen are similar in spirit and intention to the word pictures of miners by Orwell.

Yet further work can be linked to some of Orwell's other documentary type essays and books — 'Shooting an Elephant', 'How the Poor Die', *Down and Out in Paris and London* and *Homage to Catalonia*. By then students may have come to judge for themselves Orwell's integrity and achievement as a committed writer. Such delicate questions cannot be resolved in the instant and final form of a homework's essay. Truly personal judgements of tone can be sharpened by direct experience of artistic choices when the work of several artists is seen fresh from the exercise of those choices in practical explorations of the art of documentary.

RESPONSE TO DRAMA IN PERFORMANCE

It is a commonly argued point that drama texts should be regarded as printed intentions for live effects in performance, and the study of plays through some sort of dramatic exploration by students' own drama work is commonly advocated. For English students this is usually intended to help them answer examination questions about the imagined dramatic possibilities of the printed text. The alternative AEB and JMB syllabuses give provision in their coursework element for written responses to live performances. Again this is often claimed to be important in drama study on English courses, but the evidence is rarely produced for the kind of perceptions that can be gained from the linked study of text and performance.

Maria had read *Hamlet* with her class as a first experience of Shakespeare in the Lower Sixth; she had been involved in improvisations, scene performances, and discussions that had focused on the problems and insights presented to an audience by the unfolding of the play. After seeing a performance at Stratford in her second term Maria wrote in her review of that performance:

> The performance of Hamlet was interesting and sensitive, something reading the play does not always create. Hamlet's character was portrayed with understanding, his madness being given a purpose, to show the true life of the court, yet as in most human situations, showing times when it got out of control. The most realistic element of this performance was not only the perceptive manner Hamlet was given but the fact that during and after the performance his character could not be clearly assessed or defined. Like a living being he was too deep and complexed (*sic*) a character to be drawn out with mere words.

This may be escaping some complexities at this stage, yet whilst it is struggling with a sense of the dramatic enigma of Hamlet's character there is a clear view of Hamlet's role in the whole drama, 'his madness being given a purpose'.

Ashley, on the other hand, in reviewing a performance of *The Caucasian Chalk Circle*, again after prior reading and discussion of the text, was quite specific about the nature of the complexities of the character of Azdak:

> The production does not show Azdak's contradictions well. Nicky Henson, who played Azdak (at Sheffield), seems constantly to indulge the character's senses, without showing how mentally alert Azdak is. Azdak is not shocking to the audience because Henson assumes that his contradictions are simply those of a corrupt man. Azdak's apparent corruptness, however, is rational and based on logic. He is, therefore, parodying the corrupt nature of the court system. It is not until the trial involving Grusha that the audience truly sees the dominance of Azdak's shrewdness over Grusha's simple goodness.

This sense of measuring up an actor's or a director's interpretation of the same text read earlier by the student can lead to suggestions for improvement in dramatic effects that are sharp, clear and physical in their expression of an intellectual perception. At the time of writing her first account, Celestine did not know about Brecht's use of masks for the soldiers in his original production of *The Caucasian Chalk Circle*:

> In order to create the atmosphere of fear and tension on stage, and conveying the same feeling of fear which I felt while reading the play, the director should have portrayed the iron shirts wearing a black mask, shaped like a dome, smooth, with no indentations representing a mouth or ears. The back and front should have been indistinguishable so that the mask is transporting (*sic*) the image that the iron shirts have no feeling or loyalty.

In the theatre, 'Truth is concrete' is Brecht's famous motto. It must be said that in getting students to write about its enactment, rather than as a book only, practice is an advantage, and the focus of discussion on the physical and contextual nature of meaning in theatre is also necessary. We saw a play and reviewed its performance once each term, not confining ourselves to the productions of texts of which we had copies, but also choosing new plays at our local studio theatre that made full use of the vibrant liveness of performance, and of course, some that did not!

In order to achieve the subtle yet clear understanding of Azdak's character that Ashley's paragraph shows, it is necessary to accept the conditions of turmoil in which Azdak attempts to survive. Celestine's expression of the Ironshirts' lack of 'feeling or loyalty' that creates these conditions takes the form of a vivid practical image. Like Ashley she writes with a thoughtful, felt understanding of the nature of meaning in dramatic performance.

TEXT AND CONTEXT — THE GRAPES OF WRATH

The uncelebrated dramas of our students' own lives in the community are a resource for learning that is traditionally neglected most in the Sixth Form. Yet the concept of 'relevance' in relation to a text like *The Grapes of Wrath* can only be accurately applied if attention is paid as much to differences as to similarities with contemporary family life, unemployment and social change. The slide/tape sequence, '*Grapes of Wrath* and the 1930s' is an American production (EAV Inc) which brings together the classic photographs of the period, Woody Guthrie's songs, readings from the novel and an informative commentary on the economic background to the movement of migrant workers from the Mid West during the 1930s. This combination of art-forms makes the unfolding of the historical story a powerful experience in its own right. As an introduction to a study of the novel the combination of modes helps an understanding of economic and social processes to be formed in a way that is not separated from the authentic quality and response to the experience in the lives of people themselves.

We began with Part II of the sequence which deals with the wider economic and political perspectives, making notes at the second running of it so that the historical processes could be identified. An important element in the approach of this sequence is that these processes are seen to be the dynamics of the policies and motivations of men, as seen all the time in the photographs. This is an important perception to bring to a discussion of the extent to which Steinbeck reifies 'the Banks' in the novel. When we ran Part I of the sequence the focus of attention was on the direct experiences of the farmers and migrants. After a first run-through of sound and photographs the photographs alone were discussed in terms of the emotions revealed in the subjects and the stance taken by the photographers. This led to questions about pride and dignity in relation to poverty. At the end of this discussion of the photographs students were asked to write in note form all they could about the actual experience of dispossession, unemployment and poverty in America in the 1930s from the evidence of the songs, novel extracts and tape commentary as well as the photographs. Drawing from these notes they were then asked to devise questions for an interview with a person at present unemployed, in order to discover differences and similarities in the experience and responses to it among their family, friends or neighbours today.

When the students returned with the results of their interviews attention was turned to the Woody Guthrie songs on the tape. Their form was discussed and the sources of the tunes discovered. Students were then asked to use the results of their interviews to write a song that would be a contemporary English equivalent to Guthrie's songs of the 1930s in America. To the tune of 'To Be A Sheffield Grinder' from the play *The Stirrings in Sheffield on Saturday Night*, Jane's song began:

'Ballad for the Unemployed'

To be unemployed in Britain
  it is no easy trade,
No hope for long-time jobless
  whose ideals have frayed,

No hope for all the people
   whose work they cannot find,
It's alright for the miners
   they have an axe to grind.

It's hard for all those people
   to look you in the face,
But don't you employ someone
   to come and take their place.
Remember they have feelings
   although they're hard to find;
Humiliated dole queues
   where all their names are signed.

Though people think you're lazy
   What else is there to do?
What else is there to offer?
   There's no jobs to go to
Your family and friends reject you
   they say you cause them shame
But one day in the future
   they may end up the same.

The tone of bitterness and frustration that expresses the detail ('Humiliated dole queues') and trapped sense ('What else is there to do?') came to a head in the final lines quoted here. The obvious authenticity derived from the interview has found witty form in a parody of a popular local song about work.

By the time we began reading and discussing the novel itself Joe Klein's biography of Woody Guthrie (1981) was circulating; the visual ground had been prepared for our visit to John Ford's film of the novel at a later stage; some historical information had been noted to put alongside Steinbeck's political analysis; and most important, some engagement had been made with the nature of experiences of people like the Joads through other art-forms. The obvious strain and sense of indignity shown through the faces in the photographs, the last remnants of pride in the loaded cars of the migrants, the bitterness in the songs of Woody Guthrie, and making an articulation of our contemporary experiences of loss of work, all made the relevance of Steinbeck's novel obvious before we read it.

It is perhaps worth adding that in helping students to make a personal response to the novel at a first reading much use was made of students' personal reading diaries in the way suggested by David Jackson in *English in Education* (1979). Students were asked to read a section of the novel and then record in their diaries their immediate thoughts about it to bring to a class discussion or group work on that section of the book. Any class discussion thus began from points that interested or puzzled the students at first acquaintance; it then moved into areas that the teacher felt to be important if they had not been discussed already.

The diary is the place where early connections are made between the reader and the text, where the suggestions of the text are sorted out in relation to the reader's experience. Christine's comments on Chapter 19 in her reading diary *after* a class discussion represent a more reflective stage of evaluation of the text that is moving beyond a first engagement:

> Steinbeck realises that the stage is set for revolt, and assumes that it will come one day. He seems sure that he is right, and indeed the seeds of revolt are certainly present and growing, but, in the end, is he biased? Can the people really overcome their oppression? He sees from the inside as his writing of conversation shows. But the revolution is *not* inevitable. The poverty is short term, not long term as in other countries where revolution occurred. It seems to be wishful thinking on Steinbeck's part — wish for an uprising.

In our emphasis on personal engagement, stages of learning, the opening of the sympathies by integrating art-forms in a way that does not truncate students' own creativity, we have not been arguing for an emotional identification that is separate from critical judgement. In this section, for example, our treating the matter of relevance as more than simple parallels has perhaps led to this sharply perceptive evaluation in Christine's diary. Certainly she needs to develop this response in a more considered statement by referring to Steinbeck's use of language in the text. Certainly, too, further questions remain. How far can our use of worksheets of detailed questions, related to key passages of the novel, help to sustain alert and felt response through to the final examination? To what extent can the problems of the assessment of students' own creative work be met by agreement trials for teachers, together with examiners, considering through actual examples the balances between suggestion and clarity, complexity and accuracy, experimentation and communication? The answers to questions such as these are urgently needed if our teaching in the Sixth Form is to allow as much for the wholeness of the growing person as for the wholeness of fully formed art. And in the end, of course, these must go together; since art, like language, can live only through those who use, and thereby continuously renew, art and language.

REFERENCES

Brandt, B. (1936) *The English at Home* (Batsford)

Brecht, B. (1966) 'The Caucasian Chalk Circle' in *Parables for the Theatre* (Penguin)

Cobbett, W. (1830) *Rural Rides* (Penguin, 1967)

Coombes, B. L. (1939) *These Poor Hands* (Gallanz)

Defoe, D. (1722) *Journal of the Plague Year* (Penguin, 1966)

EAV Inc. 'The Grapes of Wrath and the 1930s' slide/tape sequence R2 170 (Mary Glasgow Publications)

J. Grierson's film *Drifters* (1929) available from BFI, Central Film Library, 81 Dean Street, London, W1V 6AA

Hardy, F. (1979) *Grierson on Documentary* (Faber)

Hughes, T. (1970) *Crow* (Faber)

Klein, J. (1981) *Woody Guthrie: a Biography* (Faber)

Lawrence, D. H. 'Nottingham and the Mining Country' in *Selected Essays* (Penguin, 1950)

MacFarlane, J. (ed.) (1979) *Essays from the Yorkshire Coalfield* (University of Sheffield)

Orwell, G. (1933) *Down and Out in Paris and London* (Penguin, 1962)
    (1938) *Homage to Catalonia* (Penguin, 1969)
    (1937) *The Road to Wigan Pier* (Penguin, 1962)
    (1961) 'Why I Write', 'Shooting an Elephant' and 'How the Poor Die' in *Collected Essays* (Mercury)
    (1968) 'Diary of the Road to Wigan Pier' in *The Collected Essays, Journals and Letters*, Vol. I (Secker)

Shakespeare, W. *Hamlet*

Sigal, C. (1960) *Weekend in Dimlock* (Secker)

Spender, H. photographs in *Camera Workshop* No. 11 (Mass Observation Issue) and (1982) *Worktown People* (Falling Wall Press)

Steinbeck, J. (1939) *The Grapes of Wrath* (Penguin, 1951)

Craig, D. and Heinemann, M., (1976) *Experiments in English Teaching* (Arnold)

Dixon, J. *et al.* (1979) *Education 16–19: The role of English and Communication* (Macmillan)

Dixon, J. and Roberts, N. (1978) 'Towards Changes at A Level' in *The Use of English*, Volume 29, No. 2

Gill, R. and Jackson, D. (1980) 'Students Articulating their Response to Literature' in *Schools Council English 16–19 Project Booklet No. 9*

Harding, D. W. (1977) 'Feeling Comprehension' in *The Cool Web* (ed.) Meek, M. *et al.* (Bodley Head)

Horner, S. and Allen, D. (1980) 'A Bang or a Whimper — A New 'A' Level Syllabus', in *English in Education*, Volume 14, No. 2

Jackson, D. (1979) 'A Sixth Form Approach to Seamus Heaney' in *English in Education*, Volume 13, No. 3

Leavis, F. R. (1977) *The Living Principle* (Chatto)

Newton, J. M. (1971) 'Literary Criticism, Universities, Murder', in *The Cambridge Quarterly*, Volume 5, No. 4

Potter, S. (1937) *The Muse in Chains* (Cape)

Stanton, M. (1980) 'Art Exists to Make the Stone Stoney', in *English in Education*, Volume 14, No. 3.

Witkin, R. (1974) *The Intelligence of Feeling* (Heinemann)

VII ASSESSMENT

In the opening extract, Jackson evaluates some of the basic aims of comprehension questions, considering the viewpoint of pupils as well as of teachers in his discussion.

The statement of the national criteria in English for the G.C.S.E. (42) is followed by an article by Dixon and Stratta who, sensing their moment of history, pose a series of questions as to the possible success or failure of the examination. Will it be a liberating influence?

Official certainty and the definition of the 'common core' at 'A' level is contained in (44), a precursor to John Dixon's discussion of student response in that examination. The discussion is accompanied by invaluable illustration. Some of the issues involved in teaching an alternative 'A' level are considered by Terry Gifford in the final article of the section and of the book, issues seen in terms of a case study of his teaching of Alan Garner's *Red Shift*.

41 Formulating Your Own Questions: An Approach to Comprehension

● David Jackson

THE END OF SOMETHING

In the old days Hortons Bay was a lumbering town. No one who lived in it was out of sound of the big saws in the mill by the lake. Then one year there were no more logs to make lumber. The lumber schooners came into the bay and were loaded with the cut of the mill that stood stacked in the yard. All the piles of lumber were carried away. The big mill building had all its machinery that was removable taken out and hoisted on board one of the schooners by the men who had worked in the mill. The schooner moved out of the bay towards the open lake carrying the two great saws, the travelling carriage that hurled the logs against the iron piled on a hull-deep load of lumber. Its open hold covered with canvas and lashed tight, the sails of the schooner filled and it moved out into the open lake, carrying with it everything that had made the mill a mill and Hortons Bay a town.

The one-storey bunk houses, the eating-house, the company store, the mill offices, and the big mill itself stood deserted in the acres of sawdust that covered the swampy meadow by the shore of the bay.

Ten years later there was nothing of the mill left except the broken white limestone of its foundations showing through the swampy second growth as Nick and Marjorie rowed along the shore. They were trolling along the edge of the channel bank where the bottom dropped off suddenly from sandy shallows to twelve feet of dark water. They were trolling their way to the point to set night lines for rainbow trout.

'There's our old ruin, Nick,' Marjorie said.

Nick, rowing, looked at the white stone in the green trees.

'There it is,' he said.

'Can you remember when it was a mill?' Marjorie asked.

'I can just remember,' Nick said.

'It seems more like a castle,' Marjorie said.

Nick said nothing. They rowed on out of sight of the mill, following the shore line. Then Nick cut across the bay.

'They aren't striking,' he said.

'No,' Marjorie said. She was intent on the rod all the time they trolled, even when she talked. She loved to fish. She loved to fish with Nick.

Close beside the boat a big trout broke the surface of the water. Nick pulled hard on one oar so the boat would turn and the bait spinning far behind would pass where the trout was feeding. As the trout's back came up out of the water the minnows jumped wildly. They sprinkled the surface like a handful of shot thrown into the water. Another trout broke water, feeding on the other side of the boat.

'They're feeding,' Marjorie said.

'But they won't strike,' Nick said.

He rowed the boat around to troll past both the feeding fish, then headed it for the point. Marjorie did not reel in until the boat touched the shore.

They pulled the boat up the beach and Nick lifted out a pail of live perch. The perch swam in the water in the pail. Nick caught three of them with his hands and cut their heads off and skinned them while Marjorie chased with her hands in the bucket, finally caught a perch, cut its head off, and skinned it. Nick looked at her fish.

'You don't want to take the ventral fin out,' he said. 'It'll be all right for bait but it's better with the ventral fin in.'

He looked each of the skinned perch through the tail. There were two hooks attached to a leader on each rod. Then Marjorie rowed the boat out over the channel-bank, holding the line in her teeth and looking toward Nick, who stood on the shore holding the rod and letting the line run out from the reel.

'That's about right,' he called.

'Should I let it drop?' Marjorie called back, holding the line in her hand.

'Sure. Let it go.' Marjorie dropped the line overboard and watched the baits go down through the water.

She came in with the boat and ran the second line out the same way. Each time Nick set a heavy slab of driftwood across the butt of the rod to hold it solid and propped it up at an angle with a small slab. He reeled in the slack line so the line ran taut out to where the boat rested on the sandy floor of the channel and set the click on the reel. When a trout, feeding on the bottom, took the bait it would run with it, taking line out of the reel in a rush and making the reel sing with the click on.

Marjorie rowed up the point a little way so she would not disturb the line. She pulled hard on the oars and the boat went way up the beach.

Little waves came in with it. Marjorie stepped out of the boat and Nick pulled the boat high up the beach.

'What's the matter, Nick?' Marjorie asked.

'I don't know,' Nick said, getting wood for a fire.

They made a fire with driftwood. Marjorie went to the boat and brought a blanket. The evening breeze blew the smoke toward the point, so Marjorie spread the blanket out between the fire and the lake.

Marjorie sat on the blanket with her back to the fire and waited for Nick. He came over and sat down beside her on the blanket. In back of them was the close second-growth timber of the point and in front was the bay with the mouth of Hortons Creek. It was not quite dark. The firelight went as far as the water. They could both see the two steel rods at an angle over the dark water. The fire glinted on the reels.

Marjorie unpacked the basket of supper.

'I don't feel like eating,' said Nick.

'Come on and eat, Nick.'

'All right.'

They ate without talking, and watched the two rods and the firelight in the water.

'There's going to be a moon tonight,' said Nick. He looked across the bay to the hills that were beginning to sharpen against the sky. Beyond the hills he knew the moon was coming up.

'I know it,' Marjorie said happily.

'You know everything,' Nick said.

'Oh, Nick, please cut it out! Please don't be that way!'

'I can't help it,' Nick said. 'You do. You know everything. That's the trouble. You know you do.'

Marjorie did not say anything.

'I've taught you everything. You know you do. What don't you know, anyway?'

'Oh, shut up,' Marjorie said. 'There comes the moon.'

They sat on the blanket without touching each other and watched the moon rise.

'You don't have to talk silly,' Marjorie said. 'What's really the matter?'

'I don't know.'

'Of course you know.'

'No, I don't.'

'Go on and say it.'

Nick looked on at the moon, coming up over the hills.

'It isn't fun any more.'

He was afraid to look at Marjorie. Then he looked at her. She sat there with her back towards him. He looked at her back. 'It isn't fun any more. Not any of it.'

She didn't say anything. He went on. 'I feel as though everything was gone to hell inside me. I don't know, Marge. I don't know what to say.'

He looked on at her back.

'Isn't love any fun?' Marjorie said.

'No,' Nick said. Marjorie stood up. Nick sat there, his head in his hands.

'I'm going to take the boat,' Marjorie called to him. 'You can walk back around the point.'

'All right,' Nick said. 'I'll push the boat off for you.'

'You don't need to,' she said. She was afloat in the boat on the water with the moonlight on it. Nick went back and lay down with his face in the blanket by the fire. He could hear Marjorie rowing on the water.

He lay there for a long time. He lay there while he heard Bill come into the clearing walking around through the woods. He felt Bill coming up to the fire. Bill didn't touch him, either.

'Did she go all right?' Bill said.

'Yes,' Nick said, lying, his face on the blanket.

'Have a scene?'

'No, there wasn't any scene.'

'How do you feel?'

'Oh, go away, Bill! Go away for a while.'

Bill selected a sandwich from the lunch basket and walked over to have a look at the rods.

THE STUDENTS

Four fourth year pupils — Stephen, Elspeth, Stella and Max — were asked to read Hemingway's short story, 'The End of Something', and to talk about and write down their own set of questions on the story.

The group started to talk about Max's suggestion, 'Why was the mill the end of something?' Stephen thought it was an odd way to start a story about Nick and Marjorie's fishing trip. He thought that all this stuff about the mill's machinery was not necessary. But Stella did not agree. She said the opening showed Nick's feelings towards the mill. The mill was finished and Nick was pining for the days that he had known there.

A long pause followed. Elspeth did not think Nick was doing the pining. But Stella went on, persisting that he was reluctant to talk about it after Marjorie said that the mill seemed like a castle because when he saw the old mill he remembered his earlier life.

Max thought the description of the mill set the atmosphere for the story and that a question ought to be set on it. Stephen said that Nick and Marjorie were like the mill. They were almost like a comparison.

Elspeth's second question was, 'Who is Bill, and what does he have to do with what's going on in the story?' Max did not know who Bill was but Stella said he was Nick's mate.

Elspeth thought Nick was a cunning devil who had set up the splitting scene on purpose, but Max suggested that Bill might have pushed Nick into planning it. They all seemed to agree that it was a put-up job.

Stella said she did not like Nick at all. He seemed like a yellow belly to her. He should have either told her to get lost or explained to her what he was feeling. Instead he pushed Marjorie into an argument where she had got to end it. Stella thought he just could not cope.

After an excited digression stemming from Stella's protest about cutting the fishes' heads off even while they were alive, the group decided on three questions:

1. Why was the mill the end of something?
2. Who is Bill, and what does he have to do with what's going on in the story?
3. Do you think Nick was right to end it the way he did?

As a department, some months before, the teachers had worked out their own set of comprehension questions without reference to the children's views. They provide a revealing contrast:

1. What changes took place in Hortons Bay over the period of ten years?
2. Why did the writer open his story with the description of Hortons Bay?
3. What do we learn about Nick and Marjorie's feelings for each other from the way they talk to each other and the way they go about their fishing?
4. Telling people that you want to finish with them is often a very difficult and painful thing to do. How do you think Nick copes with doing this?
5. *Either* imagine that you are Marjorie, rowing back across the lake without Nick. Describe your feelings, thoughts and sensations. This could be a free verse poem, short story or any other form of writing. *Or* imagine that you are Bill and describe the two conversations that you had with Nick about splitting with Marjorie, *before* and *after* the fishing trip.

CREATIVE ASSIGNMENTS

1. Write about a time when you parted from something or somebody close to you (e.g., moving to a new area, taking a pet to the vet to be put down, arguing with a best friend, changing schools).
2. Set out in play form the telephone conversation between a boy and a girl friend, where one of them wants to finish with the other.
3. Write a letter that ends a relationship.

4. 'It isn't fun anymore'. Write a short story.
5. Ten years later (e.g., going back to a house that you once lived in and finding it deserted).

Dissatisfied with the triviality of many literal-minded comprehension questions we were aiming at eliciting a more total response from the child than in many top-of-the-head angled questions. So that in question 5 and the creative assignments we were accepting that imaginative involvement might be a necessary pre-condition to understanding the story fully.

Also prompted by Bullock into considering a range of understanding skills we had tried to arrange the questions into an ascending hierarchy of literal, inferential, evaluative/appreciative skills but as we can see from the way the pupils tackle the story we were probably misguided in doing so. In our question 1 we were attempting to keep the response to a literal level. But children's reactions cannot be contained like this, as their talk bears out. Discussion of Max's question leads them on inevitably into inference in Stella's comment about Nick pining for the days that he had known there, evaluation in Max's point about atmosphere, and inference/evaluation in Stephen's appreciation of the correspondence between the physical setting and the state of Nick and Marjorie's relationship, 'They were almost like a comparison.' Literal, inferential and evaluative responses in children exist in a much more scrambled, interrelated state than the neat adult pigeon-holes would have us suppose.

Often, I would suggest, our teacherly concerns about appropriate critical attitudes get in the way of the pupils having time and space to find their own feeling entrance into the passage or story. Here I am not idly knocking these critical concerns because they can often deepen understanding and enjoyment, but they should work alongside the children's perceptions and not smother them. Take the department's question 3 for example. In comprehension exercises children are often confused by the special wording or syntax that prevent them from recording their full response. I suspect that the teacher choice of 'learn' here might well have signalled a school-approved right answer to the pupil rather than being interpreted as an open invitation for detailed speculations. Lying behind the question is the implicit concern that children will approach Nick and Marjorie's relationship through the story's texture and in this case should be directed to seeing how the curt, laconic exchanges establish the feeling of unease between the two people. But the facility for manipulating that kind of critical apparatus is not necessarily tied into a feeling experience of any sort. And often, in schools, we go for the premature critical approach without the lived-through dimension to make it real.

Elspeth's question about Bill has a greater directness and simplicity than the teacher's question 3, but more importantly, starting from a pupil's perspective on the story, it leads the reader straight to the heart of the most essential issues. Although superficially the question might seem peripheral it takes us on to consider Nick's character and motivation (is it a planned job?), Nick's relationship with Marjorie (if it is a planned job what is so wrong between them that he wants to break off with her?) and the structure of the whole story (as Elspeth puts it, 'what does [Bill] have to do with what's going on in the story?'). By framing a genuine question about an area of the story that puzzles her, rather than being encouraged to take over adult insights, formulations and categories, she is moving towards getting on the inside of the story's meaning, and constructing an interpretation for herself.

Instead of being confused by the special rules of the game of comprehension questions set by examiners or teachers (the difficult wording, misleading associations, ambiguous syntax, etc.), Max, Elspeth, Stella and Stephen could start with an active purpose in mind and use their own cultural focus and familiar words to make sense of what they were reading.

The role of active questioner rather than docile receiver also encouraged the children to have exploratory conversations about the story's implications — like Elspeth not standing back blankly from the story, but determinedly tackling the sudden appearance of Bill at the end by explaining that it shows how calculating Nick is in setting up this splitting scene in collaboration with Bill. This personal engagement with the story makes her want to construct her own meaning out of it.

The comparative strength of the children's social position in all this is important. Instead of being back-seat passengers taken somewhere by an adult they are much more in the driving seat, deciding which route to take and which turnings to go up. So that some of the increased incentive for making anything out of the story is attributable, I think, to the way their viewpoint is respected. The teacher is no longer dominating all the decisions and there is scope for their own investigations in a more socially potent situation.

The teacher's role would be as a tactful adviser but a significant one nevertheless. The choice of material is crucial; she has got to know enough about the common preoccupations of this age group to select stories that are rich enough in personal associations to create a motivated interest in the reader. Stories, perhaps, like Doris Lessing's 'Through the Tunnel', John Wain's 'A Message from the Pig-man', William March's 'The Prisoners', William Carlos Williams's 'The Use of Force', and John Gordon's 'The Place'.

Also, when the children have had a chance to formulate and talk through their own lines of enquiry into the story, the teacher has an important synthesizing job to do. She has to encourage and support more central and productive lines of investigation, like Stephen's suggestion that Nick and Marjorie were like the mill, and blend them into her own reactions to the story without smothering the children's initiatives and without her preconceptions about the story being unmodified by the children's response.

42 *General Certificate of Secondary Education: The National Criteria, English*

- Department of Education and Science

1. AIMS

1.1 The subject English is to be regarded as a single unified course leading to an assessment in English. It may also lead to a separate assessment in English Literature.

The course should seek to develop the ability of students to:

1.1.1 communicate accurately, appropriately and effectively in speech and writing;

1.1.2 understand and respond imaginatively to what they hear, read and experience in a variety of media;

1.1.3 enjoy and appreciate the reading of literature;

1.1.4 understand themselves and others.

1.2 For assessment purposes, two titles will be used — English and English Literature — and these are treated as separate examination subjects.*

1.3 The implications of English in a multi-cultural society are considered in what follows in this document and in the General Criteria.

[...]

---

* Only 'English Literature' is included in this extract.

English Literature

1. ASSESSMENT OBJECTIVES

1.1 The assessment objectives in a syllabus with the title English Literature must provide opportunities for pupils to demonstrate, both in the detailed study of some literary texts and in wider reading, their ability to:

1.1.1 acquire first-hand knowledge of the content of literary texts;

1.1.2 understand literary texts, in ways which may range from a grasp of their surface meaning to a deeper awareness of their themes and attitudes;

1.1.3 recognise and appreciate other ways in which writers use language;

1.1.4 recognise and appreciate other ways in which writers achieve their effects (e.g. structure, characterisation);

1.1.5 communicate a sensitive and informed personal response to what is read.

1.2 The skills listed above are clearly interrelated and interdependent and while all must be asessed, it is not envisaged that each skill need be tested in isolation.

2. CONTENT

2.1 The content of the examination syllabus in English Literature must consist of the detailed study of individual texts as well as wider reading in all of the three main literary genres of prose, poetry and drama. Examining Groups may extend the scope of what is traditionally regarded as the canon of English Literature in recognition that awareness of the richness of cultural diversity is one of the rewards of the study of literature. The majority of the works must be literary texts originally written in English which may, for example, include American and Commonwealth writing, but works in translation may also be included.

2.2 The works of detailed study need not be prescribed in a set texts syllabus of a traditional kind. For example, a wide personal choice may be offered in recommended reading of authors, themes, periods or genres. Works for wider reading may be suggested similarly. Examining Groups will need to ensure that the works for detailed study are of sufficient substance and quality to merit serious consideration and that they are selected from at least two literary genres.

3. RELATIONSHIP BETWEEN ASSESSMENT OBJECTIVES AND CONTENT

The Assessment Objectives (see 1.1.1 to 1.1.5 above) set out in general terms the abilities which are to be assessed in English Literature. The Content (see 2.1 and 2.2) above is expressed in terms of detailed study, covering at least two literary genres as well as wider reading in all three. All the stated objectives can be assessed in both areas. Since response to literature combines skills which are not always readily separated, no specific weightings for these objectives are recommended, but at least 60% and not more then 75% of the total marks in English Literature must be allocated to the assessment of detailed study of individual texts.

4. TECHNIQUES OF ASSESSMENT

4.1 Extended writing (i.e. more than a single paragraph) is valuable in English Literature in allowing candidates to articulate and develop their response to literary material and must therefore be included. While this technique may allow candidates to demonstrate their ability across the whole range of Assessment Objectives, other techniques such as structured sets of short-answer questions may also be employed to assess particular aspects of understanding or appreciation. Continuous writing must account for at least 50% of the whole scheme of assessment.

4.2 The Assessment Objectives will be tested by reference to material studied during the course; they should normally also be tested by unprepared material not previously set for study. Unprepared material can provide the candidates with opportunities to apply appropriate skills in a more spontaneous manner than reliance upon learned responses. It will be particularly important, however, to select material that will suit the range of ability to be examined.

4.3 In assessing first-hand knowledge of texts studied during the course, undue emphasis should not be placed on mere recall.

Access to texts is readily available in the assessment of course work and can also be permitted in the examination-room through the provision of lengthy extracts or complete plain texts.

4.4   Centre-based and Board-based Assessment

4.4.1   Examination by the assessment of Course Work is appropriate to English Literature in view of the variety of approaches indicated in Paragraph 2.2. Compared with a formal examination paper it provides wider evidence of candidates' achievement demonstrated on different occasions in samples of work covering the range of skills to be assessed. It can provide the flexibility needed to assess a wide range of ability in the subject. It is especially suitable for the assessment of wide reading since it may prove difficult to set satisfactory general questions in a final examination.

4.4.2   It is recommended that a combination of assessment by Course Work and by final examination should normally be used. In all syllabuses such Course Work must account for at least 20% of the total marks. It is recognised that some Examining Groups will wish to offer syllabuses which will be assessed by Course Work only. Where this is the case some of the work to be assessed must be done under controlled conditions.

4.4.3   Although the same reading material may be used in courses leading to examinations in both English and English Literature the same pieces of work may not be submitted for assessment of Course Work in both examinations.

4.5   Differentiated Assessment

Differentiation in English Literature arises from the nature of the texts studied and the tasks set and will be achieved by the use of differentiated papers; differentiated tasks within papers; or a non-differentiated component combined with a differentiated component; and by the use of differentiated tasks within course work.

43 *Unlocking Mind-Forg'd Manacles?*

● John Dixon and Leslie Stratta

A UNIQUE OPPORTUNITY

'A unique opportunity for improving the quality of education in this country'[1]: this is how the [former] Secretary of State [saw] the introduction of G.C.S.E. And we agree. It could be so, especially in English Literature — provided that teachers and exam boards work together to seize the opportunity.

For the first time in the sixty-odd years since the 'First and Second Public Examinations' were founded, national criteria are stating some of the obvious truths about assessing literature:

> Examination by the assessment of Course Work *is appropriate* to English Literature . . . *provides wider evidence* of candidates' achievement . . . *is especially suitable* for the assessment of wide reading . . .

Thus

> In all syllabuses such Course Work *must account* for at least 20% of the total marks [and] It is recognised that some Examining Groups will wish to offer syllabuses which *will be assessed by Course Work only*.[2]

So 'the general objective, as I see it,' [said Sir Keith Joseph], 'must be to give teachers all the help and support we can in order that the new examination may be as good as possible and the improvements in the quality of education and teaching may be maximised.'[3]

SHORTCOMINGS FOR SIXTY YEARS

Now is the time to remember that in 1921, as the national exam system was being set up, the Newbolt Committee commented[4]:

1 'We have heard over and over again that answers to examination papers give much evidence of (unassimilated, and therefore insincere, criticism).' How is G.C.S.E. going to eradicate this — even in coursework?

2 'Many teachers set great store by the cultivation of original work on the part of their pupils or by dramatic performance. It would be a misfortune should the examination system rule such work out of court.' Will G.C.S.E. provide for it?
3 '. . . we agree with the English Association in holding that ''if examination in . . . Literature is to be complete and thorough, some part of it at all stages should be oral''.[5]
Will there be controlled experiments by the boards on these lines?

Equally it is worth recalling that despite Newbolt — and only a decade later — L. C. Knights, writing in *Scrutiny* said:

> Any English master interested in education who has prepared a school certificate form knows that bitter feeling of waste . . . . Since the damage done to education by external, 'standardising' examinations is so gross, obvious, persuasive and inescapable, the time has come to press, firmly, for their abolition.[6]

What is NATE going to be saying about G.C.S.E. Literature by the year 2000? — 'the bitter feeling of waste' or 'a unique opportunity'?

ESCAPE FROM MIND-FORG'D MANACLES

For the past sixty years, all of us — teachers, examiners and candidates — have been through a peculiar processing that has distorted our notions of response to literature, especially through writing. Until we thoroughly understand this, we cannot escape.

The evidence is unmistakable especially for teachers of literature, who pride themselves on close reading of the text. How extraordinary it is that we have no tradition of looking equally closely at the language of typical exam questions — and how disillusioning it is when we do so. Let us scrutinise two groups of key words from 1984 G.C.E. exam papers[7]. All are concerned with character study, one of the two major topics in literature papers.[8] What are the assumptions behind them?

> '*In what ways* are X and Y *similar?*'
> '*In what ways* do X and Y *differ?*'
> '*Outline* the changes in X's attitudes to Y. . . . '
> 'Refer closely to the text *to illustrate the points* you make.'
> 'By *referring closely* to the play, *discuss this statement*. . . .'

In this group, the key words we have underlined have two major functions. Primarily they direct the student into generalisation. Characters are to be treated on the whole as a bundle of traits, which may be fixed or may change in some determinate way ('the' changes). So the essay consists in a set of 'points'. Thus, when the text is referred to it is to be treated as purely subordinate, an 'illustration' for the candidate's generalisations.

What is wrong with these instructions? If literature offers us any understanding of character or human nature, it does so by presenting people in action and interaction. Through dialogue and narrative, literature deepens our awareness of the complexity, ambiguity and even contradictions in human behaviour. Within literature, generalisation does have a place — but it arises directly from this apprehension of the subtle texture of living relationships. In effect, then, key words such as we have quoted reverse the way we learn from literature. But they do more: consider this second group.

> '*Point to the* difference in this extract. . . .'
> '*Outline the* changes. . . .'
> '*What* is *the* effect . . . upon *the* reader?'
> '*What* do *we* learn from X and Y?'
> '*Point out what is revealed* in these scenes of X's character.'
> '*What impressions* of X *can be obtained* . . .?'

The key words here are even more dangerous. They assume that the knowledge of people that we derive from literature is definitive and consensual. Thus candidates are expected to take on an authoritative role and assert the accepted position 'we' have had 'revealed'. On these assumptions readers are passive, while the text makes 'impressions' and 'reveals' the truth to them.

What is so dangerous? The student is being encouraged to deny self-evident truths about response to literature. Reading is a creative act, whereby the individual reader uses the printed words to construct an imaginary experience.

What is more, this imaginary experience depends on the thoughts, feelings and relationships readers can actively bring to bear from their own personal lives. If what we can draw on continues to develop and mature throughout our lives, then our individual readings too will change and mature. For this reason alone, no reading can be definitive. And to expect a definitive reading of 16-year-olds is nonsensical. Reading literature is problematic, subject to individual, cultural and historical change.

To judge by these two sets of key words, then, examinations are attempting to turn the reading of literature into a form of knowledge which is generalised, consensual, determinate and unproblematic. A mind-forg'd manacle indeed! And it has been there fettering all our thinking for over sixty years now. But, not surprisingly, there are signs of unease, a desire to break free perhaps? At their best, these are giving further clues to what is being unconsciously suppressed as well as what is being enforced. Consider the following set of key words, scattered much less systematically through the 1984 papers.

> 'Which of the (characters) do *you find most interesting*, and *why*?'
> 'Is there any one . . . for whom *you feel a special sympathy*?'
> 'What are *your feelings about their conflicts* . . .?'
> 'Do *you agree with her that she should* have . . .?'
> 'Do *you think he is a suitable husband* for . . .?'

What aspect of the reading process do these key words point to? In one way or another, they acknowledge that, having created an imaginative experience, readers (like spectators at a play) view a character with 'interest' or 'sympathy', their 'feelings' as well as 'thoughts' are aroused, and given the chance they will reflect upon the action from a personal standpoint. As it happens, these questions are still tied to the request to generalise, but at least they do not rule out a vital personal element in literary response, as most character questions do.

To sum up: we have taken the most frequent form of literature question — the character question — and by close analysis of the language we have tried to demonstrate the distorting assumptions behind typical key words. These assumptions deny what the imaginative student, teacher (or examiner) are trying to achieve in their day-to-day explorations of literature. We have discussed elsewhere their effects on the written work of a typical student.[9] The question is: will G.C.S.E. Literature liberate itself, or not? Will 'the unique opportunity for . . . raising standards' be taken, especially in the coursework consortia, and will the boards actively encourage it?

SIGNS OF NEW THINKING BY THE BOARDS

Over the past decade or so, we can discern two new directions in Literature exam questions: both seek to recognise fundamental processes in reading and response, and to make room for them — as far as conditions allow — in the examination.

The first arose from the Cambridge Plain Text approach. This accepted that it was wrong to base the assessment of Literature entirely on memory. With the text in the examination room, the way was open for teachers and examiners jointly to consider what processes they wanted to encourage. How could they help students in the first place to re-engage with the text, (re-)creating and extending their imaginative reading and response? What kinds of wording would offer guidance without restricting the student to a closed and pseudo-definitive view? How could the reader be encouraged to dwell on and explore particular moments from which a more general perspective and understanding might naturally emerge? These are not easy questions.

There was fresh thinking here, but some traditional assumptions seem to have been left unquestioned. In general, for instance, this approach still asks the student to take on a version of the relatively familiar university role of 'critical' analysis.

The second new direction offered students a different role; they were asked to write not as the reader but as an imaginary participant or spectator. It is a role that emerges naturally enough when students have taken part in a dramatic production, or dramatically re-enacted sections from a novel (as Dickens did). Writing allows room for the imagination to work empathically, extending the understanding of a character and situation. Film and (video-) tape open up further possibilities.[10] Exam questions that asked students to take on a role have been included intermittently by many boards (the Cambridge Plain Text among them). We have to make a careful distinction here between two poles: at the one end, using the experience of literature as a springboard for constructing (related) imaginative worlds of one's own, and at the other, dwelling on the experience of the text by imaginatively living through it in role. Both show how much students can gain from literature, but it is the latter we want to attend to here.

The question again is what processes to encourage. How can we help the student to explore tacit kinds of empathy and understanding? Is there room also for some explicit (more reflective) commentary, while still within role? Can we suggest ways of extending the language used in searching for appropriate forms? Which parameters of the text are going to be important, which incidental or peripheral (for 16-year-olds of varying abilities)?

CAN COURSEWORK LEARN FROM THE PLAIN TEXT APPROACH?

In our experience, much of what passes as 'coursework' today is still moulded by past examination traditions. 'A unique opportunity' is not being taken up. Yet, as we have just seen, some examinations are themselves moving in new directions. What has coursework to learn from them?

First, short sections of the play or novel can be a natural springboard for the student writer. In the Plain Text approach these are inevitably chosen by the examiners, but in coursework, when a class has been enacting, presenting readings, or taping key scenes, it is possible to encourage and assist students to make their own choices of a section for 'detailed study', where their 'first-hand knowledge' of the text can lead to a 'sensitive and informed personal response'[11] — with the text still in front of them, and the experience of enacting it fresh in their minds.

Secondly, if they are taking on a more reflective, analytic role, some students may welcome or need guidelines. These will have three functions, at least;

(a) to keep them actively engaged in re-creating and extending an imaginary world constructed from the text;
(b) to help them to focus on elements in that experience that they find significant;
(c) drawing on the ebb and flow of their sympathies, to help them stand back and reflect on what the experience means for them.

Thirdly, if there are going to be guidelines, or prompts, what are they going to look like? Here again Cambridge has been suggestive. Consider the effect of some of these phrasings taken from the last eight years' papers:

re-creating and   your reactions as you read through . . .
extending   . . . any lines that particularly interest or puzzle you
                . . . your feelings may vary
                . . . when you look closely at what each man says and think about how he says it
                . . . when you think of what each says and does

finding   what impression do you form (of the atmosphere . . .)
significance   . . . what do you find unexpected in their behaviour, attitude and language
                . . . explore some of the contrasts (in feeling, mood, action, character, attitude) that you yourself find interesting
                . . . what differences do you discover . . . in temperament and in the way they look at life
                . . . what hints do you see that help you to understand (later) developments (or relationships)
                . . . your understanding of the problems that confront X and Y
                . . . what portrait of X would you produce

reflecting   how well does Y cope with (the problems), do you think
on personal   . . . in your opinion, (do) they deserve pardon or
meanings and   punishment
judgements   . . . what is your own interpretation
                . . . do you think X is being fair

In our view, phrases such as these encourage the *process* of reading and response, so that discoveries can continue to be made in the course of *writing*. Writing ceases to be primarily a summary (or, worse still, a regurgitation) of past thoughts; it is an opportunity to think through and even discover afresh. In imaginative teaching, of course, such writing has the launch pad of animated 'analytical' discussions, arising as a natural corollary of presentations and enactments. Talk precedes writing and helps to shape it.

In one or two cases we find equally suggestive ideas in the Plain Text approaches to lyric poems. Although in the exam the poem was unseen, the following assignment — with adaptation — could equally have been given to a group who had chosen their own poem to explore, present, and write about:

> Read the following poem ('*Incendiary*' by Vernon Scannell) a number of times, till you feel you have begun to get inside it; then look at the questions . . ., which are intended to help you to express freely your own reactions to the poem.

What is interesting in this 'introduction' is that it not only recognises the need for 'a number of' readings 'to get inside' any poem, but also leaves the student free to accept or set aside the guidelines that follow;

> — This poem is about a small boy and a fire that he started deliberately.
> What impression of the fire does the poem create for you? Mention some
> of the details in the poem that contribute to this impression.
> — Write about your impression of the small boy and the feeling towards
> him that the poem arouses. How far does the poem enable you to
> understand why he started the fire?
> — The poet repeats the word 'frightening'. What things frighten him
> about this incident? Do you find that 'frightening' is the strongest, or the
> final, feeling that the poem expresses for you?[12]

No doubt questions like these are not beyond improvement, but it is
impressive to see their effect on students of varying articulacy and
maturity in poetic response. Let us look in turn at the opening sections
from two students:[13]

> (a) The poem give the impression that the fire ~~was~~ were great and it had
> spread all over ~~town~~ the farm. its flames spread quickly, as quickly as
> a tiger hungrily coming towards you ~~and rearing~~, the noise of the fire
> was as deafening as the roar of a tiger whilst tearing flesh. The
> brightness of the red and gold flames made the sky look red and
> fierce, and as persons chocked, you could imagine the stars up in the
> sky being chocked by the thick black smoke rising into the sky.
> My impressions of the small boy ~~is~~ are that he was lonely and
> needed some attention just to tell him that he was still loved. . . . The
> last two lines of the poem 'He would have been content with one
> warm kiss had there been anyone to offer this', made me feel
> sorrowful for the child. I wanted to reach out, ~~and~~ pull him close and
> give him the one warm kiss that he so much wanted, which no one
> would give him.

Space does not allow us to discuss here the detailed developmental
features in this staging point of written response: however, we can point
to the way she dwells on and imagines the possibilities in two dense
poetic images in the poem ('flame-fanged tigers roaring hungrily' and
'set the sky on fire and choke the stars'); to her empathic understanding
of the boy and the love he needed; to the directness of her warm, human
response. She has trusted to the guidelines and found them valuable.

> (b) The fire was huge to compare ~~to~~ with what his heart needed. His need
> for love was 'brazen, fierce and huge'. That small boy with 'a face like
> pallid cheese' seems almost under other circumstance to be an angel.
> But the fire of hatred in his heart for not being wanted has burnt out
> his eyes. People say the eyes are connected to ~~his~~ the heart his
> certainly seem to be. The colour suggests life and ~~fier~~ fierce ~~yere~~
> reactions. I don't feel it is true of the boy. He is almost ash in his
> feelings. Almost dead and gone. . . .
> And it is frightening that such a small child should carry such pain
> in his heart. That such a child could as the poem says 'set the sky on
> fire and choke the stars ~~stars~~ to heat.' It is frightening that we can
> allow such people to exist in such a state. The fear is emphasized by
> mentioning the boys actual size. The smallness of him to cause such a
> fire. 'such skinny limbs and such little heart'.

> And then we are offered the remedy. So simple as remedies usually
> are. So pure a feeling and action 'one warm kiss'.

Again, briefly, we can point to a vital element of imaginative
construction in her reading of the symbolism (the fire is not only
external but internal!); a synthesising of 'fact and metaphor'; the sense
of multiple meanings in an image like 'burnt-out little eyes' or an action
like 'one warm kiss'; a wider reflection on what 'we can allow'. The
phrasing of the assignment has been helpful to her, but — impelled by
her imagination — she has felt free to develop her own complex
response.

CAN COURSEWORK GRASP THE POTENTIAL OF IMAGINARY ROLES?

During the past decade a number of boards have experimented
intermittently — both at A level and 16+ — with the idea of asking
candidates to write in an imaginary role, rather than within the analytic
tradition. So far as we know, there has been no national review of the
lessons that have been learnt. What are the options? Let us consider, for
simplicity, a set of examples drawn from the past five years' papers in
the Cambridge Plain Text syllabus:

> — There are as many different ways of directing *Macbeth* as there are
> directors. Each director has to make crucial decisions about what
> Shakespeare's play means and how the production will bring out the
> meaning.
>
> What would you, as director, want to convey to the audience about *one* of
> the following . . . difficult problems . . . and how would you do it? (June
> '81)
>
> — Uncle Ben's appearances in (*Death of a Salesman*) have a mysterious and
> puzzling quality. What do you make of him? You may, if you wish, think
> of yourself as a director talking to the actor who will be playing the part.
> (June '81)
>
> — (In *1984*) As she sits in the cell, awaiting questioning, Julia looks back
> over her affair with Winston. What do you think her thoughts and feelings
> about their relationship would be? If you wish, you can write as if you
> were Julia. (June '84)
>
> — Explain exactly why (Bathsheba) feels unable to knock at the door and
> speak to Oak (in Chapter 43). You may write as if you were Bathsheba if
> you wish. (June '84)
>
> — Imagine you are Laura's mother (in *Lark Rise*), and say what you think
> and feel about your nine-year-old daughter. (June '81)

Coursework gives students ample opportunities to take advantage of
such approaches — and others like them. The actual experience of
working in class on the production of a scene from a play leads naturally

into exploring what can be learnt in the role of director — or actor. All the script offers is printed dialogue on the page: taking on these roles adds in such new dimensions as gestures, actions and reactions; movement, stance and juxtaposition; inner thoughts and feelings; and, crucially, the spoken interpretation of the text.

Similarly, in preparing a reading from a novel or short story, students have to imagine themselves into the role(s), in a particular era, culture and setting. Whatever the text — be it a Hemingway short story or a proposal scene from *Pride and Prejudice* — there will be massive demands on the reader to construct beyond the words. The sub-text of motive, intention, attitude and feeling may be no more than hinted at, or very obliquely indicated.

Role play associated with prepared readings, then, is a method of slowing down the reading process, allowing for a fuller imaginative creation, while at the same time giving students the responsibility and the opportunity to learn from their own discoveries. As an alternative way of getting at sub-text, 'explication de texte' from the teacher, while it certainly slows down the reading (!), is more than likely to deaden both imagination and response.

Thus, as an element in coursework writing, the 'imaginary role' approach seems to us equal in significance to analytical writing, and best viewed as a complement and parallel to it. If so, no coursework folder should exclude either.

As our final point, let us indicate briefly what may be gained: with space for no more than one example, we have chosen a piece from a C.S.E. folder, by an 'average' student, written — as it happens — in a mock exam and based on a N.W.R.E.B. question.[14]

> Imagine yourself a character in one of the books you have studied and write the full entry you make in your diary for one especially interesting and important experience.
> Include in your entry your thoughts and feelings. (May '84)

'KES'

22nd of November, something very important happened with my bird, 'Kes' he started as a chick that wouldn't kill for its food unless it was fed by me so I looked up about this in ~~library~~ books and they say that you should give ~~the~~ the bird time to get used to not having a mother and so I did, and now he's flying around and fending for himself like any other wild bird.

I took him out to the park early this morning and let him go — at first I thought he'd fly off but he came straight back to me, so I let him loose again to catch some meat which I tied to a string and spun it round my head untill 'Kes' saw it and lunged at it.

I then took a sparrow which I had caught before and ~~took~~ let it loose
'Kes' was flying so fast I thought he'd miss it, but he never missed, his aim
was superb he went straight through the skin ~~whi~~ with his sharp and
killing claws. I know this was cruel but at least I gave the sparrow a Fifty-
Fifty chance. I am glad that my training of the bird hasn't hurt its natural
instincts to kill for food, but I am also sad that I will have to let him go soon
because it belongs in the wild with the rest of the wild birds.

Its been a long time since I ~~1st~~ First found him in an old building
abandoned so it seemed, just waiting for some one to just walk along and
help it, the little chirps that meant 'help me', almost brings tears to my eyes.

The essential question to ask, it seems to us, is what kind of evidence
such writing offers of empathy with Billy Casper, and understanding of
the significance of the bird for his character. At two points, the prose
seems to be unusually responsive to feeling and thought. In the first,
there is exultation and pride, 'he never missed, his aim was superb',
followed by a more ambiguous acknowledgement of brute power, 'his
sharp and killing claws'. There is a kind of wrestling with ambivalent
judgements, 'I know it was cruel . . . I am glad . . . my training . . .
hadn't hurt its natural instincts.' In the second, the poignancy of the
coming loss of the bird is prefigured, as Billy remembers finding it. The
cadence of this final sentence suggests a writer of surprising
sophistication — 'Its been a long time since . . . abandoned so it seemed,
just waiting . . . almost brings tears to my eyes.' In order to recognise
such evidence, we have to interpret what it enacts, rather than expect
analytic fullness (of the kind our own commentary begins to offer).

Admittedly, there are two minor objections we may need to meet, in
this instance. First, writing under exam pressures, with more than one
text to cover in the session, Leslie has misremembered and
kaleidoscoped more than one incident. Does it really matter, though?
('Undue emphasis should not be placed on mere recall' as the new
National Criteria state.) Secondly, the opening reads more like a letter to
a close friend (offering contextual explanation) than a diary entry.
Neither of these takes away from the positive achievements, in our
view. The vivid external events evoked with such delicacy, the
exploration of inner thought and complex feeling, the precision of the
language and appropriateness of the rhythms, and the overall coherence
of the piece are a fitting testimony to what this writer has learned in
responding to literature.

NOTES

1. Letter from Sir Keith Joseph to Sir William Cockcroft (S.E.C.) 21 Dec. 1984.
    Para 1.
2. National Criteria for English, Jan. 1985, pp 8-9.

3. Sir Keith's letter above, para 2.

4. *The Teaching of English in England* H.M.S.O., 1921, p. 118.

5. Ibid. pp. 302–8 (see discussion in Dixon and Brown, *Responses to Literature*, 1984, obtainable from NATE, Sheffield).

6. 'Scrutiny of Examinations', in *Scrutiny*, XII, 2, pp. 157–8 — a brilliant discussion, and published in 1933!

7. Including A.E.B., J.M.B., London, Oxford, and joint W. Midlands/ Cambridge.

8. See Barnes and Seed, *Seals of Approval*, 1981, p. 24, University of Leeds, School of Education.

9. L. Stratta and J. Dixon, *Character Studies — changing the Question*, forthcoming from Southern Regional Examinations Board, Southampton.

10. See, for example, Stratta, Dixon and Wilkinson, *Patterns of Language*, 1973, chapter 2, Heinemann.

11. National Criteria for English, Jan. 1985, *Assessment objectives*, p. 8.

12. Cambridge English Literature (Plain Texts), June 1982, Q.17.

13. We are grateful to Geoff Lambert and the Cambridge Syndicate for permission to quote these extracts, and to Jane Ogborn, chief examiner, for bringing them to our attention.

14. We are grateful to Leslie Brownhill and to Bob Lever, his English teacher, at Norton Priory School, Runcorn, Cheshire, for permission to quote this piece.

English Literature

● GCE Boards of England, Wales and Northern Ireland

IMPLEMENTATION OF THE REPORT

All Boards have accepted the common core, although the JMB intends to retain its own wording of Aims and Objectives in place of the statement of Aim and Skills Tested given below.

Dates for the first examination of syllabuses implementing the core proposals are as follows:

No modifications needed	London
1984	SUJB
1985	JMB
1986	AEB, Cambridge, N. Ireland Oxford, O & C, WJEC

DEFINITION OF SUBJECT TITLE

Although the Cambridge and London Boards and the WJEC are accustomed to using the title 'English' and the remaining Boards 'English Literature' for their A-level syllabuses, the subject is common to all Boards, viz., the study of works of English Literature and development of skills of literary appreciation. The Working Party, therefore, includes in its review all Boards' syllabuses dealing with Literature in English.

The Working Party deliberately set aside A-level syllabuses which are not essentially concerned with Literature, for example the AEB Language and Literature syllabuses and the London Board's optional Language paper, although it recognised that more work might be required in the future on language components at this level.

DEFINITION OF COMMON CORE

The Working Party noted that the Secretaries of the Boards, having consulted their advisers, had agreed that there was sufficient evidence and common ground to justify a study with the aim of developing an A-level English Common Core, and that the Secretaries had suggested:

(i) that critical appreciation was the most promising area in which to seek a common core, since six of the nine Boards already set a compulsory paper in unseen critical appreciation accounting for between 20%–33⅓% of the total marks;

(ii) that an alternative common core might be sought in one of the following areas: Shakespeare; Chaucer and Shakespeare; Chaucer, Shakespeare and major authors, since all Boards set at least one paper of this type.

UNSEEN CRITICAL APPRECIATION

The representatives of the six Boards which incorporate a compulsory paper of this kind feel that it is an important discriminator within the examination which can encourage a different teaching approach. It is particularly useful for testing analysis, judgement and response. The representatives of the Cambridge Board, however, report that their optional critical appreciation paper is not a popular choice and they are, therefore, reluctant to make it a compulsory component of the examination. The Oxford Board sets passages for critical appreciation from the prescribed texts and also unseen passages in one optional paper and the Oxford and Cambridge Board sets unseen passages exclusively in the optional Special paper. These two Boards are similarly reluctant to adopt unseen critical appreciation as a compulsory common core. Some examiners believe that this paper is the most difficult to assess reliably and, although this view is not widely shared, the difficulty of finding a continual supply of suitable material is generally recognised. The Working Party acknowledges the value of providing a variety of approaches to the subject and in view of the differences of opinion and experience between Boards it does not recommend the adoption of unseen critical appreciation as a common core.

SHAKESPEARE, CHAUCER AND MAJOR AUTHORS

Having eliminated the possibility of a common unseen critical appreciation paper, the Working Party then sought common ground in the set book papers where it is agreed that it should be compulsory to include a minimum of one Shakespeare play. However, since context questions vary from tests of comprehension to critical appreciation in different Boards, standardisation of questions is not thought desirable. In practice, most candidates study at least one novel but, in order to accommodate those specialising in the early periods, it is not recommended that this should be compulsory. The Working Party feels that it should be compulsory to include some poetry as well as at least one example of another genre.

There is unanimous agreement that it would be inappropriate to recommend any writer (apart from Shakespeare) or any individual text for inclusion in the common core. It would obviously be undesirable for all A-level English students to be forced to study common texts and the Working Party feels that sufficient choice must be available to allow for differing tastes and specialised interests and to enable the skills of literary appreciation to be fostered and developed by sympathetic teaching. The Working Party agrees that all candidates should be required to offer a minimum of six books in the examination. The critical appreciation paper (if set) will be in addition to this, and it is agreed that in practice the majority of candidates will study more than six books. With the exception of the Cambridge representatives, all Boards feel that a selection of texts consisting of Shakespeare and entirely twentieth-century writing is too limited and an inadequate basis for developing the skills. There is, therefore, a strong recommendation that at least one work written before 1900 should be examined in addition to the Shakespeare play(s).

Since there is no question of a definable body of knowledge which can be packaged into a separately graded common core, grade criteria will not be required and have not been drafted.

LITERATURE AND TRANSLATION

Although English Literature has been taken to mean Literature originally written in English, (i.e., including American, African, Caribbean and Commonwealth) there has been a tendency to include the occasional work in translation. The Working Party feels that this option should continue to be available for those Boards who wish to prescribe such works and it therefore deliberately refrains from making any recommendation on the use of literature in translation.

COMMON CORE RECOMMENDATIONS

The common core thus identified is pervasive and consists of a common aim and a list of skills to be tested within a content framework which offers some flexibility of approach. It presents a clear public statement of the agreed common basis of all Boards' syllabuses, to which it could be prefaced with little or no modification. The Working Party is hopeful that the use of the statement will bring renewed clarity and direction to the study of this important subject without inhibiting or confining the teaching in any way.

AIM

To encourage an enjoyment and appreciation of English Literature based on an informed personal response and to extend this appreciation where it has already been acquired.

SKILLS TESTED

1. *Knowledge* — of the content of the books and where appropriate of the personal and historical circumstances in which they were written;
2. *Understanding* — extending from simple factual comprehension to a broader conception of the nature and signifance of literary texts;
3. *Analysis* — the ability to recognise and describe literary effects and to comment precisely on the use of language;
4. *Judgement* — the capacity to make judgements of value based on close reading;
5. *Sense of the past and tradition* — the ability to see a literary work in its historical context as well as that of the present day;
6. *Expression* — the ability to write organised and cogent essays on literary subjects.

CONTENT

Candidates will be required to offer for examination a minimum of six texts consisting of at least one play in Shakespeare, some poetry and at least one example of a genre other than poetry. (The Working Party recommends that in addition to Shakespeare at least one work written before 1900 should be offered for examination.)

45 *Taking Too Much for Granted? A Level Literature and Its Assessment*

- John Dixon

WHAT EVIDENCE OF A GENUINE ENCOUNTER?

Before we start, I would like to ask those of you teaching A Level Literature a question: as your students write their answers in mock, or in A Level itself, how strong will the evidence be that they have appreciated, and had a genuine encounter with, the novel, play or poem?

It is a serious question. Suppose the answer was: very little evidence, or next to none, for most of the paper. Would that throw in doubt the point of the course? or the examination? And, conversely, would we not be deeply satisfied if the evidence was strong and positive?

Within the tradition of literary studies that most of us grew up in, the basic assumption is that criticism arises from a living contact with the imaginative experience created from the text. It is a lot to expect, perhaps. And we all know that Literature examinations have been under attack since they were conceived. 'We have heard over and over again that answers to examination papers give much evidence of (unassimilated, and therefore insincere, criticism)' said the Newbolt committee in 1921. But they went ahead and recommended the new Second Examination, our Advanced Level, because they believed 'there is still great possibility of fresh achievement in the art of examining'. Now we know from their regular reports what modern examiners' attitudes are to a 'mechanical approach', 'unmeaning task-work', 'second-hand reactions' and so on. So it seems that things are safe. But are they?

My own doubts flared up about five years ago, during the Schools Council English 16–19 Project, when John Brown dug out some actual A

Level answers on *Lear*, published in a book called *English and Examinations*.[1] They were the only such essays publicly available at the time — and so far as I know, still are — so we studied them quite intently. After our first disappointment, even with the higher-graded work, we asked ourselves that opening question: was there any evidence of appreciation and genuine encounter with the play? Was the imaginative experience still alive as the students wrote? The answer seemed to be, very little evidence, or none.

Were these impressions simply personal, we wondered. We tried discussing some of the essays in detail, in seminars with project groups. They taught us something very important: it was possible to move beyond 'subjective' impressions and to point to precise features in the language. These indicated that the imagination was not alive; for instance, that the textual quotations were being handled in an unthinking, unfeeling way. When we introduced course work essays into our seminars (from the Leicestershire JMB group), the contrast was remarkable: you could actually see the students' imaginative thinking in progress, if you read closely.

We reported these preliminary findings in the project book, *Education 16–19: The Role of English and Communication* (Macmillan 1979). In addition, we approached the A Level committee of Schools Council, representing teachers and the boards, to ask if they would support an investigation into a sample of A Level course and examination work. They agreed. (The results were published in 1984 and 1985 by the Schools Council.[2])

GETTING LITTLE OR NOTHING . . . ?

Overall, there were roughly 400 essays in the sample, and most of them were commented on by at least two of our panel of readers. These were drawn from schools, colleges, universities and HMI, representing the whole of the UK. John Brown and I were delighted by their generous interest, and in the seminars we held with them we learnt a good deal more about the delicacy of evidence that was there in a student's essay, if one looked closely.

What were the findings? It is not possible to summarise such things statistically, except in the crudest fashion. What you really need to do is read the representative selection of essays and panel commentaries that form part 2 of our report. But what can be said is that, overall, the commentaries offer grave cause for concern, first about the examination essays, and second — to a lesser degree — about the coursework. If the 400 essays are at all representative, half the students taking A Level Literature may be getting little or nothing from their course, so far as written appreciation is concerned.

At a time when universities are already in conflict over the definition of literary studies, this possibility is not at all easy to face or respond to. Besides, school staffs have more than enough pressures on them, economically and politically. And yet, I believe, positive action can be taken, positive outcomes produced, given the will. Let me put forward three suggestions and consider each in turn, to see what they might imply:

1. Boards might publish — on a regular basis? — exemplars of strong evidence of appreciative response to literature at various grade levels. In other words, publish the good to drive out the bad. With several boards running syllabuses that include coursework folders, positive exemplars of these folders would be very valuable too.

2. The exemplar essays would need to be analysed in detail, to show where the evidence for imaginative reading lay. This work would entail further efforts to clarify what goes on in the reading of literature, drawing on the current international discussion. Here is a place for joint work by universities and schools, possibly through a national body such as NATE.

3. A major part of A Level Literature is a course in writing, as Part 1 of the research report makes clear. This is hardly mentioned in syllabuses, but the current interest in writing development suggests that rapid progress might be made in suggesting some lines of approach.

In effect, I am suggesting that in a 'discipline' such as literary criticism, standards can only be made public by exemplifying achievements, at various levels. Similarly, the teaching and assessing of that work depends on a critical understanding in the first place of reading processes, and in the second, of writing processes. In particular, students as well as teachers need as clear a sense as possible of the kinds of development in reading and writing that might be hoped and aimed for between 16 and 19.

1. HOW CAN WE MAKE STANDARDS PUBLIC?

In Literature courses, students are learning to use written language to make something of the experience of reading an imaginative text. You cannot discuss the stage they have reached in this process without looking at examples of their writing. There is no other way. This is a perfectly normal part of examiners' meetings, just as it is for coursework consortia. And the joint study of the piece of writing has to be quite detailed and scrupulous — with time for an exchange of comments, paragraph by paragraph — if a well-grounded consensus is to be reached.

What has happened in the past is that these scripts, used in standardising meetings up and down the country, have not been made public. Effectively, then, the major avenue for communicating and sharing standards of achievement has been overlooked. Recently, however, changes have begun. For their 16+ examination, two of the boards (JMB and TWYLREB) have published English Language folders as exemplars for each grade. And after studying this and further material in a series of national seminars, twenty senior and chief examiners have asked the GCE and CSE Boards to consider 'the role of exemplar material, accompanied by analysis of significant features, in giving positive advice and feedback to teachers'.[3] Could this notion not be extended, with benefit, to A Level Literature?

In our research report, John Brown and I have begun this process. For the benefit of teachers and examiners we have set out batches of exemplars for the B and D grades. Thus, among the 150 B grade essays[4], our panel found half of the examination and two-thirds of the coursework 'fairly convincing' or 'strong' evidence of literary appreciation. What they meant by that we have demonstrated by printing in Part 2 a representative selection of these essays, together with their comments. But two things should be added. First, as we show in Part 1, our own study of the panels' comments, whether in seminar or in isolation, suggested some key points in the structure and texture of the essays that a reader would be wise to check. This is just a beginning, we believe, in finding the 'significant features' that indicate to what degree the imaginative experience is still alive, there to be drawn on, in the course of critical writing.

Our second point is that even in our B grade sample, roughly half the examination essays and a third of the coursework struck our panel as 'rather thin', or 'very weak', or even as 'negative' evidence of literary appreciation. This is the key to the problem, as the panel saw it, so we have printed a similar selection of those essays together with the comments in detail. If teachers and examiners find themselves largely in agreement with those commentaries, then something must be done to ensure that such work does not get credit in future. The most obvious step seems to be for boards to publish examples.

THE SAME . . . BUT WORSE

When we turned to the D and O grades, the story was much the same — but progressively worse. This raises an important question. Is the definition of D or O grade to be couched in terms of relative failure to do what A or B grade students were doing? Or is it to be a positive definition, in terms of more limited achievements, or a more limited range? Once again the seminar group of 16+ examiners have proposed positive criteria for each grade.[3] If this were carried through to A Level, it would sharply affect the choice of exemplar material.

Part 2 of our report offers an initial basis for positive criteria: it contains a representative selection of D grade essays that showed strong or fairly convincing evidence of literary appreciation, in the view of our panel. Naturally, these essays are limited in certain respects, as our panel quite often noted in their commentaries. Nevertheless, roughly half of the 150 D grade essays[4] in the sample drew positive judgements about the evidence of a genuine encounter with the imaginative work. (And in terms of the 74 examination essays, the proportion was not so very different from that of the B grade sample.)

With the rather smaller sample of O grade work[4] (75 essays in all) the number thought to be 'strong' evidence of appreciation was too small to offer a useful guide — whether for coursework or examinations. Indeed, if those essays were representative of the wider population, they raise the question whether an O grade counts as much more than a consolation trinket for students who have gained little or nothing, so far as written evidence of appreciation is concerned. This is a serious issue for teachers and the boards to examine further.

To sum up:

1. Within this subject, public standards at A Level, and an articulate consensus about them, seem to depend on published exemplars, with detailed analysis of the (graded) achievements they represent.
2. If it is agreed that work with little or no evidence of literary appreciation is being given credit, more or less widely, that practice can only be driven out by publication of examples, with critical commentaries.

2.   WHAT GOES ON AT BEST IN READING LITERATURE?

Our focus for the moment is 16 to 19 year-olds, though there are clear implications for what goes on before and afterwards. In Part 1 of the report John Brown and I look closely at a group of essays discussed in seminars with the panel, using their comments and our continuation of the analysis to tease out strands in the reading process. We see this as a beginning to the much more searching enquiry that is needed.

An English Literature course depends on assumptions about the nature of reading, and of writing. Yet there must be many teachers of English who went through higher education without any analytic discussion of these assumptions. Such discussions seem particularly important now, at a time when new theories of reading (derived mainly from the work of Russian, German and French writers) have started to penetrate thinking about the study of literature at university level and, to a certain extent, at school level too.

In the hope of clarifying the issues, I want to propose two lines of enquiry. First, I suggest, teachers from the post-war English universities (like myself) should look back at the key texts that tried to articulate some of the (hidden) assumptions behind our courses — and thus behind most of the current tasks at A Level *at its best*. I imagine that Richards and Denys Harding would be essential, and passages from Lionel Knights, Leavis and others might well be added.

Even a preliminary survey of this territory is fruitful and suggestive. It was Richards — not Terry Eagleton! — who said in 1929 that *Practical Criticism* was 'in part . . . the record of a piece of field-work in comparative ideology' (p.6). If only he had followed up the idea — and many others of that period. It was Harding who wrote in *English in Education* (in 1968) that 'fiction is a social convention, an institutionalised technique of discussion, by means of which an author invites us to join him in discussing a possibility of experience . . .'. We need to be more aware of the cross-currents and unfulfilled ambitions of these theoreticians of 'the English school' 1930–1970. Equally Richards and Harding offer a lead where 'the Continental tradition' is lacking: they study actual readers, and are that much more in contact with what other people do, not just the idealised norms of the introspective scholar.

Still, the limitations of that tradition are increasingly obvious today, and this is the point of my second proposal. We need to consider what questions about the reading process were left unasked. Even if the *answers* are by no means complete or compelling, it is here that the Continental theorists (and others) are so valuable — in asking questions such as these:

— What are the precise stages by which the reader moves from the verbal signs to a dynamic, imaginatively present contract with people in action?
— What expectations are generated, as the cultural codes for construing reality are recognised?
— How is the reader's stored experience affected in the process of imaginative construction — and reflection on it?
— What does the reader make of harmony and dissonances in 'the discussion' with the author? and what precise forms may this take?

INTERPRETING THE SIGNS

Without in any way trying to be definitive, let me illustrate some of these questions, and their importance for English teaching at A Level and beyond.

In the 1980s we are even more aware than Richards that we must start with questions about *organising the string of verbal signs* laid out on the page. This is done progressively and in several different ways as we re-read a text. For instance, as we try to master the structure of a short poem, do the words or the syntax fall into patterns of parallelism and opposition? If so, what underlying structurings of the experience may they be pointing to? And what signs of cross-currents or ambiguities in the experience do they already offer? Think of the second verse of 'A slumber did my spirit seal':

> No motion has she now, no force;
> She neither hears nor sees,
> Rolled round in earth's diurnal course
> With rocks and stones and trees.

No . . . no . . . neither . . . nor . . . ; has no motion . . . force . . . neither hears . . . sees . . . (is) rolled . . . ; she . . . with rocks . . . stones . . . trees . . . Our mind needs to dwell on the potentialities of such patterns (and dislocations) within the matrix of the text as we quietly re-read it. Discovering them, tacitly or explicitly, seems a vital step in our apprehension of its meaning. Nevertheless, that process is still schematic, a rehearsal for something fuller.

Many further questions arise as we try to *turn print into speech*. (And there are university courses that ignore or fudge the whole issue.) What voices, what timbres and moods, what speech tunes and stress, what changes in rhythm and tempo seem appropriate to the text as laid out on the page? We have to be clear that — compared with music for singing, say — the written notation of poetry and prose leaves a great deal to vocal interpretation by the reader. There will be no single vocal rendering that is 'right'. Nevertheless, the voice cannot ignore evidence from the smallest units of sound upwards:

> A slumber did my spirit seal

To a trained ear, 'slumber . . . spirit . . . seal' already suggest where the range of appropriate moods and tempi for the opening will lie. (The tongue and lips will bear this out if you whisper the words aloud.) Decisions about stress (and all that implies for meaning) are critical and sometimes difficult, as in this poem. There is a temptation in the first verse, for instance, to stress '*human* fears' and perhaps '*earthly* years', as I heard a famous American critic do recently; but this seems to me to imply a pointless contrast with superhuman (?)/heavenly (?) fears etc. So where is the stress to go, and how prominent is it to be, to express the incomprehension of those lines?

> A slumber did my spirit seal;
> I had no human fears:
> She seemed a thing that could not feel
> The touch of earthly years.

Equally, how is the voice to change and signal the emotional shift suggested in the sound and stress of '*No motion*'? What blankness . . . stoicism . . . pain . . . lies behind those words?

In general, then, a vocal interpretation of the text has to body out the felt side of the experience. And while there are signs in the text or script that indicate a range of potential readings, they cannot — in the nature of written notations — determine the precise quality of the felt experience.

This raises a much larger question: how precisely do printed signs become a presented experience in which we the readers are personally involved? What further demands does this put on us as we read? In part, we must *use the signs of the text to construct an imaginary experience*; indeed, if we read the words aloud or act them out, we must use our own bodies and voices to *be* the persons involved. This raises important questions about how we bring relevant human experience to bear, and what the effects may be of cultural differences between ourselves and the author.

Finally, in this incomplete set of overlapping processes, let me raise our *reflective response to what the poem enacts*. Peirce, the founder of modern semiotics, claimed that each sign 'addresses somebody, that is, creates in the mind of that person an equivalent sign, or perhaps a more developed sign.' And he went on to suggest that in discussion the equivalent sign (or 'interpretant') could naturally evoke some further interpretant, and so on indefinitely.[5] This is precisely what happens in literary response; we use the 'interpretants' to point to part of the potential significance of the poem for *us*.

ABSTRACTED INTERPRETATIONS

To put this into practice; because Wordsworth's poem above absorbs me, I might say something like this, provisionally.

'A man begins by recalling the dream-like, as it seemed eternal, unchanging presence of a woman he loved — still unable to comprehend what has happened to her. Then he spells out to himself the irrevocable truths about her dead remains, their place now in the natural order, and the appalling absence that signifies in a wild landscape that was home to them.' We have only to go this far to realise that such language is at once more generalised and more analytical than the enacted experience of the poem; and it is only one of many possible 'abstracted interpretations' of that experience.[6] The test of their value lies in the way they indicate potentialities in the poem (as read), and potentialities in human experience (as we readers understand it), trying to connect the two. I could add, of course, that, even given my personal ideology, this poem — and the incomplete transition it enacts — communicates something about death that I find equally hard to recognize or acknowledge. That is part of its power for me: it affects me and my life!

I have said enough, then, I hope, to suggest that there are many questions that have to be raised, refined, and answered as best we can, if the reading of literature is to be adequately understood. Questions about printed signs and their organisation; about cultural codes and the generation of expectations; about vocal interpretation and being the poem/character; about the construction of an imaginative experience; about abstracted interpretations and their role in connecting the poem and human experience such as the reader knows it.

Much more could be said, and needs to be; but to sum up at this point:

1. Recent theories of reading might allow us as teachers to make a quantum leap in diagnosing where and how to help our students in the course of learning to read a literary work.
2. As attempts now begin to emerge to get a historical grasp of the shifts in our past understanding of reading literature and the potential in our present international enquiries, this is an appropriate time for teachers in schools, colleges and universities to set up for themselves a series of discussion seminars on the subject.

3.   A LEVEL LITERATURE AS A COURSE IN WRITING?

The principal point of having a better theory of reading is that it helps to make clear what we are trying to do — and thus what students are trying to learn. The same is true of a theory of writing. Indeed the two sides are inextricably linked. What reading processes is writing supposed to be clarifying and extending, during the A Level course? What further, reflective and analytic processes is it supposed to serve, or leave room for? And what demands does this make on the 16–19 year old student, in terms of new textures of written language and new forms of organisation to master?

At present this part of an A Level Literature course depends almost entirely upon tacit assumptions. In the space available, then, I simply want to try to demonstrate that there *are* ways of answering the opening questions, and incidentally that some at least of the prevailing assumptions are open to doubt. To do so, I will draw on three extracts from essays in the research sample.

In general terms, we can say that one major side of reading is to move from a printed text to a presented experience (and a presenting voice and consciousness). For most literature this entails giving a reading or presenting a work dramatically. It is the voice that has to express the changing feelings, emotions, moods and attitudes of a poem, let us say, and equally to convey how the narrator sees these things. With the modern emphasis on 'text', it is easy to forget how problematic decisions about such things are. How much depends on subtle signs in the 'script', how much is inevitably left open, so that the reader finally has to ask: what would it be human to feel as I say this line, in this context? Manifestly, such a question arises with even greater force when a dramatic script is being spoken and enacted. For, unlike the poem, the play usually has no narrating presence to guide us; and this very fact opens up new possibilities for a writing course.

EXAMPLE 1: *The Winter's Tale*

Here, for instance, is a 17-year-old trying to imagine how Polixenes and Camillo might behave, and what they might be thinking and feeling, as they say the lines in their scene towards the end of Act I Scene ii in *The Winter's Tale*.

> . . . Camillo who is already in the state-room but slightly in the shadows is thinking over what Leontes has asked him to do. He finds it very difficult to believe that Hermione and Polixenes are lovers.
>
> He hears Polixenes and turns round very surprised at seeing him but trying to act normally, Polixenes comes closer, Camillo starts to fidget and move awkwardly. They greet each other and Polixenes asks Camillo what could be wrong with the king as he thinks he is out of favour with him. Camillo answering that he does not know but indicating that he does.
>
> 'I dare not know, my Lord.'
>
> But the guilt shows in his face and Polixenes notices this. So Camillo must have sufficient expression to convey his guilt.
>
> Polixenes becomes angry and strolls angrily towards the audience almost appealing to them, how could Camillo not tell him but then he turns back when he says, 'Good Camillo', and becomes pleading. He says (Camillo) must be a part in this because he sees Camillo's changed complexion and that tells him he must also have changed.
>
> Camillo answers like a riddle probably breaking slightly away from Polixenes saying it very softly but precisely, wishing to get it over with. He says that Polixenes has caused a sickness, which has made many ill but that he himself is totally oblivious of this. He would then turn back and face Polixenes who replies. He is shocked and confused, he does not understand and starts to walk and talk to the audience but returning when he speaks direct to Camillo. Again he pleads with him to be more outspoken.
>
> Camillo by this time uncertain that he is doing the correct thing after all Leontes trusts him, he gives a weak answer and turns away from Polixenes.
>
> Polixenes totally tormented because he cannot think of what he has done, shakes Camillo,
>
> 'Dost thou hear, Camillo',
>
> He then lets him go. He gesticulates with his arms towards the audience,
>
> 'How far off, how near;'
>
> Camillo then very surprisingly says he will tell Polixenes . . .

Now it might be said that all this is 'mere narrative' response. And it is indeed narrative. But suppose we ask first, what does the student stand to learn in such writing? After all, this narrative is intended to be keyed into dialogue (as the student indicates from time to time), and if Shakespeare produced the dialogue is it not something of a challenge, to become the omniscient narrator who can tell what is going on behind his words? Remember that this is done mainly by inference — by taking the spoken words and considering what they might imply in terms of thought and feeling (and their outward expression). This seems to be a vital step in learning to 'read' a play, and an appropriate use of the written medium.

If so, I want to make three further observations. First, if we look in detail at such narratives and their distinguishing features, they represent a substantial development on any but the most outstanding narratives in 16+ folders.[7] Indeed, there is evidence in this extract to suggest that, with the student at full stretch in her *composing* process, there was intermittent breakdown in her control of *transcription*.[8] And that leads me to my second point. The dialogue is very much simplified, or omitted for the most part. This has the effect of focusing the student on inner thought and feeling, and on actions. We can see this as a necessary simplification, perhaps, if the task is to remain within her control. Third and finally, there is a further kind of simplification going on: I doubt if this writer comes to the task cold, without the chance to act out the scene and discuss what the words might signify. Yet her narrative offers, in the main, a single line of interpretation: she does not consider any of the alternative inferences that might well have arisen in discussion. Already, then, I can envisage two or three stages of development (at least) *within* this form of narrative, and a further stage which takes the writer beyond narrative, probably.

EXAMPLE 2: *ANTONY AND CLEOPATRA*

For my second example, I want to turn to a different side of reading. This arises as the reader begins to reflect on the presented world (and the presenting consciousness), to 'read' this as a metaphor for life, and thus to derive 'interpretative abstractions' from it. This is a process Horst Ruthrof deals with lucidly and in some detail.[6] Here, I want simply to illustrate the way students frequently have to tackle it at A Level. A typical task runs something like this: ' "All the play's complexities resolve upon a single opposition: Egypt is romantic but wrong, Rome is repulsive but right!" Discuss.' The aim is presumably to propose a discussion of *Antony and Cleopatra* at a high level of interpretative abstraction. However, difficult though that task might be, what is actually proposed is something more complex. A summary abstract judgement is quoted from some anonymous reader, and the students are presumably expected to formulate their own interpretative abstraction *in the act* of arguing for or against that judgement. Let us see what a B grade student from our sample made of a comparable task: the three opening paragraphs follow.

An essential element of 'Antony and Cleopatra' is the marked contrast between the worlds of Egypt and Rome. D. A. Traversi in his book on the

Roman plays called it the contrast between 'the sensuous luxury of Egypt . . . and the severe practical genius of Rome.' And this, I think, sums up the differences nicely.

Egypt is essentially, in 'Antony and Cleopatra' anyway, a land of beauty, sensuousness and riotous living. Charmian's idea of excellent fortune is to be 'married to three kings in a forenoon and divorce them all'. Massive feasts are described by Enobarbus as 'but as a fly by an eagle'. But, at the same time as this there are bad elements in the Alexandrian court as there are in Cleopatra's character. Warmth and beauty personified though the latter may be at some times, at others she can be ruthless and violent, as the messenger finds out to his cost. Similarly though Charmian and Iras' teasing of Alexas in Act I scene two is done with humour, it is, nonetheless, vicious. But the overall impression of Alexandria is the one of enormous feasts followed by enormous feasts.

This is exactly the opposite of Rome, there the inhabitants are never shown feasting or enjoying themselves at all. This is because the primary objectives of the Romans are quite different. They seek power and position instead of luxury and beauty. The brief interlude with Ventidius reminds us that the conquest of the Roman empire is still underway. Shakespeare deliberately makes Rome opposite in every way to Alexandria . . .

The line taken by the student simplifies his task: he accepts the Traversi contrast as his own, and proceeds to demonstrate how it arises from the presented experience of the play. Unfortunately, as we see when we come to the student's own abstractions, he does not in fact agree with Traversi, though in the heat of the moment he does not recognise the fact. His attitudes to 'Egypt' are ambiguous: he sees it as (attractive) beauty and riotous living, but also as (repulsive) viciousness and ruthless violence. But the two direct quotations suggest that he is aware of something more — though he has not time to examine it and to derive something more exact than 'riotous living', or for that matter 'sensuous luxury'.

This essay is representative of a number in our examination sample. Formally it is an argument — the rather elementary kind of argument that might be called 'advocacy'. Although the organisation of argument places new demands on a writer, this student appears on the surface to be handling them quite confidently. (Can that be why he got such a high mark — in keeping with his B grade?) Actually, at a deeper level he is floundering, as we see: the essay is unproductive, or counterproductive. Its glibness becomes a danger to further reading. How can the student learn to do better? We must acknowledge that, in the course of reading and reflection, abstract oppositions of this kind do emerge, quite naturally. Indeed, Egypt and Rome are an explicit part of the structure of the text in this case. But the play is not an allegory — not intended to body out a more abstract message, like *Animal Farm*, say. So students who recognise such abstract oppositions and feel their power have to be encouraged to go back into the presented experience of the play or novel, testing and questioning the force of this contrast — and the way it relates or jars with other contrasts that are presented. They have to learn to look for counter-evidence as well as support, hoping to emerge with a more precise but complex sense of the metaphoric power of the work. And as they do so the question arises whether they think that is true to life, and what they think of the author's stance: they begin to discuss the 'possibility of experience' as *they* see it, as well as the author.

EXAMPLE 3: *RICHARD II*

It is a complex demand, and in a 750–1000 word 'essay', written without detailed preparation, most students are condemned to failure, I would have thought. Besides, the very attempt to keep moving between abstractions and presented life, while 'discussing' with the author, calls for an extremely complex organisation of discourse. I want to end, therefore, by suggesting the need for half-way houses, and to illustrate from the coursework sample what kinds of effect they might have. In the extract that follows, the student is discussing *RICHARD II* Act IV scene i, line 162 on.

MOVEMENTS ON STAGE INITIAL LAYOUT ON STAGE	REASONS FOR STAGE DIRECTIONS AND INTERPRETATIONS OF LINES
Abbot of West + Bishop of Carlisle at stage rear	Clergy at rear of stage to symbolise the fact that the 'Divine right of Kings' and hence religious aspects have been neglected, and are out of the 'lime-light'.
King Richard + Aumerle on stage right together when they have entered from rear stage left. Stage left Bolingbroke and his collaborators: York, Northumberland + Henry Percy	King Richard & Aumerle together to show their alliance against Bolingbroke. This group on stage left rather than right, because traditionally the left hand signifies evil, hence the group trying to abolish the Divine right is on the left of the clergy group.
Richard stops at stage centre on his way from rear stage left to front stage right, and looks to Bolingbroke for line 162	Richard says line 162 questioningly looking at his oppressors in turn. After '. . . reigned?' there is a pause and silence while he waits in vain for an answer.
Richard sighs after receiving no answer and moves slowly to Aumerle at front stage right saying line 164 'I hardly . . . submission' When Richard arrives at Aumerle's side, Bolingbroke looks to York and	M. Reese's 'The cease of Majesty' claims — 'When Richard is brought in he is by turns theatrical and pathetic'. I disagree that he is pathetic, although I would agree he is theatrical, however I believe the

after a pause of thought moves to front stage centre

play on the whole to be strikingly theatrical and hence Richard's performance is not over alarming.

After finishing line ending in '. . . submission' Richard turns sharply and faces Bolingbroke who immediately stops. Richard says line 167 'Yet I well . . .'. Whilst Richard is saying line 167 Northumberland moves slowly towards H. Percy and York looking at his feet.

Line 167 is said with contempt and a vicious, somewhat disgusted grin crosses Richard's face. Richard's moods and expressions in my opinion change quickly and frequently in this short scene. At times he seems contented and accepts his fate, similarly his mood changes and he becomes very positive of his position of King. I believe he is confused by the abruptness of the swing of power. Northumberland is plainly conscious of his disloyal behaviour and moves for comfort to his fellow oppressors . . .

This is the opening of an extended analysis on the same lines. Clearly the student is beginning to think about the way groupings, movements, and displacements on the stage imply thematic structures that can be abstracted from the text (and he is rather enjoying the experience, by the sound of it!). The commentary on the right is not systematic. It is sparked off, one imagines, by the connections he is making as he writes: movement suggests interpretation, and vice versa.

At this stage, then, what the student has to say is fragmentary and incomplete. The layout acknowledges as much, while equally implying the need to keep up an interplay between the two sides (imagining the presented experience and interpreting its significance). It is a transitional form, suitable for reading and discussing further in a student group. I want to suggest that students who have carried out this kind of provisional analysis in detail are less likely to succumb when they meet authoritative critical abstractions — as we see from the response to Reese's claim. Equally, if they *do* emerge with a 'structured set' of abstractions, in Ruthrof's phrase, they have something to build on as they try to organise these into continuous discourse. At the same time, these particular comments warn us as teachers that the student has still a long way to go before that kind of *personal* achievement is possible. Nor should we be surprised.

These are tentative lines of thinking about a writing course. Perhaps the appropriate way to sum them up is in the form of questions:

1. What is the place of narrative — and more complex, developing forms of narrative — in fostering certain levels of reading and reflection?

2. What range of 'traditional' forms could encourage students as they write to keep alive to the interplay between different levels of reading (including some of those discussed in the previous section)?

3. If we want students' interpretative abstractions to be personal and exploratory, rather than dogmatic and unanalysed, what kinds of task are appropriate and what enabling contexts will be necessary at 16 to 19?

NOTES

1. *English and Examinations* F. Stevens (Hutchinson 1970).

2. *Responses to Literature: what is being assessed?* J. Dixon & J. Brown. Schools Council (Part I, 1984; Parts II and III, 1985.)

3. Achievements in Writing at 16+ Project, Booklet 4, available from Leslie Stratta, University of Birmingham.

4. Technically, in the examination scripts these were 'essays with a mark commensurate with the *overall* grade'.

5. See W.B. Gallie, *Peirce and Pragmatism* (Penguin 1952) for a useful explanation of this point.

6. Horst Ruthrof's ideas in *The Reader's Construction of Narrative* (Routledge 1981) have been a useful stimulus to me here.

7. Achievements in Writing at 16+ Project, Booklets 1 & 3.

8. Frank Smith *Writing and the Writer* (Heinemann 1982).

46 *Teaching Garner's Red Shift for an Alternative A level: Case Study*

● Terry Gifford

THE GROUP

Yewlands School, Sheffield, is an eleven-to-eighteen mixed comprehensive of eight hundred pupils. It serves one part of a large council estate in the north of the city together with a small area of private housing. All of its sixth-formers who apply for places in higher education are the first generation to do so.

In English lessons pupils are taught in mixed-ability classes from the first to the fifth year. All are entered for the NEA 16+ Syllabus B course-work assessment. One or two groups are formed each year by option choices to follow a course leading to English Literature CSE Mode 3 course-work assessment or the Cambridge Plain Texts examination. This option is really regarded as 'extra literature' since literature has a strong presence in the 'unitary English' approach throughout the school.

A-level English Literature is popular at Yewlands, attracting an initial group of between twelve and sixteen students each year. Students are entered for the JMB's Sheffield Alternative syllabus. This requires that students answer the same examination paper on two Shakespeare plays and a paper of practical criticism as candidates for the conventional JMB A-level English Literature syllabus. In addition there is an open-book examination on a set text novel and collection of poetry selected from a list of six texts chosen by the Sheffield group of schools. (Other groups work this syllabus independently in West Yorkshire and Newcastle.) One-third of the final grade is assessed by a sample of course-work. In this, Wide Reading and Composition are compulsory, but free choice of texts is allowed for the study of poetry, drama or novels. For four years I have used Alan Garner's *Red Shift* as a text for study, leading to a piece of writing (maximum of 2,000 words) to be assessed as a course-work novel study.

Girls have been in a majority in each of the groups that have worked on *Red Shift*. Their future expectations are generally lower than their potential achievements, although they are self-confident and assertive in their personal relationships. In different ways they often tend to make some form of identification with Jan in the novel. These students do not have a depth of experience of literature to draw from outside what school has provided. It cannot be assumed that as readers they will recognise the most important sign systems in the novel concerning matters of love and identity.

THE TEXT

Red Shift is a deliberately difficult book. It is also a consciously problematic text, which is not quite the same thing. I chose the book in the belief that the difficulties can be overcome in order to enjoy an engagement with what is problematic in the text. Let me explain. The narrative shifts between three historical periods, but the actions are placed in one locality at those different times. Garner does not immediately make it obvious that, although one period is the present, the action of the other two strands of narrative are set in the Roman period and the Civil War period. If the deliberate confusion of the reader at the beginning can be overcome, it will be realised that the relationships developed in those three different periods have some features that are parallel: a love relationship in which the male character of the pair is experiencing an identity crisis, whilst the relationship is threatened in different ways by a rival lover.

I chose the book because its themes are fundamental — indeed, archetypal in Garner's awareness of them — and because their exploration in the novel is revealingly complex. I find discussion of them in their problematic form in this book to be an important learning experience. The fact that Tom and Jan in the novel are contemporary sixth-formers ought to make it an obvious text to consider with this age group. The fact that it is a problematic text ought to make it a suitable challenge, an extending reading experience for students who are writers as much as readers. All this depends upon avoiding the danger of initial alienation from the book's difficulties.

INTENTIONS

As a teacher of literature for examinations I am inevitably a mediator of a text. My organisation of the group's study of the text will be dictated by my attitude towards the text. That I have a particular perception of the text will already be evident from my description of it. Indeed it is important that I do have, not only an individual reading of the text, but a particular view of its potential value for students, since my role as an educationalist is the development of students' personal growth rather than a guide in the deconstruction of texts for its own sake.

All this is especially pertinent to Garner's text since I might seem, to some readers, to be spoiling my students' chances of a reading of the text as Garner intended it. I believe not only that Garner created unhelpful difficulties in his text, but that my responsibility as a teacher of it is to my students rather than to the writer.

Alan Garner's *Red Shift* in its economy of narrative style, which requires the reader to 'read between and across the lines' so much, might be regarded as a classic example of the notion that reading is a creative act. Ironically I find that the danger for my students is that they can become, in Barthes's terms, 'consumers' rather than 'creators' of the text. The initial difficulties in 'placing' the different narrative strands can become a rather distracting hunting for clues about basic information with an emphasis on 'When is this happening?' rather than 'What is going on here between these people?'

What complicates this low-level search for meanings by students is that the teacher knows the answers. It is inevitably the case that whilst students are responding to a first reading of the text the teacher has the advantage of more than one reading. A second reading of *Red Shift* is a different experience, and I believe a much more profitable one, but it places the teacher in danger of being the mediator of the students' consumption of narrative information.

I deal with this problem in the classroom by admitting that I have some information and giving it up as readily as it is needed by the group, in order to allow attention to be directed to what is importantly problematic rather than frustratingly difficult for each particular group of readers. They monitor their engagement with the immediate delights and distractions of the book in their personal reading journals.

These journals are used for all their reading in the course, whether it is of individually chosen texts, which might eventually be considered in an essay sampling their Wide Reading, or reflections on group discussion of the set Shakespeare texts, or individual poems they might be personally exploring. The purpose of the journal is to provide space for personal sorting out of ideas between first responses and a final structured essay. So first responses can be revisited in more reflective writing during a second reading. This journal is the source of the material that will, after a second or third reading of *Red Shift*, be used to produce an essay on an aspect of the novel that particularly interests each student.

THE PROGRAMME OF WORK

The first section of *Red Shift* never fails to move me as I read it aloud to a group, continuously, without questions or comment, at our first session on the novel. I know that scenario of moral tension between parents and indignant eighteen-year-olds. I know those characters and have their voices distinct. When, at the height of the row with Tom's 'prurient mother', Jan says, 'I bet you've flattened some grass in your time', a gasp comes from the group, but the tension is not released. I read on across the space on page 20 (Fontana Lions edition), exploiting the emotional and grammatical continuity of Garner's story-telling technique, crossing what is actually a shift of time, place and characters. I stop at the top of page 22 after 'we're still the Ninth, not brickies. Right?'

We discuss individual perceptions of what has just been happening. About the first section we can easily reach some agreement, although individual judgements need identifying as such. About the brief latter section there are widely different versions. This is important. Different readers emphasise different details, notice different cues, read between the lines differently. This is going to be a feature of this book particularly. However, the writer does depend upon the reader noticing some clues. Is this section set in the same time as the first? 'Cloaks' and 'arrows' — no. Is it set in the same place? 'Rudheath' — yes. Have you heard of the Ninth? 'Stonemasons', 'brickies', an 'army' and its 'roads' — Roman Britain; and 'Cats' are a Celtic tribe. Does the language of these soldiers ring any bells? 'Hardware', 'goofball', 'busted' — Americans in Vietnam fighting a guerrilla war? What was the effect of my reading across the time space? Tom became Macey. Macey's inward emotional tension continued Tom's.

Helen's first entry in her journal reads:

> The writer's time-spans are at first confusing, but it is interesting finding the different things that link them all up. There is a sense of confusion and mystery about the characters and a little more information would make the book more enjoyable.

Confusion but mystery; finding links but aware that the writer is being coy with his clues: this response characterises a student's first reading of the book. So to help keep this balance of tensions satisfying we read the book together, with students taking the lines of different characters. I hope it helps that I read Macey's speech and Thomas's and Tom's, with voices that dramatise my attempt to convey their vulnerability, confusion and often intense, trance-like vision.

At page 46 we pause for the first taking-stock, listing the links between the three time periods. By this point in the book the unities of place, Orion and the stone axe that link all three periods have been introduced.

Some parallels in the relationships between Tom and Jan, Macey and the goddess, and Thomas and Madge can be identified, partly suggested by another emotional continuity across the time gap on page 35, together with the strength of Madge in protecting Thomas, which draws attention to the female roles in each of the love relationships.

By page 87 a second pause to note recurring phrases that have begun to seem significant an alertness to Garner's language at work on the reader. The dramatic emotional tensions have been enjoyed for themselves in each self-contained episode as a first priority at this first reading, but there is a need to pause and note the continuities that are resurfacing in passing phrases.

By the time Thomas Venables has saved Margery and Thomas from the massacre at page 144 a fourth discussion can extend the common pattern of relationships in each period to that of a pair threatened, but in some ways saved, by another man. On the last page of the book lines of speech from the three parallel periods are fully integrated and provoked an immediate discussion of purpose, which ranges back over the whole book. Just what has Garner been about in this book? Judgements about the nature of the key relationships are stimulated by speculation about which of the three pairings students think will now survive in the future beyond the end of this narrative.

Following this group discussion at the end of a first reading of *Red Shift* students are asked to make a second reading, noting particularly what they feel to be significant to one aspect of the book that fascinates them, knowing that this will be the basis of a final essay on the book. Some students know that they want to examine Garner's treatment of time, or the role of the women, or religion when they begin a re-reading.

But for some, the journal notes will help them discover something worth exploring only towards the end of their second reading, like Helen's journal note after page 147:

> Logan protects Macey's relationship with goddess.
> German wine grower gives money for Jan and Tom's relationship.
> Thomas Venables helps protect Madge and Thomas.

This train of thought is further extended by a note stimulated by a comment from Thomas Venables on the next page of the book. The journal reads:

> p. 148 the Venables sanctuary isn't safe — you can't live in/on sanctuary.
> Insisting that Madge doesn't stay there forever. She can't be alone all the time, needs a community.
> Roman Ninth can't live forever on sanctuary of Mow Cop. Each one has turned mad.
> Can't live in a pretence of sanctuary — it is not real.
> Tom can't accept Jan living outside their sanctuary.
> In Venables's sanctuary no one will help you — slashing his leg.
> Also the love relationship can't exist in isolation. Always third person.
> Goddess having a role with other people outside (other men raped her).

> Madge with John (but not a threatening lover) and Thomas Venables.
> Jan with the wine seller.

The circle traced by those thoughts is fascinating, the freedom of space in the personal journal being used to get the parallels clear. These notes became the core of an essay that began:

> Throughout all the different time spans the role of women has a major influence on the other characters. Firstly looking at Tom and Jan's relationship, Tom can't see himself living in modern society and it is Jan that has to be patient with him. Jan is more mature than Tom and it is this maturity that Tom relies on.

The process I have been describing aims at facilitating personal possession of the book. Jane, in her essay on religion in *Red Shift*, reveals another side to Jan's comparative maturity. In commenting on Jan's attachment to the stone axe, which Jan calls a 'Bunty', Jane writes:

> For her it seems to symbolise stability and permanence which she otherwise lacks in family life — parents are constantly away from home and she flits numerous times from town to town depending on where her parents' work takes them.

An individually chosen essay theme can throw up quite different perceptions, which are, of course, equally valid. The fact that Jane's essay contains both aspects of Jan's 'maturity' means that it is ultimately better for having a more complete view of the complexities.

Some students never fully resolve their initial puzzlements in re-reading and indeed deepen them in an interesting way in the process of carrying them through from the journal to the essay. Diane wrote about love in the novel and came to a point where she made an interesting admission:

> It seemed strange to me why the women preferred the weak-willed, vulnerable men rather than the mature, in-control men like Thomas Venables and the German. They seemed to find the weaker qualities in them more attractive and realised that these men needed them more than the stronger ones.

Sometimes points that have arisen in our first reading together are repeated in the essays in a way that reveals how much further on is the thinking around that initial simple point. Here Tracey reveals her grasp of the writer's intentions in the book (however awkwardly expressed) and goes on to use a point from our very first session as a springboard for sharp observations of her own:

> The timelessness of relationships is one of the most important aspects of this book, linked directly with the timelessness of language. The Romans speak noticeably in American slang and the action in this period is representative of the Americans in the Vietnam war; people fighting 'tribes' far from home for a cause they have little interest in. A classic example of the language is:

'I don't give a toss what some minging stonemason does because he thinks he can run an army. Let him build his goddam wall, and all the rest of the crap, but we're still the Ninth, not brickies. Right?'

The songs sung by Thomas Venables and on 'Cross Track' [Tom's tape] have many similarities, but the most interesting part is these lines sung by Venables:

> I'll dye, I'll dye my petticoat red
> For the lad I love I'll bake my bread
> And then my daddy would wish that I were dead.'

The first line could apply to Thomas and Margery, the second to the goddess and Macey and the third maybe to Tom and Jan.

The culmination of these ideas arises in the cathartic ending of the novel. All the different periods of the book join as one, the words could be applied to everyone: 'He felt the child move' could be relevant to each age. However, only Tom and Jan must say goodbye; they repeat the words spoken by Thomas and Madge, but it is only the absolute end for *them*. This is shown in the final sentence, which has been given previously in the book: 'It doesn't matter. Not really now not any more.' This makes all the past and the relationship seem futile, everyone was in the rat race, fighting a losing battle against time.

I think the development shown here exemplifies what I am hoping for in this course-work process of studying a novel. After guidance given at the early stages to make the dramatic power of the novel accessible, the stages of journal-thinking and re-reading should encourage a personal engagement with the text, concluding in a critical exploration of an area of meanings in the book. Tracey's criticism of the feeling of futility left at the end concerning Tom and Jan's relationship happens to agree with that of Neil Philip in his study of Garner (*A Fine Anger*, Collins, 1981). Tracey's final sentence in her essay, however, does not reflect a negative feeling about her experience of reading the book: '*Red Shift* is compulsive reading, the ideas explored and their implications for society are as timeless as its action.'

Lee was also tempted to struggle with the language of abstraction to sum up his feelings in the final paragraph of his essay:

Finally I feel the tone of the book is a very suppressed one, all the characters are aggrevated, which then produces violence. Again the visionary fits which occur are a reaction to a suppressed feeling of desolation. The feeling of being caged in comes across strongly, and I feel the book is a comment on humans realising their insignificance, which stimulates relationships to overcome this depression. If however relationships aren't forged, then the depression leads to a subconscious break-out: the fits which contain no time, therefore no desolation, but violent nature.

As an ending to an essay that examined Garner's achievement in the 'merging of time' it is remarkable how much personal human understanding is revealed here, arising out of a comment about the tone of the book. Lee's final paragraph represents what course-work can make possible: a personal response to the writer's use of language (in this case 'tone'), whilst exploring a theme of interest to the individual (in this case 'time'), expressed with more thought, personal discovery and individuality than is possible or encouraged in an instant essay against the clock.

AFTERWORD

I first used *Red Shift* in the middle of the first term of the lower sixth as a shared challenge for a newly formed group. The effect of the book on that occasion was to unite the group against it. I have subsequently used it in the first term of the upper-sixth year with much greater success. More maturity and security seem to make all the difference.

I have not found Neil Philip's book *A Fine Anger* of much help to students or myself. It is too concerned with sources and clue-spotting rather than evaluating the implications of the themes. I have used it with two groups to give as full information as possible about both Delta Orionis (p. 92) and the documentation of the massacre at Bartholmley church in 1643 (p. 95), but this detailed information has been so simply taken for granted by all these students that verbal explanation from me seems all that is needed in future. Responding to the text on its own terms seems to be what my unscholarly students prefer, and the strength of their personal engagement is what I want to encourage in their reading, talking and writing about *Red Shift*.

Index